Palgrave Studies in Workplace Spirituality and Fulfillment

Series Editors

Satinder Dhiman
School of Business
Woodbury University
Burbank, CA, USA

Gary Roberts
Robertson School of Government
Regent University
Virginia Beach, VA, USA

Joanna Crossman
International College of Management
Sydney, NSW, Australia

Satinder Dhiman
Editor-in-Chief

Gary Roberts and Joanna Crossman
Associate Editors

By way of primary go-to-platform, this Series precisely maps the terrain of the twin fields of *Workplace Spirituality and Fulfillment* in the disciplines of business, psychology, health care, education, and various other allied fields. It reclaims the sacredness of work—work that is mind-enriching, heart-fulfilling, soul-satisfying and financially-rewarding. It fills the gap in scholarship in the allied disciplines of Workplace Spirituality and Flourishing. Using a comprehensive schema, it invites contributions from foremost scholars and practitioners that reflect insightful research, practices, and latest trends on the theme of workplace spirituality and fulfillment. The uniqueness of this *Series* lies in its anchorage in the moral and spiritual dimension of various positive forms of leadership—such as Authentic Leadership, Servant Leadership, Transformational Leadership, and Values-Based Leadership.

We welcome research monographs and multi-authored edited volumes representing myriad thought-positions on topics such as: Past, Present and Future Directions in Workplace Spirituality; Workplace Spirituality and World Wisdom/Spiritual Traditions; Culture Studies and Workplace Spirituality; Spiritual, Social and Emotional intelligence; Nature of Work; Mindfulness at Work; Personal Fulfillment and Workplace Flourishing; Workplace Spirituality and Organizational Performance; Inner Identity, Interconnectedness, Community and Transcendence; Managing Spiritual and Religious Diversity at Work; Spirituality and World Peace Imperative; Sustainability and Spirituality; Spirituality and Creativity; and Applied Workplace Spirituality in Health Care, Education, Faith-based Organizations, et al.

More information about this series at
http://www.palgrave.com/gp/series/15746

Satinder Dhiman
School of Business
Woodbury University
Burbank, CA, USA

Palgrave Studies in Workplace Spirituality and Fulfillment
ISBN 978-3-319-67572-5 ISBN 978-3-319-67573-2 (eBook)
https://doi.org/10.1007/978-3-319-67573-2

Library of Congress Control Number: 2018958763

This Palgrave Macmillan imprint is published by the registered company Springer Nature Switzerland AG
The registered company address is: Gewerbestrasse 11, 6330 Cham, Switzerland

Satinder Dhiman

Bhagavad Gītā and Leadership

A Catalyst for Organizational Transformation

palgrave
macmillan

त्वदीयं वस्तु गोविन्दः
तुभ्यमेव समर्पये

tvadīyaṁ vastu govinda
tubhyameva samarpaye

O Lord! I offer unto Thee
What is really Thine only!

|| एतेन मे निबन्धेनार्पिता वै गुरुदक्षिणा ||

|| *etena me nibandhena*
arpitā vai gurudakṣiṇā ||

Whatever I have composed here,
I offer as a tribute to all my revered teachers.

श्री कृष्णार्पणमस्तु

Śrī Kṛṣṇārpaṇamastu

This book is humbly dedicated to Śrī Kṛṣṇa, *the master creator of the Song Celestial who, more than 5000 years ago, proactively impelled change from the prevailing unjust order to that of righteousness and showed the path of liberation through Self-knowledge.*

Acknowledgments

The goal of life is to manifest the Divinity already within us. (Swami Vivekananda)

Śrī Śaṅkara (788–822 CE), the preeminent Vedānta philosopher, counts association with great seer-saints among the rarest of the rare blessings:

> दुर्लभं त्रयमेवैतद्देवानुग्रहहेतुकम् ।
> मनुष्यत्वं मुमुक्षुत्वं महापुरुषसंश्रयः ॥ ३॥
>
> *durlabhaṁ trayamevaitaddevānugrahahetukam /*
> *manuṣyatvaṁ mumukṣutvaṁ mahāpuruṣasaṁśrayaḥ //3//*

These are three things which are rare indeed and are due to the grace of God—namely, a human birth, the longing for liberation, and the protecting care of a perfected sage.[1]

I have been very fortunate to have the blessed opportunity to sit at the lotus feet of a few such illumined sages.

This book is the direct result of the abiding Grace of the Lord, received in the form of the holy association with these seer-saints. In these pages, I have tried to be an "empty reed," just echoing what I have received from the lips of my preceptors in life and spirit. They *gave* me what *cannot* be taken. The effect of their teachings can only be described by the Biblical phrase, "The scales fell off from my very eyes."

But how can one recount one's debt to the Supreme Lord Nārāyaṇa[2]:

Thy Benediction has made me captive of Thee;
No ransom will ever be sufficient to redeem my debt.

[1] Swami Madhavananda, trans., *Vivekacūḍāmaṇi of Śrī Śaṅkarācārya*: Text with English Translation, Notes, and Index (Calcutta, India: Advaita Ashrama, 2007 reprint), 2.

[2] *Nara* meaning "human" and *āyaṇa* means "direction/goal." *Narāsya-āyaṇa iti Nārāyaṇa*: That which is the final goal, the ultimate end, of all humans is *Nārāyaṇa*.

Likewise, my debt to Śrī Śaṅkarācārya is ineffable. His illuminating commentaries on the triple canon of Vedānta—the Bhagavad Gītā, Upaniṣads, and Brahma Sūtras—have been the guiding light and solace of my life.

I am particularly indebted to Paramśraddheya Swāmī Rāmsukhdāsjī Mahārāj, whose commentary on Śrīmad Bhagavad Gītā, entitled, "*Sādhaka-Sañjīvaṇī*," is unparalleled in the Hindi language;[3] Swāmi Śharṇānandjī Mahārāj, whose revolutionary spiritual teachings illumine my path, every step of the way;[4] Swāmī Brahmātmānand Saraswati, my root Vedānta teacher, whose profound silence continues to echo in my soul; Swāmī Gyānajīvandāsjī and Śrī Dyālu Swamījī, whose simplicity, blessed love, and affection continue to be the source of my strength; Swāmī Dayānanda Saraswati jī and Swāmī Paramārthānanda, whose discourses on the Gītā and Upaniṣads represent some of the finest traditional Vedānta teachings currently available in the English language; Br. Shri Pranipāta Chaitanya, who patiently taught me the Bhagavad Gītā Śaṅkara Bhāṣya over Skype for a period of three years; and Swāmī Satchidānandendra Saraswati, whose writings in Sanskrit, Kannada, and the English language present Śaṅkara's liberating teachings in their most pure, pristine form.

I would like to express my deepest gratitude to Pujya Śrī Sreenivāsa Mūrthy jī—my present Vedānta teacher, who has been generously and lovingly teaching me the art and science of realizing the truths of Vedānta in one's own direct, intuitive experience (*svānubhava*), by taking a stand in the Self, the changeless, conscious principle. His objective, "threadbare" analysis of the deepest truths of Vedānta has provided an alchemic crystallization to my four decades of relentless spiritual search. Using himself as a mirror and a sounding board, he vividly demonstrated the difference between being a *mantra-vit*, a mere knower of the

[3] I was given the blessed opportunity to translate some of Swāmījī's writings, which are as follows:

S. Dhiman, trans., *Kripāmayi Bhagavad Gītā: The Benedictory Gītā* (selection and compilation, Rajendra Kumar Dhawan) (2014). Based on Paramśraddheya Swāmījī Shrī Rāmsukhdāsjī Mahārāj's discourses (Gorakhpur, India: Gita Prakāshan). http://gitaprakashan.com/englishbook/1.pdf

S. Dhiman, trans., *Sahaja-Gītā: The Essential Gītā* (selection and compilation, Rajendra Kumar Dhawan) (2013). Based on Paramśraddhey Swāmījī Shree Rāmsukhdāsjī Mahārāj commentary on *Śrimad Bhagavad Gītā*, entitled, *Sādhaka-Sannjīvanī* (Gorakhpur, India: Gītā Prakāshan). http://gitaprakashan.com/englishbook/3.pdf

[4] I was provided the opportunity to translate some of Swāmījī's books into English:

S. Dhiman, trans., *Krāntikārī Santvānī: Alchemic Aphorisms of a Revolutionary Saint: Precious-Select Sayings of the founder of "Mānav Sevā Sangh,"* Brahmaleen Pujaypād Swāmī Shrī Sharnānandjī Mahārāj (Karnal, India: Karnal Manav Seva Sangh, 2018).

S. Dhiman, trans., *Prashnōttarī (Santvānī): Answers to Questions Asked by Spiritual Aspirants to the Founder-Saint of "Mānav Sevā Sangh," Sant Pravar Brahmaleen Pujaypād Swāmī Shrī Sharnānandjī Mahārāj*. E-book. (print-version, in preparation, 2015).

S. Dhiman, trans., *Sant Jīvan Darpaṇ: Inspirational Episodes and Reminiscences of the Founder-Saint of "Mānav Sevā Sangh,"* Swāmī Shrī Sharnānandjī Mahārāj. E-book (2014).

S. Dhiman, trans., *Prabodhani: A Brief Introduction of the Founder-Saint of Mānav Sevā Sangh: Brahmleen Pujaypād Swāmī Shrī Sharnānandjī Mahārāj*. Compilation by Devakījī. E-book (2014).

S. Dhiman, trans., *Sant Hridayōdgār: Brahmleen Pujaypād Swāmī Shrī Sharnānandjī Mahārāj ke Hridyasaparashī Udgār* (2014).

These books can be accessed in pdf form, free of charge, here: http://www.swamisharnanandji.org/

Also see Swāmījī's *wiki* page for more information: https://en.wikipedia.org/wiki/Swami_Sharnanandji

scriptural lore, and being an *ātma-vit*, a knower of the truth of the Self. For, only knowers of the Self, says mother *Śruti*, transcend sorrow.[5]

In fine, the wisdom belongs to my teachers; I claim only the errors as my own. The following Sanskrit verse splendidly captures my sentiment:

> यदत्र दोषनम् किन्चत्तन् तेषाम् मामेव तत् ।
> यदत्र भूषणम् किन्चित् तत्तु तेषाम् न एव मम् ॥
>
> *Yadatra doṣanam kincattan teṣām māmeva tat /*
> *Yadatra bhūṣaṇam kincit tattu teṣām na eva mam //*

Whatever deficiencies are found in this work, they do not belong to the masters—they are verily mine; whatever excellence is found here is theirs and certainly not mine.

In the Gītā's view, the selfless performance of actions, as a service to the Supreme, purifies the mind and makes it a fit vessel for the reception of Self-knowledge, which alone is the direct and immediate means to *mokṣa*, spiritual freedom.[6] Śrī Kṛṣṇa, the teacher par excellence in the Gītā, does not merely want to make us philosophically learned, but aims to help us realize the Truth *experientially* (*jñānaṃ vijñānasahitaṃ*, knowledge *combined* with immediate intuitive experience: 9.1)[7]—not to merely *instruct* but to make us *wise* and *free*.

The Gītā teaches us that only the knowers of the Self are truly wise and ever free from grief (2.11).

Śrī Kṛṣṇa, the Infinite One, identifies with Arjuna (*pāṇḍavānāṃ dhanaṃjayaḥ*), with Veda Vyāsa (*munīnām apy ahaṃ vyāsaḥ*), and with the Vāsudevaḥ (*vṛṣṇīnāṃ vāsudevosmi*) as well (10.37). The listener, the writer, and the speaker—and the reader(s)—are all part of one single unitary movement, the Vāsudevaḥ, that is All, *sarvam* (7.19)—*Tad ekam* (That Alone)![8]

As Śrīmad Bhāgavatam, another sacred Indian text that comprises the divine acts and teachings of Śrī Kṛṣṇa, puts it, "To know the Truth is to see the oneness of the Self with God."

Unless one realizes this oneness (*aikyam*), one may read a million commentaries on the Bhagavad Gītā, or even write books about it, but the realization of the truth of the Self of All will still be far away.

Salutations to the Supreme Self (*paramātmā*) that dwells in all of us!

May the Divinity bless us with this vision of Oneness; may we all be so blessed!

[5] तरति शोकमात्मवित् *tarati śokam ātamvit*: Chāndogya Upaniṣad, 7.1.3.

[6] See Śaṅkara's commentary on Brahma Sūtra 1.1.12: सद्योमुक्तिकारणमप्यात्मज्ञानम *sadyomuktikāraṇamapy ātmajñānam*. "Self-knowledge leads to instant liberation": V. Panoli, trans., *Prasthanathraya, Volume VI—Bramasutra* (Kozhikode, India: Mathrubhumi Printing & Publishing Co. Ltd., 2011), 90.

[7] In the opening verse of chapter 9, Śrī Kṛṣṇa declares: "Now, I will clearly expound this most secret knowledge and its realization, knowing which you will be released from all that is inauspicious" (*yaj jñātvā mokṣyaseśubhāt*). Śrī Śaṅkara's comment: "On realizing this knowledge, you will be liberated from the bondage of *saṁsāra*, conditioned existence." See: Alladi Mahadeva Sastry, trans., *The Bhagavad Gītā with the commentary of Sri Shankaracharya* (Chennai, India: Samata Books, 2001), 238–239.

[8] It is interesting to note that the English word "sm*all*" contains "all."

Contents

1 Prolegomena: The Bhagavad Gītā: A Timeless Manual for Self-Mastery and Leadership 1

2 Introduction: Text and the Leadership Context of the Gītā 23

3 The Real Message of the Gītā: Decoding the Text 39

4 Advaita Vedānta: The Science of Reality 71

5 Karma Yoga: The Path of Enlightened Action 103

6 Being-Centered Leadership: Leader as an Enlightened Sage 127

7 Bhakti Yoga: Love and Faith in Leadership 157

8 Mind: A Leader's Greatest Friend and Foe 179

9 Doing the Right Thing: Leaders' Moral and Spiritual Anchorage 207

10 Be the Change: The Making of a Servant Leader 233

11 Epilogue: Timeless Teachings of the Gītā—Maxims for Life and Leadership 263

Index 287

Pronunciation/Transliteration Key of Sanskrit Terms[1]

Sanskrit is written in a script called *Devanāgarī*. It is written from left to right. Sanskrit is perhaps the oldest and the most systematic language in the world.[2] Its vast structure, refined construction, and rhythmic compactness are hard to duplicate in any translation. The subtle cultural nuances are almost always lost in most translations. Highlighting the role of language in culture, Rajiv Malhotra avers in his recent book, *The Battle for Sanskrit* (HarperCollins, India, 2016), that there is no *sanskriti* (culture) without Sanskrit. For those unfamiliar with *Devanāgarī* script, and who might nevertheless like to enjoy the efflorescent splendor of the original—*albeit in a Romanized version*—we provide below the transliteration key using the International Alphabet of Sanskrit Transliteration (IAST) scheme to denote words written in *Devanāgarī* script. IAST is the most widely used Sanskrit transliteration key[3]:

[1] Compilation: Professor Satinder Dhiman.

[2] The great American historian Will Durant (1885–1981) has noted in his book, *The Case for India*:

> "India was the motherland of our race, and Sanskrit the mother of Europe's languages: she was the mother of our philosophy; mother, through the Arabs, of much of our mathematics; mother, through the Buddha, of the ideals embodied in Christianity; mother, through the village community, of self-government and democracy." Will Durant, *The Case for India* (New York: Simon and Schuster, 1931), 4. In the footnote to this quote, Will Durant writes "the first volume of the author's *Story of Civilization* will substantiate this claim."

[3] In the Word document, inserting these diacritical marks (such as ¯ ̣ ˜) is quite easy. It can be done by choosing the "Insert" dropdown menu and using the "Symbol" option to insert various diacritics. By saving the "Symbol" option on your top menu bar, you can access these marks quite easily and efficiently.

Vowels

अ a—as u in but
आ ā—as a in father
इ i—as i in pin
ई ī—as i in police
उ u—as u in full
ऊ ū—as u in boot
ऋ ṛ—as *ri* in rim
ए e—as e in evade
ऐ ai—as *ai* in aisle
ओ o—as o in over
औ au—as *ou* in out

Consonants

k—as k in king
kh—as kh in blockhead
g—as g in goal
gh—as gh in log-house
n—as n in noun
c—as ch in chair
ch—as chh in thatch-hut
j—as j in jug
jh—as dgeh in hedgehog
n—as in nut
ṭ—as t in tongue
ṭh—as in anthill
ḍ—as in dark
ḍh—as dh in God-hood
ṇ—as n in Monday
t—as t in tub
th—as th in thumb
d—as th in then
dh—as theh in breathe
n—as n in nut
p—as p in pan
ph—as ph in phone
b—as b in bed
bh—as bh in abhor
m—as in mother
y—as in yes
r—as in race

l—as in light
v—as v in avert
ś—as sh in sure (short palatal sibilant)
ṣ—as sh in bush (cerebral sibilant)
s—as s in sun
h—as in hall
ḷ—as in curl

CHAPTER 1

Prolegomena: The Bhagavad Gītā: A Timeless Manual for Self-Mastery and Leadership

Introduction

सर्वोपनिषदो गावो दोग्धा गोपालनन्दनः ।
पार्थो वत्सः सुधीर्भोक्ता दुग्धं गीतामृतं महत् ॥४॥

sarvopaniṣado gāvo dogdhā gopālanandanaḥ /
pārtho vatsaḥ sudhīrbhoktā dugdhaṁ gītāmṛtaṁ mahat //4//

All the Upaniṣads are cows, Śrī Kṛṣṇa the son of the cowherd chief is the milkman, Arjuna the son of Pritha is the calf, and the intelligent people are the drinkers of the milk, the great nectar of the Bhagavad Gītā.

This book demonstrates how the Bhagavad Gītā[1] (embedded within the great Indian epic, the *Mahābhārata*) can be approached as a powerful tool for change management and as a catalyst for organizational transformation. It presents time-tested leadership strategies drawn from the Bhagavad Gītā that are highly relevant for today's leaders. It focuses on how to harmonize the needs of the individual with the needs of society and, by extension, how to harmonize the needs of the employees and the organization. Drawing upon the wisdom of the Gītā, Gandhi once said that "the best way to find yourself is to lose yourself in the service of others." The Gītā teaches that selfless service is the highest principle of life and leadership.

[1] For distinctiveness, and in order to retain some flavor of the original, the book will present Sanskrit terms and phrases in transliteration, using diacritics according to the International Alphabet of Sanskrit Transliteration (IAST) convention, with characters encoded in Unicode. For example, a small bar drawn over a word (ā) indicates elongated sound: as "a" in the word "park." At the beginning of the book, a pronunciation key has been included for easy reference. The Gītā is comprised of 18 chapters comprising a total of 700 verses. They are referenced in the chapter/verse order format. For example, 2.11 refers to 11th verse of the second chapter—presented parenthetically either as (2.11) or (BG 2.11).

S. Dhiman, *Bhagavad Gītā and Leadership*,
Palgrave Studies in Workplace Spirituality and Fulfillment,
https://doi.org/10.1007/978-3-319-67573-2_1

This book employs an inside-out leadership development approach based on Self-knowledge[2] and Self-mastery—two highly important areas for practicing effective self-leadership. The entire Indian spiritual tradition is a "series of footnotes" to the Bhagavad Gītā. It is the scripture of scriptures and contains the essence of all spiritual disciplines and philosophies.

The Bhagavad Gītā expounds a threefold path to Self-realization: (1) the path of selfless action (*karma yoga*); (2) the path of devotion (*bhakti yoga*); and (3) the path of knowledge (*jñāna yoga*). Meaning literally "Lord's Song," the Bhagavad Gītā unfolds as a dialog between Śrī Kṛṣṇa, the divine incarnation, and his warrior-disciple, Arjuna, on the eve of a historic battle of cosmic proportions.

Different commentators have read different meanings in interpreting the Bhagavad Gītā based on their own tradition (*sampardāya*) and philosophical leanings. Some say that it teaches *karma yoga* (path of selfless action), others observe that it teaches *bhakti yoga* (the path of devotion), and still others state that it teaches *jñāna yoga* (the path of Self-knowledge). Some commentators believe that the 18 chapters of the Bhagavad Gītā cover three broad categories of themes: (1) the first six chapters, called *karma-ṣaṭkam*, deal with the concept of selfless actions as a path to liberation; (2) the next six chapters, called *bhakti-ṣaṭkam*, deal with the topic of love of the personal God as a path to liberation; and (3) the final six chapters, called *jñāna-ṣaṭkam*, deal with the path of Self-knowledge as a means to spiritual liberation.

Relevance of the Gītā for Contemporary Leadership

The wisdom of the Bhagavad Gītā is as relevant in the boardrooms of the twenty-first century as it was on the battlefields of ancient times. Although traditionally interpreted as a religious-spiritual text, the Gītā encompasses great practical life lessons for modern leaders. Within the compass of 18 dynamic chapters, it presents the whole spectacle of human drama full of challenges met, victories won, and freedom attained. It teaches us how to emerge from a state of utter apathy, gloom, sorrow, and dejection to a state of perfect engagement, understanding, clarity, wisdom, renewed strength, and triumph. Meaning literally "Lord's Song," the Gītā unfolds as a dialog between Śrī Kṛṣṇa, regarded by the Hindus

[2] "Self" is capitalized throughout this book to denote our highest Self, Ātman, our "true" or "essential" nature. Accordingly, "Self-knowledge" denotes knowledge of our "true" nature—as Pure Awareness or Consciousness. Used as lower case, "self" denotes the "ego," or "psychosomatic apparatus" or "personality" that we generally take ourselves to be. Perhaps the most often used word in the English language is "I." We rarely pause to consider what this "I" really means. For the most part, we take it to mean our "ego" or the "me-notion." Self-knowledge is a journey from the pseudo "me" to the real "I." As we shall see in the next chapter, the central theme of the Gītā is spiritual freedom through Self-knowledge (*ātma-jñāna*) or the knowledge of the Absolute Truth or Reality (*tattva-jñāna*). Throughout the book, the words "Self" and "Reality" are used interchangeably, for the truth of our being (*Ātman*) and the truth of the universe (*Brahman*) are essentially one. This understanding of the essential oneness of the individual and the universal—called the Truth of truth (*satyasya satyam*), what is really Real—is the harbinger all individual happiness and social harmony.

as the Lord in human form, and his warrior-disciple, Arjuna, on the eve of a historic battle of cosmic proportions.

The Gītā contains timeless leadership lessons for the contemporary organizations. Modern leadership concepts such as vision, motivation and empowerment, self-awareness, self-mastery, excellence in work, importance of ethical means in achieving righteous ends, meaning and fulfillment at work, service before self, and wellbeing of all beings, are all lucidly discussed in the Bhagavad Gītā. Likewise, many contemporary leadership constructs such as authentic leadership, servant leadership, transformational leadership, and values-based leadership, were already hinted, in the Bhagavad Gītā thousands of years ago.

Author's Preparation for This Book Project

This book represents a culmination of and a sequel, as it were, to three of my recent books: *Seven Habits of Highly Fulfilled People: Journey from Success to Significance* (Personhood Press, USA, 2012), *Gandhi and Leadership: New Horizons in Exemplary Leadership* (Palgrave Macmillan, 2015), and *Holistic Leadership: A New Paradigm for 21st Century Leaders* (Palgrave Macmillan, 2017). During the course of my research for these books, it dawned on me that the Gītā contains compelling leadership lessons of much greater depth and scope, *meriting a systematic book-length exposition in its own right.*

During 2012–2015, I also renewed and solidified my lifelong interest in the Bhagavad Gītā by systematically and concertedly studying its traditional and modern commentaries with a Sanskrit scholar-teacher from India, Br. Pranipata Chaitanya.[3] During this period, as a part of my spiritual practice, *sādhanā*, I also

[3] It is with much sadness that I write that my revered guide and teacher suddenly left his mortal coil for his heavenly abode on November 3, 2015, at around 4.30 am, when he was about to take up morning classes. He was an accomplished scholar of Advaita who believed in maintaining the pristine purity of the Vedic tradition. His knowledge was deep; his devotion to his Guru was deeper. By way of tribute and a kind reminder, one member of the Advaitin Yahoo group shared a poem by William Cowper (1731–1800): sunderh@yahoo.com [advaitin].

God Moves in Mysterious Ways!

God moves in a mysterious way,
His wonders to perform;
He plants his footsteps in the sea,
And rides upon the storm.

Deep in unfathomable mines
Of never failing skill,
He treasures up his bright designs,
And works his sovereign will.

Ye fearful saints, fresh courage take,
The clouds ye so much dread
are big with mercy, and shall break
In blessings on your head.

attempted a translation of one of its versions into English.[4] In addition, I was given the rare opportunity of working with my Sanskrit teacher, Br. Pranipata Chaitanya, in revising, editing, contributing a scholarly introduction, and publishing the Sanskrit-English translation of one of the most important philosophical treatises of Vedānta called *Vivekacūḍāmaṇi: The Crest Jewel of Wisdom.*[5]

This author has published three peer-reviewed journal articles on the leadership lessons of the Bhagavad Gītā;[6] has served as a lead editor of a recently edited volume entitled *Bhagavad Gītā and Management: Timeless Lessons for Today's Managers* (Springer, USA, 2018); has conducted several management development programs around the world using the Gītā as a foundational text; has co-organized, moderated, and presented at international conferences dedicated to the Bhagavad Gītā, such as the 2017 Global Bhagavad Gītā Convention organized by the Center for Inner Development Resources, North America, held at UC Irvine during September 9–10, 2017 and the 9th and 10th World Confluence of Humanity, Power & Spirituality held in Delhi and Kolkata, India, during December 16–17, 2016 and December 22–23, 2017, respectively; and has presented on this topic at various national and international academic conferences, including a presentation titled *The Bhagavad Gītā: Old Text, New Leadership Context* at the 2016 Academy of

Judge not the Lord by feeble sense,
But trust him for his grace;
Behind a frowning providence,
He hides a smiling face.

His purposes will ripen fast,
Unfolding every hour;
The bud may have a bitter taste,
But sweet will be the flower.

Blind unbelief is sure to err,
And scan his work in vain;
God is his own interpreter,
And he will make it plain.

[4] Satinder Dhiman, trans., *Kripāmayi Bhagavad Gītā: The Benedictory Gītā* (Gorakhpur, India: Gītā Prakāshan, 2014). Download e-book version at: http://Gītāprakashan.com/englishbook/1.pdf

Satinder Dhiman, trans., *Sahaja-Gītā: The Essential Gītā—Simplified* (Gorakhpur, India: Gītā Prakāshan, 2013). Download e-book version at: http://gitaprakashan.com/englishbook/3.pdf

[5] Pranipata Chaitanya, trans., and Satinder Dhiman, *revised* and *edited with notes* and an *Introduction. Śri Śaṅkara's Vivekachudamani: Devanāgari Text, Transliteration, Word-for-Word Meaning, and a Lucid English Translation.* (Burbank, CA: House of Metta, 2012). http://www.lulu.com/shop/pranipata-chaitanya-and-satinder-dhiman/sri-sankaras-vivekachudamani/paperback/product-20465360.html

[6] S. Dhiman, Bhagavad Gītā & the art of leadership: Old text, new context! *The Journal of Values-Based Leadership*, 2015, 8 (1), 7.

S. Dhiman, The ethical and spiritual philosophy of the Bhagavad Gītā: A Survey. *Interbeing: The Journal of Personal and Professional Excellence*, 2013, 6 (1), 19–39.

S. Dhiman, The universal message of the Bhagavad Gītā. *Business Renaissance Quarterly*, 2013, 8 (1), 37–48.

Management Annual Conference in the All Academy-Theme Symposium: *Looking into the Bhagavad Gītā for Managing Organizations to Become Meaningful*.

The ongoing preparations for this project also entailed several visits to various key spiritual centers in India such as Kundaldhām (Gujarat), Sri Ramana Ashram (Tiruvannamalai, Tamil Nadu), Sri Aurobindo Ashram (Pondicherry), Sri Ramakrishna Math, (Mylapore, Chennai, Tamil Nadu), Kailash Ashram (Rishikesh, Uttarkashi, Uttarakhand), Gītā Bhavan Ashram (Swargashram, Rishikesh, Uttarakhand), and Narayana Gurukulam (Edappally-Varkala, Kerala), and personally meeting, discussing, and learning with many eminent Vedānta teachers, seers, and saints, such as Swami Brahmatmanand Saraswati, Swami Dayananda Saraswati, Swami Paramarthananda, Swami Gyanajivandasji, Br. Shri Pranipāta Chaitanya, and Muni Narayana Prasad.

These explorations, discussions, and translations have helped me to understand and appreciate the larger context of spirituality in general and the universality of the message of the Gītā in particular. During the course of my search and research, I also discovered that, currently, there are hardly any titles that *systematically* and *synergistically* attempt to apply the message of the Gītā to leadership, primarily from the standpoint of Advaita Vedānta.[7] This further spurred my interest in developing this book project.

Approaching the Teachings of the Gītā

The Bhagavad Gītā is an endearing dialog (*saṁvād*) between two friends—the warrior prince, Arjuna, and the Lord in human form, Śrī Kṛṣṇa. So, if we want to really understand the true import of the Gītā, we have to befriend Śrī Kṛṣṇa. There is no room for contention, *vivād*, among friends.

The Bhagavad Gītā is probably the only scripture in human history where the reader is not asked to accept anything on faith. Every question is examined insightfully, and diverse perspectives are presented for reflection. It offers food for thought *without* interfering with the intellectual appetite of the reader. At every step, the freedom of choice of the listeners/readers is respected. "Do as you wish" (not as I say), Arjuna is told at the end (BG 18.63). Teachers only open the door; we have to enter by ourselves.

Throughout, Arjuna asks good questions (*paripraśnena*) and Śrī Kṛṣṇa answers them lovingly and objectively, without becoming upset or deprecating. The student has humility and has respect for the teacher, and the teacher has caring concern for the wellbeing of the student. This makes the Gītā a great treatise on the art and science of effective communication. The real beauty of the Gītā lies in its ability to harmonize the spiritual and the temporal, in the art

[7] The philosophy of Advaita Vedānta is crest jewel of Indian spiritual wisdom and deals with the knowledge and realization of Ultimate Reality that is One, without a second. Please see Chapter 4, entitled "Advaita Vedānta: The Science of Reality."

and science of attaining the highest good (*param-śreyas*) while remaining fully engaged in everyday practical matters. This blend of the spiritual and the practical is the key to the Gītā's universal appeal over the centuries.

The Gītā uses a very special teaching methodology. It presents the highest teachings—the "big picture"—first. Arjuna's was confused about his duty and wanted to know "the right thing to do" (*śreyas*). Śrī Kṛṣṇa starts the teaching with the highest good (*param-śreyas*)—the nature of the Self. Arjuna was mostly worried about the outer kingdom; Śrī Kṛṣṇa points him to the inner Kingdom—the abiding inner treasure of the fullness of our being (*puraṇattvam*).

The message of the Gītā is for everyone who is interested in attaining spiritual freedom. The sole purpose of the Gītā is the salvation of all of humankind. Regardless of one's race, religion, or philosophical orientation, one can attain one's spiritual welfare by following its simple teachings. The Gītā introduces a unique viewpoint, in that if someone does not believe in God, they too can seek their highest spiritual welfare by following the teachings of the Gītā![8]

This is the uniqueness of the Gītā: it teaches the art of seeking the highest good in the ordinary practical matters (*vyavahār mein paramārth ki kalā*). It urges us to perform our duties, in the spirit of detachment and sacrifice (*yajña*) for the mutual benefit of each other. By cherishing each other in this manner, we will attain the "Supreme Good" (BG 3.11). It further assures us that "by properly performing one's duty, everyone attains perfection" (BG 18.45). While many scriptures enjoin the renunciation of the world to attain God, the Gītā states that one can attain perfection by worshiping God (who is the source of all creation and is all pervading) through the performance of one's prescribed duties—*svakarmaṇā tam abhyarcya siddhiṃ vindati mānavaḥ* (BG 18.46).[9]

Developing Right Orientation to Cognize the Truth!

> *Inwardness of spirit, cultivated through self-control and contemplation, enables the student of the scriptures to grasp their subtle meaning, which otherwise remains hidden from the merely intelligent reader.* (Huston Smith, the great American scholar of comparative religion)

The telling phrase at the end of the above quote is noteworthy: "the merely intelligent reader." It is not to decry the role of intellect in understanding spiritual things. It implies that we need to bring *more* than mere *buddhi-kauśaltā* (intellectual competence) to imbibe the deep truths of great wisdom texts.

We need *inner eyes* and *inner ears* to cognize and hear the truth, which is our true nature. We need both the sharp mind and the subtle intellect.

A student of astronomy will not get very far if s/he reads the manuals of astronomy with the commonly-held notion that earth is flat and stationary

[8] Satinder Dhiman, trans., *Sahaja-Gītā: The Essential Gītā*, 12–13.
[9] Ibid., 13.

while the sun rises, moves, and sets. S/he has to acquire astronomy-*driṣti* (vision) to intuit and unravel the truth of the heavenly bodies. Similarly, to a common person, the world appears in the form of multiple, discrete, separate solid objects. Whereas, for a physicist, at the sub-atomic level at least, there are no discreet, separate, solid objects.

Quantum physics tells us that separation is only an optical illusion. According to Bohm, Einstein's colleague and successor at Princeton, this is the natural state of the human world—*separation without separateness.* It is all a play of cosmic energy in the form of a quantum soup of particles vibrating at the speed of light. However, we continue to delight in differences and fail to see that which is essentially the same in all of us. It is abundantly evident that divisions of race, religion, color, creed, and culture have contributed to the most heinous horrors of humankind. This will continue unabated, as history testifies, until we see the tyranny of our disempowering stance and become mindful of our hidden wholeness.

One can never understand the Vedāntic teachings of Oneness if one regards oneself as mere physical body (*deha-buddhi*). A seeker of Self-knowledge has to take his/her firm stand in the conscious principle that illumines the activities of the body, mind, and intellect. Otherwise, the subtle teachings of non-duality as described in the scriptures, *śāstras*, will always elude the seeker.

The Sanskrit word for scripture is "*śāstra.*" *Śāsti ca trayate ca iti śāstram*: that which rules and protects is a *śāstra*. One has to approach the subject, under the guidance of a competent preceptor, with the *śāstra-dṛśti* (the eye of the scriptures). What is the *śāstra-dṛśti* that Vedānta exacts? That I am not the body-mind complex I normally take myself to be. I am the change-less principle, the Witnessing Consciousness, of the objective world (*dṛśya-prapañca*) that inheres and enlivens the body-mind complex. Only then one can arrive at the true knowledge of the boundless Ultimate Reality, which is nothing but our true Self.

Therefore, if we want to understand the Gītā, we have to take our stand in the changeless principle of existence—the Supreme Self. We have to view it from the same height from which the Gītā was discoursed by Śrī Kṛṣṇa. As pointed out above, a student of astronomy will remain foreign to the deeper truths of astronomy if s/he insists, based on common observation, that the Sun rises in the East in the morning and sets in the West in the evening. From the astronomer's standpoint, the Earth moves whereas the Sun is relatively fixed within the context of the solar system. A critical student of astronomy, therefore, has to take the correct standpoint of the astronomer to understand the truths of astronomy. The standpoint of a common person will not help.

Likewise, we have to understand the truths presented in the Gītā from the standpoint of the Self. We have to examine our belief system in the light of the truths presented in this light rather than scrutinizing its truths in the light of our preexisting notions. We have to dare to be on the side of the truth, rather than insisting for the truth to be on our side.

This is the most important key to understanding any profound work of philosophy, including the Gītā.

The Gītā extols equanimity (*samatvaṃ*) above all. In all the three main *yogas* presented in the Gītā, *samatā* is offered as the benchmark of their perfection (*siddhi*). No matter what the path, if evenness of the mind is not attained, the goal is still far away. Favorable or unfavorable, success or failure, gain or loss—these epithets do not sway the one steady in the wisdom of the Self (*sthita-prajñaḥ*: BG 2.55–57). Such a person remains unshaken amidst even the greatest sorrow (*na duḥkhena guruṇāpi vicālyate*: BG 6.22).

The Gītā says that all our existential problems ultimately stem from self-ignorance—not knowing who we truly are. Realizing our true Self as the "immutable, eternal, and conscious principle" constitutes [Self-] knowledge according to the Gītā. Simply put, Self-knowledge is knowledge that you are the Self and *not* the body and the mind. According to the Gītā, realizing that one is not the body or the mind is the first and foremost step on the spiritual journey.

In the final analysis, the Bhagavad Gītā teaches us that true peace can only come by surrendering to the Divine *within* us.

On War and Peace in the Gītā

The first chapter of the Gītā lays out the setting in which armies have been drawn on both the sides. The war of epic proportions is about to begin. Precisely at that critical moment, Arjuna, the warrior prince, develops misgivings about the war and gets grief-stricken. He becomes confused about his true duty and beseeches Śrī Kṛṣṇa, the Supreme Lord in human form, to teach him about the right thing to do (BG 2.7). The remaining 17 chapters are devoted to dispelling Arjuna's confusion and the grief caused by it.

Arjuna was no ordinary fighter; he was a consummate warrior. He knew exactly what his dilemma was.

A fighter fights with others; a warrior's war is with himself. A fighter is focused on the results; a warrior's concern is the process. A warrior knows that when the process is sound, the right results follow inevitably. A fighter quarrels with the inexorable laws of the universe. A warrior has a deep trust in the divine order—an order modulated by the cosmic laws of cause and effect.

In every loss, the fighter *labels* the universe as unfair and unjust. A warrior *knows* that the universe has a structural bias toward goodness. A fighter keeps on collecting *needless* karma by fighting with the inevitable; a warrior triggers no unwanted causes and fears no unintended consequences.

A fighter always thinks in terms of *ends*, namely, winning or losing; a warrior focuses on perfecting the *means*. At every failure, the fighter gets into the blame game and contemplates quitting; the warrior confronts the enemy *within*, resolutely perseveres, and finally prevails.

The fighter spends all life in chasing outer success, blissfully oblivious to the fact that it is temporary and transient. The warrior focuses on the significance of inner victory that is permanent and lasting.

When a master archer fails to hit the target, s/he does not blame the target. S/he steps back, realigns the purpose, works steadfastly on the technique, and comes back—*extra* renewed.

By all thy becoming, *become* a warrior—a peaceful warrior of spirit!

This is one message of the Bhagavad Gītā.

The warrior metaphor is appropriate since the Gītā is a dialog between the warrior-prince Arjuna and Śrī Kṛṣṇa, God in human form. Many scholars/practitioners believe that the war is just an allegory representing the eternal duel of good and bad on the battlefield of our mind.[10] The outer battlefield mirrors the inner battleground of desires and conflicts, ever presenting a perennial choice between the right and the wrong, between proper and improper conduct. The inner landscape represents a field of possibilities for both the good and the bad to manifest; *what actualizes depends upon what we care to feed and nurture.* Noting the multivalence "suggestiveness of the book" to be "almost without limit" when "read with the right attitude of mind," Huston Smith presents his allegorical reading as follows:

> The Gītā can be read as history, but it lends itself readily to being an allegory. In this mode, Arjuna represents the individual soul, and Sri Krishna the Supreme Soul that dwells in every heart. Arjuna's chariot is the body. The blind king Dhṛtarāṣṭra is the mind under the spell of *māyā*, ignorance, and his hundred sons are man's numerous evil tendencies. The battle is an eternal one that is always going on between the powers of good and the powers of evil. The warrior who listens to the advice of the Lord speaking from within will triumph in this battle and attain the Highest Good.[11]

The whole Gītā is presented to enlighten us, through the example of Arjuna, about how to live authentically, how to lead a just cause, and how to fully engage in our duties efficiently, effectively, and ethically while at the same time ensuring our highest goal, that is, spiritual freedom. It demonstrates how leaders achieve lasting influence by exercising Self-knowledge, compassion, and selfless service.

Skilled or Skillful According to the Gītā

Most people merely aim at being "skilled." To be "skillful" is something quite different. Skillful is what is good for one and good for all. This is also the main difference between a fighter and a warrior: A fighter is *skilled*; a warrior is *skillful.*

[10] See: Mahatma Gandhi & John Strohmeier (Ed.), *The Bhagavad Gītā According to Gandhi* (Berkeley, CA: North Atlantic Books, 2009), 16.

[11] Huston Smith, Foreword. In Winthrop Sargeant, trans., *Bhagavad Gītā*, the 25th anniversary edition (New York, NY: New York State University Press), x.

Hence, the Buddha's use of the word "skillful" which in turns depends upon *samma sati*, "right" mindfulness.[12] Not just mindfulness, but *right* mindfulness. A sniper is also mindful and focused; but a sniper's mindfulness will not pass the Buddha's test of "right" mindfulness.

The Gītā defines *yoga* in the same manner: Yoga is skillfulness in action (योगः कर्मसु कौशलम्) (2.50). Earlier in 2.48, the Gītā had defined yoga as *samatā*, "equanimity": समत्वं योग उच्यते. After all, mindfulness is nothing if not equanimous. The exact parallel between "*samma*" of *samma sati* and "*samatā*" of the Gītā is noteworthy.

Skillfulness has a moral valence—right, *in the right measure*. It is *just* right. It is *right* in the dual sense: it is equanimous and non-harming. Since it is equanimous, it is also non-harming.

This perspective is sorely needed in the present turbulent times. Only such right awareness/mindfulness can harbor "peaceful co-existence of all species." The ultimate fulfillment of human life lies in making it worthy for Self-knowledge/realization. Accordingly, the usefulness of an idea, an ideology, or a book depends upon how far it succeeds in helping us attain this supreme goal. The rest is spiritual entertainment or spiritual tourism.

The Subject Matter of the Gītā[13]

What is the subject matter of the Gītā? To start with, we briefly offer three perspectives:

Conjoining the last word of the last verse of the Gītā (18.78) मम (*mama*) with the first word of the first verse of the Gītā (1.1), धर्म (*dharma*), we get "मम धर्म," signifying "my duty." Thus, the Gītā accords great importance to performing one's innate duty (*svadharma*) for the good of others, *without* expecting anything in return.[14] And if we rearrange the first two words of the Gītā "धर्मक्षेत्रे कुरुक्षेत्रे" (*dharmakṣetre kurukṣetre*) as "क्षेत्रे क्षेत्रे धर्मम् कुरुः" (*kṣetre kṣetre dharmam kuruḥ*), we get the following meaning: in every sphere of life, do the *right* thing—in the full wakefulness of Self-knowledge.[15] Doing the right thing brings one under the protective care of Dharma, the cosmic moral order. We have a Vedic injunction: धर्मो रक्षति रक्षिताः *Dharmo rakṣati rakṣitāḥa*: Dharma protects those who uphold Dharma.

Another perspective in approaching the timeless message of the Gītā is to look at the first and last words of Śrī Kṛṣṇa's teachings in the Gītā (that is, verses 2.11 and 18.66). The very first word of the teaching is *aśocyāna* (अशोच्यान 2.11)—not

[12] Right Mindfulness is the seventh of the eight path factors in the Noble Eightfold Path, and belongs to the concentration division of the path. See: http://www.accesstoinsight.org/ptf/dhamma/sacca/sacca4/samma-sati/index.html

[13] For further details, see Chapter 3 entitled "The Real Message of the Gītā."

[14] The Gītā tells us that although the Supreme Lord of universe has nothing to attain personally in all the three worlds, still, the Lord keeps on performing the duties for the benefit of all (3.22). Even so, those in power should model their behavior since majority of people follow whatsoever an important person does (3.21). What an object lesson for the leaders to follow!

[15] To study the Gītā is to study yourself—the *real* "YOU," with "Y" capital, "O" capital, and "U" capital, as my present Vedānta teacher is wont to say.

worthy of grieving over; and the last word is *mā śucaḥ* (मा शुचः 18.66)—do not grieve. The first *śloka* (2.11) further declares that the wise, the knowers of the Self, do not grieve: *nānuśocanti paṇḍitāḥ* (नानुशोचन्ति पण्डिताः).[16] In the Gītā's view, suffering is optional and therefore avoidable. The knowers of the Self overcome all grief. The Gītā expounds the truth of the essential nature of the Self as unborn, indestructible, immutable, eternal, and imperishable (2.16–30). The idea is that the wise, knowing the Self *as such*, do not grieve (2.11,13, 2.25–27, 30; 18.54). Thus, the Gītā offers the highest security system that there is, in the form of Self-knowledge (*ātma-vidyā* or *brahma-vidyā*).

Śrī Rāmakrishna Paramahansa, the great seer-saint of modern India, used to say that one could understand the essential meaning of the Gītā by repeating the word "Gītā, Gītā Gītā Gītā." If the word Gītā is repeated several times, one finds oneself uttering "*ta-Gi ta-Gi ta-Gi…*," and it comes to sound like *tāgi—tāgi* (*tyāgi*–one who renounces, the unreal in favor of the Real).

This is the teaching of the Gītā—"Realize the Real by letting go of the unreal."[17]

The *leitmotif* of the Bhagavad Gītā is the vision of a sage who is pure in heart and steady in mind, and who, having cast off all self-centered desires, moves about free from personal likes and dislikes (*rāga-dveṣa*), established in the Oneness of all existence,[18] even-minded in success and failure.[19] Having attained the highest knowledge of the Supreme Self (*brahma-vidyā*), such a person has "accomplished all that has to be accomplished" (*kṛtakṛtya* 15.20).[20] The Gītā boldly declares that this Self-knowledge (*ātma-jñāna*) or the knowl-

[16] In the Gītā's view, the wise, *paṇḍitāḥ*, are those who know the true nature of the Self—as immortal, who have clear discernment regarding what is real and unreal; that is, those who display *viveka-vati-buddhi* or *kuśāgra-buddhi*.

[17] See: BG 2.16: नासतो विद्यते भावो नाभावो विद्यते सतः *nāsato vidyate bhāvo nābhāvo vidyate sataḥ*: The unreal never is; the Real never ceases to be.

A.R. Orage, the great British philosopher and critic, was a great admirer of Indian wisdom. He is reported to have requested that this half-verse should be inscribed on his gravestone. He considered this verse the highest expression of perennial philosophy, *philosophia perennis*. Orage, whom George Bernard Shaw once called the "the most brilliant English editor and critic of last 100 years," studied the Mahābhārata concertedly for 15 years. He believed that it embodied absolute truths emanating from the Objective and Universal Consciousness. See: Philip Mairet, *A.R Orgage: A Memoir* (New Hyde Park, NY: University Books, 1966), 121. Also see: Wallace Martin, *The New Age under Orage: Chapters in English Cultural History* (New York, NY: Manchester University Press, 1967).

[18] Īśa Upaniṣad declares: What sorrow or delusion for the one who is established in universal Oneness? तत्र को मोहः कः शोक एकत्वमनुपश्यतः ॥ ७ ॥ *tatra ko mohaḥ kaḥ śoka ekatvamanupaśyataḥ //7//*.

[19] What can be favorable or unfavorable for the wise? The wise welcome all situations and experiences as opportunities for self-learning and growth.

[20] Verse 14.3 of *Pañcadaśi*, a philosophical sub-text of Vedānta, declares, "A Self-realized person is ever-blissful on four counts—absence of sorrow (*duḥkhābhāvaś*), the fulfillment of all desires (*kāmāptiḥ*), the satisfaction of having done all that was to be done (*kṛtya-kṛtyo*) and the satisfaction of having achieved all that was to be achieved (*prāpta-prāpyo*)." See: H.P. Shastri, trans, *Panchadashi: A Treatise on Advaita Metaphysics by Swami Vidyaranya* (London: Shanti Sadan, 1982, reprint edition), 448.

edge of the Ultimate Reality (*tattva-jñāna*) is so special that, having known it, nothing else remains to be known here in this world (*yaj jñātvā neha bhūyo'anyaj jñātavyam avaśiṣyate* 7.2).[21] Having nothing here left to be achieved for oneself, such a person works concertedly for the wellbeing of all beings (*sarvabhūtahite ratāḥ*: 5.25; 12.4) and revels in harnessing the coherence of the world order by bringing the world communities together (*lokasaṃgraham* 3.20, 3.25).

We discover that this conception of an *engaged* sage lies at the heart of all wisdom traditions of the world as well. In the first chapter of his masterly work *A Short History of Chinese Philosophy*, Dr. Yu-Lan Fang describes the character of the Chinese Sage as that of "sageliness *within* and kingliness *without*" (emphasis added). Similarly, we find the same theme in Plato's conception of the Philosopher-King, who, having cultivated the wisdom, is *fit* to rule. An unexamined life, said Socrates, is not worth living. This self-examination is called discernment, the art of living attentively. The Buddha's last words were: "Act without inattention."[22]

Life, said Aristotle, is a gift of nature. Beautiful living is a gift of wisdom. In his book, *Nicomachean Ethics*, Aristotle asks a question: What is the essence of life? He then provides the answer: The essence of life is *to serve others and do good*.[23] Thus we see that wisdom has its natural flowering in compassion—selfless benevolence for all beings. In fact, wisdom and compassion are two sides of the same coin.

The wisdom of the Gītā is available to everyone who is interested in it. It transcends all distinctions and boundaries.[24] It is humbly offered in the spirit of "to whom it may concern" and not imposed on anyone (18.67–69).[25] After the entire teachings of the Gītā had been given, Śrī Kṛṣṇa offers Arjuna the complete freedom of choice to decide for himself:

> *iti te jñānam ākhyātaṃ guhyād guhyataraṃ mayā /*
> *vimṛśyaitad aśeṣeṇa yathecchasi tathā kuru* //18.63//

Thus has the wisdom, more secret than all that is secret, been declared to you by Me; reflect over it all and act as you please.[26]

[21] See also BG 6.22:

> *yaṃ labdhvā cāparaṃ lābhaṃ manyate nādhikaṃ tataḥ /*
> *yasmin sthito na duḥkhena guruṇāpi vicālyate* //

Having attained which, one does not reckon any gain greater than that, and established in which one is not affected by even a great sorrow.

[22] *Digha Nikāya* II. 156. Cited in Roberto Calasso, *Kā: Stories of the Mind and Gods of India* (New York, NY: Alfred A. Knopf, 1999), 396.

[23] Retrieved June 10, 2017: https://www.quora.com/What-are-some-great-quotes-of-Aristotle

[24] Throughout the book, the masculine pronoun is used in its universal sense to reflect both the genders. The teachings of the Gītā are gender-neutral and are universally applicable.

[25] The verses of the Gītā are referenced in the chapter, verse format: 18.67 denotes chapter 18, verse 67. All translations are the author's unless otherwise stated.

[26] Alladi Mahadeva Sastry, trans., *The Bhagavad Gītā with the commentary of Sri Shankaracharya*, 497.

Do as you wish, *not* as I say. At best, teachers can only open the door; students have to enter of their own volition.

Thus, the Gītā expounds the art of attaining the highest good (*param śreyas*) while remaining fully engaged in the everyday practical matters. It demonstrates that we can achieve the highest perfection by being true to ourselves (*svakarmaṅā/svadharma* 18.46).

The Bhagavad Gītā teaches that the greatest project you will ever work on is YOU! It says that, ultimately, all our existential problems stem from Self-ignorance—not knowing who we truly are. Realizing our true Self as the immutable, eternal, and conscious principle constitutes [Self-] knowledge according to the Gītā. In the Gītā's view, only those who know themselves are truly wise (*paṇḍitāḥ*).

Knowing the Self, the wise find fulfillment working selflessly for the welfare of the world. What an object lesson for life and leadership!

The Gītā recognizes that much stress in life comes from misalignment of our actions and results. It explains that all actions are orchestrated by the interplay of the threefold properties of the material Nature (*triguṇātmika prakṛti*). Only those who are confused about the true nature of the Self *mis*-appropriate all actions to themselves (3.27). The Gītā teaches us to do our allotted duty diligently and selflessly and leave the results to the workings of the Cosmic Order.

The Gītā teaches us that true peace can only come by surrendering to the Divine *within*.

What is the gist of the message of the Bhagavad Gītā?

Always and in everything, keep your mind fastened on the Truth of the Self and fight the battle of life.[27] Then your actions will become creative expressions of the Divine and you will become *nimita-mātra* (11.33), a mere instrument, for the willing service of the Supreme.

Perhaps no better pointers for making our life divine can be conceived!

There are only a few books worthy of being called "*whole*" and "*holy*." The Gītā is one such book. The final message of the Gītā is, "*Know* yourself, *serve* all, and *surrender* to the Divine within."[28] This is the wisdom we all need in the present turbulent times.

Choosing the Good Over the Pleasant

The Upaniṣads and the Gītā have one central theme or teaching: Complete cessation of sorrow (आत्यंतिक शोक निवृत्ति). According the Gītā 6.23, that state is called yoga which is free from the contact of sorrow (*duḥkhasaṃyogaviyogaṃ yogasaṃjñitam*).

[27] सर्वेषु कालेषु माम् अनुस्मर युध्य च: *sarveṣu kāleṣu mām anusmara yudhya ca* (8.7).

[28] This captures the essence of all three paths, *yogas*: *jñānayoga*, *karmayoga*, and *bhaktiyoga*—the paths of knowledge, selfless action, and devotion. In short, *jñāna* culminating in *bhakti*: Self-knowledge culminating in surrender to the Divine within. When this occurs, *niṣkāma karma*, selfless action, happens on its own accord.

These *yogas*, paths/disciplines, and their application to life and leadership, is the subject matter of this book.

It urges us to know that yoga (*taṃ vidyād*) and to practice it with a resolute and unwearied mind. Sorrow is caused by lack of knowledge about our true Self: We suffer because of self-ignorance. The Gītā aims to remove this sorrow by removing the self-ignorance that is causing it. The lot of an ignorant person is that he goes through life blaming others for all the bad in life while pocketing all the credit for the good. When told about Self-knowledge, one gets upset because one is accustomed to knowing things other than oneself, although it is presumed that a person knows who s/he is. The removal of self-ignorance is the fruit of true Self-knowledge (विद्या फलं असत् निवृत्ति) and that, which liberates, is called knowledge (सा विद्या या विमुच्यते).

According to the Upaniṣads and the Gītā, two type of happiness are available to us: the *preyas* (the worldly, the pleasant) and the *śreyas* (the spiritual, the good). *Preyas* happiness is *caused* by the fulfillment of some desire. *Śreyas* is uncaused happiness—the happiness of realizing our true nature or the fullness of our being (*puraṇattvam*). The fulfillment we drive from the *preyas* goals is at best short-lived and ultimately unsatisfying whereas the fulfillment that results from pursuing the *śreyas* goals is long-lasting and deeply satisfying. Our experience and reflection dictate that wealth and happiness are not related to each other as cause and effect. The very fact that we are constantly in pursuit of happiness shows that we are not content with the current situation.

The Bhagavad Gītā starts with Arjuna's admittance of his confusion with regards to what is decidedly "good" (*śreya*) in life (2.7). This also represents the universal human dilemma—the conflict between duty and desire. Another Indian wisdom text that has close affinity with the Gītā, *Kaṭhopaniṣad* (I.ii.3), speaks about the importance of choosing the right goals over the pleasant in this manner: "Both the good and the pleasant present themselves to a man; the wise man examines them well and distinguishes the two. Wisely does he prefer the good to the pleasant, but the fool chooses the pleasant for its worldly good."[29] The Gītā teaches the path of the *śreyas* that is good in the beginning, good in the middle, and good in the end. The *śreyas*, according to the Gītā, is not any material good or worldly attainment, but realizing the immortal nature of the Self through Self-knowledge.

Three Key Dimensions of Leadership: Knowing, Doing, and Being

The book uses a unique framework of for self-mastery that highlights three key dimensions of leadership: Knowing, doing, and being.

These dimensions can be expressed as:

1. *Know* yourself.
2. *Do* good.
3. *Be* fulfilled.

[29] Swami Nikhilananda, ed. and trans., *The Upanishads: A One Volume Abridgement* (New York, NY: Harper & Row, 1964), 71. [Slightly revised].

The message of the Gītā starts with the Self-knowledge, with the wisdom of our authentic Self, unruffled by the pulls and pushes of the commanding ego. The spirituality of the Gītā is firmly rooted in the ethical values. There is no progress on the path of spirituality if there is no harmony and unity between our *vicāra* (thought process) and *ācāra* (conduct). This book takes it as axiomatic that leadership is a voyage of inner discovery and that Self-knowledge is the key to leading from within. This journey begins with *knowing* oneself and culminates in *living* one's deepest values at the personal, team, and organizational level for the common good. This book is built on the premise that enlightened leaders holistically engage the body, mind, heart, soul, and spirit of those whom they lead.

According to the Gītā, the quest and conquest of Self-knowledge must integrate with life and blossom into the good of all. Only then does it lead to inner freedom and fulfillment. This is the Gītā's path to freedom and fulfillment: Fulfillment is a voyage of inner discovery, a natural state of wellbeing infused with inner joy and peace, independent of any external props. In Gītā's abiding vision, enlightened leaders achieve lasting influence by exercising self-wisdom, compassion, and selfless service.

Unless otherwise stated, the translation of the Gītā's verses and Sanskrit phrases quoted in this book is author's own. Given that all pronouns in the Gītā are masculine, the translation has retained that wherever a neutral term was not possible without sounding linguistically awkward. It purely reflects a convention, and not author's gender bias. The teachings of the Gītā are equally applicable to men as well as women. More importantly, the terms for the Ultimate Reality, the Imperishable, the Supreme Being (*Purṣottama*) have occurred in the Gītā in all the three forms (masculine, feminine, and neuter).

A Brief Overview of the Book and Its Chapters

Focusing on the moral and spiritual dimensions of leadership, this book will present key leadership lessons and concepts as enunciated in the Bhagavad Gītā. Specifically, this book will focus on demonstrating how leaders achieve lasting influence by harnessing Self-knowledge, compassion and selfless service—the three cardinal teachings of the Gītā. It shows why leaders need to be aware of the self and the surroundings, why mind matters most in self-leadership, why leaders need right knowledge and right intention, and how character is the key ingredient of effective leadership.

This book will frequently utilize teaching stories to underscore and clarify various leadership concepts. Stories have been used universally to crystallize an abstract idea since time immemorial. The stories, anecdotes, and metaphors presented in this book are used somewhat in the manner of Jungian *archetypes* for their deeper impact. A story is like a "zip file" that needs to be "unzipped" through deep reflection. These tales are not "bedtime stories" meant to lull us to sleep; they are designed to wake us up.

The author of this book has sought to present each chapter as a complete, independent unit. Accordingly, some repetition of the concepts has been unavoidable. In Vedānta, repetition is a part of learning. Each chapter of the book is presented integrally as an independent whole, and yet the teachings of the Gītā are unfolded in a progressive manner.

Chapter 3, titled "The Real Message of the Gītā," and Chapter 4, titled "Advaita Vedānta," are integral to understanding the deeper import of the Bhagavad Gītā and its application to life and leadership. The author's goal in these two foundational chapters has been to provide a comprehensive overview of all the important concepts to facilitate the understanding of the text. One must first strive to understand a great text fully before one attempts to apply it. Otherwise, one may fall prey to the pervasive syndrome of the "blind leading the blind."

We present below the synoptic overview of the book chapters:

Chapter 1 introduces the Bhagavad Gītā (which literally means the "Song of the Supreme Being") as a timeless manual for Self-mastery and leadership. After briefly recounting the author's preparation for this book, it offers pointers on how to approach the teachings of the Gītā. It lays out the setting by providing an overview of the subject matter of the Gītā and its relevance for contemporary leaders and organizations. Finally, it provides a synoptic overview of all the chapters of this book. Each chapter of the book is presented integrally as an independent whole and yet the teachings of the Gītā are unfolded in a progressive manner.

Drawing upon the wisdom of the Gītā, Gandhi once said that "the best way to find yourself is to lose yourself in the service of others." The Gītā teaches that selfless service is the highest principle of life and leadership. This book focuses on how to harmonize the needs of the individual with the needs of society, and by extension, how to harmonize the needs of the employees and the organization. It demonstrates how the Bhagavad Gītā can be approached as a powerful tool for change management and as a catalyst for organizational transformation. It briefly presents time-tested leadership strategies drawn from the Bhagavad Gītā that are highly relevant for today's leaders.

Chapter 2 establishes the text and the leadership context of the Bhagavad Gītā. The Gītā is a non-sectarian spiritual text with a universal message for living a life of meaning and purpose and for leading from our authentic self. Although traditionally interpreted as a religious-spiritual text, the Gītā encompasses great practical life and leadership lessons for modern times. It shows how to manage oneself, as a necessary prelude to leading others. The Bhagavad Gītā's call for selfless action inspired many leaders of the Indian independence movement including Gandhi, who regarded it as his "spiritual dictionary."

The Bhagavad Gītā, a philosophical poem par excellence, has been extolled as "the scripture of scriptures" within the corpus of Indian spiritual texts. Its unusual battlefield setting, highly practical orientation, and deep philosophical import have endeared it to people from all walks of life looking for guidance in both the sacred and secular realms. While there are many books that aspire to present spiritual truths in practical terms, perhaps there is no other book that presents such an integral vision of attaining the ultimate purpose of life (*mokṣa* or liberation) while fully engaged in the proceedings of life.

In Chapter 3, we will attempt to determine the central theme of the Gītā by applying a three-step interpretative process. First, we will analyze the colophon at the end of each chapter of the Gītā. Secondly, we will apply an exegetical analysis methodology called hermeneutics, a qualitative methodology involving an in-depth interpretation of a key text, to the Bhagavad Gītā, to determine its main message. Finally, we will provide a brief summary of each of the 18 chapters of the Gītā to introduce the text and to synergistically determine its emergent message.

Following the literal meaning of the Gītā is not hard; the real challenge lies in understanding its true spirit. Understanding the true spirit of its message clearly will provide a sure footing for applying its teachings to the leadership domain, as enunciated in the subsequent chapters of this book.

Chapter 4 presents an in-depth survey of Advaita Vedānta as an essential framework to unfold the profound message of the Gītā. To facilitate the comprehension of the text, it will review the key tenets of Vedānta, the earliest and the most refined science of Self-knowledge. This chapter also presents the Vedic ontology and epistemology to explain what is real and how we know what is real. If the first job of a leader is to define reality, as Max Depree once remarked, then understanding what is real can furnish important clues to defining the context and reality of leadership. The Gītā unfolds the vision of the Vedas, the world's foremost and perhaps oldest texts of wisdom. Advaita Vedānta represents the culmination of Vedic wisdom, both historically and philosophically.

By way of a holistic approach to life and leadership, the chapter unfolds the vision of Oneness as propounded by Advaita Vedānta, the non-dual philosophy enunciated in the Bhagavad Gītā, the Upaniṣads, and Brahma Sūtra—the three principal source wisdom texts (*prasthāna-traya*) of Vedānta. It shows that Self-knowledge, as the knowledge of our true nature, is a self-evident, self-established fact. Due to Self-ignorance, we are unaware of this vital fact. The goal of Vedānta is to help us *dis*-cover Self-knowledge and fulfillment, right here and now, as our essential nature. Vedānta boldly declares that there is only one Reality. The world is an expression of it. That art thou! *Know* the Limitless Awareness, Brahman, as your inmost Self, Ātman, and *be* free! This is the promise of Vedānta.

Chapter 5 presents the teachings of the Bhagavad Gītā regarding *karma yoga*, the path of enlightened action, and its application to leadership. The words—*karma* and *yoga*—have become a regular part of everyday discourse in the West, and this chapter proposes to contribute to the understanding of these ubiquitous terms. In this chapter, we will also focus on the path of detached action as a framework for performing selfless service. Many scholars and practitioners believe that the philosophy of disinterested selfless action, *niṣkāma karma*, is the most distinctive contribution of the Gītā to the field of practical spirituality. It is perhaps true that nowhere else is the doctrine of disciplined action enunciated with such clarity and granularity as it is in the Bhagavad Gītā. This path of enlightened action is explored in great depth as an alchemy of sage-hood, the realization of one's Highest Self.

The universality and pervasiveness of action in human life is a veritable fact—nobody can remain action-less even for a moment. Indian philosophy postulates that all actions performed with the desire for self-referent results cause bondage. If we cannot remain without performing actions, and all self-centered actions lead to bondage, is there a way out of this relentless cycle of action and reaction? This chapter presents the Gītā's well-ascertained answer to this enigmatic question. This chapter also briefly discusses the law of karma, since a proper understanding of *karma yoga* also assumes a clear grasp of the operation of this inexorable law, as conceived within the framework of the Indian spiritual paradigm. The doctrine of karma is far more complex than its popular characterization: "What goes around comes around."

Chapter 6 takes as axiomatic that leadership is a voyage of inner discovery and that Self-knowledge is the key to leading from within. This journey begins with knowing oneself and culminates in living one's deepest values and selflessly working for the common good. This chapter presents a unique conception of a leader as an enlightened sage who operates from a higher stance of being, effortlessly anchored in Self-knowledge and self-mastery. As a prelude to the conception of a sage steady in the wisdom of the Self (*sthitaprajña*), this chapter also highlights the need, the importance, and the application of Self-knowledge. Self-knowledge is also essential for leading a fulfilled life. Since happiness is sought for the sake of the self, it stands to reason that the quest for fulfillment should begin with knowing the Self.

By way of illustrating the ideal of being-centered leadership, this chapter briefly profiles three leaders—Steve Jobs, Nelson Mandela, and Gandhi—who directly or indirectly embodied the values of self-actualization, service, contribution, humility, forgiveness, and higher purpose, as articulated in the Gītā.

Chapter 7 presents the pursuit of divine love and devotion (*bhakti yoga*), one of three main *yogas* taught in Bhagavad Gītā. In Hinduism, the *bhakti yoga* is a spiritual path of loving devotion to a personal God. The Gītā postulates two main paths to spiritual freedom—*karma yoga*, the pursuit of enlightened action; and *jñāna yoga*, the pursuit of Self-knowledge (BG 3.3). Bhakti yoga is considered a concomitant to both the *karma yoga* and *jñāna yoga*, for without loving devotion to the ideal of action or knowledge, it is not possible to succeed in either the pursuit of action or Self-knowledge. Through equanimity, service, detachment, and surrender, the Gītā teaches the art of spirituality while being deeply engaged in worldly conduct.

One of the most important applications of *bhakti yoga* is by way of treating everything as sacred and invested with intrinsic goodness and meaning. *Bhakti yoga* bestows the perspective that everyone and everything has a purpose. Essentially, it means a feeling of oneness (at-one-ment) with the whole existence (*sarvātmabhāva*) and seeing God in everything and everything in God. This understanding lends a certain sanctity to all of our activities and helps foster an environment of empathy, kinship, and solidarity. This reclaiming of the sacred dimension of life is sorely needed in the present-day world plagued by distrust, disengagement, and disharmony. The chapter will conclude with leadership lessons based on the path of loving devotion.

Chapter 8 presents the teachings of the Gītā on understanding and restraining the mind and emotions. Given the growing importance of mindfulness and meditation in fostering workplace wellbeing, this chapter also presents the guidelines that the Gītā provides for mastering the mind through practice of meditation. The Gītā unfolds as an infallible guide for those higher-order individuals who externally live a life of full engagement with the world, while internally always remaining steadfastly anchored in the wisdom of their Higher Self and its awareness. It is common knowledge that mental strength and determination are the keys to leadership success; leaders who are mentally weak and wayward cannot achieve a durable and consistent organizational vision or mission.

The Gītā reminds us that an unruly mind is our greatest foe, and a stable mind our greatest friend. It places great emphasis on self-restraint and mental discipline. The outcome of an unrestrained mind is a life given to selfish desire, anger, and greed leading to disempowering culture. These three traps (excessive desire, anger, and greed) are present in every dysfunctional organization, manifested to the highest degree in its leaders. Given the need and importance of meditation during these stressful times, this chapter will also present the teachings of the Gītā on the art and science of stilling the mind.

Chapter 9 presents the ethical and spiritual philosophy of the Bhagavad Gītā as a pathway to a leader's self-mastery and freedom. The first part of the chapter presents an axiomatic fact that the fundamental seeking of all human beings is security, peace/happiness, and liberation. By gently pointing out that our whole problem is a misdirected search due to self-ignorance, the Gītā tells us that the only place where permanent and complete happiness and fulfillment can be found is within ourselves—in the fullness of our own being.

To create a context, this chapter will also provide an essential overview of various *yogas* presented in the Gītā. It mainly focuses on its teachings regarding the discipline of selfless action (*karma yoga*) and the discipline of Self-knowledge (*jñāna yoga*) as two basic archetypes of ethics and spirituality presented in the Gītā. In addition, it presents the essence of *bhakti yoga*, the path of loving devotion, since devotion is a necessary concomitant to success in both *karma yoga* and *jñāna yoga*.

Embedded within these three paths to liberation, it will provide a brief overview of the psychological make-up of individuals comprising three basic modes of nature—*sattva* (purity/goodness) that brings truth/harmony; *rajas* (movement/passion) that kindles action/activity; and *tamas* (ignorance/inertia) that leads to delusion/confusion. The teaching of selfless service and three psychological types have direct application for the field of management and leadership. The chapter will conclude with the five culminating practices for fostering inner security, peace, and harmony in life and leadership.

Chapter 10 focuses on the core message of the Gītā, as interpreted by Gandhi and the practical lessons in life and leadership that Gandhi drew from his lifelong study of this timeless spiritual classic. It traces the influence of the Gītā in the fashioning of Gandhi as a servant leader. It demonstrates why the Gītā exercised such a singular hold on Gandhi's mind and heart. The Gītā was a spiritual reference book for Gandhi. He studied it all his life; he lived, worked and died according to the spirit of the Gītā. It is well known that Gandhi modeled his life upon the teachings of the Gītā and "constantly referred to it as his 'spiritual dictionary,' 'the mother who never let him down,' or his '*kāmdhenū*,' 'the cow that grants all wishes.'" The Gītā played a pivotal role in guiding, shaping, and solidifying his beliefs and actions.

Gandhi's firm and sustained belief in spiritual freedom (*mokṣa*) and Self-realization was almost entirely shaped by the teachings of the Gītā. As Gandhi himself tells us in his autobiography and other writings, the Gītā's emphasis on Self-realization and selfless service were the primary sources of inspiration for his life and leadership. This chapter will also examine the question of whether the Gītā advocates war, especially in the light Gandhi's interpretation of the Gītā and the epic of Mahābhārata.

Finally, Chapter 11 distills the essential teachings of the Gītā on life and leadership. It draws together all the myriad strands presented in the foregoing chapters and offers pointers on the path of action (*karma yoga*), knowledge (*jñāna yoga*), meditation (*dhyāna yoga*), and devotion (*bhakti yoga*). The path of Self-knowledge as taught in the Gītā garners self-awareness, an essential quality of effective leadership. This self-awareness makes us aware of the fact that, at its very core, all life is essentially one. The diversity and multiplicity that we see is an expression of that one Reality in which everything is irrevocably connected to everything else. According to the Gītā, this understanding helps us live a life of selfless service and contribution, the key to personal happiness and social harmony. The Gītā teaches us that true peace can only come by serving the common good and surrendering to the Divine *within* us.

The path to leading others starts with self-awareness through self-discipline and ends with self-transcendence through selfless service. The Gītā calls it enlightened leadership. Enlightened leadership is essentially servant leadership. It represents a shift from followers serving leaders to leaders serving followers. Enlightened leaders are not motivated by personal desires or interests. They become instruments of the whole and selflessly serve for the wellbeing of all beings (*sarvabhūta hitae*, BG 5.25; 12.4). Only those who have relinquished personal ambition can truly serve. According to the Gītā, the path to enlightened leadership is paved with authenticity, humility, service, and compassion. The Gītā teaches us that our choice lifework, *svadharma*, is a supreme means to discover who we are. The goal is Self-knowledge; service is the means.

This culminating chapter presents 101 maxims of life and leadership according to the teachings of the Gītā.

Concluding Thoughts

The Bhagavad Gītā is a quintessential manual of Self-awareness and Self-knowledge. Self-awareness has become the hallmark of recent leadership writings on authentic leadership and emotional intelligence. Self-awareness is rooted in Self-knowledge. Self-knowledge, the knowledge of our true nature, may seem simple but it is not easy. The following verse in the Bhagavad Gītā points out the rarity of the individuals who strive for the knowledge of the Ultimate Reality, and the extreme rarity of the ones who truly arrive:

> *manuṣyāṇāṃ sahasreṣu kaścid yatati siddhaye /*
> *yatatām api siddhānāṃ kaścin māṃ vetti tattvataḥ* //7.3//
>
> Among thousands of people, a rare person strives for perfection or freedom (*mokṣa*). Even among those who strive and are perfect, only a rare person comes to know Me in truth.

The Gītā then goes on to provide the greatest pointers on the path:

> *tad viddhi praṇipātena paripraśnena sevayā /*
> *upadekṣyanti te jñānaṃ jñāninas tattvadarśinaḥ* //4.34//
>
> Know that (i.e., attain Self-knowledge) by humble reverence, by asking proper questions and through service (to the wise). The wise, who have seen the Truth, will teach you that knowledge.

Would-be leaders will do well to take heed.

How rare and special is the message of the Gītā? We can appreciate this better by reading the following dialog between Arjuna and Śrī Kṛṣṇa, as narrated in the Anu Gītā:

> Said Arjuna: "O! mighty-armed one! Your greatness became known to me upon the approach of the battle. O son of Devaki! Your form, as the Lord of the universe, then became known to me! What your holy self said to me at that time, O Kesava, through affection, has all been forgotten by me, O chief of men, in consequence of the fickleness of my mind. You, O Madhava, will repair to Dwaraka soon."

Vasudeva (Śrī Kṛṣṇa) said: "*I discoursed to you on the Supreme Brahman, having concentrated myself in Yoga*....It is impossible for me, O Dhananjaya, to repeat, in detail, all that I said on that occasion. That religion (about which I discoursed to you then) is more than sufficient for understanding the Brahman. I cannot discourse on it again in detail....I made you listen to truths that are regarded as mysteries. I imparted to you truths that are eternal. The recollection of all that I told you on that occasion will not come to me now."[30]

We bow down to the sage Veda Vyāsa (literally, the "arranger" of Vedas) for immortalizing and bequeathing this incomparable scripture to all future generations.

[30] *The Mahabharata*: SECTION XVI (*Anugita Parva*)—Book 14: Aswamedha Parva (Adapted and emphasis added). See: The Mahabharata of Krishna-Dwaipayana Vyasa translated by Kisari Mohan Ganguli. Retrieved June 24: http://www.sacred-texts.com/hin/m14/m14016.htm

CHAPTER 2

Introduction: Text and the Leadership Context of the Gītā

Introduction

A man is pulled in two different directions: towards the realisation of Brahman the absolute and towards the ignorant acceptance of the reality of the world. That which he strives to realise with great intensity wins![1]

This opening quote establishes the need and importance of determining our highest purpose. Life presents a choice of choosing between the absolute good and the relatively pleasant. What we attend to, wins. This chapter establishes the text and the leadership context of the Bhagavad Gītā. The Gītā is a non-sectarian spiritual text with a universal message for living a life of meaning and purpose and for leading from our authentic self. Although traditionally interpreted as a religious-spiritual text, the Gītā[2] encompasses great life and leadership lessons for modern times. Some commentators, including Mahatma Gandhi, view the setting of the Gītā in a battlefield as an allegory for the moral struggles of the human life. It shows how to manage oneself, as a necessary prelude to leading others. The Bhagavad Gītā's call for selfless action inspired many leaders of the Indian independence movement, including Gandhi, who regarded it as his "spiritual dictionary."[3]

Its message fosters the holistic development of human personality in all its dimensions—physical, psychological, emotional, intellectual, and spiritual. The

[1] Swami Venkatesananda, trans., *Vāsiṣṭha's Yoga* (New York, NY: State University of New York Press, 1993), 87.

[2] Abbreviated form of the Bhagavad Gītā.

[3] Mohandas K. Gandhi, *Autobiography: The Story of My Experiments with Truth* (New York, NY: Dover Publications, 1983), 233. See also: Mohandas Karamchand Gandhi article in *Encyclopedia Britannica*. Retrieved May 15, 2017: https://www.britannica.com/biography/Mahatma-Gandhi/Resistance-and-results

S. Dhiman, *Bhagavad Gītā and Leadership*,
Palgrave Studies in Workplace Spirituality and Fulfillment,
https://doi.org/10.1007/978-3-319-67573-2_2

Gītā unfolds as an infallible guide for those higher-order leaders who *externally* live a life of full engagement with the world, while *internally* always remaining steadfastly anchored in the wisdom of the higher Self. Anchored in moral and spiritual values, such leaders seek meaning and purpose through insight, service, and contribution.

Applying the text of the Gītā to the context of leadership, the book addresses the greatest leadership dilemma: What is the right thing to do in a given situation? It views the leader as an "enlightened sage" who operates from a higher stance of being anchored in authentic self, guided by Self-knowledge and Self-mastery. The book presents a unique framework for understanding the psychological make-up of leaders and followers. It presents an effective approach to workplace engagement through a comprehensive analysis of empowering and disempowering stances. The book provides a clear roadmap of developing winning leadership values such as humility, selfless service, compassion, Self-knowledge, self-discipline, and resilience. It concludes with how leaders seek freedom and fulfillment in life and leadership working selflessly for the good of others.

Though in its ultimate bidding a manual for spiritual freedom, the Gītā speaks eloquently to leaders' unremitting commitment to deep spiritual quest—the hallmark of all *good* and *great* leaders. It is not an esoteric treatise on spirituality. In its practical bearing, the Gītā is a great manual for practical living. As A. Parthasarathy has rightly noted, "The Bhagavad Gītā is a technique, a skill for dynamic living, not a retirement plan."[4] The Gītā's ideal is not indifference to the world, but enthusiastic engagement in the full wakefulness of Self-knowledge, love, and compassion born out of realizing one's self *as* the Self of all beings.

This book leverages the wisdom of the Bhagavad Gītā to managing and leading organizations effectively. It innovatively synthesizes the empirical research, best practices, and the latest trends in transitioning toward a more fulfilling and spirituality-oriented workplace. This book is built on the simple premise that it is hard to lead others if one is not able to manage oneself. In the final reckoning, leadership remains an art of self-transformation and our leadership style is an expression of who we are. The transformation of self is also a sine qua non for bringing about larger social change. Lives of exemplary world leaders such as Gandhi, Martin Luther King, Jr., Nelson Mandela, Rosa Parks, Mother Teresa, the Dalai Lama, and Desmond Tutu clearly show that leadership for social change requires cultivation of inner moral and spiritual qualities. These leaders have constantly drawn abiding inspiration from their spiritual roots and moral convictions.

The Buddha once said: "Carpenters fashion wood; fletchers fashion arrows; the wise fashion themselves."[5] Fashioning oneself is a lifelong process and there

[4] A Parthasarathy cited in Dennis Waite, *Back to the Truth: 5000 Years of Advaita* (Winchester, UK: John Hunt Publishing, Ltd., 2007), 519.

[5] As quoted in Lou Marinoff, *Plato, Not Prozac! Applying Philosophy to Everyday Problems* (New York, NY: Harper, 1999), iii.

are no short cuts. For Gandhi, it meant a relentless struggle of 56 long years; for Nelson Mandela, it meant spending 10,000 days in jail; and for Mother Teresa, it meant dedicating her whole life in serving the poorest of the poor! Though some leaders self-develop in the wake of life's crucibles, many need guidance in the art of "fashioning themselves." The Gītā provides the time-tested wisdom for today's leaders.

Perennial Appeal of the Gītā

The Bhagavad Gītā is "one of the most studied and most translated texts in the history of world literature."[6] It holds a special place in the world's sacred and philosophical literature and has wielded an enduring influence on the spirit of humankind over the centuries. Count Hermann Keyserling, a German philosopher, hailed it as "perhaps the most beautiful work of the literature of the world."[7] It is the most popular and widely read text among the followers of Hindu philosophy and religion.[8] According to Aldous Huxley, "The Gītā is one of the clearest and most comprehensive summaries of Perennial Philosophy ever to have been made. Hence, it's enduring value, not only for Indians but for all mankind. The Bhagavad Gītā is perhaps the most systematic scriptural statement of the Perennial Philosophy."[9] According to a preeminent modern Sanskrit scholar, J. A. B. van Buitenen, "No other Sanskrit text approaches the Bhagavad Gītā in the influence it has exerted in the West."[10]

Henry David Thoreau has stated that "in comparison to the Bhagavad Gītā our modern world and its literature seem puny and trivial." A. L. Basham and other Sanskrit scholars agree that the significance of the Bhagavad Gītā in India is comparable to that of the New Testament in Western civilization.[11] Noting its widespread appeal and popularity, Robert N. Minor, a modern exegetical commentator, states that the Bhagavad Gītā has become "the most translated text after the Bible."[12]

[6] Christopher Key Chapple, Editor's Preface with a User's Guide to the Word-by-Word Analysis of the Bhagavad Gītā. In Winthrop Sargeant, trans., *Bhagavad Gītā*, the 25th anniversary edition (New York, NY: New York State University Press), ixx.

[7] Cited in Will Durant, *The Case for India* (New York, NY: Simon and Schuster, 1930), 6.

[8] Naranjan Saha, Bhagavad Gītā: A bird's eye view of its historical background, formation, and teaching. *Indian Council of Philosophical Research*. Published online: Feb 2017. https://doi.org/10.1007/s40961-017-0098-6

[9] Swami Prabhāvananda & Christopher Isherwood, trans., *The Song of God: Bhagavad- Gītā/* with an introduction by Aldous Huxley (New York, NY: Harper, 1951/2002), 22.

[10] J. A. B. van Buitenen, ed. and trans., *The Bhagavad Gītā in the Mahabharata: A Bilingual Edition* (Chicago, IL: University of Chicago Press, 1981).

[11] K. W. Bolle, *The Bhagavad Gītā: A New Translation* (Berkeley, CA: University of California Press, 1979), 224.

[12] R. N. Minor (Ed.), *Modern Indian Interpreters of the Bhagavad Gītā* (Albany, NY: State University of New York Press, 1986), 5.

Steve Jobs' credo "Actualize yourself" seems to have come directly out of the Bhagavad Gītā's philosophy of Self-realization. Peter Senge, one of the preeminent management thinkers of our time, has quoted the Gītā in two of his celebrated books, *The Fifth Discipline* and *Presence*.[13] Mahatma Gandhi regarded it as a spiritual *vade mecum*, a "spiritual reference book"[14] that provided moral and spiritual solace in the vicissitudes of his life:

> When disappointment stares me in the face, and all alone I see not one ray of light, I go back to the Bhagavad Gītā. I find a verse here and a verse there and I immediately begin to smile in the midst of overwhelming tragedies—and my life has been full of external tragedies—and if they have left no visible, no indelible scar on me, I owe it all to the teachings of the Bhagavad Gītā.[15]

Gandhi regarded the Gītā as the nourishing mother and it became the basis for all his moral and social actions. Some scholars believe that Gandhi's autobiography is an extended ode to the Bhagavad Gītā.[16] Speaking about its historical significance and uncommon popularity, Professor A. L. Herman, a philosopher-cum-orientalist, states:

> There is truly something for everyone who comes to the *Gītā* seeking knowledge of an ancient people and their culture, or an understanding of the self as it relates to the world and to God, or an appreciation of another people's moral and religious dilemmas in another time and another place that is strangely and peculiarly contemporary. The greatness of the *Gītā* lies in this universal appeal, its marvellous refusal to be consistently one thing, one message, one way, its ability to relate historically, theologically, philosophically and personally to any people, at any time and any place.[17]

Herman rightly points out that the Gītā's message is highly contemporary, practical, and universal for it speaks endearingly to people from all walks of life who are in search of abiding answers to the fundamental questions of life. He rightly notes how, in times of earthly trouble, suffering, and chaos, the Lord assumes human form and comes to earth to provide solace, comfort, and

[13] See Peter M. Senge, *The Fifth Discipline: The Art & Practice of The Learning Organization* (New York, NY: Doubleday, Revised and updated edition, 2006), 76. Peter M. Senge, C. Otto Scharmer, & Joseph Jaworski, *Presence: Human Purpose and the Field of the Future* (New York, NY: Crown Books, 2008), 92.

[14] Mahatma Gandhi & John Strohmeier (Eds.), *The Bhagavad Gītā According to Gandhi* (Berkeley, CA: North Atlantic Books, 2009), xvi.

[15] Cited in S. Radhākrishnan, *The Bhagavad Gītā: With an Introductory Essay, Sanskrit Text, English Translation, and Notes* (London, Great Britain: George Allen and Unwin, Ltd., 1958), 10.

[16] See: Kay Koppedrayer, Gandhi's "Autobiography" as commentary on the "Bhagavad Gītā." *International Journal of Hindu Studies*, 2002, 6 (1), 47–73.

[17] A. L. Harman, *The Bhagavad Gītā: A Translation and Critical Commentary* (Springfield, IL: Charles C. Thomas Publishers, 1973), vii–viii.

understanding.[18] The practical appeal of the Gītā lies in the fact that it describes at least three ways to spiritual liberation, called *yogas*, to conform to the three basic human types: virtuous, energetic, and indolent. "Simply knowing what kind of human being one is," says Herman, "and using the *yoga* appropriate to one's own nature or personality, leads one ultimately to liberation, freedom, and happiness."[19] The message of the Gītā is not a sectarian dogma; it is a perennial philosophy of universal significance applicable to all of humanity. Just as Arjuna was, we are all confused about who we are and what we should do to attain full and complete happiness. This shows that the teachings of the Gītā are universal and timeless, and *not* specifically given to Arjuna about war.

The Bhagavad Gītā, a philosophical poem par excellence, has been extolled as the scripture of scriptures within the corpus of Indian spiritual texts. The Bhagavad Gītā is the most popular and widely read text among the followers of Hindu philosophy and the religion.[20] Its unusual battlefield setting, highly practical orientation, and deep philosophical import have endeared it to people from all walks of life looking for guidance in both the sacred and secular realms. While there are many books that aspire to present spiritual truths in practical terms, perhaps there is no other book which presents such an integral vision of attaining the ultimate purpose of life (*mokṣa* or liberation) while fully engaged in the proceedings of life.[21] Huston Smith rightly avers, "Truth being one, the Gītā's teachings find their parallels in the other revealed scriptures, but nowhere else are its teachings so succinctly stated."[22] It has been hailed as the philosophy of God-realization.[23] The Gītā

[18] यदा यदा हि धर्मस्य ग्लानिर्भवति भारत।
अभ्युत्थानमधर्मस्य तदात्मानं सृजाम्यहम् ॥ ४.७ ॥

yadā yadā hi dharmasya glānirbhavati bhārata/
abhyutthānamadharmasya tadātmānaṁ sṛjāmyaham // 4.7//

Whenever righteousness is on the decline, and unrighteousness in on the rise,
I send Myself forth into the world—to protect the good (*paritrāṇāya sādhūnāṁ*),
to destroy the wicked (*vināśāya ca duṣkṛtām*), and
to re-establish the sacred *dharma* (*dharmasaṁsthāpanārthāya*): 4.8.

[19] A. L. Harman, *The Bhagavad Gītā*, op. cit., viii. Prof. Harman is improvising on BG 18.46: *svakarmaṇā tam abhyarcya siddhiṁ vindati mānavaḥ*: By performing one's work as an offering to the Creator, one attains supreme fulfillment.

[20] Naranjan Saha, Bhagavad Gītā: A bird's eye view of its historical background, formation, and teaching. *Indian Council of Philosophical Research*. Published online: Feb 2017. https://doi.org/10.1007/s40961-017-0098-6

[21] Swāmī Rāmsukhdās jī, a modern saint-seer who pondered over its mysteries for over nine decades, used to say that the Gītā teaches the art of seeking the sacred in the temporal, *vyavahār mein paramārtha ki kalā*.

[22] Huston Smith, Foreword. In Winthrop Sargeant, trans., *Bhagavad Gītā*, the 25th anniversary edition (New York, NY: New York State University Press), x.

[23] R. D. Rānāde, *The Bhagavad Gītā as a Philosophy of God Realization* (Bombay, India: Bharatiya Vidya Bhavan, 1982).

is a non-sectarian spiritual text with a universal message for living a life of meaning and purpose and for leading from our authentic Self.[24]

The Text and Context of the Gītā

It is believed that the Bhagavad Gītā was composed about 3000 years before the present era (a little over 5000 years ago). The date and authorship of the Gītā is a hotly debated topic among Western scholars and Indian pundits. We shall not burden this chapter with a recounting of the divergent views, for, from the standpoint of this chapter, it is a futile exercise—"a veritable counting of the leaves in place of eating the mangoes after entering a mango garden." In matters of the spirit, what matters is that the content and the context of the text is real and meaningful! Concluding his insightful study on the Gītā, Eliot Deutsch, states "This is indeed a teaching that has meaning and value for all times and places."[25] According to the Indian tradition, the authorship of the Bhagavad Gītā is attributed to the great sage, Veda Vyāsa (literally, the "arranger" of the Vedas).

The Gītā occurs within the great Hindu epic, Mahābhārata, in chapters 25–42 of the Bhīṣma Parva (*The Book of Bhīṣma*), which describes the first part of the great Kurukṣhetra War, a battle between the Kauravas and the Pāṇḍavas, with Bhīṣma as commander-in-chief of the Kauravas and his fall on the bed of arrows. The Mahābhārata contains "107,000 octameter couplets—seven times the length of the *Iliad* and the *Odyssey* combined."[26] The Mahābhārata is believed to be the first written document in the world to theorize the concept of cloning, test tube babies, and surrogate mothers. It is one of the two major epics of ancient India, the other being the Ramāyaṇa. There are 18 main *Purāṇas*, 18,000 *śalokās* of *Śrīmad Bhāgavatam*, and 18 *parvas* (sections) of the epic Mahābhārata; in the *Mahābhārata* war, the army consisted of 18 *akshauhini* (divisions: the Kauravas controlled 11 while the Pāṇḍavas controlled 7); the Kurukṣhetra battle lasted for 18 days; in the same manner, there are 18 chapters in the Bhagavad Gītā.

The Gītā is a sublime song sung by the Lord, Śrī Kṛṣṇa. It is a dialog between Śrī Kṛṣṇa and His dear friend Arjuna, who was a warrior prince. Ever since the great commentator, Ādī Śaṅkarācārya, fixed the total number of its verses to be 700, this number has been considered to be the most authentic, and all modern editions of the Gītā contain 700 verses, although some Kashmiri editions contain up to 742 verses. Some scholars believe that the original Gītā contained 745 verses, conforming to the Gītāmāna Verse (verse giving the message of the Gītā) of the Mahābhārata.[27]

[24] Throughout this book, capital "S" in the word "Self" denotes our real Self—our true nature—while lower case "s" in the word "self" refers to the ego or empirical personality.

[25] Eliot Deutsch, *The Bhagavad Gītā, Translated with Introduction and Critical Essays* (New York, NY: Holt, Rinehart and Winston, Inc., 1968), 190.

[26] Will Durant, *The Story of Civilization Part 1: Our Oriental Heritage* (New York, NY: Simon and Schuster, 1963), 561.

[27] See: Sunil Kumar Bhattacharjya, *The Original Bhagavad Gītā* (Complete with 745 verses, including all the rare verses) (Delhi, India: Parimal Publications, 2014), 11.

The Gītā is one of the most translated books of the world. The first English translation of the Bhagavad Gītā was done by Sir Charles Wilkins in 1785 CE. Sir Edwin Arnold published a beautiful translation of the Bhagavad Gītā in verse in 1885 CE. Since then, more than a thousand translations and commentaries have appeared.[28] The *Purāṇas* and *Itihāsas*, including the Mahābhārata, have been called Panchama Veda or the fifth Veda in the Chandogya Upaniṣads, belonging to the Sama Veda. The Bhagavad Gītā, which is in Mahābhārata, is considered to be the essence of all the Vedas.[29]

The spiritual text, the Bhagavad Gītā, is embedded within the *Bhīṣma Parva* (the Book of Bhīṣma) of the great epic, Mahābhārata, within chapters 25–42. A. R. Orage, an eminent British philosopher and literary critic, extolls the glory of the Mahābhārata as follows:

> The Mahabharata is the greatest single effort of literary creation of any culture in human history. The Iliad and the Odyssey are episodes in it; and the celebrated Bhagavad Gītā is simply the record of a single conversation on the eve of one of its many battles....(It is) the most colossal work of literary art ever created. It contains every literary form and device known to all the literary schools, every story ever enacted or narrated, every human type and circumstance ever created or encountered.
>
> Unlike the reading of derivative works of art, the reading of the Mahabharata is a first-hand experience. One ends it differently, just as one emerges differently from everything real. The Mahabharata towers over all subsequent literature as the pyramids look over the Memphian sands....More real Mysticism can be gathered from the Mahabharata than from the whole of modern mystical writings.[30]

The setting of the Gītā is the austere battlefield of Kurukṣhetra, where the armies have been drawn between the Kauravas and Paṇḍavās, representing two clans of the same descent. The teachings of the Gītā take place right before the war and are presented as a dialog between its warrior-hero, Arjuna, and God in human form, Śrī Kṛṣṇa. Some commentators including Mahatma Gandhi view the setting of the Gītā in a battlefield as an allegory for the moral struggles of the human life.

Christopher Key Chappel splendidly captures the essential setting and context of the Gītā within the compass of a brief paragraph as follows:

> The Bhagavad Gītā tells a story of great crisis, a crisis that is solved through the interaction between Arjuna, a Pāṇḍava warrior hesitating before battle, and Krishna, his charioteer and teacher. The Gītā is included in the sixth book (*Bhīsmaparvan*) of the Mahābhārata and documents one tiny event in a gargantuan epic tale. The

[28] Ibid., 11.

[29] Ibid., 17–18.

[30] See Avin Deen's response: Mahabharata (Hindu epic): Why do some Indians think Mahabharata is superior to all other epics ever written? Retrieved June 21, 2017: https://www.quora.com/Mahabharata-Hindu-epic/Why-do-some-Indians-think-Mahabharat-is-superior-to-all-other-epics-ever-written

main plot of the larger work involves a dispute between cousins over rulership of the Kurukṣetra kingdom in north central India. The kingdom had been lost by five brothers, the Paṇḍavas, during a dice game and ceded to their cousins, the hundred sons of the blind king Dhṛtarāṣṭra. By prearranged agreement, the latter group was due to give back rulership to the five Paṇḍavas brothers, but refused to abide by the contract. The Paṇḍavas are forced to wage war in order to regain their rightful territory. However, these two sets of cousins were raised together and shared the same teachers. The prospect of war between the two camps is especially repugnant because so many good friends and close relatives must be killed. Thus, we arrive at the opening of the Bhagavad Gītā, the moment just before the battle begins. Arjuna is thrust into crisis; he must face the anguish of killing his relatives and friends or allow himself to be killed.[31]

In this chapter (as well as throughout this book), we will unfold the vision of Advaita Vedānta, the non-dual philosophy enunciated in the Bhagavad Gītā, the Upaniṣads, and Brahma Sūtra, the three source texts of Vedānta.

Mahābhārata: A Great Philosophy of Life[32]

The Mahābhārata is an epic, a ballad, perhaps a reality, but definitely a philosophy.

It is said in the texts that 80% of the fighting male population of the civilization was wiped out in the 18 days of the Mahabharata war.

Sanjay, at the end of the war went to the spot where the greatest war took place: Kurukshetra.

He looked around and wondered if the war really happened, if the ground beneath him had soaked in all that blood, if the great Pandavas and Krishna stood where he stood.

"You will never know the truth about that!" said an aging soft voice.

Sanjay turned around to find an old man in saffron robes appearing out of a column of dust.

"I know you are here to find out about the Kurukshetra war, but you cannot know about that war till you know what the real war is about." the old man said, enigmatically.

"What do you mean?"

The old man smiled luring Sanjay into more questions.

"Can you tell me what the philosophy is then?"

Sanjay requested.

"Sure," began the old man.

"The Pandavas are nothing but your five senses:

[31] Christopher Key Chappel, Editor's Preface with a User's Guide to the Word-by-Word Analysis of the Bhagavad Gītā. In Winthrop Sargeant, trans., *Bhagavad Gītā*, the 25th anniversary edition (New York, NY: New York State University Press), ixx.

[32] The Real Meaning of the "Mahabharat". Retrieved July 15, 2018: https://literaryyard.com/2017/04/06/the-real-meaning-of-the-mahabharat/

sight,
smell,
taste,
touch,
and sound…,

And do you know what the Kauravas are?" he asked narrowing his eyes.

"The Kauravas are the hundred vices that attack your senses every day, but you can fight them…and do you know how?"

Sanjay shook his head again.

"When Krishna rides your chariot!"

The old man smiled brighter and Sanjay gasped at that gem of insight.

"Krishna is your inner voice, your soul, your guiding light, and if you place your life in his hands, you have nothing to worry about."

Sanjay was stupefied but came around quickly with another question.

"Then why are Dronacharya and Bhishma fighting for the Kauravas, if they are vices?"

The old man nodded, sadder for the question.

"It just means that as you grow up, your perception of your elders changes. The elders who you thought were perfect in your growing up years are not all that perfect. They have faults. And one day, you will have to decide if they are for your good or your bad. Then you may also realize that you may have to fight them for the good. It is the hardest part of growing up, and that is why the Gītā is important."

Sanjay slumped down on the ground, not because he was tired, but because he could understand, and was struck by the enormity of it all.

"What about Karna?" he whispered.

"Ah!" said the old man. "You have saved the best for last. Karna is the brother to your senses, he is desire, he is a part of you but stands with the vices. He feels wronged and makes excuses for being with the vices as your desire does all the time.

Does your desire not give you excuses to embrace vices?"

Sanjay nodded silently. He looked at the ground, consumed with a million thoughts, trying to put everything together and then when he looked up the old man was gone…disappeared in the column of dust…leaving behind the great philosophy of life!

This is an interesting way to unlock the hidden meaning of this great epic and its main characters. However, it is important not to press the metaphors too far.

The Gītā and Advaita Vedānta[33]

Advaita Vedānta is considered to be the crest-jewel of Indian wisdom.[34] "Advaita" is Sanskrit for "non-dual"—one-without-a-second—and "Vedānta" literally means "the end or inner core of the Vedas," the books of knowledge.

[33] For fuller exposition of the philosophy of Advaita Vedānta, refer to Chapter 4 titled "Advaita Vedānta: The Science of Reality."

[34] "On the tree of Indian wisdom, there is no fairer flower than the Upanishads and no finer fruit than the Vedanta philosophy." ~Paul Deussen, *Outline of the Vedanta System*, vii.

Vedānta is the most widely known system of Indian philosophy, both in the East and the West.[35] It is a philosophy of non-duality based on the Upaniṣads, which are the concluding portions of the Vedas.[36] The word "*Veda*," derived from the Sanskrit root *vid* (to know), means that which makes us know.[37] The Vedas are among the oldest sacred texts in the world. The Upaniṣads, the Brahma Sūtra, and the Gītā form the "triple standard" (*prasthāna-traya*) on which Vedāntic schools of philosophy are based.[38]

Although there are more than 108 Upaniṣads[39] extant, Ādi Śaṅkara (788–820 CE),[40] the great commentator, has written commentaries on 11 principal Upaniṣads. The Vedas are vast like an ocean, and the Gītā represents

The Upaniṣads, the *Brahma Sutra*, and the *Gītā*—form the "triple standard" (*prasthāna-traya*) on which Vedāntic schools of philosophy are based.

[35] See: Eliot Deutsch, *Advaita Vedanta: A Philosophical Reconstruction* (Honolulu, HI: The University of Hawaii Press, 1973), 3.

[36] K. Satchidananda Murty, *Revelation and Reason in Advaita Vedanta* (New York, NY: Columbia University Press, 1959), 3.

[37] Ibid., xvii.

[38] See: K. Satchidananda Murty, *Revelation and Reason in Advaita Vedanta*, xvii.

[39] Once a seeker, approached a great soul, a *Mahātmā*, and asked, "Revered Sir, how many Upaniṣads do I have to study to know myself?" The *Mahātmā* replied with a question: "How many mirrors do you need to look at yourself?"

[40] Professor Karl Jaspers, a preeminent German philosopher of the last century, once told Professor K. Satchidananda Murty, that "*there was no metaphysics superior to that of Śaṅkara.*" See: K. Satchidananda Murty, *Revelation and Reason in Advaita Vedanta* (New York, NY: Columbia University Press, 1959), xvii. [emphasis added].

"In his short life of thirty-two years Sankara," wrote Will Durant, "achieved that union of sage and saint, of wisdom and kindliness, which characterizes the loftiest type of man produced in India. Sankara establishes the source of his philosophy at a remote and subtle point never quite clearly visioned again until, a thousand years later, Immanuel Kant wrote his Critique of Pure Reason." See: Will Durant, *Story of Civilization: Our Oriental Heritage* (New York, NY: Simon and Schuster, 1954), 546–547.

Śaṅkara's fundamental Vedāntic stance can be summarized as follows: That the Brahman (Absolute) is One, without a second, and is of the nature of Pure Consciousness and bliss; that It is always, absolutely, one with the Ātman (Self). ब्रह्म सत्यम् जगन्मिथ्य जिवो ब्रह्मैव न परः। *brahma satyam jaganmithya jivo brahmaiva na paraḥ:*—ब्रह्मज्ञवलि २० (brahmajñavali 20)—Brahman is real, the world is unreal; the individual self and the Supreme Reality are one and the same. Śaṅkara, in his commentary to Brahma Sūtra 3.2.7, explicitly states, "At no time has the *Jiva* ever not been one with Brahman" (न कदाचिज्जीवस्य ब्रह्मणा सम्पत्तिर्नास्ति *na kadācit jīvasya brahmaṇa sampattir nāsti*); that the manifold world of appearance is verily an expression/projection of Brahman alone (*sarvam hi nānatvam Brahmani kalpitameva*) and is *ultimately* non-real (*mithyā*); that Brahman (Ultimate Reality) is of the nature of *satyam-jñānam-anantam*—existence, consciousness, infinitude; that self-less actions (*nishkāma karma*) play a preparatory role in purifying the mind to receive the wisdom of Self-knowledge; that ignorance (*avidyā*) alone is the cause of human bondage; Self-knowledge (*ātam-jñānam*) alone is the means to liberation; and that the spiritual freedom or liberation (*mukti or mokṣa*) is not possible until one realizes or attains the knowledge of oneness of the Self, Ātman, and the Absolute, Brahman (*brahmātma'aikya-bōdham*). All this, of course, is from the empirical standpoint (*vyavahārika-dṛśti*); however, from the transcendental standpoint (*paramārthika dṛśti*), the Self is ever-free and does not need to be liberated. This freedom is eternal and is the very nature of the seeker indeed: *nityatvānmokṣasyasādhakasvarūpāvyatirekācca* (*Bṛhadāraṇyaka Upaniṣad.* 3.3.1).

the essence of the entire corpus of the Vedas. Ādi Śaṅkara (788–820 CE), the great commentator, has aptly observed, "From a clear knowledge of the Bhagavad Gītā all the goals of human existence become fulfilled. *Bhagavad Gītā is the manifest quintessence of all the teachings of the Vedic scriptures.*"[41]

It is important to keep in mind that the teachings of the Gītā stem from the Vedas, as Śrī Kṛṣṇa has himself stated at the beginning of the fourth chapter:

> The *yoga* that I have taught you (in the second and third chapters) is not something new. Rather, it is eternal. First, I revealed this imperishable *yoga* to the Sun-God....This tradition of *Karmayoga* was transmitted in succession among the royal sages, *rājarṣis*. But after a long lapse of time, that *yoga* became lost to the world. You are My devotee and a dear friend; so I have imparted the very same ancient *Karmayoga* to you. For, this (*Yoga*) is the supreme secret.[42]

Therefore, throughout this book, we will draw upon the Vedas, and their concluding portions, the Upaniṣads, to highlight and corroborate the teachings of the Gītā. Understanding the teachings of the Gītā in the backdrop of Vedāntic philosophy is the correct approach to realize the profound message of the Gītā.[43] Perhaps the most distinctive and exalted spiritual tenet one can learn from the Gītā is the truth of One Reality that pervades all and everything in the universe (*vāsudevaḥ sarvam*: 7.19). This Reality is called Brahman[44] (the Absolute, the Totality) and is the very Self (*ātmā*) of everyone and everything. According to the Gītā, those who experience the unity of everything and have the vision of sameness everywhere, see their own Self in all beings, and all beings in their own Self:

> *sarvabhūtastham ātmānaṃ sarvabhūtāni cātmani /*
> *īkṣate yogayuktātmā sarvatra samadarśanaḥ* // 6.29//
>
> Established in the Oneness with Totality,
> the Illumined sage sees with equanimity
> the Self in all beings, and all beings in the Self.[45]

The knowledge of this truth, that we are essentially One Reality or Brahman, "strikes at the very root of narrow views based on selfishness and is the foundation of ethics. This higher Self is of the nature of Bliss, as displayed in our instinctive

[41] तत्इदम्गीता-शास्त्रं समस्त-वेदार्थ-सारसङ्ग्रह-भूतं *tat idam gītā-śāstraṁ samasta-vēdārtha-sārasaṅgraha-bhūtaṁ.*

[42] Gītā 4.1–3. See: *Sahaja-Gītā: The Essential Gītā—Simplified*, p. 53.

[43] See Swami Paramarthananda, *4 Discourses on the Gītā*, Discourse no. 1: Introduction.

[44] Brahman refers to the Absolute Reality or Pure Existence-Consciousness. Not to be confused with Brahmin, which denotes the priestly caste in Hinduism.

[45] Improvising on this theme, Rabindranath Tagore, India's poet Laureate, avers, "He alone knows Truth who realizes in his own soul those of others, and in the soul of others, his own." Quoted in Louis Fry & Mark Kriger, Towards a theory of being-centered leadership: Multiple levels of being as context for effective leadership. *Human Relations*, 2009, 62 (11), 1667–1696.

love of Self; and to recognize it in others is to bring social harmony for no one will be inclined to harm himself."[46] Thus, the Gītā's spirituality is deeply rooted in ethics, for, according to a well-known Indian dictum, "Scriptures do not cleanse the ethically unworthy." There is no spirituality without morality. Hence, ethics forms the very foundation of spiritual life and leadership, according to the Gītā.

The Gītā and Buddhism

Some scholars assert that the use of the word *nirvāṇa* in the Gītā is indicative of its being post-Buddhist. According to a preeminent scholar and translator, Swāmī Gambhīrānanda, "That the Gītā is pre-Buddhist follows from the fact that it does not refer to Buddhism. Some scholars believe that the mention of the word *nirvāṇa* indicates that the Gītā, is post-Buddhist. But the word *nirvāṇa* in the Gītā occurs compounded with brahma as *brahma-nirvāṇaṃ*—meaning identified with or absorbed in Brahman—or with *paramāṃ* as in *nirvāṇa-paramāṃ*, which means culminating in Liberation. The Buddhist Nirvana, on the other hand, is used in the sense of being blown out or extinguished."[47]

Let us look at this issue more closely.

The term *nirvāṇa* occurs five times in the Bhagavad Gītā[48] (verses 2.72; 5.24, 5.25, and 5.26; 6.15), as follows:

> *eṣā brāhmī sthitiḥ pārtha naināṃ prāpya vimuhyati /*
> *sthitvāsyām antakālepi brahmanirvāṇam ṛcchati* //2.72//

> This is the eternal state, O Pārtha (Arjuna). Attaining this, one is no more deluded. Abiding in it even at the time of death, one passes to the Bliss of Brahman (Brahmanirvāṇa).

> *yontaḥsukhontarārāmas tathāntarjyotir eva yaḥ /*
> *sa yogī brahmanirvāṇaṃ brahmabhūtodhigacchati //*
> *labhante brahmanirvāṇam ṛṣayaḥ kṣīṇakalmaṣāḥ /*
> *chinnadvaidhā yatātmānaḥ sarvabhūtahite ratāḥ //*
> *kāmakrodhaviyuktānāṃ yatīnāṃ yatacetasām /*
> *abhito brahmanirvāṇaṃ vartate viditātmanām* //5.24–26//

> He who is happy within, whose joy is within—that is he who enjoys within himself the delight of the Self—and whose light is within, that *yogin* becomes Brahman and reaches the bliss of Brahman. The seers whose sins are destroyed,

[46] K. A. Krishanswamy Iyer, *Collected Works of K. A. Krishnaswamy Iyer* (Holenarasipur, India: Adhyatma Prakash Karyalaya, 2006), 239.

[47] Swāmī Gambhīrānanda, *Bhagavad Gītā with the commentary of Śaṅkarāchārya* (Calcutta, India: Advaita Ashrama, 1984), 15.

[48] R. D. Rānāde, *The Bhagavad Gītā as a Philosophy of God Realization* (Bombay, India: Bharatiya Vidya Bhavan, 1982), 108.

whose doubts (dualities) are dispelled and who rejoice in the welfare of all beings, attain to the bliss of Brahman, who is all peace. To those austere souls (*yatis*) who are free from desire and anger, who have subdued their minds, and know the Self, near to them lies the bliss of the Brahman.

yuñjann evaṃ sadātmānaṃ yogī niyatamānasaḥ /
śāntiṃ nirvāṇaparamāṃ matsaṃsthām adhigacchati //6.15//

Thus always disciplining himself, with his mind restrained, the Yogin attains to peace, the supreme peace (*nirvāṇa*), that abides in Me.

Thus, it is clear from the above verses that the word *nirvāṇa* in the Gītā is used either in the sense of communion (as in BG 2.72) or in the sense of bliss or peace (as in 5.24–26 and 6.15).[49] However, W.D.P Hill clarifies that "the word *nirvāṇa*, familiar in Buddhist literature…occurs several time in the Epic (Mahābhārata), both in the sense of 'calm bliss' and in that of 'extinction.'"[50] Professor Ranade sums up the issue thus, "So when the Bhagavadgītā makes bliss the supreme ideal at which all human effort is to aim, it differs fundamentally from the conception of Nirvana in Buddhism which speaks of annihilation of desire or annihilation of being itself."[51]

Finally, the fundamental platform of Buddhism, says Ranade, is "*sarvam duhkham duhkham, kshanikam kshanikam*"—all things are full of suffering, all things are momentary. The Bhagavad Gītā does not uphold pessimism in any way in that sense. Even when the Bhagavad Gītā speaks of *janmamṛtyujarāvyā dhiduḥkhadoṣānudarśanam* (13.8)—a perception of the evil of birth, death, old age, sickness, and pain—it also speaks of the end of this grief on an optimistic level: *duḥkhāntaṃ ca nigacchhati* (18.36)—whereby one comes to the end of suffering. But if the Bhagavad Gītā stands for anything in particular, it stands for optimism, particularly spiritual optimism.[52]

Nevertheless, there is a fundamental difference between the ontology of Buddhism and Vedānta. Buddhism maintains that since everything is constantly changing, therefore, nothing can have a true nature. In other words, things are "empty" of any abiding essence or self. This doctrine of no-self (*anattā)*, is one of the cardinal tenets of Theravada Buddhism (doctrine of the Elders), the oldest form of Buddhism.

Vedānta says that if we examine our experience closely, we come to know that the consciousness in us that witnesses all the changes—and by virtue of which we are able to *know* about the changes—is the unchanging principle. It is the substratum in which all changes appear and disappear. For in the absence

[49] See also, BG 6.28: *brahmasaṃsparśam atyantaṃ sukham aśnute*: experiences the ultimate bliss of union with Brahman, the Absolute.

[50] W. D. P. Hill, *The Bhagavad Gītā: A Translation and Commentary* (Madras, India: Oxford University Press, 1928/1953), 72.

[51] R. D. Rānāde, *The Bhagavad Gītā as a Philosophy of God Realization,* 108–109.

[52] Ibid., 109.

of this unchanging principle, that is, consciousness, we will not be able to perceive any changes. By definition, the knower of the changes has to be changeless.

Ira Schepetin (a.k.a. *Ātmachaitanya*), a modern Vedānta scholar-teacher in the tradition of Swami Satchidanandendra Saraswati, explains this important point at great length in one of his talks on the Bhagavad Gītā, as follows:

> If you examine your own experience, you will come to understand that, the consciousness in you in which all the changes are occurring—on the basis of which you cognize all changes—that consciousness is not changing. That consciousness in you is aware of every change, of every phenomenon, of every thought, of every objective thing that is always changing. The only way you know that they are changing is because you are the unchanging light in which these changes are appearing and disappearing. That unchanging light, that unchanging consciousness, that unchanging knower—in which all changes are known—can never change. Because the only way to know that things are changing is because there must be some unchanging principle, on the basis of which you are able to know all the changes. You know all the changes because you are permanently there.
>
> That unchanging light is the Self. That is the only reality. Why? Because it never changes. This is the unique teaching of Vedānta, of the Bhagavad Gītā.[53]

Ira Schepetin uses common day-to-day experiences, our own awareness that witnesses all changes, to establish the great axioms of Vedānta—the Changeless Principle, our essential nature. The Gītā 2.16 uses the same definition of determining what is real: The unreal never is; the real never ceases to be (*nāsato vidyate bhāvo nābhāvo vidyate sataḥ*). That unchanging consciousness is our true nature, our real Self.

Then Schepetin goes on to contrast the Vedāntic definition of reality with the Buddhist concept of emptiness and is able to show where the Buddhist standpoint seemed to have erred:

> Buddhists argue that if a thing had a true nature, if it really existed, that true nature could never change. Buddhists do not accept that there is unchanging consciousness. Based on this reasoning—that everything is changing—they argue that nothing has a true nature. Everything is empty. In Vedānta, we say, Sorry sir, there is one thing that never changes. That is not even in time because time itself appears and disappears in that consciousness. That consciousness can't change. It has no parts, it cannot modify itself. It is not in space. It cannot go anywhere. That unchanging consciousness, which is in everyone, is the Self. When you know it, you will know that you are immortal. That knowledge will bring about immortality. You will know the immortal nature of your own Self. That is the only Reality. For the definition of reality is that which never changes. And that which changes cannot be real.

[53] Ira Schepetin, IRA Schepetin gives a talk about The Bhagavad Gītā. Published on YouTube on October 13, 2017. Retrieved May 30, 2018: https://www.youtube.com/watch?v=D5Vl6OUezVY&t=239s

> When you come to know that unchanging principle in you, you will get rid of the idea that I was born, that I am getting old, that I am getting sick and that I am going to die. For the Self is never born, and never dies. That is the teaching of the Bhagavad Gītā (2.20).[54]

We have provided these two extended extracts because they represent the most succinct and clearest explanation of the nature of Self in the entire body of Vedāntic literature. Through this analysis, Schepetin has been able to effectively establish the great truth of Vedānta—that we are the unchanging consciousness behind all changes—in our own experience. When we realize this unchanging principle to be our own Self, we realize our immortal nature, the *summum bonum* of Vedānta and the Bhagavad Gītā.

Concluding Thoughts

> I raise my arms and I shout—but no one listens!
> From dharma comes success and pleasure:
> Why is dharma not practiced? (The Mahābhārata)[55]

The foregoing concluding quote underscores the value of living a life of *dharma* (righteousness). The Gītā, which is a part of the Mahābhārata, likewise highlights the value of living a life of values, a life dedicated to doing our duty for duty's sake. The very first word of the Gītā is *dharma*, meaning duty (Gītā 1.1). The last word of the Gītā is *mama,* denoting "my" (Gītā 18.78). Conjoined they signify "*mama dharma*" (my duty). Therefore, the Gītā takes place within the domain of human conduct or duty. In the final reckoning, the Gītā is a book of Self-knowledge, as the colophon at the end of each chapter of the Gītā states: ब्रह्मविद्यायां योगशास्त्रे, a treatise of "yoking" (योगशास्त्रे) one's mind to the Supreme, the Absolute Reality, through Self-knowledge (ब्रह्मविद्या). All the "yogas" presented in the Gītā are different "yoking" devices to "fasten" oneself to the Supreme Reality. This is the master key to understanding the Gītā.

The goal of all spiritual quest is twofold: happy individuals and harmonious society. A Vedic verse captures this sentiment succinctly: आत्मनो ज्ञानार्थम् जगत् हिताय च[56]:

> For the Knowledge of the Self,
> For the Wellbeing of All Beings.

[54] Ibid.

[55] P. Lal, *The Mahabharata of Vyasa: Condensed from Sanskrit and Transcribed into English* (Lake Gardens, Kolkata: Writers Workshop 2010), 370.

[56] Mission statement of Ramakrishna Order, *slightly* modified: *Ātmano mokṣārtham jagat hitāya ca* (आत्मनो मोक्षार्थम् जगत् हिताय च) is a mantra in the *Rig Veda*. Literally, it means, "for the freedom of the Self and for the welfare of the world." Since the Self, *ātmā*, is never bound and is ever-free, by "Self-freedom" the mantra really means "Self-knowledge." Through Self-knowledge, one realizes one's intrinsic freedom. See Karan Singh, *Hinduism* (New Delhi, India: Sterling Publishers Pvt. Ltd., 2005), 71.

Gaining the knowledge of Real, our True Self, is the main message of the Gītā. Acting for the good of others in the full wakefulness of Self-knowledge is the culmination of the Gītā. No higher ideal for authentic leadership can be conceived.

Throughout this book, a sincere attempt has been made to present the essential teachings of the Gītā in clear and simple language. Having presented them in the correct light, the teachings are then applied to harness the self-awareness and self-mastery dimensions of leadership. The Gītā garners a view of the leader as an "enlightened sage" who operates from a higher stance of being anchored in authentic Self, performing actions in a spirit of offering to the Supreme for the good of all.

According to the Gītā, all virtues obtain in a mind that has cultivated equanimity. Whatever the spiritual practice, says the Gītā, if evenness of mind (*samatā*) is not attained, the goal is still far away. It represents the culmination of *wisdom in action* informed by Self-knowledge and guided by selfless service. Self-knowledge transforms our motivation and liberates us from the narrow confines of self-centered action to the freedom of serving others. Self-knowledge enables one to act in the world with a deep sense of peace and inner fulfillment. Such leaders work selflessly for the wellbeing of all beings and attain the highest felicity of Self-realization, the supreme goal of the Gītā.[57]

Does our life/work comprise what is true, beautiful, and good? The question is not how to live longer; the question is how to live well longer. The Gītā answers the question with a counter-question: How can I serve the world with my gifts? How can I grow in goodness? That's all, says the Gītā, you need to know to live well. *Be* Good. *Do* Good. All blessings, says the Gītā, will follow on their own accord.

May the Light of Goodness hold you, the concerted reader, in everything you do, and auspiciously pave your way everywhere you go.

[57] See: Gītā 5.25 & 12.4. *labhante brahmanirvāṇam…sarvabhūtahite ratāḥ:* 5.25: Working for the wellbeing of all beings, sages attain liberation in the Absolute. We have Gandhi's testimony inspired by the teachings of the Gītā: "What I want to achieve,—and what I have been striving and pining to achieve these thirty years,—is Self-realization, to see God face to face, to attain *Moksha*. I live and move and have my being in pursuit of this goal. All that I do by way of speaking and writing and all my ventures in the political field are directed to this same end." See: M. K. Gandhi, *An Autobiography: The Story of My Experiments with Truth* (New York, NY: Dover Publications, 1983), viii.

CHAPTER 3

The Real Message of the Gītā: Decoding the Text

Introduction

Scriptures are endless and there is much to study.
Time is short and there are too many hindrances.
What is essential must be acquired and practiced.
Like the swan separating milk mixed with water.[1]

This opening quote highlights the importance of discernment in pursuing our quest for knowledge. Since, art is long and life is short, we need to have a fine discriminating intellect—*viveka*—which can separate the kernel from the husk. In Indian tradition, a mythical swan is believed to have the ability to extract only milk from a mixture of milk and water. Such should be the sense of discernment of an astute seeker after truth.

Within the Indian religious-philosophical tradition, the Gītā forms a part of "the triple foundation" texts or *prasthāna-traya*, the other two texts being the

[1] अनन्त शास्त्रं बहुलाश्च विद्याः स्वल्पश्च कालो बहुविघ्नताच |
यत्सारभूतं तदुपासनीयं हंसो यथा क्षीरमिवाम्बुमध्यात् ||

ananta śāstraṁ bahulāśca vidyāḥ svalpaśca kālo bahuvighnatāca /
yatsārabhūtaṁ tadupāsanīyaṁ haṁso yathā kṣīramivāmbumadhyāt //

See: Minati Kar, ed. and trans., *Uttara-Gītā* (Calcutta, India: Ramakrishna Institute of Culture, 2007), 40.

One is also reminded of a famous quotation by Francis Bacon (1561–1626) that occurs in an essay titled, *Of Studies*: "Some books are to be tasted, others to be swallowed, and some few to be chewed and digested: that is, some books are to be read only in parts, others to be read, but not curiously, and some few to be read wholly, and with diligence and attention." See: Francis Bacon, *The Essays* (New York, NY: Penguin Classics, 1986), 209.

The Gītā is indeed one such book whose wisdom needs to be thoroughly "chewed" and "inwardly digested."

S. Dhiman, *Bhagavad Gītā and Leadership*,
Palgrave Studies in Workplace Spirituality and Fulfillment,
https://doi.org/10.1007/978-3-319-67573-2_3

Upaniṣads and the Brahma Sūtras. Although, technically, it belongs to a class of literature called "*smṛti*"—"remembered" or "traditional texts"—it has the status in Hindu culture of "*śruti*"—"scripture" or "revelation."[2] Śrī Śaṅkarācārya (ca. 788–820), the great Indian philosopher, lifted it up from the vast ocean of the *Mahābhārata*, fixed its verse-content at 700 and wrote the oldest extant commentary on it.[3] There is a sort of consensus among scholars today that the text of the *Bhagavad* Gītā, as fixed by Śaṅkarācārya long ago at 700, is a unitary text.[4]

The Gītā is universal in its message, comprehensive in its outlook, and concrete in its suggestions. It is a non-sectarian spiritual text, completely free from sectarian dogma. As Scott Teitsworth has rightly observed:

> There is no vengeful God in it, only a benign and loving principle, called Brahman, or the Absolute. It is replete with the finest spiritual advice tendered without compunction or guilt....There are no chosen or cursed souls, only more or less damaged and confused ones. The game here is to rectify the damage and dispel the confusion with clear thinking and action....In learning from the Gītā, we have to find and express our own inner motivation.[5]

It is important to remember that, though in its ultimate bidding the Gītā is essentially a manual for spiritual freedom (*mokṣa śāstra*)—as Śaṅkarācarya, its greatest commentator and exponent reminds us—however, in its practical aspect, it is also a great manual for living and not an esoteric treatise on spirituality. As A. Parthasarathy has rightly noted, "The Bhagavad Gītā is a technique, a skill for dynamic living, not a retirement plan."[6]

Determination of the Subject Matter of the Bhagavad Gītā

Why is it important for us to determine the central theme of the Gītā? It is because before we set out to suggest its practical application in the field of leadership, we first need to precisely know its main message. Additionally, we need to understand it in the total context of Mahābhārata, the grand epic of which it forms an important part. For, like every important text, its teachings can be easily taken out of context and misinterpreted. *Following the literal meaning of the Gītā is not hard; the real challenge is understanding its true spirit.*

[2] Eliot Deutsch, *The Bhagavad Gītā, Translated with Introduction and Critical Essays* (New York, NY: Holt, Rinehart and Winston, Inc., 1968), 3.

[3] See: Swami Tapasyānanda, *Śrīmad Bhagavad Gītā* (Madras, India: Śrī Ramakrishna Math, 2010), vii; S. Radhakrishnan, *The Bhagavad Gītā: With an Introductory Essay, Sanskrit Text, English Translation, and Notes.* (London, Great Britain: George Allen and Unwin, Ltd., 1958), 15.

[4] See: Eliot Deutsch, *The Bhagavad Gītā*; A. G. Krishna Warrier, trans., *Śrīmad Bhagavad Gītā Bhāṣya of Ādi Śaṅkarācārya* (Madras, India: Śrī Ramakrishna Math, 1983), ix.

[5] Scott Teitsworth, *The Path to the Guru: The Science of Self-Realization According to the Bhagavad Gītā* (Rochester, VT: Inner Traditions, 2014), 3–4.

[6] A. Parthasarathy cited in Dennis Waite, *Back to the Truth: 5000 Years of Advaita* (Winchester, UK: John Hunt Publishing, Ltd., 2007), 519.

Determining the True Message of the Gītā

Although one can enjoy the beauty of a flower from a distance; to enjoy its perfume, one needs to get closer to it. However, if one wants to savor its real nectar, one will need to approach the flower with the precision of a honey bee. Even more so, it is with understanding the key message of a profound scripture such as the Bhagavad Gītā. To appreciate the true splendor of the Song Celestial, we need to delve deeper into its profounder harmonies.

In this chapter, we will attempt to determine the main import of this text, applying a series of formative and summative interpretative processes.

The Bhagavad Gītā, literally "Song of the Lord," often referred to simply as the Gītā, is the most important spiritual text of the Hindus. It is one of the three main source texts (*prasthāna-traya*) of Vedānta—the Upaniṣads and the Brahma Sūtras being the other two. It has been aptly described as the Bible—the scripture par excellence—of the Hindu tradition. In fact, the Gītā is "the most translated Indian book."[7] According to a conservative estimate, "the Gītā has been translated over 2,000 times in 75 languages."[8] Over the course of centuries, many sages, experts, and lay people have written commentaries on it, suggesting both its sacred and secular significance. Every commentary, classical or contemporary, *claims* to embody the *real* message of the Gītā. The sheer volume of commentaries and sub-commentaries on the Gītā could leave a reader overwhelmed and often bewildered.[9] Commenting on the reasons for the diversity of interpretations of the Gītā, Mysore Hiriyanna observes:

> It is one of the hardest books to interpret, which accounts for the numerous commentaries on it each differing from the rest in—some essential point or other. Part of this diversity in interpretation is due to the assumption that the Gītā not only concerns itself with the problem of conduct whose solution is a pressing need for man if he is to live without that inner discord which arises from consciousness of the ideal unaccompanied by mastery over self, but also is a treatise on metaphysics.[10]

The Gītā is not only one of the most translated books, it is also one of the most commented upon books of the world. Since the subject matter of the Gītā is highly subtle and profound, one often needs the help of various commentaries to understand its deeper import. As stated above, myriad commentaries by clas-

[7] The Gītā is among the most translated and most commented upon book of the world's sacred texts. See: Koti Sreekrishna & Hari Ravikumar, trans., *The New Bhagavad-Gītā* (Mason, OH: W.I.S.E. Words Inc., 2011), 35.

[8] Ibid., 36.

[9] Ādi Śaṅkara, perhaps the most important commentator on the Gītā, says that he undertook to write his commentary precisely for the reason that there were many highly conflicting meanings (*atyanta-viruddha-anēka-arthatvēna*) and that the real meaning of the Gītā is hard to fathom (*durvijñēyārthaṁ*).

[10] Mysore Hiriyanna, *Outlines of Indian Philosophy* (Delhi, India: Motilal Banarsidass Publishers, 2005, reprint Indian Edition), 117.

sical and contemporary authorities exist, and the sheer volume of those commentaries can be bewildering to a seeker. It is beyond the scope and intent of this chapter to evaluate various commentaries. However, it may not be amiss to list a few noteworthy English translations of the Gītā's most famous commentator, Ādi Śaṅkarācārya. Although translations by Swami Gambhirananda and Dr. A. G. Krishna Warrier present Śaṅkarā's *bhāsya* (commentary) in a contemporary English idiom, yet Alladi Mahadeva Sastry's translation—even though, strictly speaking, it is not a complete translation—seems closer to the intent and purpose of the original. If you do not mind some interpretive theosophical leanings, then this translation can convey the gist of Śaṅkarācārya's commentary in a simple, pure, and unvarnished way. Sastry usually gets to the essence of the original in the most direct way.

Huston Smith, the great religious studies scholar, calls the Gītā "literally a pager-turner" and a "multivalent book," for "there is something in it that will reward every serious reader."[11] In this chapter, we will use a three-step interpretive process to determine the main theme of the Gītā. First, we will analyze the colophon at the end of each chapter of the Gītā. Secondly, we will employ scriptural exegesis called hermeneutics,[12] a qualitative approach involving an in-depth interpretation of a key scriptural text, to the Bhagavad Gītā, to determine its main message. Finally, we will provide a brief summary of each of the 18 chapters of the Gītā to introduce the text and to determine its progressive message synergistically.

For most Indian people, the Gītā is a scripture blessed with God's Grace (*ek prasādik grantha*).[13] The Lord Himself has declared it to be His very own

[11] Huston Smith, Foreword. In Winthrop Sargeant, trans., *Bhagavad Gītā*, the 25th anniversary edition (New York, NY: New York State University Press, 2009), ix.

[12] Originally, an approach used for the interpretation of ancient and biblical texts, hermeneutics has, over time, been applied to the human sciences more generally. Hermeneutics as an interpretive methodology of understanding has much to offer those interested in qualitative inquiry, and is especially suitable for work of a textual and interpretive nature. Given that the emphasis in qualitative research is on understanding and interpretation, as opposed to explanation and verification, the connection between qualitative research and hermeneutic thought becomes self-evident. Hermeneutics employs the art of interpretation, and the transformative possibilities within, to seek in-depth understanding of a key text. The goal of hermeneutics is to arrive at a deeper sense, hidden under the surface—*hypónoia*, that is, *underlying* meaning.

See: Elizabeth Anne Kinsella, Hermeneutics and critical hermeneutics: Exploring possibilities within the art of interpretation. *Forum Qualitative Sozialforschung/Forum: Qualitative Social Research*, 2006, 7 (3), Article 19. Retrieved March 6, 2017: http://nbn-resolving.de/urn:nbn:de:0114-fqs0603190

[13] Satinder Dhiman, trans., *Kripāmayi Bhagavad Gītā: The Benedictory Gītā*: Selection and compilation, Rajendra Kumar Dhawan (Gorakhpur, India: Gītā Prakāshan, 2014), 39. Based on Paramśraddheya Swāmījī Shrī Rāmsukhdāsjī Mahārāj's Discourses. (Gorakhpur, India: Gītā Prakāshan, 2014), 39.

Heart: "*Gītā mey hṛdyam Pārtha.*"[14] Extolling the glory of the Gītā, Ādi Śaṅkara (788–820 CE), its most renowned commentator, states: "From a clear knowledge of the Bhagavad Gītā all the goals of human existence become fulfilled....Bhagavad Gītā is the compendium of the quintessence of all the teachings of the *Vedic* scriptures."[15]

We first look at the colophon at the end of each chapter of the Gītā to understand the subject matter of this text.

The Colophon of the Bhagavad Gītā

The colophon that occurs at the end of each chapter of the Gītā signals the basic theme of *each* chapter. In addition, it highlights the central theme of the *entire* text to be both "the knowledge of Brahman and *yoga*": ***Brahmavidyāyāṁ yogaśāstre śrīkṛṣṇārjunasaṁvāde*** (ब्रह्मविद्यायां योगशास्त्रे श्रीकृष्णार्जुनसंवादे). The colophon is not found in the Mahābhārata, but is conventionally used in reciting the Gītā. Literally, this colophon means: a treatise of "yoking" (*yogaśāstre*) one's mind to the Supreme, the Absolute Reality, through Self-knowledge (*brahmavidyāyāṁ*), presented in the form of a dialog between Śrī Kṛṣṇa and Arjuna (*śrīkṛṣṇārjunas aṁvāde*). So, what does the Gītā teach? It teaches two things mainly: ***knowledge*** of the Absolute Truth/Reality and the ***practice*** of yoga (***brahmavidyāyām yogaśāstre***).[16] Since reality is non-dual, the knowledge of Absolute Reality (Brahman) also signifies knowledge of the Self (Ātman). Thus, the colophon signifies that the Gītā is a treatise comprising a dialog between Śrī Kṛṣṇa and Arjuna about yoking the Self to the Supreme—through the knowledge of the Self or Ultimate Reality.

This is the first important clue to the central message of the Gītā.

The colophon also refers to the Gītā as an Upaniṣad, ***śrīmadbhagavadgītās ūpaniṣatsu*** (श्रीमद्भगवद्गीतासूपनिषत्सु), thus, signifying the essence of the Upaniṣads and placing it at the same level as these most sacred of Hindu texts (Upaniṣads) representing the concluding portions of the Vedas. The Upaniṣads contain highly developed—and the earliest available—spiritual philosophy about the true nature of our Self.

[14] Ibid., 19.

[15] *yataḥ tadartha-vijñānē samasta-puruṣārtha-siddhiḥ ataḥ...*
tat idam gītā-śāstraṁ samasta-vēdārtha-sārasaṅgraha-bhūtaṁ.

[16] In the Western world, normally, the word "yoga" is commonly taken to mean bodily postures, to say nothing of the yoga mats and yoga pants! Even within Patañjali's progressive stages of *aṣṭāṅga yoga*, bodily postures (*āsanas*) form one of the eight components of this yoga system, occurring after the ethical don'ts (*yamas*) and do's (*niyama*) have been observed. Nevertheless, yoga is about ***straightening the mind*** and not ***twisting the body***. As the following chapters will show, the word ***yoga*** is used in myriad ways in the Gītā, such as ***karma yoga, bhakti yoga, rāja yoga, dhyāna yoga, and jñāna yoga***. In a special sense, it is also used to denote certain skillfulness, ***kauśalam***. For further details, please refer to the section titled, "The Gītā is a Treatise of Yoga, a Yoga Śāstra."

Brahma-Vidyā: Ātman = Brahman: Identity of Self-Knowledge (Ātma-Jñāna) and the Knowledge of Absolute Reality (Tattva-Jñāna)

The spiritual journey is from "me" to "I."[17]

> *Brahma-vidya* is the science of the Absolute—that system of thinking which is enabled to comprehend within itself at any time the *total* structure of things.... The reality of a particular thing is not only in itself; it is also in that which determines it, restricts it, influences it, conditions it, defines it, and makes it what it is....Brahma-vidya is the art and the science of educating oneself in the manner of *correctly perceiving* the world as such, including one's own self, in the totality of relations, so that no partial vision of things can be regarded as a passport to the concept of the Absolute.[18]

The above extract suggests that the knowledge of Absolute Reality, *Brahma-vidyā*, entails, above all, correctly perceiving things simultaneously from an individual as well as from a holistic perspective—in their entirety, in totality. That is, looking at the big picture without losing sight of the underlying details. Throughout all its chapters, the Gītā never loses sight of this dialectic of the absolute and empirical standpoint. However, by way of highlighting its *leitmotif*, the Gītā underscores the absolute standpoint of the Self and provides pointers to intuit it. Therefore, in order to understand the true import of the Gītā, one needs to take one's stand in the highest truth[19]—the changeless conscious principle in whose presence and association all empirical transactions take place.

In the Gītā, wherever the Lord refers to Himself as "I," or "Me" or "My," It should be taken to mean the Absolute Reality and Its expression or Absolute Supreme Self.[20] As Sri Krishna Prem writes, "It is thus not a person who is speaking in the Gītā but the great Brahman out of which all beings come and into which all will in time return."[21]

[17] My esteemed Vedānta teacher, Śrī Sreenivāsa Murthy-jī of Bangalore, has always reiterated this point: The spiritual journey is from "me" (body-mind-senses complex) to "I" (the changeless, conscious principle).

[18] Swāmī Krishnananda, *Commentary on the Bhagavadgita:* Discourse 1: The Colophon of the Bhagavadgita. Emphasis added. Retrieved March 7, 2017: http://www.Swāmī-krishnananda.org/bgita/bgita_01.html

[19] The expression "taking a stand in the highest truth" is not used in any dogmatic sense. It means having a correct *perspective* about the nature of Ultimate Reality—as Limitless Existence-Consciousness. This is the most important point to bear in mind in studying all profound texts. Only when our standpoint is correct can we expect to draw right conclusions.

[20] Ira Schepetin, Bhagavad Gītā Talk, September 14, 2017. Retrieved February 19, 2018: https://www.youtube.com/watch?v=VHbiTNsoYi4&t=19s

[21] Sri Krishna Prem, *The Yoga of the Bhagavadgītā* (Sandpoint, ID: Morning Light Press, 2008), 127.

We list below some examples where the Gītā directly points to the knowledge of the Absolute Reality (*brahma-vidyā*):

1. Know That alone to be imperishable by which all this (universe) is pervaded.[22]
2. There is nothing else besides Me, the Supreme Lord.[23]
3. I am the Self seated in the heart of all being.[24]
4. That which has to be known, I shall describe, knowing which one attains immortality.[25]
5. Knowing which nothing else remains to be known in this world.[26]
6. Knowing which one is released from all that is inauspicious.[27]
7. The Absolute has eyes everywhere, has feet everywhere, and has hands everywhere, because it is neither a subject nor an object.[28]

The Gītā presents the characteristics of the Ultimate Reality both in its individual expression as the *Ātman*, our innermost Self, as well as in its absolute sense, the *Paramātman*. For example, in chapter 2 verses 24–25, the Self *Ātman*, is described as eternal, all-pervading, immovable, constant, unmanifest, incomprehensible, immutable, and everlasting. Similarly, in chapter 12 verses 3–4, the characteristics of the Supreme Self, *Paramātman*, are stated to be: omnipresent, indefinable, indestructible, eternal, immovable, unmanifest, and changeless. There is a striking similarity between the characteristics of the individual self and the universal spirit, indicating the unity and identity of the Self, *Ātman*, and the Supreme Self, *Paramātman* or Brahman. Brahman and Ātman are one and the same "limitless-conscious-existence." Brahman is the knowing Self/Subject within us—the unchanging conscious principle that illumines all and everything. Realizing the identity of the individual Self and the universal Self constitutes Self-knowledge (*ātma-jñāna*) or *tattva-jñāna*, the knowledge of Ultimate Reality.

[22] *avināśi tu tad viddhi yena sarvam idaṃ tatam* (2.17). See also, BG 8.21 & 8.22.

[23] *Mattaḥ parataraṁ nānyat kiñcid asti* (7.7).

[24] *aham ātmā guḍākeśa sarvabhūtāśayasthitaḥ* (10.20).

Sri Ramana Maharshi, the great modern Sage, regarded verse BG 10.20 as representing the quintessence of all 700 verses of the Gītā: "Bhagavan was speaking once with a visiting pandit about the great merits of the Bhagavad Gītā, when a devotee complained that it was difficult to keep all the seven hundred verses in mind and asked if there was not one verse that could be remembered as the quintessence of the Gītā. Bhagavan thereupon mentioned chapter 10, verse 20: 'I am the Self, Oh Gudakesa, dwelling in the Heart of every being; I am the beginning and the middle and also the end of all beings.'" See *The Collected Works of Sri Ramana Maharshi* (Tiruvannamalai, India: Sri Ramanasramam, 2002), 153.

[25] *jñeyaṁ yat tat pravakṣyāmi yaj jñātvāmṛtam aśnute* (13.12).

[26] *yaj jñātvā neha bhūyo.anyaj jñātavyam avaśiṣyate* (7.2).

[27] *yaj jñātvā mokṣyaseśubhāt* (9.1).

[28] *sarvataḥ- pāṇipādaṁ tat sarvatokṣiśiromukham, sarvataḥśrutimal loke sarvam āvṛtya tiṣṭhati* (13.13).

The "kernel of Upaniṣad teaching" can be presented as follows:

1. The *ātman*,[29] [the Self], is the consciousness, the *knowing* subject within us.
2. The *ātman*, as the knowing subject, is itself unknowable as an object.
3. The *ātman* is the sole reality.[30]

Put differently,

There is one Ultimate Reality.
The world is an expression of It.
That *art* Thou!
This is the declaration, *udaghōsha*, of Vedānta and the Gītā.

The main purpose of the Bhagavad Gītā is to highlight this knowledge of the real nature of the Self, *ātma-jñāna*, knowing which one crosses over sorrow.[31] Arjuna is grieving over the dreadful consequences of the imminent war—death of his relatives and others. He is thinking in terms of the relative standpoint of an individual. He forgot that he is a warrior fighting a righteous war, a war that has been imposed upon him as a last resort. The Lord knew that nothing short of the absolute knowledge (*Brahma-vidyā*) regarding the immutability of soul would assuage Arjuna's sorrow.

This liberating knowledge of the eternal Self is the subject matter of the Gītā.

Self-knowledge is not a matter of accumulating information, but rather, of removing mistaken notions about the Self.[32] You are already the Self and your true nature is already limitless awareness. You simply haven't seen yourself in the right light, so to speak. Once the mind is exposed to the teachings, the teachings do the work of correcting the mind's misapprehension.[33] When scriptures speak of someone attaining enlightenment, it is only "figuratively speaking." As A. J. Alston clarifies, "Enlightenment implies no change of state,

[29] *Ātman*, the Self, is the unchanging conscious principle that illumines the senses, the mind and the intellect.

[30] See: Paul Deussen, *The Philosophy of the Upanishads* (New York, NY: Dover Publication, 1966), 399–400.

[31] Chāndogya Upaniṣad 7.1.3: *tarati śokam ātamvit*: The knower of Self crosses over sorrow.

[32] My Vedānta teacher, Śrī Sreenivāsa Murthy, is wont to say "Vedānta is about demolishing the wrong notions regarding the Self. We do not build (or add anything to) the Self. It is all about subtracting." Strictly speaking, Self-realization is not an attainment. As James Swartz explains, "the self cannot be gained because you are the self already. Self-knowledge is only a loss of ignorance, not a gain of the self." See: James Swartz, *How to Attain Enlightenment* (Boulder, CO: Sentient Publications, 2009), 275. See also, the opening sentence of *Tao Te Ching*, poem 48: "In the pursuit of knowledge, everyday something is added. In the pursuit of Tao, everyday something is dropped." Stephen Mitchell, trans., *Tao Te Ching: A New English Version* (New York, NY: Harper Perennial, 1992), 54.

[33] Ted Schmidt, *The Event of "Enlightenment" Versus Self-Actualization*, September 1, 2015 Satsang. Retrieved March 22, 2017: http://www.nevernotpresent.com/satsangs/the-event-of-enlightenment-versus-self-actualization/

but only the correction of an error."[34] As Pure Awareness, we are already free. Self-knowledge corrects the error of taking ourselves to be a limited "body-mind-senses" complex. It helps us to realize our true nature and own up to it.

Self-realization and God-realization are one and the same because the essential nature of God and the Self is the same. When you have realized the nature of wave,[35] you have also realized the nature of ocean, namely, water. The truth of microcosm is the truth of macrocosm. If a person says I have realized the Self and thinks that I have not realized God, it means he has not realized either the Self or God. Analogically speaking, God or Brahman is like referring to water as ocean; Self or *Ātman* is like referring to water as wave.[36]

The Gītā Is a Treatise of Yoga, a Yoga Śāstra

Although some Western scholars believe that the Gītā is a loose collection of thoughts of different schools, Madhusudana Saraswati divides the Gītā into three systematic sections of six chapters, each section dealing successively with ***karma-yoga***, ***bhakti-yoga***, and ***jñāna-yoga***, the first leading to the second and the second to the third.[37] In the third chapter of the Gītā,[38] however, only two yogas (***karma yoga*** and ***jñāna yoga***) are mentioned. ***Bhakti yoga*** is not mentioned since ***bhakti*** is essential for attaining success in both ***karma yoga*** and ***jñāna yoga***. For example, in chapter 10, we have two important verses that show

[34] A. J. Alston, trans., *Śaṅkara Source-Book, Volume VI: Śaṅkara on Enlightenment* (London, UK: Shanti Sadan, 2004), 224.

[35] The wave is busy with "mergers and acquisitions" without realizing that it is ocean only. As water, both the wave and the ocean are essentially one. However, practically speaking, a wave is a wave and an ocean is an ocean: one can navigate a ship in the ocean, but not in the wave. Strictly speaking, ocean and wave are water only, but water is neither wave nor ocean. In other words, water can exist without wave and ocean, whereas ocean and wave cannot exist independent of water. Likewise, subject, the Self, exists even in the absence of objects of experience, as in deep sleep. An object cannot exist independent of the conscious subject. This is an important distinction to keep in mind with reference to subject and object. Hence, concludes Vedānta, the world of objects is ***dependently*** real (***mithyā***) while the subject alone is really real (***satyasya-satyam***).

[36] See Ted Schmidt, *Non-Duality Is the Basic Tenant of Vedanta*, February 14, 2017 Satsang. Retrieved March 22, 2017: http://www.nevernotpresent.com/satsangs/non-duality-is-the-basic-tenant-of-vedanta/

[37] Swami Gambhīrānanda, trans., *Bhagavad Gītā with Commentary of Saṅkarācārya* (Calcutta, India: Advaita Ashrama, 1984), 21.

Most commentators, however, agree that the chapters of the Gītā conform to the Upaniṣadic statement "*Tat Tvam Asi*" or "You are that." The first six chapters cover the "Tvam" or the "you" aspect, the next six cover the "Tat" or the "That" aspect, and the final six chapters cover the "Asi" or the "are" aspect. That is, the Gītā first explains the truth of the eternal Self (***ātman***) in chapters 1–6; then, it explains the truth of the Supreme Self (***Paramātman***) in chapters 7–12; and finally in chapters 13–18, it underscores the identity of Self and the Supreme Self.

[38] In this world, a twofold path was taught by Me in the beginning, the path of knowledge (for ***jñāna-yogis*** who have clear knowledge of the Self and the non-Self) and the path of action (for ***karma-yogis*** who are inclined to action). (3.3). Śaṅkara's comment: The path of action is a means to the end, a ***preparatory step*** leading to the path of knowledge. The path of knowledge leads to the goal (***mokṣa***) directly.

that *jñāna* is the reward of *bhakti*: "For those who are always committed to Me, seeking me with loving-devotion, I bestow that vision whereby they reach me. For them alone, out of compassion, I, obtaining in the thought of their mind, destroy the delusion born of ignorance by shining the lamp of knowledge."[39] Similarly, we find an important verse in chapter 8 that presents *bhakti* (devotion) expressed in the form of *karma-yoga*: "Always and in everything, keep your mind fastened on the Truth of the Self and fight the battle of life."[40]

The setting of the Gītā's message is highly meaningful. It takes place on the battlefield, on the eve of a war of epic proportions. The genesis of the teachings in the battlefield signifies the great practical orientation of the Gītā. It is an applied treatise on the art of living, a *yoga-śāstra*. The word "*yoga*" is used in a very special sense in the Gītā, unlike its meaning in the context of the *Yoga Sūtras of Patañjali*.[41] Etymologically, the word *yoga* comes from the Sanskrit root "*yuj*," which is cognate with the word "yoke." The *yoga*, "yoking," that is intended in the Gītā is the union of individual self, *jīvātmā*, with the Supreme Self, *Paramātmā*. According to the preeminent Sanskrit scholar, J. A. B. van Buitenen, "The word *yoga* and cognates of it occur close to 150 times in the Gītā, and it needs attention."[42] It is also helpful to bear in mind that in the Gītā, *karma* (action) does not always equate with "*karmayoga*," and *jñāna* (knowledge) does not always signify "*jñānayoga*." A spiritual practice becomes "*yoga*" only if it leads to communion with the Divine. Otherwise, it is a mere mundane activity. This basic fact should not be lost sight of in the study of the Bhagavad Gītā.

"*Yoga*" is a multivalent word with several shades of meanings in the Gītā. The root meaning of the word is "union." However, at two places, Śrī Kṛṣṇa presents the word "*yoga*" in its truest meaning: BG 2.48 and BG 6.23. In BG 2.48, Śrī Kṛṣṇa states "*samatvaṁ yoga ucyate*"—the evenness of mind is called *yoga*. The second important sense in which the word "*yoga*" is used in the Gītā occurs in verse BG 6.23: *taṁ vidyād duḥkhasaṁyogaviyogaṁ yogasaṁjñitam*—the state of *disassociation from association with sorrow* should be known as *yoga*.

[39] The Gītā 10.10–11. Based on Swami Dayananda Saraswati, trans., *Śrīmad Bhagavad Gītā*: Text with Roman Transliteration and English Translation (Chennai, India: Arsha Vidya Research and Publication Trust), 131–132.

[40] The Gītā 8.7: सर्वेषु कालेषु माम् अनुस्मर युध्य च: *sarveṣu kāleṣu mām anusmara yudhya* ca. Śaṅkara's comment: तस्मात् सर्वेषु कालेषु माम् अनुस्मर यथाशास्त्रम्। युध्य च युद्धं च स्वधर्मं कुरु: "therefore; always think of Me, in the way prescribed by the scriptures and engage yourself in war, which is your own duty."

[41] Considered the foundations of classical yoga philosophy of Hinduism, the *Yoga Sūtras of Patañjali* were compiled prior to 400 CE by the sage Patañjali. According to Swāmī Krishnananda, "This is the whole yoga of Patanjali, for instance, which summarizes in two *sutras—yogaḥ cittavṛtti nirodhaḥ* (I.2); *tadā draṣṭuḥ svarūpe avasthānam* (1.3): 'The restraint of the mind is yoga; and then there is establishment of self in its own self.' Here is the whole of yoga in two sentences." The Gītā captures the essence of meditation in less than half a verse: *ātmasaṃsthaṃ manaḥ kṛtvā* (6.25): Resolving the mind in the Self.

[42] See: J. A. B. van Buitenen, ed. and trans., *The Bhagavad Gītā in the Mahābhārata: A Bilingual Edition* (Chicago, IL: University of Chicago Press, 1981), 17. In the original Sanskrit text, the word *yoga* occurs in the Bhagavad Gītā eighty-one times as a noun and twenty-five times in its verbal form as *yukta* or *yuktā*. See Swāmī Rāmsukhdās jī, *Gītā Jñāna Praveśikā* (Gorakhpur, India: Gītā Press, 2000), 246–247. [This book in Hindi is a veritable treasure trove of some very important information about the structure and composition of the Gītā. See also Swāmījī' authoritative book of philosophical essays on the Gītā entitled *Gītā Darpaṇ*].

Here, the word *yoga* is used in the sense of *viyoga* (disassociation). According to the Gītā, *the complete freedom from sorrow is possible only when one is established in the Supreme Self (Paramātman).* This meaning of the word *yoga* should not be confused with the Rāja Yoga taught in the Yoga Sūtras of Patañjali "where the goal may either be supernormal perception or supernormal powers—only *within* the phenomenal world—or the complete *suppression* of all the activities of the mind."[43] The only *yoga* that the Gītā recommends can be described as "*adhyātma-yoga*," that "spiritual discipline," whereby one withdraws the mind from sense-objects and concentrates it on the Self[44]:

> *śanaiḥ śanairuparamedbuddhyā dhṛtigṛhītayā /*
> *ātmasaṁsthaṁ manaḥ kṛtvā na kiñcidapi cintayet* //6.23//
>
> With the intellect endowed with perseverance, may one slowly resolve the mind (in *ātman*). Making the mind abide in the Self,[45] may one not think of anything else.[46]

When used in the form of *karma yoga, bhakti yoga, jñāna yoga,* and so on, it primarily means "discipline," a "method," or a "way." Swāmī Rāmsukhdās jī used to say that the word *yoga* (union) should more properly be used in the context of *karmayoga* because, with regard to the disciplines of knowledge (*jñānayoga*) and devotion (*bhaktiyoga*), the "union" is quite natural. The Seer, after realizing that God is all, remains naturally established in the experience of Oneness; and the devotee likewise constantly experiences reverential union with the Lord by keeping mind and thoughts fixed on God. It is because the path of actions is marred by selfish desire and attachment to results that we need to "attain union"—*yoga*—through the discipline of *karmayoga*. All the "*yogas*" presented in the Gītā are different "yoking" devices to "fasten" oneself to the Supreme Reality.

The following story splendidly points out the path and the goal of all the *yogas*:

How the Little Fish Discovered the Ocean, Finally!

Once upon a time, a deep curiosity arose in the mind of a little fish that used to live in the ocean. She asked her mother, "For many days now, I have been hearing this word 'ocean.' What is this thing called 'ocean' and where can I find it?"

The mother-fish replied, "O, my dear, I too likewise have been hearing about this word called 'ocean' since my early childhood, but I do not know anything about it. Nor have I ever pondered over it. Let me ask my friends." The mother fish asked her friends the same question; they also replied that they too had not thought about this matter.

(*continued*)

[43] A. J. Alston, trans., *Śaṅkara Source-Book, Volume VI: Śaṅkara on Enlightenment*, 93.
[44] Ibid., 94.
[45] *Making the mind abide in the Self*—this telling phrase sums up the entire art and science of not only meditation but also Self-realization.
[46] Swami Dayananda Saraswati, trans., *Śrīmad Bhagavad Gītā*: Text with Roman Transliteration and English Translation (Chennai, India: Arsha Vidya Research and Publication Trust), 90.

(continued)

However, her friends advised the mother-fish that there was a wise old fish; perhaps she would know about the ocean. They decided to go and ask her.

Some fishes left the search and did not accompany them, saying, "You go ahead and meet with this wise old fish. We have nothing to do with this thing called 'ocean!'" Some fishes accompanied the mother-fish and the little fish just out of curiosity.

They all went to see the wise old fish to inquire about the ocean. They said to the old fish, "What is this thing called 'ocean?' Do you know anything about it?"

The wise old fish had a big laugh hearing all this and addressed them, solemnly: "O, dear ones, that in which we all are born, that in which we all live day and night, that in which we will subside one day, that which pervades inside and outside of us all, that in whose being we find our sustenance, that from which we can never ever be separated, and that which is present all around us—that verily is the ocean!"

Many fishes who heard it did not understand this abstract explanation and started staring at each other in utter disbelief. Some wise ones were wonder-struck in awe.

But that little "seeker-fish" (jijñāsu)*, absorbed in the deep contemplation of the ocean, became utterly silent! For she had now truly "experienced"/"realized" the ocean, firsthand, in her direct experience!*

Six Markers Signifying the Main Message of the Gītā

It is clear from the foregoing that the principal subject matter of the Gītā is Self-knowledge (*ātma-jñāna*) or the knowledge of the Absolute Reality (*brahma-vidyā* or *tattva-jnana*). In this section, we will employ a sixfold exegetical analysis methodology to arrive at the central message of the Gītā. This characteristic of the teaching revealing one central theme is called *samanvaya*, convergence. In the case of the Bhagavad Gītā, the convergence is on Self-knowledge. To show convergence, we have to employ the exegetical analysis (*mīmāṃsā*) of sixfold criteria (*chaṭa liṁgāni*). Thus, from sixfold criteria, convergence is proved; from convergence, a central theme is proved.[47]

An important Mīmāṃsā lists six signs (*liṁgama*) or criteria to look for in order to determine the true and ultimated purport (*tātparya nirṇaye*) or central theme of any text[48]:

[47] See: Swāmī Paramārthānanda, *Brahma Sūtras*, Summary Discourse No. 388. Retrieved June 12, 2017: http://hinduonline.co/AudioLibrary/Discources/CommentaryOnBrahmaSutraParamarthananda.html

[48] उपक्रमोपसम्हारौ अभ्यासोऽपूर्वताफलम् ।
अर्थवादोपपत्तिश्च लिङ्गं तात्पर्यनिर्णये ॥

upakramopasamhārau abhyāso'pūrvatāphalam/
arthavādopapattiśca liṅgaṁ tātparyanirṇaye //

upakramopasaṁhārāvabhyāso'pūrvatāphalam /
arthavādopapattī ca liṅgaṁ tātparyanirṇaye //

In ascertaining the meaning, the characteristic signs are—the beginning and the conclusion, repetition, originality, result, eulogy, and substantiation.

According this verse, the six determining signs, *chaṭa liṁgāni*, of a text are:

1. The beginning and the conclusion (*upakramo upasaṁhāra*)
2. Repetition (*abhyāsa*)
3. Originality or novelty or uniqueness (*apūrvatā*)
4. Result (*phalaṁ*)
5. Eulogy (*arthavāda*)
6. Demonstration through examples and illustrations (*upapatti*)

The Beginning and the Conclusion of the Text (*upakramo upasaṁhāra*)

An analysis of the beginning and conclusion of the Gītā reveals that Self-knowledge, or the knowledge of the Absolute Reality, is the key message that the Gītā wants to convey. The Gītā starts with Arjuna's question to know the highest good. Arjuna is a warrior-king and is the main character of the Gītā. He came to the battle knowing well who he would be fighting. However, after taking a look at the armies arrayed for battle, his mind became confused about his duty (*dharmasaṃmūḍhacetāḥ*: 2.7). A deep sense of pity overpowered his heart and he started expressing all kinds of doubts about the purpose and the outcome of the war. He confessed that his mind was confused regarding his duty and beseeched Śrī Kṛṣṇa, his charioteer,[49] to guide him. Arjuna's mind was

This section is primarily based on Swāmī Tejomayananda jī's six masterly discourses on the Bhagavad Gītā titled *Geeta at a Glance*—Melbourne—2012 MP3 6 Talks (Discourse no. 2). This author is especially indebted to Swāmījī for this succinct *six-point analysis* of the text. He has not come across similar analysis of the Gītā's contents in terms of the sixfold criteria elsewhere in the literature. To get a deeper understanding of this unique presentation, the readers may like to listen to these talks that were given in English—especially talk number 2 that focuses on the discussion of these six determinants of the central theme of a given text. The following text that also presents the analysis of the six signs (*liṁgama*) of the Bhagavad Gītā arrived quite late in this author's hands to fully benefit from its remarkable exegesis: Śrī Śrī Swāmī Ātmānandendra, *Gītā Sādhana Sōpāna: Steps to Self-Realization as Taught in the Bhagavad Gītā* (Woodstock, NY: Vedāntic Light Publishers, 2017), 58–93.

[49] The role of Śrī Kṛṣṇa, the Lord in human form, acting as the charioteer of Arjuna is deeply symbolic. The Lord, seated in the hearts of all beings as the Self of all (BG 10.20; 18.61), is indeed the inner director of all activities. The chariot metaphor also occurs in *mantras* three and four in chapter 1, section three (*Adhyāya*-1, *Vallī*-3) of *Kaṭhopaniṣad*, an *Upaniṣad* which has a few verses common with the Bhagavad Gītā. Plato also uses the chariot allegory in his dialog *Phaedrus,* to explain the journey of human soul toward enlightenment. The *Kaṭhopanisạd* 1.3.3–4 likens the human body to a chariot (*ratha kalpanā*) to describe the position of individual Self (*ātmā*) *vis-à-vis* senses (*indriya*), mind (*manas*), and intellect (*buddhi*). The mind is the reins and the five senses are the horses. The objects perceived by the senses represent the chariot's path. The intellect is the driver, and the Self as the passenger acts as the enjoyer or sufferer in the association of the mind and senses. Whereas an ordinary person is constantly driven by the wayward mind and unruly desires for sense objects, a wise

under the spell of ignorance and misplaced pity. Arjuna wanted *to know* what is decidedly good (*yac chreyaḥ syān niścitam*: 2.7). Ānanda Giri states that the word *niścitaṃ* here signifies "that which is absolutely true." Thus, Arjuna is here beseeching Śrī Kṛṣṇa for imparting the knowledge of the Absolute Reality, the Self, which leads to liberation, *mokṣa*.

After the teachings of the Gītā have been thoroughly imparted, Śrī Kṛṣṇa asked Arjuna at the end of the last chapter if his (Arjuna's) *delusion born of ignorance* had been dispelled (*ajñānasaṃmohaḥ pranaṣṭaste*: 18.72). Arjuna's response was succinct: "My doubts and delusion are gone; by Thy Grace, I have now regained the remembrance of my true nature (*ātma-smṛti*). I am steady in my understanding and will do Thy bidding" (18.73). The teachings of the Gītā end at this point. From analyzing these two verses occurring respectively at the beginning and the end of the Gītā, we come to know that the highest teaching that the Gītā wants to impart is the knowledge of the true Self that dispels delusion born of ignorance of the Self (*ātma/tattva-jñānena ajñāna-nivṛtti*). Thus, we find that the subject matter of the Gītā is removal of ignorance by imparting the knowledge of the Self or the Absolute Reality.

What Is Repeatedly Emphasized Throughout the Text (*abhyāsa*)

The second point that needs to be analyzed to determine the subject matter of a text is *abhyāsa*. That which the author repeatedly emphasizes in a text to bring to our notice is called *abhyāsa*. When Arjuna said: "O Lord, please teach me," the very first word[50] of teaching spoken by Śrī Kṛṣṇa was, "*aśocyān*": *not* worthy of grief; and the last words were, "*do not* grieve" (*mā śucaḥ*: 18.66). The first *śloka* (2.11) with which the teachings of the Gītā starts further declares that the wise do not grieve (नानुशोचन्ति पण्डिताः). The Gītā expounds the truth of the essential nature of the Self as unborn, indestructible, immutable, eternal, and imperishable (2.16–30). The idea is that the wise, knowing the Self *as such*, do not grieve (2.11,13, 2.25–27, 30; 18.54).

As stated above, the teachings of the Gītā begin from verse 11 of chapter 2, after Arjuna admitted his confusion and beseeched Śrī Kṛṣṇa to teach him[51]:

person uses the power of intelligence to discern between what is pleasant (*preyas*) and what is good/right (*śreyas*).

[50] To be precise, the very first words spoken by Śrī Kṛṣṇa occur in chapter 1 verse 25. After placing the chariot in the middle of two armies—right in front of the Great Bhīṣma and Drōṇa, Śrī Kṛṣṇa addressed, "Arjuna! Behold these Kauravas assembled here." Swāmī Rāmsukhdāsjī in his famous Hindi commentary on the Bhagavad Gītā entitled *Sādhaka-Sañjīvānī* states: "Arjuna only wanted the chariot to be placed in between two armies. If the Lord had placed the chariot anywhere, the teachings of the Gītā would not have started at all. But the Lord placed the chariot right in front of Bhīṣma and Drōṇa, and said, 'Behold these Kauravas assembled here.' If the Lord, instead of saying 'behold these Kauravas assembled here,' had said, 'Behold the sons of Dhaṛtarāṣtra,' Arjuna would not have felt the sorrow, without which the teachings of the Gītā would not have begun. For, Arjuna was certainly ready to engage in the battle with the sons of Dhaṛtarāṣtra." See *Kripāmayi Gītā*, p. 11.

[51] In the Bhagavad Gītā, Śrī Kṛṣṇa's teachings begin at 2.11 and end at 18.66. Ādī Śaṅkara also begins his masterly commentary from verse 2.10 onward. He says that the purpose of verses

aśocyān anvaśocas tvaṃ prajāvādāṃś ca bhāṣase /
gatāsūn agatāsūṃś ca nānuśocanti paṇḍitāḥ //2.11//

You grieve over those who should not be grieved for and yet speak like the wise. The wise do not grieve over the dead or the living.

The upshot of this verse is that "the wise do not grieve." In other words, wisdom and grief do not go together. Arjuna was grieving and Śrī Kṛṣṇa essentially told Arjuna that his grief was due to ignorance. It is clear from this first verse that to grieve over anything or any person is not wise. The Sanskrit word "*paṇḍitāḥ*" comes from the root "*paṇḍā*," which means "knowledge of the Self"—a discerning intellect capable of discriminating between the real and the unreal,[52] between the eternal and the ephemeral. Those in whom this wisdom, that is, sense of discrimination, is highly developed are called "*paṇḍitāḥ*." Throughout the Gītā (2.11; 4.19; 5.4, 5.18), the word "*panḍitāh*" refers to the knowers of the Self, to those endowed with the ability to discern between the real and the unreal. After all, there is nothing to grieve about the [unchanging] real; for, the real (the Self) never ceases to be (2.16). And there is nothing to grieve about the [changing] unreal, for it is transient anyway. It is only when we mistake the unreal *as* real that we grieve and suffer.[53]

The reason the wise do not grieve is that they are well aware of the distinction between the eternal Self and the ephemeral body. Arjuna was grieving because of his ignorance about this vital distinction between the real and the unreal. This Self-ignorance can only be removed by Self-knowledge. Hence, based on the foregoing analysis of this seminal opening verse, we ascertain that the main purpose of the Gītā's teachings is to remove this ignorance through Self-knowledge.

Ādī Śaṅkarācārya, in the introduction to his masterly commentary on the Gītā, states that the teachings of the Gītā were imparted to Arjuna, who was drowning in the vast ocean of sorrow and delusion (शोक-मोह).[54] Delusion and sorrow are two undeniable features of our conditioned human existence. The Gītā teaches that sorrow is caused by delusion born of ignorance (*ajñānavimohitāḥ* अज्ञानविमोहिता: 16.15; *ajñānasaṁmohaḥ* अज्ञानसंमोह: 18.72). This theme of delusion (and resultant sorrow) caused by ignorance is repeated several times in the

1.2–2.9 of the Gītā is to establish that delusion and sorrow lead to the misery of conditioned existence, *saṁsāra*—a cycle of repeated births and deaths.

[52] *Paṇḍā*: means wisdom about the Self; and those who know the Self are indeed (*panḍitāḥ*) (पण्डिता: आत्मज्ञा: *panḍitāḥ ātmajñāḥ*). See Śaṅkara's commentary on verse 2.11. Ānanda Giri, an immediate disciple of Ādī Śaṅkarācārya, in his sub-commentary, *Tika*, on BG 2.11 clarifies that "the second half of the verse is intended to show that Arjuna's delusion was due to his ignorance of the true nature of the Self." See: Alladi Mahadeva Sastry, trans., *The Bhagavad Gītā with the commentary of Sri Shankaracharya* (Chennai, India: Samata Books, 2001), 30.

[53] See: Swāmī Śrī Rāmsukhdāsji Mahārāj, *Sādhaka-Sañjīvanī* (Gorakhpur, India: Gītā Press, 2002), 78.

[54] *śōka-mōha-mahā-udadhau nimagnāya* (शोक-मोह-महा-उदधौ निमग्नाय).

Gītā.[55] For example, the Gītā 5.15 states that "knowledge is covered by ignorance and due to that (ignorance) people are deluded."[56] Here, ignorance means ignorance of one's true Self. Wherever the word ignorance, *ajñāna*, is used in the Gītā—and, for that matter, in this book—it refers to Self-ignorance and *not* to the ignorance of any branch of knowledge, such as physics or chemistry or any other worldly information.

Arjuna was confused about his duty; he was also concerned about the death of his relatives. Whenever we are confused about our duty, it mostly springs from confusion about our true identity. When one is confused about one's identity, one is also confused about one's duty. And one's duties depend upon one's position or identity in a given situation, such as one's job or family. Arjuna did not look at himself as one representing the cause of righteousness (*dharma*).[57] He looked at himself as an individual, as Arjuna. Even from the relative standpoint, he looked at himself as Arjuna related to so many people and got confused about his duty. So, the confusion about the duty (*dharmasaṃmūḍhacetāḥ*: 2.7) arose only because of Arjuna's confusion about his absolute as well as relative identity.

In the second chapter, Śrī Kṛṣṇa has pointed out repeatedly to Arjuna that it was due to delusion alone that he (Arjuna) was feeling the sorrow; and that he should not grieve, both from the absolute as well as from the relative standpoint: The wise do not grieve (2.11); the wise person does not get deluded about this (2.13); knowing the Self as immutable, you should not grieve (2.25); you should not grieve like this (2.26); and you should not grieve over the inevitable (2.27).[58] Arjuna felt that even if death is certain for the born, why he should become the cause of anyone's death. Let them die their natural death. After all, it is not right to kill people just because they are going to die eventually.

Śrī Kṛṣṇa points out that this type of thinking is based on the standpoint of the doer of an action, taking oneself to be an entity. From the standpoint of the highest Absolute Reality, the Lord points out to Arjuna that "he is *not* the doer." Your true nature is Pure Awareness or Consciousness in whose presence the body, mind, intellect, and so on, get their sentiency. The Self, Consciousness, itself does not do anything. From the Absolute standpoint, you are non-doer. Therefore, why should you grieve over it? Does that mean that one should go killing because, as Pure Awareness, one is non-doer? No, not at all! From the

[55] See BG 2.11; 2.13; 2.30; **5.15**–16; 14.16; **16.15**; **18.72**–73.

[56] BG 5.15: *ajñānenāvṛtaṁ jñānaṁ tena muhyanti jantavaḥ* (अज्ञानेनावृतं ज्ञानं तेन मुह्यन्ति जन्तवः).
See: Swāmī Dayananda Saraswati, trans., *Śrīmad Bhagavad Gītā*, 77.

[57] The word "*dharma*" has no single equivalent in the English language. It is often translated as righteousness, duty, religion, ethics, norms of conduct, and so on. Literally, *dharma* means "what holds together"; thus, it is the basis of all order—social, moral, cosmic, and so forth. Essentially, *dharma* means the intrinsic nature or specific quality of a thing—such as heat is the *dharma* of fire, wetness is the *dharma* of water, and sweetness is the *dharma* of sugar. The primary meaning of the word *dharma* is the "*ness,*" the inner law or intrinsic being of a thing. Only in its secondary sense, *dharma* refers to virtue or moral duty.

[58] Swāmī Tejomayananda, *Geeta at a Glance*—Melbourne—2012 (Discourse no. 2).

relative standpoint, this killing is *not* an injunction, "Thou shall kill." Here, Śrī Kṛṣṇa speaks to Arjuna's relative identity as a warrior. Thus, if a righteous war is forced on you, in that situation, as a warrior, Arjuna, it is your duty (*svadharma*) to fight.[59] It will be regarded as only a performance of your duty; it may appear violent or unpleasant, but duty is duty.

Arjuna's grief was that, in the war, so many people would die, including his relatives. So, the main cause of his grief was death. At the very beginning of the second chapter, Śrī Kṛṣṇa provides several reasons both from the relative and absolute standpoints as to why it is not wise to grieve over death. From the absolute standpoint, Śrī Kṛṣṇa points out that there are two entities—the body and the eternal Self. All bodies are subject to end while the soul is eternal and indestructible.[60] Therefore, there is no reason to grieve over for that which is going to end any way (body) or that which is eternal (the Self or the soul).

Arjuna's basic problem is grief and delusion, *śōka-mōha*. The Gītā *repeatedly* points out that grief (*śōka*) is the result of delusion (*mōha*) born of Self-ignorance. According to the Gītā, the fundamental ignorance that everyone has is taking oneself to be the body. The Gītā removes this self-ignorance through Self-knowledge. Self-knowledge means the knowledge that we are not the body that we take ourselves to be; we are the Self, the unchanging awareness that illumines the body, mind, and senses. The body is subject to birth, decay, and death not the Self, which is the imperishable principle in us. One who knows the Self to be imperishable, eternal, and free from birth and decay—how and whom can that person kill or cause to kill?[61] By referring to our absolute identity (our true Self) as well as our relative identity (as social beings), the Gītā presents a permanent way out of delusion through Self-knowledge. Śrī Kṛṣṇa assured Arjuna: "Gaining this knowledge, you will not be deluded again";[62] and, finally, "this is the state of a Self-realized person; having attained which one is not deluded again."[63] Thus applying the test of *abhyāsa*, we discover that the subject matter of the Gītā is the removal of delusion (and the resultant sorrow) through Self-knowledge.

Originality, Novelty or Uniqueness of the Text (*apūravatā*)

Apūravatā means novelty or specialty of the knowledge that the Gītā teaches. It refers to the uniqueness of Self-knowledge that is not available through any other commonly known means of knowledge. The scripture is not required to know what can be known through the common means of knowledge such as perception or inference. What is the uniqueness of the knowledge that the Gītā

[59] BG 2.31: *svadharmamapi cāvekṣya na vikampitumarhasi* (स्वधर्ममपि चावेक्ष्य न विकम्पितुमर्हसि): From the standpoint of your own duty, you should not waver, for there is nothing greater for a warrior than a righteous war.

[60] BG 2.18: *antavanta ime dehā* (अन्तवन्त इमे देहा) The bodies are subject to end. See also BG 2.20.

[61] BG 2.21.

[62] BG 4.35: *yajjñātvā na punarmohama* (यज्ज्ञात्वा न पुनर्मोहम).

[63] BG 2.72: *eṣā brāhmī sthitiḥ pārtha naināṁ prāpya vimuhyati* (एषा ब्राह्मी स्थितिः पार्थ नैनां प्राप्य विमुह्यति).

reveals? Every person has the feeling that "I am." However, whenever we say, "I am"—by this "I am," we mostly refer to our body or our bodily existence.[64] For this, no special knowledge is required, for everybody knows "I am this body." In fact, Ādi Śaṅkarācārya says that as far as identification with the body is concerned, there is no difference between a human being and an animal. An animal also knows that "I am this body."[65]

A teaching is required for something that is special which is not otherwise known. "I am" is known to everybody. That "I am" different from the body and the mind—that "I am unborn, that my nature is imperishable and eternal"—and that I have to look at myself and the world from this standpoint, this is not commonly known. This is the *apūravatā* or novelty of this knowledge. And this knowledge is given in the Bhagavad Gītā.

The uniqueness of the Gītā is also evident from the fact that in the Anugītā, which occurs in the *Aśvamedha Parva* of Mahābhārata, Arjuna asked Śrī Kṛṣṇa to repeat the Bhagavad Gītā since he (Arjuna) has forgotten much of it due to the fickleness of his mind. Śrī Kṛṣṇa said it was not possible to repeat it since He was established in union (yoga) with Supreme Brahman at time of the Bhagavad Gītā's recitation[66]:

> The recollection of all that I told you on that occasion will not come to me now….It is impossible for me, O Dhanañjaya, to repeat, in detail, all that I said on that occasion. That religion (about which I discoursed to you then) is more than sufficient for understanding the Brahman. I cannot discourse on it again in detail. I discoursed to you on the Supreme Brahman, having concentrated myself in Yoga (*yogayuktena*).[67]

[64] In Vedānta, the identification with the body is considered to be the greatest obstacle on our way to the realization of our true nature as limitless Pure Awareness.

[65] Ānanda Giri, an immediate disciple of Ādī Śaṅkarācārya, in his *Tika*, sub-commentary, on BG 15.19, defines "undeluded" as one who "never looks upon the physical body, and so on, as himself or as belonging to himself." See: Alladi Mahadeva Sastry, trans., *The Bhagavad Gītā with the commentary of Sri Shankaracharya* (Madras, India: Samta Books, 1995/1897), 412. Though not a word-for-word translation of Śaṅkara's commentary, Mahadeva Sastry's translation gets to the heart of the text perhaps like no other translation. See this author's review of Sastry's translation on Amazon: https://www.amazon.com/Bhagavad-Gītā-Commentary-Sri-Sankaracharya/dp/0910261032#customerReviews

[66] शरावितस तवं मया गुह्यं जञापितश च सनातनम |
धर्मं सवरूपिणं पार्थ सर्वलोकांश च शाश्वतान ||9||
स हि धर्मः सुपर्याप्तो ब्रह्मणः पदवेदने |
न शक्यं तन मया भूयस तथा वक्तुम अशेषतः ||11||
परं हि ब्रह्म कथितं योगयुक्तेन तन मया ||12||

śrāvitas tvaṃ mayā guhyaṃ jñāpitaś ca sanātanam /
dharmaṃ svarūpiṇaṃ pārtha sarvalokāṃś ca śāśvatān //9//
sa hi dharmaḥ suparyāpto brahmaṇaḥ padavedane /
na śakyaṃ tan mayā bhūyas tathā vaktum aśeṣataḥ //11//
paraṃ hi brahma kathitaṃ yogayuktena tan mayā //12//

[67] Kisari Mohan Ganguli, trans. *The Mahabharata, Book 14: Aswamedha Parva: Anugita Parva: Section XVI*: 16.9, 11, 12. Retrieved June 16, 2017: http://www.holybooks.com/wp-content/uploads/MahabharataOfVyasa-EnglishTranslationByKMGanguli.pdf

It is also indicated at several places in the Gītā that this knowledge is a profound secret as follows:

1. This knowledge is a deeply profound secret (*rahasyaṁ*) (BG 4.3)
2. This most secret knowledge (*guhayatamaṁ*) (BG 9.1; 15.20)
3. The greatest secret knowledge –centered on the Self (*guhyam*) (BG 11.1; 18.68; 18.75)
4. More mysterious than any secret (*guhyād guhayataraṁ*) (BG 18.63)

The conclusion of these statements is this: Śrī Kṛṣṇa is telling Arjuna that the knowledge He was imparting to him is not commonly known; it is only available through the teacher-disciple tradition (*guru-śiṣya-paramparā*).[68] The secret here refers to the fact that this knowledge is not available through the normal means of knowledge such as perception or inference. Through perception and inference, one can only know about the world of objects—gross or subtle. How can one know the knower, the subject?[69] Self is the subject that cannot be objectified. This knowledge is so difficult that even when we are told—that we are not the body-mind-senses complex, but limitless Awareness—we are not able to appreciate it. The novelty or uniqueness of the Gītā lies in imparting the knowledge of the Knower, the Self, the knowledge of the origin of creation, and the knowledge of Absolute Reality. Even when the Gītā speaks about *karma*, its uniqueness lies in imparting the knowledge about the *attitude* with which we need to perform our actions so that they become *yoga*, a pathway to union with the Supreme. In short, based on the test of uniqueness or novelty, the main theme of the Gītā is imparting the knowledge of the Self or the Absolute Reality.

Result (*phalaṁ*)

The indication of result or benefit also points out to the subject matter of a text. As mentioned above, at the end of the section on the state of an enlightened person in chapter 2, Śrī Kṛṣṇa underscores the benefit of Self-knowledge: "This is the state of a Self-realized person; having attained which one is not deluded again" (2.72). Similarly, in chapter 4, the result of this knowledge is pointed out again: "Gaining this knowledge, you will not be deluded again" (4.35). In other words, Self-knowledge will bestow such clarity of vision that you will be able to deal effectively with any situation of life. And at the conclusion of chapter 15, Śrī Kṛṣṇa reiterates that the Gītā reveals the most profound knowledge, understanding which one becomes truly *fulfilled* in life:

[68] See BG 4.34.

[69] *Bṛhadāraṇyaka Upaniṣad* 4.5.15: येनेदं सर्वं विजानाति, तं केन विजानीयात्। विज्ञातारमरे केन विजानीयात्.... Through what should one know That owing to which all this is known. How should one know the Knower?

> Arjuna! The sinless one! Thus, the utmost secret scriptural doctrine has now been revealed by Me. Knowing this, a person becomes truly enlightened. [For such a person, there remains nothing else here whatsoever to be known, to be done, or to be attained]. His human birth becomes fulfilled (*kṛtakṛtya*) for he has realized the Highest Goal of human life.[70]

The Gītā says that this is highly unique knowledge, having known which, there remains nothing else to be known here (7.2). This sense of fulfillment is not present in the pursuit and attainment of materialistic objects.[71] As observation and experience reveals, our pursuit of the worldly goods leaves us with a deep sense of incompleteness in its wake—a feeling of something missing—no matter what the nature or level of achievement may be. Consider this poignant observation of Tolstoy who, at the height of his career—with wealth, fame and power, all accomplished—finds it all sham and mockery:

> All this took place at a time when so far as all my outer circumstances went, I ought to have been completely happy. I had a good wife who loved me and whom I loved; good children and a large property which was increasing with no pains taken on my part. I was more respected by my kinsfolk and acquaintance than I had ever been; I was loaded with praise by strangers; and without exaggeration I could believe my name already famous….And yet *I could give no reasonable meaning to any actions of my life*. And I was surprised that I had not understood this from the very beginning. My state of mind was as if some wicked and stupid jest was being played upon me by someone. *One can live only so long as one is intoxicated, drunk with life; but when one grows sober one cannot fail to see that it is all a stupid cheat.*[72] (emphasis added)

One can perfunctorily dismiss Tolstoy's assessment as "too pessimistic" or "too cynical," yet one cannot deny the tyranny of life as laid bare in his analysis. If we carefully look at the pursuits of pleasure, wealth, fame, and security, we realize that they are all limited and time-bound in the ultimate bidding. Even when one has them all, one still feels, with Tolstoy, the gnawing sense of incompleteness that something is still missing. Eventually, however, every discerning human being comes to realize with Simone Weil that "there is no true good here below, that everything that appears to be good

[70] BG 15.20:

iti guhyatamaṁ śāstramidamuktaṁ mayānagha /
etadbuddhvā buddhimānsyātkṛtakṛtyaśca bhārata //

[71] Strictly speaking, everything other than the Self is an object. Experience and observation show that objects, howsoever exalted, cannot provide lasting fulfillment. They cannot satisfy the soul's hunger for full and complete freedom. If objects cannot provide lasting and complete fulfillment, the only other place to look for it is the Subject, the Self. See: James Swartz, *How to Attain Enlightenment* (Boulder, CO: Sentient Publications, 2009).

[72] Quoted in William James, *The Varieties of Religious Experience* (Collector's Library New Edition, 2006), 160.

in this world is finite, limited, wears out, and once worn out, leaves necessity exposed in all its nakedness."[73]

In the world of objects, there is no gain which is not subject to loss or which does not involve loss of something else at the same time. Life is a package deal, a zero-sum game. You cannot have your cake and eat it too, at least not at the same time. You cannot beat the system. It is set up that way. There is no upside that does not have a downside.[74] Vedānta says that the real gain is that which is not subject to loss and which does not involve loss of something else. There can only be one thing that is not subject to any loss, which is our own eternal Self. The Gītā says that there is no gain greater than the gain of the truth of the Self, established in which one is not shaken by the greatest sorrow (6.22). Only Self-knowledge is capable of removing our delusion, sorrow, and fear. Our own Self is ever-attained and cannot be lost. How can one move away from the truth of oneself? This gain is of the nature of supreme knowledge of our infinite Reality, our limitless Being—which is our true nature. That which is eternal, that which is infinite cannot be lost. And in the infinity, all finite things are also included. To facilitate this knowledge of the eternal Self is the central theme of the Gītā.

The unique benefit of this knowledge is that one becomes completely fulfilled in life. The Gītā teaches us that the fundamental human problem is the lack of Self-knowledge and the resultant extroverted-ness of our search for happiness and the mistaken way we relate to the world. In all our quests, we approach people, objects, and situations through the prism of our likes and dislikes (*rāga-dvēṣa*), which leads to attachment or aversion. Attachment leads to sorrow and sorrow leads to delusion, which in turn compounds our misery. When the Self-knowledge (*ātam-jñāna*) dawns, we realize that whatever we have been seeking is already within us. It is in fact our own nature or Self, which is of the nature of Sat-Chit-Ananda, Truth, Consciousness, Bliss—Fullness of Being, *puraṇattvam*. What can be added to fullness? How can one improve upon infinity? When we realize the fullness of our being, our seeking/suffering comes to an end. We are able to experience the calm bliss of the fullness of our Self and intuit the harmonious oneness of all existence.

What is the practical value of this understanding? When the false divisions and distinctions based on our narrow personal likes and dislikes disappear, we are able to extend our benevolence without preference or prejudice in all directions and our very existence benefits the whole universe. Our whole existence then becomes an offering to the Supreme, a *yajña*—a penance of knowledge (*jñānatapasā* 4.10) or actions burnt up by the fire of knowledge/wisdom

[73] Quoted in Huston Smith, *The World's Religions*, 20.

[74] James Swartz, a contemporary teacher of traditional Vedānta, who studied with the great Swāmī Chinmayananda ji, categorically states this in one of his talks during the Vedānta Retreat held at Westerwald, 2014, Part 2, titled *Motivations, Objects and Happiness*: "You cannot proceed on the path of enlightenment as long as you think that the joy is coming from the objects." He defines *mokṣa*, spiritual freedom, as "freedom from dependence on objects for happiness." Video Retrieved April 17, 2017: https://www.youtube.com/watch?v=QQZTTNdk3dU&index=2&list=PLjYJW23pwZdjqOTpWQCY_tUDAnqzRivGu

(*jñānāganidagdhakarmāṇaṁ* 4.19). And our feet get firmly planted on the path that leads to peace, happiness, and freedom. This is the fruit (*phalaṁ*) of Self-knowledge or the Supreme Science of Reality, *brahmavidyā*, that the Gītā teaches.[75] Thus, from the result (*phalaṁ*) that is indicated, we determine that the central theme of the Gītā is Self-knowledge.

Eulogy (*arthavāda*)

The indication of result or benefit derived from the study of the Gītā also suggests its praise and purport. We notice at several places in the Gītā that the glory of Self-knowledge is especially extolled:

- There is indeed no purifier like knowledge;[76] Swāmī Tejomayananda explains that while other means such as charity and pilgrimage may help purify one's *sins*, only Self-knowledge purifies the *sinner*, by removing the false sense of doership.
- Having gained this knowledge, one immediately attains supreme peace.[77]
- All actions in their entirety get resolved in knowledge.[78] All actions are performed to attain happiness. Lasting happiness does not lie in the objects. When through the knowledge of the Self we realize that happiness is our own nature, the pursuit of happiness through actions comes to an end.

Śrī Kṛṣṇa has extolled Self-knowledge in so many ways: This knowledge is the king of all knowledge, the king of secrets, supreme purifier, directly comprehensible, attended with virtue, most excellent, easy to accomplish, and imperishable.[79] And those who have no faith in this Self-knowledge, not gaining Me, remain subject to the cycle of conditioned existence (*saṁsāra*), which is fraught with death (9.2). From all these, it is clear that the main message of the Gītā is to impart Self-knowledge, the king of all knowledge.

[75] These observations about the fundamental human problem and our quest for happiness are primarily inspired by Swāmī Paramārthānandajī's discourses on the Bhagavad Gītā. Throughout this book, we will also draw upon Swāmījī's sublime teachings as available in his extensive repertoire of discourses on the Gītā and other texts and sub-texts of Vedāntā.

[76] BG 4.38: *na hi jñānena sadṛśaṁ pavitramiha vidyate* (न हि ज्ञानेन सदृशं पवित्रमिह विद्यते). See *Geeta at a Glance*, Talk no. 2.

[77] BG 4.39: *jñānaṁ labdhvā parāṁ śāntimacireṇādhigacchati* (ज्ञानं लब्ध्वा परां शान्तिमचिरेणाधिगच्छति).

[78] BG 4.33: *sarvaṁ karmākhilaṁ pārtha jñāne parisamāpyate* (सर्वं कर्माखिलं पार्थ ज्ञाने परिसमाप्यते). Ibid.

[79] BG 9.2:

राजविद्या राजगुह्यं पवित्रमिदमुत्तमम् ।
प्रत्यक्षावगमं धर्म्यं सुसुखं कर्तुमव्ययम् ॥

rājavidyā rājaguhyaṁ pavitramidamuttamam /
pratyakṣāvagamaṁ dharmyaṁ susukhaṁ kartumavyayam //

Demonstration by Examples and Illustrations (*upapatti*)

The Gītā provides several examples and illustrations to indicate the immutability of Self. Just as man changes clothes when worn out (BG 2.22), even so when the worn-out bodies are given up, the Self remains immutable. Again while pointing out the nature of Self which is not a doer, and remains immutable, illustrations of Sun and space are given (BG 13.32, 33): Just as one sun illumines everything, even so the Self, Ātman, illumines everything; just as the all-pervading space never gets affected due its subtlety, in the same way Ātman, though dwelling in the body, never gets tainted by the results of actions of the body.

Thus, proper reasoning is provided for Arjuna, through such illustrations, not to grieve.

As the foregoing discussion reveals, all six criteria presented above *converge* on the subject of Self-knowledge (*ātma-jñāna*) or the knowledge of the Absolute Reality (*Brahma-vidya*). Thus, we come to know that the main purpose of the Bhagavad Gītā is to enlighten us about our true nature and about the discipline (*yoga*) of action performed in the full wakefulness of Self-knowledge. When enlightenment dawns, the delusion, sorrow, fear—root, branch, and all—are gone. Therefore, we undertake the study of the Bhagavad Gītā to gain Self-knowledge (*ātma-jñāna*), or the knowledge of Absolute Reality (*tattva-jñāna*).

Essence of the 18 Chapters of the Gītā

The Gītā consists of 18 chapters comprising 700 verses. To facilitate understanding of the message of the Gītā, we present a brief summary of the subject matter of each chapter.[80] The word "*yogah*" at the end of each chapter simply signals its topic or subject matter. It reflects a skillful means of *integrating* oneself through a particular method as explained in a given chapter. In essence, each of the 18 chapters of the Gītā presents a unique discipline or *yoga* of connecting with the Supreme.

Essence of the First Chapter (अर्जुनविषादयोग: *arjunaviṣādayogaḥ*) (47 Verses)

The first chapter is titled as the *yoga* of Arjuna's dejection or anguish, *arjunaviṣādayogaḥ*. Arjuna came to the war, knowing very well that he would have to fight with his own kith and kin. But when he actually saw his relatives, elders, teachers, and friends lined up on the other side, ready to fight, it brought about a confusion between duty and desire, reason and emotion. The intensity of Arjuna's anguish created a deep dispassion in him which is a necessary condition for understanding the deeper truths of life. Essentially, Arjuna is archetypical of all of us struggling in the battle of life. Overpowered by the delusion born of ignorance, we get confused about our real duty and get caught up in this dilemma,

[80] Partially adapted from *Sahaja Gītā*. Print edition, 175–178.

"What should I do and what should I not do." The force of such a dilemma brings us face to face with a spiritual guide—just as despairing Arjuna who sought guidance from Śrī Kṛṣṇa, the Supreme Being, the Lord in human form.

Essence of the Second Chapter (साङ्ख्ययोग: *sāṅkhyayogaḥ*) (72 Verses)

The body is perishable and the Self (soul) which knows it is imperishable (2.13, 2.16, 2.18, 2.120). By giving importance to this discriminating reasoning (*viveka*) and diligently fulfilling one's allotted duty, worries and sorrows come to an end. This chapter is generally considered as the summary of the entire Gītā. It presents all the *yogas* in a seed form—*karma yoga*, *jñāna yoga*, and so on—which are further developed in the later chapters. This chapter introduces an important touchstone of wisdom—equanimity of mind (*samatvam* 2.48), which is later presented as a touchstone of perfection in all the *yogas* in the Gītā (2.48, 53, 57; 5.6, 18–20; 12.13–19; 14.24, 25; 18.10, 26). So, *samatā* is the crest-jewel of perfection (*siddhi*) in all the paths to God-realization. All virtues obtain in a mind that has cultivated equanimity. Whatever the spiritual practice, if evenness of mind (*samatā*) is not attained, the goal is still far away.

Essence of the Third Chapter (कर्मयोग: *karmayogaḥ*) (43 Verses)

Fulfilling one's duty selflessly for the wellbeing of others leads to liberation. Śrī Kṛṣṇa explains the essence of the path of action as the performance of one's prescribed duties without attachment to results. Actions prompted by desire, and attachment to results of actions, can lead to bondage. *Karma yoga* is the *yoga* of "attitude" toward actions and their results: performance of actions as an offering to the Divine and acceptance of results as a Divine Grace. This attitude signifies *yoga*, union, with the Supreme through actions. This is the skillfulness (*kauśalam*) in actions and *yoga* in *karma*, *karmayogaḥ*.

Essence of the Fourth Chapter (ज्ञानकर्मसंन्यासयोग: *jñānakarmasaṁnyāsayogaḥ*) (42 Verses)

There are two ways to be free from the bondage of actions: Performing actions unselfishly as an offering by understanding the true essence of actions or by realizing (or attaining) the knowledge of the essential Reality *(tattva-jñāna)*. This chapter also stresses the importance of learning the science of Self-knowledge from the wise ones (*jñāninasta*) who have realized the truth in their direct experience (*tattvadarśinaḥ* 4.32).

Essence of the Fifth Chapter (संन्यासयोग: *saṁnyāsayogaḥ*) (29 Verses)

A person should not become happy or unhappy due to favorable or unfavorable circumstances. One who becomes happy or unhappy due to circumstances cannot rise above the mundane world and experience the Bliss Supreme. This chapter explains what is action, what is inaction, who is the doer of action, and what is true renunciation. True renunciation is renunciation *in* action, not *of* actions. Renunciation in action occurs by renouncing the "doer-ship"—the false sense that "I am the doer." This is the true *yoga* in the performance of actions.

Essence of the Sixth Chapter (आत्मसंयमयोगः *ātmasaṁyamayogaḥ*) (47 Verses)

This chapter presents the path of meditation (*dhyānayoga*) by which mastery of the mind might be gained. Resolving the mind in the Self (आत्मसंस्थं मनः कृत्वा *ātmasaṁsthaṁ manaḥ kṛtvā* 6.25) is the essence of meditation and is the best spiritual practice. The wise see all things in God and God in all things (6.29–30). This chapter contains some of the most important verses about the path of knowledge (6.29–32) and the path of devotion (6.30, 6.47) and provides the most succinct definition of yoga as "dissociation from association with sorrow" (6.23). Whatever be the spiritual practice, one should attain equanimity *(samatā)* of mind. Without equanimity of mind, a person cannot become completely free from the agitations of the mind (or the sway of the thoughts).

Essence of the Seventh Chapter (ज्ञानविज्ञानयोगः *jñānavijñānayogaḥ*) (30 Verses)

Śrī Kṛṣṇa explains the nature of Absolute Reality and the illusory nature of *Māyā*, the creative Divine energy responsible for the appearance of the variegated world of name and form. God is all there is (वासुदेवः सर्वमिति: *vāsudevaḥ sarvamiti* 7.19): to accept this and live a God-centered life is the best spiritual practice. The Gītā adds that such a wise person is very hard to come by (स महात्मा सुदुर्लभः *sa mahātmā sudurlabhaḥ* 7.19).

Essence of the Eighth Chapter (अक्षरब्रह्मयोगः *akṣarabrahmayogaḥ*) (28 Verses)

The fate of an embodied soul is determined according to its state of mind at the time of death. Therefore, remembering God at all times, we should perform our allotted duties (सर्वेषुकालेषु मामनुस्मर युध्य च *sarveṣukāleṣu māmanusmara yudhya ca* 8.7). Only then shall we be able to remember God during our critical last moments.

Essence of the Ninth Chapter (राजविद्याराजगुह्ययोगः *rājavidyārājaguhyayogaḥ*) (34 Verses)

The chapter presents the path or *yoga* of the most secret royal knowledge. The alchemy of this knowledge is presented as the highest devotion thusly: Fix your mind on Me (the Lord), with Me as thy support (मन्मना भव...मत्परायणः *manmanā bhava...matparāyaṇaḥ* 9.34) and whatever you do, please do it as an offering to Me (यत्करोषि...ततमदर्पणम् *yatkaroṣi...tatamadarpaṇam* 9.27). If you do so, it is assured that the Lord will take care of what you need to get and protect it too (योगक्षेमं वहाम्यहम् *yogakṣemaṁ vahāmyaham* 9.22).[81]

Essence of the Tenth Chapter (विभूतियोग: *vibhūtiyogaḥ*) (42 Verses)

This chapter reveals that God is the primal source of all and everything in the universe. Wherever any uniqueness, special quality, beauty, prominence, brilliance, strength, and so on are observed in the world, considering them to have sprung from the Lord, one should constantly contemplate on the Lord alone.

Essence of the 11th Chapter (विश्वरूपदर्शनयोग: *viśvarūpadarśanayogaḥ*) (55 Verses)

This chapter presents the vision of the Universal Form of the Lord. It explains how the Supreme Being pervades the entire cosmic creation. By regarding this universe verily as God's cosmic form, everyone can have a vision of God's universal form constantly. The last verse of this chapter is considered to be the quintessential verse summarizing the essential import of the entire Gītā: The one who does all actions for My sake, regards Me as his Supreme Goal, who is devoted to Me, free from all attachments and free from malice towards all beings, comes to Me, O Arjuna! This verse also prepares the ground for the culminating chapter on the yoga of loving devotion to the Lord (*bhaktiyogaḥ*).

Essence of the 12th Chapter (भक्तियोग: *bhaktiyogaḥ*) (20 Verses)

This chapter explains the exalted path of devotion or divine love. It states that a devotee, who fully surrenders himself to God, with his body, senses, mind, and intellect, is extremely dear to God (ऽतीव मे प्रिया: *'tīva me priyāḥ* 12.20). The Gītā regards the *yoga* of loving devotion/service to and relationship with the Lord as the highest form of *yoga*.

Essence of the 13th Chapter (क्षेत्रक्षेत्रज्ञविभागयोग: *kṣetrakṣetrajñavibhāgayogaḥ*) (34 Verses)

This chapters presents 20 preparatory marks of knowledge. There is only One Supreme Reality *(Paramātama-tattva)* that pervades the entire universe. This Supreme Reality, which is the Light of all lights (ज्योतिषाम ज्योति *jyotiṣāma jyoti* 13.17) is to be known; knowing which, one attains to immortality. Such a person has realized that the Divine resides equally in all and everything (13.27)

[81] According to Swami Ram Tirath ji, verse 9.22 is the watershed, since it represents the *mid-point* of the Gītā, and hence, its unique importance. It was explained to this author that, in this context, *yogakṣemaṁ* (योगक्षेमं) does not refer to the provision and protection of worldly things by the Lord. Rather, it means that to those ever united in thought with the Lord, the Lord ensures that what is needed for the spiritual progress of the seeker will be provided (योग) as well as protected (क्षेमं). That is the true import of verse 9.22.

and that the Self in me is the Self in all. This chapter is considered to be the most important chapter from the standpoint of the path of knowledge, *jñāna yoga*.

Essence of the 14th Chapter (गुणत्रयविभागयोग: *guṇatrayavibhāgayogaḥ*) (27 Verses)

This chapter explains the three modes, *guṇas,* of material nature—*sattva* (purity), *rajas* (passion), and *tamas* (inertia)—how they bind, and how can one transcend them. *Sattva* binds one through attachment to pleasure and knowledge, *rajas* to actions and their fruit, and *tamas* to apathy and sloth (14.6–9). To be free from the bondage of the threefold properties of material nature (*prakṛti*), one has to rise above the triad of purity, passion, and inertia. One becomes free from these three modes through knowledge of, and unswerving devotion to, the Supreme.

Essence of the 15th Chapter (पुरुषोत्तमयोग: *puruṣottamayogaḥ*) (20 Verses)

The sole source and support of this universe, the infinitely Supreme Person (***puruṣottama***) is the One Lord only. All splendor, glory, and excellences belong to this Supreme Being, the inner essence of all. Knowing the Lord as the Self of all thusly, one should worship the Lord with exclusive and unswerving devotion. Knowing this, a person becomes wise and has accomplished all that has to be accomplished (बुद्धिमान्स्यात्कृतकृत्यश्च *buddhimānsyātkṛtakṛtyaśca* 15.20). The Gītā extolls the teaching revealed in this chapter to be the most profound scripture (गुह्यतमं शास्त्रम *guhyatamaṁ śāstrama* 15.20).[82]

Essence of the 16th Chapter (दैवासुरसम्पद्विभागयोग: *daivāsurasampadvibhāgayogaḥ*) (24 Verses)

In this chapter, Śrī Kṛṣṇa identifies the human traits in terms of divine and the demonic natures that can be understood as empowering and disempowering dispositions. He counsels that, to attain the supreme destination, one must give up the disempowering traits such as desire, anger, and greed, and cultivate favorable traits such as truthfulness, purity of mind, modesty, authenticity, fortitude, and compassion. To discriminate between right and wrong action, let discernment (*viveka*) and the injunctions of the scripture (*śāstra*) be our guides.

[82] Ādī Śaṅkarācārya's comment: "Though the whole of Gītā is called Science (Sastra) yet from the context it appears that the fifteenth discourse alone here is spoken as the Science, for the purpose of extolling it. In fact, the whole teaching of the Gītā-Sastra has been summed up in this discourse." See Alladi Mahadeva Sastry, trans., *The Bhagavad Gītā with the commentary of Sri Shankaracharya*, 412.

Essence of the 17th Chapter (श्रद्धात्रयविभागयोग: *śraddhātrayavibhāgayogaḥ*) (28 Verses)

The operative word in this chapter is *śraddhā*, which is hard to translate. It is commonly translated as faith, but *śraddhā*[83] is more than faith and includes an element of loving-devotion. Śrī Kṛṣṇa enunciates the three divisions of faith, thoughts, and deeds corresponding to the three modes (*guṇas*). Whatever auspicious task one begins with loving-devotion, one should begin it by remembering God and by uttering His holy name. The chapter concludes with the explanation of "*Oṁ tat sat*," the threefold expression of *Brahman*, the Absolute Reality.

Essence of the 18th Chapter (मोक्षसंन्यासयोग: *mokṣasaṁnyāsayogaḥ*) (78 Verses)

This culminating chapter is the longest and sums up the entire teachings of the Bhagavad Gītā. The Vedas are the essence of all scriptures; Upaniṣads are the essence of all Vedas; the Gītā is the essence of Upaniṣads; and the essence of the Gītā lies in taking refuge in God (*Bhagavān ki śarnāgati*). One who takes refuge exclusively in the Lord, the Lord frees that person of all the sins.

Arjuna conveys his understanding of the final message of the Gītā in the following concluding verse:

नष्टो मोहः स्मृतिर्लब्धा त्वत्प्रसादान्मयाच्युत ।
स्थितोऽस्मि गतसन्देहः करिष्ये वचनं तव ॥

naṣṭo mohaḥ smṛtir labdhā tvatprasādān mayācyuta /
sthito'smi gatasandehaḥ kariṣye vacanaṁ tava //

O Changeless One (Śrī Kṛṣṇa), by Thy Grace, my delusion has been dispelled and I have regained my memory[84] (of my true Self). I now stand firmly established (in my *svarūpa*, my true nature), with my doubts all cleared, ready to do Thy bidding.

Every word here is worth its weight in gold: With Thy Grace; my delusion is gone; I have regained remembrance (आत्म-स्मृति, *ātma-smṛti*); all my doubts have cleared; I am now firmly established in my essential nature; and ready to do the inner, Divine Command (हुक्म, *hukam*). What a complete picture of all that is essential in a spiritual journey!

[83] In one of his discourses on the Gītā, Swāmī Akandānand jī Mahārāj explains that the word "*śraddhā*" (*sad+dhārana*) signifies the capacity to embrace truth (सत्य को धारण करने की क्षमता).

[84] In the realm of Self-realization.

ना पाना है, ना छोड़ना है
बस प्राप्त को समझना है

Neither to attain, nor to relinquish;
Just to understand the ever-attained.

With this key verse, we have come full circle in the teachings of the Bhagavad Gītā: Śrī Kṛṣṇa started the teaching declaring that "the wise do not grieve" (2.11: *nānuśocanti paṇḍitāḥ*) and concludes it with an assurance: "do not grieve" (18.66: *mā śucaḥ*). So, if you want to overcome the sorrow, attain to the liberating wisdom of the Self. What is this liberating wisdom? Just this: perform your actions as an offering to the Supreme (*Ishvara-arpanabhāvanā*), performing your duties without the expectation of any reward. Be an instrument of the Divine in all that you do. Let all your actions be for the wellbeing of all beings (*sarvabhūtahite ratāḥ*: 5.25); be a role model for bringing the world communities together and the maintenance of the world order (*lokasaṃgraham evāpi saṃpaśyan kartum arhasi*: 3.20).

Above all, accept the results of your actions with graceful equanimity, as a Grace of the Lord (*Iśhvara-prasādabhāvanā*). Then your actions will never taint you. Attain the highest pure knowledge by which the One Imperishable Being is seen in all the existences, undivided in the divided (18.20). In this manner, with the Divine Grace, you will attain the communion of the individual self with the Supreme Self.

Concluding Thoughts

In the scheme of the Bhagavad Gītā, ethical conduct (*dharma*) furnishes the essential foundation for the quest for spiritual freedom. It is interesting to note that the very word of the first verse, *śloka,* of the Gītā—"*dharma*" (1.1)—when conjoined with the very last word of the last verse of the Gītā—"*mama*" (18.78)—virtually form the word "*mama dharma*" denoting "my duty." Thus, the Gītā addresses the most fundamental question any leader can ask: What is the right thing to do? Hence, *dharma* (innate moral duty or righteousness) is the province of the entire Gītā!

Swāmī Tejomayananda captures the essential message of the Gītā within the compass of a short paragraph as follows:

> Śrīmad Bhagavad Gītā is a Song of Enlightenment. It enlightens us about life in its totality. It makes us understand our essential and absolute identity and also our relative identity. Accordingly, all duties and responsibilities associated with the relative identity are also explained. Since we live in this world, the Gītā also enlightens us about its cause and composition and our relationship with it. It contains many practical teachings regarding living a happy and successful life. In short, the main theme of this scripture is Self-knowledge or knowledge of Absolute Reality (*Brahma-vidyā*). Every teaching presented in the Gītā either directly highlights the necessity of Self-knowledge or is designed to prepare the mind to receive this knowledge.[85]

[85] Swāmī Tejomayananda, "Geeta at a Glance," 6 Discourses, Melbourne, 2012. Discourse 3.

It is important to remember that though in its ultimate bidding, the Gītā is essentially a manual for spiritual freedom (*mokṣa śāstra*[86])—as Ādī Śaṅkarācarya, its greatest commentator[87] and exponent, reminds us—however, in its practical aspect, it is also a great manual for living and not an esoteric treatise on spirituality. As A. Parthasarathy has rightly noted, "The Bhagavad Gītā is a technique, a skill for dynamic living, not a retirement plan."[88]

At what point of one's life should one pursue the goal of Self-realization or *mokṣa*? Many believe that spiritual quest is something to be pursued during the last phase of one's life. Dispelling this popular notion, Gandhi tells us in his autobiography that people had a "superstition" that Self-realization could be attained only in the last stages of life. Those who deferred it until then attain not Self-realization, but "a second and pitiable childhood living as a burden on this earth."[89]

Self-knowledge transforms our motivation and liberates us from the narrow confines of selfish action to the freedom of serving others. Through this rediscovery of our intrinsic freedom, we are also able to experience the calm bliss of the fullness of our Self and intuit the harmonious oneness of all existence. When the false divisions and distinctions based on our narrow personal likes and dislikes disappear, we are able to extend our benevolence without preference or prejudice in all directions, and our very existence benefits the whole universe. Our very existence then becomes an offering to the Supreme, a celebration to the Whole. And our feet get firmly planted on the path that leads to peace, happiness, and liberation. The teachings of the Gītā gently guide us toward this supreme desideratum of all human quests and pursuits.

In keeping with the tradition of Indian philosophy, the Gītā starts with presenting the highest human goal to be reached first: Access the Inner treasure-house of Self-sufficiency: *ātmanyevātmanā tuṣṭaḥ* (2.55), everything else will follow on its own accord. At the heart of the Gītā, there lies the conception of a sage of steady wisdom (*sthitaprajña*) who has gone beyond the pair of opposites such as pleasure and pain, success and failure, virtue and vice. Steady in wisdom, the seer, *sthitaprajña*, enjoys the constant bliss of the Self, regardless of the changing circumstances. The Gītā (2.55) defines *sthitaprajña* as follows: "When a person completely casts away all the desires of the mind, *satisfied in the Self alone by the Self*, then that person is said to be one established in steady wisdom." This wisdom (*prajña*) has two aspects: fullness (*puraṇattvam*) of

[86] *Mokṣa* is a Sanskrit word that means freedom from bondage. *Śāstra* is a Sanskrit word that means a manual of instruction, a book of knowledge, a technical treatise on a specialized subject. "That which commands" is *śāstra: śāsti iti śāstraḥa*. In this context, it means a sacred book or a scripture.

[87] My Vedānta teacher would often express his great appreciation for Ādī Śaṅkarā, stating: "Śaṅkarā is Śaṅkarā!"

[88] A. Parthasarathy cited in Dennis Waite, *Back to the Truth: 5000 Years of Advaita* (Winchester, UK: John Hunt Publishing, Ltd., 2007), 519.

[89] M. K. Gandhi, *An Autobiography: The Story of My Experiments with Truth* (New York, NY: Dover Publications, Inc., 1983), 302.

being and equanimity (*samatvaṁ*) of the mind. Only when one has experienced the inner fullness can one be free from the servitude of the ever-growing desires. And only when one is able to approach the ups and downs of life with an *equanimous* mind can one free oneself from the sway of favorable and unfavorable experiences. This wisdom is the only security worth seeking and the sure-fire armor to human sorrow and suffering.

In sum, become an instrument of the Divine in all that you do (*nimittamātraṁ bhava*: 11.33). Let all your actions be an offering to the Divine (*brahmaṇy ādhāya karmāṇi*: 5.10), performed *without* attachment, for the purification of the Self (*saṅgaṁ tyaktvātmaśuddhaye*: 5.11), and for the wellbeing of all beings (*sarvabhūtahite ratāḥ*: 5.25); and be a role model for the bringing of the world communities together and for maintenance of the world order (*lokasaṃgraham:* 3.20). Above all, accept the results of your actions with engaged equanimity, as a Grace of the Lord (*Īśhvara-prasādabhāvanā*). Then your actions will never taint you.

The fundamental teaching of the Gītā can be summarized as follows: the unreal has no existence and the real never ceases to be (2.16); the soul is indestructible (*avināśi*), eternal (*nitya*), unborn (*aja*), undiminished (*avyava*), all-pervasive (*sarva-gatah*), immovable (*achala*), ancient (*sanātana*), unmanifest (*avyakta*), unthinkable (*achintya*), and immutable (*avikṛya*). The soul is immortal and eternal; it is neither born nor does it die; it does not perish along with the body (2.20). Attain the Highest Knowledge, *Brahma-vidya*, by which the One Imperishable Being is seen in all the beings, the undivided in the divided, *avibhaktaṃ vibhakteṣu* (18.20). This knowledge of the essential oneness of all existence (*sarvabhūteṣu yenaikaṃbhāvam*), the Gītā regards as the purest (*sāttvik*) knowledge: *taj jñānaṁ viddhi sāttvikam* (18.20). Śrī Kṛṣṇa succinctly points out this fact in the Gītā 13.27:

> *samaṁsarveṣu bhūteṣu tiṣṭhantaṁparameśvaram /*
> *vinaśyatsv avinaśyantaṃ yaḥ paśyati sa paśyati //*
>
> He alone truly sees who sees the Supreme Lord abiding equally as imperishable amidst the perishable.

Strive to know yourself as the unchanging, Limitless Awareness, and be free. Once this realization becomes an *existential fact*, not just an *idea in the mind* but a *living truth in the heart*, the goal has been realized.[90] Living with this understanding, by the Divine Grace, one attains the communion of the individual Self with the Supreme Self, the *summum bonum* of human existence.

This is the timeless message of this manual for life, leadership, and liberation.

At the conclusion of his magnum opus, *Sādhaka-Sañjīvani*, Swāmī Rāmsukhdās jī had only this to say about the ultimate message of the Gītā:

[90] My Vedānta teacher used to reiterate: "With Self-knowledge, one can weather all existential storms aplomb and can swim in any ocean."

"Taking refuge in the Lord (*śaraṇāgati*) is the quintessence of the entire message of the Gītā. In surrendering to the Lord lies the culmination of the Gītā's teachings. Then the devotee becomes forever free from the pangs of fear, sorrow, worry, etc." The *Vedas* are the essence of all scriptures; the *Upaniṣads* are the essence of all *Vedas*; the Gītā is the essence of *Upaniṣads*; and the essence of the Gītā lies in taking refuge in Divine (*Bhagavān ki śaranāgati*). One who takes refuge exclusively in the Lord, the Lord frees that person of all the sins.

S. K. Maitra, erstwhile Honorary Professor of Philosophy at Benares Hindu University, fully concurs with this assessment. On the subject of "right attitude toward God," the Gītā's teachings may be summed up in one word: "Surrender."[91]

This is then the final teachings of the Gītā to Arjuna:

> Occupy thy mind with Me, be devoted to Me, sacrifice to Me, bow down to Me. Thou shalt reach Myself; truly do I promise unto thee, (for) thou art dear to Me. Relinquishing all dharmas, take refuge in Me alone; I will liberate thee all sins; grieve not. (BG 18.65–66)
>
> This is the ultimate testament of the Gītā, the most secret teaching of all: *sarvaguhyatamaṃ...paramaṃ vacaḥ* (BG 18.64)

In the final reckoning, Bhagavad Gītā remains a manual for spiritual freedom, as S. K. De has rightly observed:

> While philosophers of diverse schools interpret it in accordance with their own conceptions, and critical scholars quarrel over the question of its consistency, its deep ethical and religious fervour lifts it above sectarian and scholastic considerations and supply nourishment to devout minds as a gospel of deliverance.[92]

This is the net result, the ultimate finding, of the teachings of the Gītā: to live equanimously and act selflessly in the full wakefulness of Self-knowledge—dedicating all and everything to the Divine. Then, every step you take will bring you to the path that leads to wisdom, service, and freedom.

[91] S. K. Maitra, *The Spirit of Indian Philosophy* (Benares, India: Published by the Author; printed at The Indian Press Limited, Allahabad, 1947), 66.

[92] S. K. De, Some aspects of the Bhagavad-Gītā. *IC*, 1942–1943, IX, 21–35.

CHAPTER 4

Advaita Vedānta: The Science of Reality

Introduction

The Bhagavad Gītā is the summation of the Vedānta, and…stands out as one of the most direct formulations possible of what constitutes the very essence of our spirituality.[1]

As the opening quote clarifies, the Bhagavad Gītā is the essential summation of the key tenets of Vedānta, which is the culmination of Indian philosophy and spirituality. Advaita Vedānta furnishes the philosophical framework to comprehend fully the profound teachings of the Gītā. The Gītā unfolds the vision of the Vedas (BG 4.1–3), the world's foremost and perhaps oldest wisdom texts. Advaita Vedānta represents the culmination of Vedic wisdom, both historically and philosophically. By way of a holistic approach to life and leadership, the chapter unfolds the vision of Oneness[2] as propounded by Advaita Vedānta, the non-dual philosophy enunciated in the Bhagavad Gītā, the Upaniṣads,[3] and Brahma Sūtra—the three principal source wisdom texts (***prasthāna-traya***) of

[1] Huston Smith, Foreword. In Winthrop Sargeant, trans., *Bhagavad Gītā*, the 25th anniversary edition (New York, NY: New York State University Press), x.

[2] Oneness here refers to non-duality. Vedānta says that reality which appears to be dual, many, is essentially non-dual, one. This "One" in the word "Oneness" is ***not number*** 1, which implies 2 or even zero. Vedanta's "one" (***ekam***) is one, without-a-second (***ekam evādvitiyam***). See Chāndogya Upaniṣad 6.2.1.

[3] Although there are 108 Upaniṣads that are extant, out of these, 10 Upaniṣads are considered more important because the great commentator, Ādi Śaṅkara, wrote elaborate commentaries on these: Bṛhadāraṇyaka Upaniṣad; Chāndogya Upaniṣad; Māṇḍūkya Upaniṣad; Kena Upaniṣad; Kaṭha Upaniṣad; Muṇḍaka Upaniṣad; Aitareya Upaniṣad; Taittirīya Upaniṣad; Praśna Upaniṣad; and Īśa Upaniṣad.

Once a seeker, so the story goes, approached a Mahātmā ("a great soul") and asked, "Revered Sir, how many Upaniṣads do I have to study to know myself?" The Mahātmā replied with a question: "How many mirrors do you need to look at yourself?!" ~Narrated by Swāmī Tejomayānanda, *Discourses on Brahm-Sūtras*, No. 1.

S. Dhiman, *Bhagavad Gītā and Leadership*,
Palgrave Studies in Workplace Spirituality and Fulfillment,
https://doi.org/10.1007/978-3-319-67573-2_4

Vedānta. It shows that Self-knowledge, as the knowledge of our true nature, is a self-evident, self-established fact. Due to Self-ignorance, we are unaware of this vital fact.

The goal of Vedānta is to help us *dis*-cover Self-knowledge and fulfillment, right here and now, as our essential nature. Vedānta boldly declares: "*Know* the Limitless Awareness, Brahman, as your inmost Self, Ātman, and *be* free!" Advaita Vedānta is considered to be the crest-jewel of Indian wisdom.[4] "Advaita" is Sanskrit for "non-dual"—one-without-a-second—and "Vedānta" literally means "the end or inner core of the Vedas," the books of knowledge. Vedānta is the most widely known system of Indian philosophy, both in the East and the West.[5] It is a philosophy of non-duality based on the Upaniṣads, which are the concluding portions of the Vedas.[6]

The word "*Veda*," derived from the Sanskrit root *vid* (to know), means that which makes us know.[7] The Vedas are among the oldest sacred texts in the world. The Upaniṣads, the *Brahma Sūtra*, and the Gītā form the "triple standard" (*prasthāna-traya*) on which Vedāntic schools of philosophy are based.[8] Although there are more than 108 Upaniṣads[9] extant, Ādi Śaṅkara (788–820 CE),[10] the great commentator, has written commentaries on 11 principal Upaniṣads. The Vedas are vast like an ocean and the Gītā represents the essence of the entire corpus of the Vedas. Ādi Śaṅkara has aptly observed, "From a clear knowledge of the Bhagavad Gītā all the goals of human existence become fulfilled. *Bhagavad Gītā is the manifest quintessence of all the teachings of the Vedic scriptures.*"[11]

[4] "On the tree of Indian wisdom, there is no fairer flower than the Upanishads and no finer fruit than the Vedanta philosophy." ~Paul Deussen, *Outline of the Vedanta System*, vii.

The Upaniṣads, the *Brahma Sutra*, and the Gītā form the "triple standard" (*prasthāna-traya*) on which Vedāntic schools of philosophy are based.

[5] See: Eliot Deutsch, *Advaita Vedanta: A Philosophical Reconstruction* (Honolulu, HI: The University of Hawaii Press, 1973), 3.

[6] K. Satchidananda Murty, *Revelation and Reason in Advaita Vedanta* (New York, NY: Columbia University Press, 1959), 3.

[7] Ibid., xvii.

[8] See: K. Satchidananda Murty, *Revelation and Reason in Advaita Vedanta*, xvii.

[9] Once a seeker, approached a great soul, *Mahātmā*, and asked, "Revered Sir, how many Upaniṣads do I have to study to know myself?" The *Mahātmā* replied with a question: "How many mirrors do you need to look at yourself?"

[10] Professor Karl Jaspers, a preeminent German philosopher of last century, once told Professor K. Satchidananda Murty, that "*there was no metaphysics superior to that of Śaṅkara.*" See: K. Satchidananda Murty, *Revelation and Reason in Advaita Vedanta* (New York, NY: Columbia University Press, 1959), xvii. [emphasis added].

"In his short life of thirty-two years Sankara," wrote Will Durant, "achieved that union of sage and saint, of wisdom and kindliness, which characterizes the loftiest type of man produced in India. Sankara establishes the source of his philosophy at a remote and subtle point never quite clearly visioned again until, a thousand years later, Immanuel Kant wrote his Critique of Pure Reason." See: Will Durant, *Story of Civilization: Our Oriental Heritage* (New York, NY: Simon and Schuster, 1954), 546–547.

[11] तद् इदं गीता-शास्त्रं समस्त-वेदार्थ-सार-सङ्ग्रह-भूतं *tad idaṃ gītā-śāstraṃ samasta-vedārtha-sāra-saṅgraha-bhūtaṃ.*

Leaders who understand the reality of their context and proceed from the standpoint of Self-knowledge can lead organizational transformation efforts more effectively. They proactively recreate reality no less than reality recreates them.

Basic Tenets of Advaita Vedanta[12]

As rivers flow into the sea and in doing so lose their name and form, even so a wise person, freed from the identification of name and form, attains the Self-effulgent Being, beyond the very highest.[13]

This seminal quote from the Muṅḍaka Upaniṣad provides the *modus operandi* of Advaita philosophy. By overcoming the inveterate identification with the limiting body-mind-senses complex through the supreme knowledge of our true Self, we attain to our true nature which is the self-illumining light of our Pure Consciousness. The term "Vedānta" literally means the "end of the Veda" and refers, within the Indian philosophical tradition, to the teachings of the Upaniṣads, the *Brahma sūtras*, and the *Bhagavadgītā*.[14] Vedānta has been hailed as "the most sublime of all philosophies and the most comforting of all religions"[15] "On the tree of Indian wisdom," says Paul Deussen in his Prefatory Note, "there is no fairer flower than the Upanishads and no finer fruit than the

[12] Vedānta is one of the six classical schools of Indian philosophy, traditionally grouped in three pairs: Nyāya-Vaiśeṣika, Sāṅkhya-Yoga, and Pūrva-Mīmāṃsā-Uttara-Mīmāṃsā (or Vedānta). Each of these schools is known as *darśana*, a term derived from the Sanskrit root, *dṛś*, meaning "to see." It signifies a direct *vision* of Reality—an immediate insight into the nature of Truth. Upaniṣadic philosophers were not mere *knowers*, but *seers*, of truth (*ṛṣis*). They are called *mantra-draśtās*, the "seers" of the mantras. That is why the Gītā speaks in terms of knowers-seers of truth (*jñāninas tattvadarśinaḥ:* 4.34). As Eliot Deutsch elegantly puts it: "The Avaitin is convinced that '*to know*' is *to be*." See: Eliot Deutsch, *Advaita Vedānta: A Philosophical Reconstruction* (Honolulu, HI: The University Press of Hawaii, 1973), 4. [Emphasis added].

[13] Muṅḍaka Upaniṣad 3.2.8:

यथा नद्यः स्यन्दमानाः समुद्रेऽस्तं गच्छन्ति नामरूपे विहाय ।
तथा विद्वान्नामरूपाद्विमुक्तः परात्परं पुरुषमुपैति दिव्यम् ॥ ८ ॥

yathā nadyaḥ syandamānāḥ samudre'staṁ gacchanti nāmarūpe vihāya /
tathā vidvānnāmarūpādvimuktaḥ parātparaṁ puruṣamupaiti divyam //

The Upaniṣad concludes stating the glory of this knowledge: "the knower of Brahman *becomes* Brahman" (*brahma veda brahmaiva bhavati:* ब्रह्म वेद ब्रह्मैव भवति). Passing beyond sorrow and evil, and freed from the knots of his heart, such as person becomes immortal (Muṅḍaka Upaniṣad 3.2.9). See: Patrick Olivelle, trans., *Upaniṣads* (New York, NY: Oxford University Press, 1996), 276.

[14] Eliot Deutsch, *Advaita Vedānta*, 3.

[15] Cited in Swāmī Paramānanda, *Principles and Purpose of Vedanta* (Boston, MA: The Vedanta Center, 1910), 35. See also: Max Muller, India: *What Can It Teach Us: A Course of Lectures Delivered Before the University of Cambridge* (London, UK: Longmans, Green & Co., 1883), 253.

Vedanta philosophy."[16] Vedānta is the most widely known system of Indian philosophy, both in the East and the West. Advaita Vedānta is the non-dualistic system of Vedānta expounded primarily by Śaṅkara (ca. 788–820).[17] Advaita means *not two* or non-dual—the One only, without a second. It postulates one single reality, *Brahman*, as the absolute or ultimate truth of the world. It then equates this reality with the sole reality of our own self, called *Ātman*. The goal of Vedānta is to establish the reality and identity of *Ātman-Brahman*—the identity of the individual and the universal.

However, strictly not its founder, Śaṅkara was undoubtedly the greatest expounder and systematizer of Advaita. Karl Jaspers (1883–1969), the famous Austrian existentialist philosopher, once told Professor K. Satchidananda Murthy that, "there is no metaphysics superior to that of Śaṅkara."[18] "In his short life of thirty-two years Sankara," wrote Will Durant, "achieved that union of sage and saint, of wisdom and kindliness, which characterizes the loftiest type of man produced in India. Sankara establishes the source of his philosophy at a remote and subtle point never quite clearly visioned again until, a thousand years later, Immanuel Kant wrote his Critique of Pure Reason."[19]

Śaṅkara's fundamental Vedāntic stance can be summarized in a series of progressive axioms, as follows:

1. Brahman (Absolute) is One only, without a second[20] and is of the nature of Pure Existence, Consciousness,[21] and Bliss.[22]
2. Brahman is always, absolutely, one with the Ātman (Self). Śaṅkara explicitly states, "At no time has the *jiva* ever not been one with Brahman."[23]

[16] See: Paul Deussen, *Outline of the Vedanta System of Philosophy According to Shankara* (Cambridge, MA: Harvard University Press, 1906/1927; reissued by Leopold Classic Library, 2017), vii.

[17] Eliot Deutsch, *Advaita Vedānta,* 3.

[18] See: K. Satchidananda Murty, *Revelation and Reason in Advaita Vedanta* (New York, NY: Columbia University Press, 1959), xvii.

[19] See: Will Durant, *Story of Civilization: Our Oriental Heritage* (New York, NY: Simon and Schuster, 1954), 546–547.

[20] Chandōgya Upaniṣad 6.2.1. (*ekam eva advitiyam*).

[21] Aitareya Upaniṣad 3.3. (*Prajñānam Brahma*).

[22] Taittirīyopaniṣad 2-7-1 declares, "It is the essence, for only when one has grasped that essence does one attain bliss" (*raso vai saḥ | rasaṁ hyevāyaṁ labdhvānandī bhavati*: रसो वै सः। रसं ह्येवायं लब्ध्वा आनन्दी भवति). See Patrick Olivelle, trans., *Upaniṣads* (New York, NY: Oxford University Press, 1996), 188. Bliss is spoken of here in the sense of fullness (*puraṇattvam*) of our being, in the sense of *anantam*, limitlessness. Whenever we are sorrowful, we are missing something. That is, sorrow signifies a sense of limitation. What we are all ultimately pursuing is freedom from all limitations; and that freedom can only be found in something that is limitless. This limitlessness is spoken of as bliss. Chāndogya Upaniṣad 7.23.1 declares: यो वै भूमा तत्सुखं नाल्पे सुखमस्ति *yo vai bhūmā tatsukhaṁ nālpe sukhamasti*—That which is Infinite is joy. There is no joy in the finite.

[23] *Brahma Sūtra Bhāṣya* 3.2.7. (*na kadācijjīvasya brahmaṇā sampattirnāsti*: न कदाचिज्जीवस्य ब्रह्मणा सम्पत्तिर्नास्ति).

3. The manifold world of appearance is verily an expression/projection of Brahman alone—all plurality is but imagined in Brahman[24] and is *ultimately* non-real (*mithyā*).[25]
4. Brahman (Ultimate Reality) is of the nature of Existence, Consciousness, Infinitude.[26]
5. Self-less actions (*niṣkāma karma*) play preparatory role in purifying the mind to receive the wisdom of Self-knowledge (*ātma-jñāna*).
6. Self-ignorance (*avidyā*) alone is the cause of human bondage.[27]
7. Self-knowledge (*ātam-jñānam*) alone is the direct means to liberation (*mokṣa*).[28]
8. The highest good (*param śreyas*) or the ultimate end of life is spiritual freedom or liberation (*mukti or mokṣa*).[29]
9. Spiritual freedom (*mokṣa*) consists in the knowledge of oneness of the individual Self, *Ātman*, with the Absolute, Brahman (*brahmātma'aikya-bōdham*).[30]
10. Self-knowledge does not *produce* the Self *anew*; it only *reveals* the *ever-existing* Self by removing the self-ignorance.
11. All this, of course, is from the empirical standpoint (*vyavahārika-dṛṣti*); however, from the transcendental standpoint (*paramārthika dṛṣti*), the

[24] Śaṅkara's commentary to Bṛhadāraṇyaka Upaniṣad 1.4.10. (*sarvaṁ hi nānātvaṁ brahmaṇi kalpitameva* सर्वं हि नानात्वं ब्रह्मणि कल्पितमेव). See also Bṛhadāraṇyaka Upaniṣad 4.4.19: *neha nānāsti kiñcana* (नेह नानास्ति किञ्चन): There is here no multiplicity at all.

[25] Śaṅkara himself presents his entire philosophy in the following half verse:

brahma satyam jagan-mithyā jivo-brahmaiva naparāḥ

[26] Taittirīya Upaniṣad 2.1.1. (*satyam-jñānam-anantam Brahma*).

[27] Due to the ignorance of our true nature—which is infinite, pure consciousness—we limit our self to a particular body-mind-senses complex. It is like trying to limit infinite space in to a particular cup or jar. Liberation consists of being free from this misconstrued limitation. This is attained through the essential knowledge of our true nature.

[28] Strictly speaking, we do not "attain" liberation, *mokṣa*, through knowledge, *jñāna*. *Jñāna* just removes the wrong notion that we are bound. Through Self-knowledge, we come to know that *mokṣa* need *not* to be attained. It is our very nature, *svarūpam*.

[29] See: Kaṭha Upaniṣad 1.2.2: Both the good and the pleasant approach a person. The wise ones, pondering over them with discernment, choose the good in preference to the pleasant. The simple-minded, for the sake of worldly expediency, prefer the pleasant.

[30] Sri Atmananda, a preeminent modern Vedānta teacher of the Direct Path, says, "It is the realization of oneself and the entire world as one Consciousness that is known as realization of Truth." See: Sri Atmananda, *Atma Darshan: At the Ultimate* (Austin, TX: Advaita Publishers, 1991), 6. As Greg Goode avers, "Sri Atmananda (Krishna Menon, 1897–1981) is increasingly recognized as one of the great sages in modern India, along with Ramana Maharshi (1979–1950) and Nisargadatta Maharaj (1897–1981)." For further details, see: Greg Goode'a blog entry, The Teachings of Atmananda and the Direct Path: http://awakeningtoreality.blogspot.com/2009/12/teachings-of-atmananda-and-direct-path.html

Self is ever-free and does *not* need to be liberated.[31] This freedom is eternal and is the very nature, *svarupa*, of the seeker indeed (*nityatvānmokṣasya sādhakasvarūpāvyatirekācca*).[32]

Śaṅkara succinctly presents his entire philosophy in the following verse, *śloka*:

ślokārdhena pravakṣyami yaduktam granthakoṭibhiḥ /
brahma satyam jagan-mithyā jivo-brahmaiva naparāḥ //[33]

I shall express within the compass of half a verse the quintessence of the teachings expounded in innumerable scriptures and that is:

Brahman alone is real; the world is non-real; and
the individual Self is essentially not-different from Brahman.

Brahman alone exists at all times as the Existence/Consciousness principle in all living beings. This is the quintessence of Śaṅkara's supreme metaphysics.

What is the practical significance of the value of oneness? In a world where intolerance is on a rise, Śaṅkara's non-dual philosophy can serve as a great unifying force. Nations which are blessed with immense diversity can establish unity in diversity with this understanding. In an age of moral ineptitude, a practical philosophy highlighting unity can harness truthfulness, understanding, and empathy. Vedānta defines reality as the unchanging essence underlying all existence: That alone is real which exists by itself, which reveals itself by itself, and which is eternal and unchanging.[34] All our experience—of the outer and the inner worlds—takes place as ripples in the quantum soup of this limitless unchanging awareness. When we *realize* this to be our true nature, we are *freed* from the self-imposed and limiting strictures of name and form.

[31] न निरोधो न चोत्पत्तिर्न बद्धो न च साधकः ।
न मुमुक्षुर्न वै मुक्त इत्येषा परमार्थता ॥ ४.२.३२ ॥

na nirodho na cotpattirna baddho na ca sādhakaḥ /
na mumukṣurna vai mukta ityeṣā paramārthatā //4.2.32//

[From the standpoint of Absolute Reality]: There is no dissolution, no birth, none in bondage, none aspiring for wisdom, no seeker of liberation and none liberated. This is the absolute truth. Śaṅkara's commentary on this important verse: "When duality is known to be illusory and *Ātman* alone is known as the sole Reality, then it is clearly established that all our experiences, ordinary and religious, verily pertain to the domain of ignorance." See Swāmī Nikhalānanda (trans.), *Māṇḍūkyopaniṣad with Gauḍapāda's Kārikā and Śaṅkara's Commentary* (Calcutta, India: Advaita Ashrama, 1995), 119.

[32] Bṛhadāraṇyaka Upaniṣad 3.3.1: नित्यत्वान्मोक्षस्य साधकस्वरूपाव्यतिरेकाच्च ।

[33] श्लकार्धेन प्रवक्ष्यमि यदुक्तम् ग्रन्थकोटिभिः ।
ब्रह्म सत्यम् जगन्-मिथ्या जिवो-ब्रह्मैव नपराः ॥

[34] Advaita Vedānta defines Ultimate Reality as the self-evident, self-existing, self-luminous, eternal, unchanging *Conscious Principle*, which is the source and substratum of all and everything.

Seeker Is the Sought

What you seek is so near you that there is no place for a way.[35] (Nisargadatta Maharaj)

This terse observation of Nisargadatta Maharaj points out the essential irony of spiritual quest for seeking one's true nature. A pathway presupposes distance. Since one can never be separated from one's true nature, there is no place for a path to it. It is a journey of no-journey; a self-discovery, a homecoming. It is like looking for one's eyes.

While what we seek keeps on changing, the seeker in us continues to be the same. Self-knowledge reveals the radical fact that the *seeker is the sought.*[36] The following traditional tale[37] illustrates the point splendidly by highlighting both the predicament of Self-ignorance and a way to end it:

The Missing Tenth Man

Ten monks crossed a river, and one of them counted their number to see if everyone had safely crossed. To their dismay, one was found missing. Then everyone took their turn at counting, but the result was the same. So they began to lament, when a kind passer-by inquired what it was all about.

On being told what had happened, he readily understood the situation, and asked one of them to count again. When he stopped at nine, the passer-by said to him, "You are the tenth man." This he repeated with the rest of them. Then they saw their mistake and went away happy. Everyone had left himself out in the counting!

This story highlights that the uniqueness of Self-knowledge lies in the fact that, unlike all other forms of knowledge, it does not entail any new acquisition of information. It only involves freedom from Self-ignorance. Like the tenth man in the story, gaining the essential Self means *realizing* our mistake of self-forgetfulness or Self-ignorance. The Self, like the tenth man in the story, appears initially to be not known through ignorance, but subsequently becomes known through knowledge. From an absolute standpoint, again—like the tenth man in the story—the essential Self was never lost to begin with and is ever-attained.

Sri Ramana Maharshi underscores this point succinctly in the following important passage:

[35] Maurice Frydman, trans., *I Am That: Conversations with Sri Nisargadatta Maharaj* (Durham, NC: The Acorn Press, 2nd American revised edition, 2012), 196.

[36] One sage says, "What one is searching *for* is what one is searching *with*."

[37] Swāmi Mādhavānanda, trans., *The Bṛhadāraṇyaka Upaniṣad with the commentary of Śaṅkarācārya* (Mayavati, Almora, Himalayas: Advaita Ashrama, 1934/2008), 83–84.

> There is no greater mystery than this, that we keep seeking reality though in fact we are reality. We think that there is something hiding reality and that this must be destroyed before reality is gained. How ridiculous! A day will dawn when you will laugh at all your past efforts. That which will be the day you laugh is also here and now.[38]

Strictly speaking, we cannot objectively *know* our Self because we *are* the Self. *The seeker is already the sought*! We are the knowing self—the pure awareness—the subject; and the knowing *subject*, by definition, can never become the *object* of knowledge. John Wheeler clarifies this important point that "you *are* what you are seeking," succinctly:

> Trying to focus on your true nature is something like looking for your eyes, when the whole time you are looking through them. If you try to focus on your being or aware presence, you will be trying to turn it into an object. Since you are not an object, you will be looking in vain. Just see this point and pause. Being-awareness is here in all of its immediacy and clarity. *That* is it. Why should you try to focus on it, when you *are* it? See the false concept and the error contained in it. Your being is not to be obtained. It is pointed to as a present fact.[39]

The Self seems *as though* veiled currently due to certain inhibiting factors, primarily, ignorance. This ignorance does not denote any lack of information or knowledge in any general sense. The ignorance that is referred to here is actually Self-ignorance, the ignorance or unawareness of our essential nature. The entire quest of fulfillment therefore is of the nature of awakening, a journey of recognition without distance from *here* to *here*. The following story[40] splendidly underscores the paradox of missing our reality, while riding on it, metaphorically speaking:

Lost Donkey?
A man bought 4 donkeys and rode home on one of them.
When he reached home, his wife came out to greet him.
While sitting on one donkey, he started counting and found he had only 3 donkeys.
He said to his wife that he was missing one donkey!
His wife asked him, "How many donkeys did you buy?"
He said, "I bought four, but now I only see three."
His wife smiled and said: "I see five!"

[38] Cited in Swami Rajeswarananda (Ed.), *Thus Spake Ramana*, 111. See: *Talks with Sri Ramana Maharshi* (Tiruvannamalai, India: Sri Ramanasramam, 2000), 134.

[39] John Wheeler, *Full Stop! The Gateway to Present Perfection* (Salisbury, UK: Non-Duality Press, 2012), 31. [emphasis in the original].

[40] A traditional Sufi tale, transcribed by the author.

The man in the story is Mulla Nasruddin Hodja, a populist philosopher, and a consummate jester. He is known to poke fun at our common incongruities, using himself as an example. Our search for the Self may be "likened" to looking for the fourth donkey in the story: We have been at it all along, so to speak, yet failing to recognize it while comfortably riding on it! Paradoxically, avers Anthony de Mello, "Wisdom tends to grow in proportion to one's awareness of one's ignorance."[41]

Attainment of the ever-attained Self, therefore, essentially means letting go of our false notions about what we take ourselves to be; that is, a limited body-mind-senses complex subject to mortality and unhappiness. It is about chipping away, so to speak, the fabricated edifice of the false "I," the imposter ego, posing itself to be the real Self. This special understanding requires subtle discernment to reclaim our true heritage. And this requires *knowledge*, not any special effort or *action*. We just have to *know* ourselves as we truly are.

Wave-Ocean-Water![42]

No Wave. No Ocean. Water Only!

Once upon a time, a wave felt inadequate and insecure. It felt daunted confronting the vast expanse of the ocean. It used to brood over the meaninglessness of its existence, the futility of it all and get depressed with a very low self-esteem.

Then one day a *guru* wave came along and said, "Hey! Why do you look so depressed?"

"I feel so small and frail amidst all these big waves and the vast ocean," replied the tiny wave.

"But you are not what you take yourself to be. In essence, you are not any different from the ocean!"

"Me? Ocean?!! You must be kidding!!!"

"No, I am serious. Actually, you *are* the ocean! Tell me, what does the ocean consist of?"

"Water."

"And you?"

"Water."

"So, both you and the ocean are really the selfsame water. In fact, there is no wave or ocean *apart from* water."

"Realize your essential nature to be water indeed, and *be free*."

So saying, the guru wave took leave and resolved into the big ocean.

No wave. No ocean. Only Water! Bingo!

Right at that very moment, the tiny wave became en-*light*-ened. It became playful and carefree. It stopped feeling small, limited, and inadequate. It stopped comparing itself to the surrounding waves or seeking validation from them. All struggle of becoming this or that came to an end. Its self-esteemed soared and its

[41] Anthony De Mello, *One Minute Wisdom* (New York, NY: Doubleday, 1988), 97.

[42] Based on the Vedāntic teachings of Swami Dayananda Saraswati as presented during *13 Discourses on Ānanda Mīmāṃsā*. Audio Retrieved July 15, 2015: https://archive.org/details/AnandaMimamsa

job dissatisfaction vanished. The wave attained the highest security and felicity in realizing that "no matter what, I can never cease to be water. Best of all I do not have to *do* anything to become water. All along, I have *been* water only. Realizing itself to be water indeed, it *dis*-covered the ever-flowing, abiding joy of the fullness of its being!

The guru wave further explained, "No need to be in awe of this big ocean: In essence, you and ocean are not different at all, but only water! For interacting with other waves—at home and at work—you can *still* continue to *play* the *role* of *being* a wave. But *always remember your real nature to be only water*, and *be free*."

The wave tried to express thanks to this guru wave with folded hands and a deep bow, in reverence.

The *guru* wave said, "You are still missing the point! There is no need to feel grateful. We are both waves, and, in essence, only water. There is no real difference at all. Water is water is water. Let's just *be friends*."

Then, before resolving into the ocean, finally, the *guru* wave said, "I will send you a friend request on Facebook soon."

Both waves burst into laughter and submerged into the vast space of the ocean.

The foregoing observations reveal a cardinal fact about our existence—that happiness or fulfillment that we seek is our own essential nature. This fact remains hidden from us due to Self-ignorance. Hence the importance of Self-knowledge in the quest for fulfillment. What if someone were to offer us wealth equal to the value of the Earth's weight in gold? Sages say that the value of Self-knowledge is even more precious than that.[43] One should stake one's salvation on no less a treasure than the supreme wealth of the Self.

This, then, is the considered conclusion of Vedānta: *You are already what you are seeking*. Know your true Self and be fulfilled. We have come full circle! We conclude this section with a quote that encapsulates the essence of the quest for Self-knowledge:

The spiritual quest is journey without distance
You travel from where you are right now
To where you have always been
From ignorance to recognition.[44] (Anthony de Mello)

Anthony de Mello distils the gist of all spiritual seeking in stating that it more a rediscovery, a recognition of an intrinsic truth. It is a journey of no-journey; it is a homecoming! The reader will recall an earlier quote by Nisargadatta

[43] In the famous Upaniṣadic dialog, Maitreyī asks her husband, Yajñāvalkya, "Venerable Sir, if indeed the whole earth full of wealth belonged to me, would I be immortal through that or not?" "No," replied Yajñāvalkya, "your life would be just like that of people who have plenty of wealth. Of immortality, however, there is no hope through wealth." For the complete dialog, see: *Bṛhadāraṇyaka Upaniṣad* 2.4.1–14.

[44] Larry Chang (Ed.), *Wisdom for the Soul: Five Millennia of Prescriptions for Spiritual Healing* (Washington, DC: Gnosophia Publishers, 2006), 436.

Maharaj. When it comes to Self-knowledge, all paths are essentially detours; they lead the seeker away from home. Save the trouble. Just be. This is the ultimate purpose of all Vedāntic teachings.

Door to Self-Realization

The goal of Advaita Vedānta is to establish the reality and identity of *Ātman-Brahman*. The object of Indian philosophy is not idle speculation, but to *see* the Truth, to realize it in one's own direct intuitive experience. In Indian philosophy, enlightenment is spoken of as Self-realization, the attainment of the Supreme Self. However, it is important to understand the exact sense in which the word "realization" is used. Sri Ramana Maharshi, the great Indian sage, clarifies:

> We loosely talk of Self-Realization, for lack of a better term. But *how can one realize or make real that which alone is real?* All we need to do is to give up our habit of regarding as real that which is unreal. All religious practices are meant solely to help us do this. When we stop regarding the unreal as real, then reality alone will remain, and we will be that.[45]

Vedānta takes it as axiomatic that "the highest aim of religion is…Self-knowledge."[46] The knowledge of the Self (*ātma-jñāna*) and the knowledge of the Ultimate Reality (*tattva- jñāna*) are identical. They represent the individual and the universal aspects of the same non-dual Reality. Ādī Śaṅkara, the great Advaita philosopher, urges that "you must realize absolutely that the *Ātman* [the Self] is Brahman [the All-Self]."[47] Vedānta employs several methodologies (*prakriyās*) to establish the identity of Ātman with the Brahman.

According to the Gītā and Upaniṣads, Self-realization is not a matter of intellectual acquaintance, but a living fact to be realized in one's direct experience moment-to-moment, here and now.[48] If Self is our very own nature, why do we not know this self-evident fact? It is quite natural, given the extroverted nature of our senses, reveals the Lord of Death in Kaṭhopaniṣad 2.1 to Natchiketas, perhaps history's first seeker of truth:

> God made senses turn outward, man therefore looks outward, not into himself. Now and again a daring soul, desiring immortality, has looked back and found himself.[49]

[45] A. Devaraja Mudaliar, *Day By Day with Bhagavan* (Tiruvannamalai, India: Sri Ramanasaramam, 2002), 181. [emphasis added].

[46] Sri Yukteswar Giri, *The Holy Science* (Los Angeles, CA: Self-Realization Fellowship, 1984), 6.

[47] See Swami Prabhavananda & Christopher Isherwood, trans., *Shankara's Crest-Jewel of Discrimination* (Hollywood, CA: Vedanta Press, 1975), 68–72.

[48] My Vedānta teacher always used to emphasize this point: these teachings are not only to be appreciated, but also should be *interiorized*, that is, *cognized* or *actualized* within oneself.

[49] Shree Purohit Swāmī & W. B. Yeats, trans., *The Ten Principal Upanishads* (London, UK: Faber and Faber, 1938), 33.

The "daring soul" is the person who wants Self-knowledge, *Brahma-vidyā*, who wants to know the knower. The following extract presents the methodology to intuit the reality of our true nature within the compass of a few succinct paragraphs:

Maharaj: When you use the word "I" what exact image do you have about yourself? When you were a child you considered yourself nothing other than a child and were happy enough to play with toys. Later, you were a young man and you thought you could face anything or anyone in this world. You are now in your middle age, a little mellower but nonetheless enjoying life and its pleasures, and you think you are a happy and successful man, blessed with a nice family. At present you have an image about yourself that is quite different from the images you had earlier. Imagine yourself ten years hence and further twenty years later. The image you will then have about yourself will be different from all the earlier ones. Which one of these images is the real "you"? Have you ever thought about it? Is there any particular identity that you can call your very own and which has remained with you throughout, unchanged and unchangeable?

Maharaj in this dialog points out a vital fact of our experience. During all our stages of life—childhood, young age, middle age, old age, and so on, obviously our body-mind complex undergoes complete change. If so, can we call any of these stages of our life, howsoever important they may seem to be at the time, to be our very own essential Self? Is there something that has remained unchanged amidst these changes? That is the subject matter of the following dialog:

Visitor: Now that you mention it, I admit that when I use the word "I", I have no particular idea about myself and I agree that whatever idea I have had about myself has been changing over the years.

Maharaj: Well, there is something which has remained unchanged all these years, while everything else has been changing. And that is the constant sense of *presence*, the sense that you *exist*. This sense or feeling "I am" has never changed. This is your constant image. You are sitting in front of me. You know it beyond doubt, without any need of confirmation from anyone else. Similarly you *know* that you *are*, that you *exist*.[50]

Although we experience that every stage of our life has come and gone, however, there is something that has not changed at all. If we look at our pictures when we were 5, 10, 20, or 30 years old, they all look different. At no point in our life do we doubt that they *are* our pictures. This is called the unchanging presence, the sense that I exist, that I am. Indeed, that sense of presence, of "I am," is the one constant throughout our life—the awareness of

[50] Ramesh S. Balsekar, *Pointers from Nisargadatta Maharaj* (Durham, NC: Acorn paperback, 1998), 20.

being aware. One modern teacher of non-duality calls it "Presence-Awareness"—the sense of being present and its awareness.[51]

The dream analogy is very helpful in understanding our true nature. When we dream, our awareness slips into different dimension. Let's just say that we see a tiger in the dream. We get afraid of it and start running away. Now, obviously, the tiger is outside (our mind) and the fear is inside (our mind). However, our experience of the dream—tiger/outside/fear/inside/running away—seems seamless: it is all taking place on the "screen" of cognitive awareness. And it seems very real, very vivid, as long as it lasts. In the same manner, our experiences take place during the walking state. Our mind "creates" all we see during the waking state just like it creates the objects/experiences of the dream world. Qualitatively, there is no difference. This is a paraphrase of verse 170 of *Vivekacūḍāmaṇi* of Sri Saṅkarācārya, also a favorite of Sri Ramana Maharshi.

When we get the real taste of this pulsating emanation of the unchanging Consciousness principle "I-I"—सफूरना, *safūranā*, all seeking subsides on its own accord.

It is important to bear in mind that Self-realization is not an event—it is a self-established, existential fact. These days, one comes across claims such as "someone got 'enlightened' triggered by this or that event—some sort of a big *aha moment*!" The Self is our very own nature. Its realization is not an accomplishment or an event, but a matter of discovery, recognition, or remembrance.[52] One doesn't get "enlightened" as a person or as an entity. The mind attains knowledge of its true nature and *realizes* that the Self was never a person after all. One understands that the true nature of one's Self is limitless awareness, not the limited psychosomatic apparatus, the body-mind-sense complex, that the ego takes itself to be. This very knowledge itself—that I am limitless awareness—is Self-realization or spiritual freedom. As Paul Deuseen put it succinctly, "Deliverance is not effected by the knowledge of the *ātman*, but this knowledge is itself already deliverance."[53]

Really Real or Apparently Real?

Is your gold ring real? Of course, yes! But is it *really* real? To find out, let's look at it more closely.

[51] Perhaps of all modern teachers of neo-Vedanta, John Wheeler's books carry the intrinsic authority of genuine experience and insight. See: John Wheeler, *Full Stop! The Gateway to Present Perfection* (Salisbury, UK: Non-Duality Press, 2012); *Clear in Your Heart* (Salisbury, UK: Non-Duality Press, 2010); *The Light Behind Consciousness* (Salisbury, UK: Non-Duality Press, 2008); *You Were Never Born* (Salisbury, UK: Non-Duality Press, 2007); *Right Here, Right Now: Seeing Your True Nature as Present Awareness* (Salisbury, UK: Non-Duality Press, 2006); *Shining in Plain View* (Salisbury, UK: Non-Duality Press, 2005); *Awakening to the Natural State* (Salisbury, UK: Non-Duality Press, 2004).

[52] In the last verse of the Gītā 18.73, Arjuna states his realization as follows: *naṣṭo mohaḥ smṛtir labdhā*: My delusion is gone, and I have gained recognition of my true nature.

[53] Paul Deussen, *The Philosophy of the Upanishads* (New York, NY: Dover Publications, 1966), 409.

If we melt the gold ring, what do we get? Gold. Where did the ring go? Well, ring was just a "name" and "form" which got resolved into gold upon melting. If we take out the gold from the ring, what is left? Can the ring exist separate and apart from the gold. No. So, properly speaking, ring is "dependently" real. Does the existence of gold depend upon the existence or non-existence of the ring? No. Gold can exist, just as gold or can be re-shaped into a ring, a bracelet, or an amulet. Therefore, gold is *really* real, or independently real, while all objects made out of gold are dependently real.

Vedānta uses the word "*mithyā*" to denote dependently real objects. In its vision, from the tiniest atoms to grandest galaxies, all creation is dependently real, *mithyā–real and unreal* at the same time. At the relative level, the world is real since it is experienced. At the absolute level, it is *mithyā* since it has a borrowed existence. It depends upon the observing Consciousness to reveal its existence. The Absolute Consciousness which is One, without a second, is called Brahman. This Conscious-Principle, Brahman, is our inmost self and is referred to as Self or Ātman.

It was in this sense that Ādī Śaṅkara famously quipped, "*Brahma satya, jagan mithyā, jivo bhahmeva nā paraḥ*": The Brahman is real, the world is non-real, and individual self is non-different from the universal Reality. This is one summary of Vedānta.

Vedānta says, "*Know* the Brahman as your inmost Self and *be* free!"

Vedic Vision: What Is Real and How Do We Know It?

Vedic Ontology

Vedānta defines real as that which never changes; for that which is ever changing cannot be real. Put differently, the unreal has no existence; the real never ceases to exist (*nāsato vidyate bhāvo nābhāvo vidyate sataḥ*: B.G. 2.16). The first part of the statement—the unreal does not exist—is easy to understand. The mirage in the dessert is not real and the city in the sky is not real either. They are mere appearances and hence do not exist.

That brings us to the next part of the statement: the Real never ceases to exist. This part requires some elaboration.

It is our common experience that everything that we perceive is ceaselessly changing. Our body is constantly changing; our mind (thoughts/feelings) is constantly changing; and everything in the external world is continuously changing. They cannot be *real* according to the above definition of reality.

Does that mean that there is nothing *really* real (*satyasya satya*)?

Vedānta says that the Witnessing Consciousness in everyone that perceives the entire changing phenomenon is the only unchanging reality. Everything else that is constantly changing is a mere "appearance" in the Pure Consciousness.

This Pure Consciousness is the *observer* of all the changes; it is the substratum in which all changes appear and disappear! By definition, the observer has to be changeless to be able to perceive the changes. Vedānta calls it the innermost Self (*pratyagātmā*) of all beings.

Vedānta declares that You *are* the Self (*tat tvam asi*: Chāndogya Upaniṣad 6.8.7)—the unchanging Witnessing Consciousness that perceives the changes in the body-mind-senses, the three states (waking, dream, and deep sleep), and the phenomenal world.

This unchanging Consciousness is the Absolute Reality. It is called Brahman in its universal aspect. The same universal Consciousness experienced as the Self in all beings is called Ātman.[54] There is an absolute identity of Brahman and Ātman, for Reality is One, without a second (*ekam evādvitīyam*, Chāndogya Upaniṣad 6.2.1). Ātman and Brahman are two designations of the same Absolute Reality (*Tad Ekam*—That One), the unchanging Witnessing Consciousness. That One is denoted by the primordial sound "OM" and is the only thing, which is really real: *Om Tat Sat*! *This is the ontology of Vedānta.*

To know this unchanging Pure Consciousness as our very own Self is to attain immortality (*amṛt tattvam*)—*yaj jñātvāmṛtam aśnute*: B.G. 13.12; knowing which one becomes free from all that is inauspicious (*yaj jñātvā mokṣyaseśubhāt*: B.G. 9.1). Anything other than the Self is ephemeral.[55] According to the Vedic vision, this is the *summum bonum*, the Supreme Goal (*carma-lakṣya*) of human life.

Real and *Really* Real? Wave, Ocean, Water!

Earlier in this chapter, the wave-ocean-water illustration was presented. The wave is busy with "mergers and acquisitions" without realizing that it is ocean only. As water, both the wave and the ocean are essentially one. However, practically speaking, a wave is a wave and an ocean is an ocean: one can navigate a ship in the ocean but not in the wave. Strictly speaking, ocean and wave are both only water, but water is neither wave nor ocean. In other words, water can exist without wave and ocean whereas ocean and wave cannot exist independent of water.

Likewise, subject, the Self, exists even in the absence of objects of experience, as in deep sleep. An object cannot exist independent of the conscious subject. This is an important distinction to keep in mind with reference to subject and object. Hence, concludes Vedānta, the world of objects is dependently real (*mithyā*) while the subject alone is really real (*satyasaya-satyam*).

[54] Śaṅkara, in his commentary to *Brahma Sūtra* 1.1.6, remarks: आत्मा हि नाम स्वरूपम्। Ātman means one's own nature.

[55] Bṛhadāraṅyaka Upaniṣad 3.7.23: ऽतोऽन्यदार्तं *ato'nyadārtaṁ*.

Who Am I, Really?

Vedic Epistemology

First realize that your world is a reflection of yourself and then stop finding fault with the reflection. (Nisargadatta Maharaj)

Nisargadatta Maharaj never disappoints. In this penetrating observation, he solves the basic riddle of us versus them. If we realize that the world is but a reflection of us, we stop finding fault with the world. The moral of the story: Transform yourself to transform the world. The spiritual quest begins and ends with the question, "Who Am I?" The whole purpose of Vedāntic study is to discover our true nature, who we truly are. The simplest way to know who you *are* is to find out who you are *not*.

Almost everyone takes oneself to be the body-mind-senses complex. It is quite natural (*naisargika*) and necessary for functioning in the world (*loka-vyavahāra*).[56]

When someone asks you who you are, you tend to say, "I am so and so," referring to your name and some form of identity (related to your work or profession). We generally answer such questions from the standpoint of our personality or ego-entity. Is that who we really are?

As a starting point, it is important to understand the simple difference between the subject and the object. Can you be the subject (the perceiver) and the object (the perceived) at the same time?

The answer is no.

For example, I see/perceive my car. I cannot be the car. Similarly, I perceive this body. This body, like my car, appears as an object to me. I am the subject and the body appears to me as an object. And the subject *cannot be* the object. They are of totally different natures, like light and darkness, and cannot be present at the same place, same time (*tama-prakāshavata viruddha-svabhāva ekatra samāvesha asambhava*).[57] And yet, we all quite naturally *mis*-take our body, mind, and so on to be our real self in our day-to-day affairs.[58] This mutual superimposition of the real Self and the unreal non-Self is called

[56] Śaṅkara in his introduction to *Brahma Sūtra*.

[57] Brahma Sūtra Bhaṣya 1.1.4.

[58] Ibid. सत्यानृते मिथुनीकृत्य 'अहमिदम्' 'ममेदम्' इति नैसर्गिकोऽयंलोकव्यवहारः ॥ *satyānṛte mithunīkṛtya 'ahamidam' 'mam-edam' iti naisargiko'yaṁlokavyavahāraḥ* // Human mind by virtue of its natural inclination is liable to mix up both the real "Self" and the unreal non-self and instinctively thinks in the form of "I am this"; "This is mine." Here, the word "I" refers to the real "Self" and "this" corresponds to the not-self such as the body. Man rarely suspects that this "me" includes the real as well as the not-self, body, and so on. And "this is mine" refers to everything, that is other than the self, including the mind, senses, and the body. See: Swami Satchidanandendra Saraswathi, *Śaṅkara's Sūtra-Bhāshya Self-Explained* (Holenarasipura, India: Adhyātmaprakāsha Kāryālaya), 14.

adhyāsa, nescience, *avidyā*, in Vedānta. The only purpose of studying Vedānta is to remove this misconception about our true nature.

I ***cannot be*** this body—for, I am the subject, and the body is an object to me.

Vedānta says that the spiritual quest begins with understanding this vital point—that, I am *not* this body.

Let us carry our self-inquiry a bit further.

I am aware of my thoughts and feelings. They ceaselessly come and go out of my awareness. I perceive my thoughts (as objects). Therefore, I cannot be my thoughts and feelings—my mind. But I remain, as the perceiver of their presence and absence. If I were the thoughts, then when they disappear, I will disappear too.

When you say, "My mind is calm or restless," you are referring to your mind as an "object." You, the subject, are aware of your calm or restless mind, the object. Therefore, you are *not* the mind either.

What about the intellect, the seat of logic and reasoning?

Am I my intellect?

Let's say a friend asks you, "Do you understand Einstein's Special Theory of Relativity?" You may reply, "No, it is too difficult or too complex for me" Or "My intellect cannot grasp it or figure it out." When you say so, you, the subject, are objectifying your intellect.

Hence, you *cannot* be the intellect either.

Now we see the problem with Descartes' famous assertion, "I think, therefore, I am." (Cogito ergo sum)

Did the great French philosopher mean to say that, when he is *not* thinking, he *ceases* to exist? We hope not.

"I am, therefore, I think" (*Sum ergo cogito*) seems to be more in line with the way the things are. I have to be *there* first, before I can think any thoughts. I experience my thoughts. The experiencer, by definition, is prior to the experience.

Let us recapitulate:

I am not the body, nor am I the mind or the intellect.

What about the ego? Am I my ego, the me-notion, the seat of my transactional personality?

Often, we refer to others as vain and proud and ourselves as humble. In this manner, we are *unwittingly* "objectifying" our ego.

What is ego, anyway? Does it really exist? Or is it just a concept, an "I-notion" or "I-thought," that appears and disappears in the mind, like any other thought?

If ego is just another thought appearing in the mind, then I *cannot* be the ego. Ego is the imaginary self that we *mis*-take ourselves to be. This, says Vedānta, is the root of all evil.

If I am not the body, nor the mind, the intellect, or the ego, then who am I?

As is clear from the foregoing analysis, the body, the mind, the intellect and the ego—all are objects to ME. I am the Subject. They come and go. But I remain—I do not come and go with them. I am prior to them (*agrayam*). They ceaselessly change. I am the unchanging substratum, the witnessing Consciousness that lends existence to all objects, perceptions (of the body-mind and the world), thoughts, and feelings. Their existence depends upon me. My existence does not depend upon them. I exist, regardless.

What is the practical utility of this knowledge or understanding?

If I am not the body-mind-intellect-ego-complex, then I am not conditioned by them—I am not limited by them. Their limitations are not my limitations and I am not affected by them.

What are the limitations of the physical body? The body is born at a certain time, grows ill, old, and eventually dies. If I am NOT the body, then birth, old age, death, and so on, do not belong to me. They belong to the body. In my essential nature (*svarupa*), I am not affected by them.

As the Self, I am never born; as the Self, I never die. I am eternal (*nitya*) (B.G. 2.20), changeless, ever the same.

Since my true Self is of the nature of Pure Awareness, the limitations of the mind and intellect do not limit me either. My true Self is all-pervading (*sarva-gatah*) like space (*vyōm-vat*). Can space ever become impure? So, I do not need to "purify" my mind. How can you purify space, which is ever pure?

This puts an end to the whole self-improvement business!

I, the Self, do not need to be liberated. How can the space be bound?

Our "being" does not need any liberation or awakening because it is never bound, to begin with.

This puts an end to the whole enlightenment business.

I, in my true nature as the Witnessing Consciousness, am ever pure and liberated (*nitya-shuddha-bhudda-mukta-svabhāva*).[59]

This is who I am, right now, and right here.

This puts an end to all spiritual seeking and existential suffering, once and for all!

Then, one lives one's life, naturally and spontaneously, without needing to be on the ceaseless treadmill of self-improvement or becoming enlightened.

Who wants to improve, to get better, or become enlightened? The imposter ego wants all these frills because it feels small, limited, and separate.

This knowledge frees us from the servitude of the commanding ego (*nafs-e-ammārā*). We welcome all and everything as it comes, choicelessly, without attachment or aversion (*rāga-dveśa*). The undue attachment with the objects has ceased; and the sense of separation, limitation is gone. There is only effortless joyful playfulness.

You go with the flow, with the Divine Play (*līlā*), without identifying with it or considering it as *your* play.

You have arrived HOME, which you had never left in the first place!

This is the promise, and the fulfillment, of Vedānta.

[59] Śaṅkara in his introduction to *Gītā-Bhāṣya*.

Vedānta: The Supreme Science of Reality

As stated earlier, this chapter primarily draws upon Advaita Vedānta which is considered to be the crest jewel of Indian wisdom.[60] "Advaita" is Sanskrit for "non-dual," and "Vedānta" literally means "the end or inner core of the Vedas," the books of knowledge. Vedānta is the most widely known system of Indian philosophy, both in the East and the West.[61] It is a philosophy of non-duality based on the Upaniṣads, which are the concluding portions of the Vedas.[62] The word "*Veda*," derived from the Sanskrit root *vid* (to know), means that which makes us know.[63] The Vedas are among the oldest sacred texts in the world. The Upaniṣads, the *Brahma Sūtra*, and the Gītā form the "triple standard" (*prasthāna-traya*) on which Vedāntic schools of philosophy are based.[64]

Advaita Vedānta is widely considered by Western scholars of religion, and Hindus themselves, to be the philosophical culmination of the Indian spiritual tradition.[65] As a system of Self-knowledge, Advaita Vedānta is free from any narrow sectarian dogma or doctrine. Its tenets are rational, universalistic, and scientific in spirit and there is much Advaita metaphysics in contemporary quantum physics. It reveals the oneness of humanity and the intrinsic divinity, infinity, and immortality of the soul. It presents its message through logical axioms that are self-evident. There are no creeds to follow and no dogmas to adhere to. All that is required is an open mind and the willingness to understand objectively the truth of our own existence. Vedānta does not posit happiness as a future possibility, but helps the seeker to appreciate it as an ever-attained fact in the present.

Advaita Vedānta teaches that the phenomenal world, though real at a relative level, is merely the manifestation of the one underlying Absolute Reality, known as Brahman. At the individual level, this reality is experienced as pure awareness or Consciousness, the Self (*ātman*), which is essentially an expression of Brahman itself (the Absolute). There is one limitless Consciousness which is the substratum of all and everything. This vision of the essential oneness of our reality (*ātman*) and the reality of the world (Brahman) provides a sound foundation and *raison d'être* for acting for the good of others. Once understood clearly, it becomes a lived experience, nay, a living reality, serving as

[60] "On the tree of Indian wisdom, there is no fairer flower than the Upanishads and no finer fruit than the Vedanta philosophy." ~Paul Deussen, *Outline of the Vedanta System*, vii.

The Upaniṣads, the *Brahma Sutra*, and the Gītā form the "triple standard" (*prasthāna-traya*) on which Vedāntic schools of philosophy are based.

[61] See: Eliot Deutsch, *Advaita Vedanta: A Philosophical Reconstruction* (Honolulu, HI: The University of Hawaii Press, 1973), 3.

[62] K. Satchidananda Murty, *Revelation and Reason in Advaita Vedanta* (New York, NY: Columbia University Press, 1959), 3.

[63] Ibid., xvii.

[64] See: K. Satchidananda Murty, *Revelation and Reason in Advaita Vedanta*, xvii.

[65] See: Eliot Deutsch, *Advaita Vedanta: A Philosophical Reconstruction* (Honolulu, HI: The University of Hawaii Press, 1973).

both the path and the goal for our quest for fulfillment, in the form of Self-knowledge and selfless service respectively.

The basic truth of Vedānta is the Self, which is essentially of the nature of pure Consciousness. This truth of the Self is self-existent and self-evident: we *know* that we exist and we are *conscious* of our existence. No further proof is required to prove that we exist. Nor can the existence of the Self ever be denied, for to deny the Self is to actually prove its existence! Representing the culmination of all secular and sacred knowledge, Vedānta has been aptly called the *philosophia perennis*—the perennial philosophy—whose truth is found in many different traditions of the world that emphasize "oneness of the being."[66] As Swami Nikhilananda has noted, "The existence of the Self, or Consciousness, cannot finally be doubted, because the doubter himself is the Self, or Conscious Entity. It cannot be denied, because the denier himself is the Self, or Conscious Entity."[67] In a similar vein, Sureśvarācārya, a ninth century Advaitin, explains:

> Wheresoever there is a doubt, there, the wise should know, the Self [the Real] is not. For no doubts can arise in relation to the Self, since its nature is pure immediate Consciousness.[68]

In the form of Consciousness-presence, our Self is an indubitable, undeniable, self-established, and self-evident fact.

As a primary spiritual practice, Vedānta recommends a process of Self-inquiry (*ātma-vicāra*)—a methodology of inquiring into the essential nature of our self—discerning the real by separating it from the unreal: *nitya-anitya-vastu-viveka*. It requires a certain level of preparation on the part of the seeker to appreciate the subtlety of this methodology. It is recommended that one should learn the truth of Vedānta in close association with a teacher who is well versed in this teaching tradition (*sampardāya*).[69] It is believed that when a seeker is really ready, the Divinity so arranges that a teacher will cross paths with the seeker.

To discern what is "I" and what is "not-I" (*ātmānātma-vicāra*), Vedānta uses several methodologies to intuit our true self, such as *adhyāropa—apavāda* (Superimposition and Negation), *dṛg-dṛśya viveka* (Seer-Seen Discrimination), *panca-kośa viveka* (discrimination of the five sheaths), *avasthā-traya viveka* (discrimination of the three states), and *anvaya-vyatireka*

[66] For example, the Sufi doctrine of *waḥdat al-wujūd* literally means the "Unity of Existence" or "Unity of Being." This, along with its corresponding doctrine of the "Oneness of Perception" (*wahdat al-shuhud*), was formulated by Ibn al-Arabi (1165–1240 AD), which postulates that God and His creation are one, since all that is created preexisted in God's knowledge and will return to it.

[67] Swami Nikhilananda, *Self-Knowledge: Atmabodha* (New York, NY: Ramakrishna-Vivekananda Center, 1987), 45.

[68] Cited in Eliot Deutsch, *Advaita Vedanta*, 19.

[69] *Samapardāya*, a Sanskrit word, denotes more than just a tradition. It means a system that hands over the knowledge properly *as is*, in an unbroken chain of the teacher-student relationship—*samyak pradiyate iti sampardāya*.

nyāya (method of co-presence and co-absence). For the purpose of this chapter, we will now briefly focus on *anvaya-vyatireka* as a choice method to cognize our Self.

Who Am I?[70] Discerning What Is "I" and What Is "Not-I" (*Ātmānātma-vicāra*)

Vedānta says that there is only one question worth asking and answering: "Who Am I?" Through the simple process of self-exploration called Self-inquiry ("who am I?"), Vedānta points out that we are not what we normally take ourselves to be: a limited body-mind-senses complex. Vedāntic wisdom tells us that we are in fact limitless Consciousness that inheres and enlivens the body, mind, and senses. Generally, we take ourselves to be a separate and limited body-mind-senses complex. Vedānta says that this is the basic misconception we have regarding our true identity. Vedānta declares that I am not the limited and changing psychosomatic apparatus I mistake myself to be; I am indeed the limitless and unchanging Consciousness principle. However, I experience myself as a limited entity, limited by time, space, and causality. How does Vedānta establish this fact that I am limitless Consciousness, which is quite contrary to my direct experience?[71]

Vedānta recommends Self-inquiry (*ātma-vicāra*) to reconcile this apparent contradiction between what I take myself to be and who I am in reality. This inquiry is conducted in two stages, using two methodologies (*prakriyas*) as follows:

1. *Anvaya-vyatireka* (co-presence and co-absence)
2. *Adhyaropa-apavāda* (superimposition-negation)

Anvaya-vyatireka (Co-presence and Absence)

The *anvaya-vyatireka* analysis is generally used to establish cause-effect relationships between two events or things. Here, we use a special form of *anvaya-vyatireka prakriyā* called *anuvarta-vyāvratta* (अनुवर्त-व्यावृत्त): to show that one thing has continued existence (*anuvarta*) while the other thing comes and goes (व्यावृत्त). What is invariably present in all our experience and what is not subject to change is *anvaya* or *anuvarta*. What is sometimes present and sometimes absent and what is, therefore, subject to change is *vyatireka* or *vyāvratta*.

For example, gold is present when the necklace is present. This is *anvaya*. When gold is absent, the necklace is also absent. This is *vyatireka*. So, when the necklace exists, gold also exists. When the necklace is broken, the gold still exists. From this analysis, it is concluded that gold is *real* while the necklace is non-real

[70] Based primarily on Swāmī Paramārthānanda jī's discourses titled "Essence of Vedanta." [Discourse number one].

[71] There is no law which says that which is experienced is a valid knowledge. For example, a blue sky is experienced; it is not a valid knowledge; Sunrise and Sunset is experienced; it is not a fact; and flat Earth is experienced, it is not a fact.

(*mithyā*). In other words, gold is *really* real while necklace is *apparently* real. This analysis can also be applied to the three states of waking, dream, and deep sleep to arrive at the understanding of the Self as the invariable Witness of these states. During waking state, I experience myself and the physical body. During dream state, the Self experience is there and mind is experienced also, but the body experience is not there. In deep sleep, I continue to experience myself,[72] but the mind and the body are not experienced. Thus, I, the Self, continue to exist in all three states while body and mind and the world do not exist in the deep sleep. Therefore, body-mind are the incidental features that I have which are subject to arrival and departure. What is incidental (and comes and goes) cannot be my true nature. Therefore, from the analysis of three states (*avasthā-traya-viveka*), I find out that I am different from my body and mind. That I am different from the world, I know. For that, there is no need of any inquiry (*vicāra*). I, the Self, subsist as the invariable Conscious principle in and through all states and stages of life.

Śrī Dakṣiṇāmūrti Stotram, a short devotional text attributable to Śrī Śaṅkarācārya, distills the entire teaching on the subject in a short compass of few lines in verse 7 as follows:

> Self persists in all stages of life like boyhood and so on, in all states like waking and so on, and all other conditions—among all these conditions which constantly manifest, the Self continuously illumines them as "I am."[73]

This technique is very important to arrive at our true nature. The *Catuḥślokī Bhāgavatam* 2.9.32–35 states, "He who wants to know the truth of the Self should investigate as to ascertain what it is *that exists everywhere and always*, for that is the Self."[74] That which is invariably and ubiquitously present in all states and times is the Self, the Ultimate Reality.[75]

[72] It is everyone's direct experience that we *exist* during sleep, otherwise, we will not be able to wake up. Mind completely subsides (otherwise we will still be in the dream state) and there is no awareness of the body at all. Besides, everyone talks about their sleep experience as blissful. That means I, as the Self, is present during deep sleep to experience bliss.

[73] Translated with explanation by Br. Pranipata Chaitanya. Retrieved October 30, 2016: http://advaita-academy.org/shri-dakshinamurti-stotram-part-5/ [Adapted by the author] Br. Pranipata Chaitanya, my revered teacher, who patiently taught me the Bhagavad Gītā with Śaṅkara-Bhāṣya over Skype for a period of three years. His dedication to the tradition of Vedānta was truly inspiring.

बाल्यादिष्वपि जाग्रदादिषु तथा सर्वास्ववस्थास्वपि
व्यावृत्तास्वनुवर्तमानमहमित्यन्तः स्फुरन्तं सदा ॥७॥

bālyādiṣvapi jāgradādiṣu tathā sarvāsvavasthāsvapi
vyāvṛttāsvanuvartamānamahamityantaḥ sphurantaṁ sadā //7//

[74] N. Raghunathan, trans., *Śrīmad Bhāgavatam*, vol. 1 (Madras, India: Vighneswara Publishing House, 1976/1981), 118. [emphasis added].

[75] एतावदेव जिज्ञास्यं तत्त्वजिज्ञासुनात्मनः ।
अन्वयव्यतिरेकाभ्यां यत्स्यात्सर्वत्र सर्वदा ॥ ०२.०९.०३५ ॥ *Catuḥślokī Bhāgavatam*

etāvadeva jijñāsyam tattva-jijñāsunātma-naḥ /
anvaya-vyatirekābhyām yat syāt sarvatra sarvadā //

Thus, through *anvaya-vyatireka* analysis, I come to know that I, the Self, am different from body, mind, and the world.[76] Body, mind, and the world are of the same order and referred to as non-self, *anātmā*, in Vedānta. But there is still duality (*dvaita*) between I, the Self, and body-mind-world, the non-self. There is still no *advaita siddhi*. Therefore, the second stage of inquiry is conducted.

Adhyaropa-apavāda (Superimposition-Negation)

This inquiry is conducted to find out the relationship between the Self (*ātmā*) and the non-self (*anātmā*). This methodology involves understanding cause (*kārṇa*) and effect (*kārya*). First, we provisionally accept (*adhyaropa*) the reality of the effect. Next, we recognize the cause in the effect. Finally, we negate (*apavāda*) the effect as being dependent and non-different from cause. Cause is regarded as really real (*satyasya satyam*) while the effect is only dependently real (*mithyā*). Let's take the example of clay and pot. Clay perspective: Clay exists as a cause of all varieties of pot. Pot perspective: Pot exists, but only as an effect of clay. The existence of pot depends upon clay but clay exists independent of the pot. So, clay is real while pot is *mithyā*. We now extend this logic to Self and non-self.

It is our common experience that any observed object is proved only through the existence of the subject, the observer.[77] If I, the subject, do not exist as the observing consciousness, the world cannot be known to exist as an object. Therefore, through *adhyaropa-apavāda* analysis the Self is shown to be the substratum (*adhiṣthānam*) of the appearing and disappearing of the three states.[78]

The Self, the subject, can exist without the world. So, I, the Conscious Principle, lend existence to the waking world, just as I, the Self, lend existence to the dream world. I am the cause; the world is the effect. Here, Vedānta makes another beautiful observation: the effect cannot limit the cause. The non-self (body-mind, and the world) cannot limit me, the Self. Therefore, I am free from limitations. This freedom from limitations is called Brahman. Vedānta points out that we experience this limitlessness every day, during our deep sleep (*śuṣupti*). During my waking state (*jāgrat avasthā*), due to my identification with the non-self (the body-mind-complex), I feel limitations.

Vedānta says we should own up to our true status of Limitless, unchanging Consciousness (*nirdoṣam Brahma*) and be free.

What the seeker after Truth has to grasp is that Substance which persists always through all its Transformations into its various effects or forms, but suffers no diminution in the process. The Supreme Self is the ultimate Substance. [Translation adapted from Swami Tapasyananda, *Srimad Bhagavata*, vol. 1 (Chennai, India: Sri Ramakrishna Math, 1980)]

[76] *Anvaya-vyatireka bhyām ātmana-anātma vilakṣanattva nirṇayaḥ.*

[77] *dṛik adhīna driṣya siddihi.*

[78] *adhyaropa-apavāda bhayām ātma-anātmana adhiṣthānam nirṇayaḥ.*

Waking, Dream, and Deep Sleep States[79]: *Intuiting the True Nature of the Self*

Although we experience three states everyday—waking, dream, and deep sleep—we tend to confine our observations and conclusions about reality to waking state only. This is called a mono-basic view of life. We consider the dream state as some sort of illusory experience and relegate deep sleep to a state of unconsciousness. Vedānta, the science of Reality, takes a tri-basic view of life and regards our experiences during all three states to be equally important to understanding life in a comprehensive manner.

One of the clearest statements about the Self *vis-à-vis* three states comes from John Wheeler, a neo-Vedānta teacher in the tradition of Śrī Nisargadatta Maharaj and Sailor Bob Adamson:

> When you awake in the morning, consciousness dawns. In this state of being conscious, you perceive a body, mind and world. These are appearances only, not what you are in essence. To identify oneself with any of these appearances gives rise to the notion of being a separate person, self or individual entity. This is the cause of all seeking, suffering and doubts. Consciousness is a state that comes and goes. In sleep, unconsciousness or under anesthesia, the experience of being conscious subsides….However, before you awoke and became conscious of anything else, including the fact of being conscious, you existed.[80]

John Wheeler points out the basic human error in interpreting all our experience: identification with appearances. This fundamental error is responsible for all our doubts, seeking, and suffering. Our psychological suffering is a sort of optical illusion. Please note that John Wheeler uses the term consciousness in a relative sense. In its absolute sense, consciousness does not come and go. One cannot ever say that I am unconscious. He continues to explain that essential nature (Pure Consciousness) is *prior* to the arising and subsiding of all states. It is non-perceptual, non-conceptual cognizing awareness:

[79] This section is partially based on KAK Iyer's masterpiece, *Vedanta or the Science of Reality* (Holenarasipur, India: Adhyatma Prakash Karyalaya, 1930/1991). It is perhaps the most important book in English language on the topic of *avastha-traya prakriya*, the methodology of three states. Also see: Sri Devarao Kulkarni, *Avasthātraya Viveka* (Calcutta, India: Manas Kumar Sanyal, 1990); Swamiji Sri Satchidānandendra Saraswati, *Avasthatraya or The Unique Method of Vedanta* (Holenarasipur, India: Adhyatma Prakash Karyalaya, 1938/2006). This writer feels blessed to have come in contact with Sri Sreenivasa Murthy of Bangalore, who studied Vedānta for several years with Sri Devarao Kulkarni (who in turn was a gifted disciple of Swamiji Sri Satchidānandendra Saraswati). During his daily *Satsangs*, Mr. Murthy explained and clarified some complex Vedantic concepts—nay, "showed" them, in the author's own direct experience—in a manner that one seldom comes across these days. Mr. Murthy joyfully taught me how to take a correct standpoint in the unchanging Witness Principle while studying Vedānta. My gratitude is too deep for words.

[80] John Wheeler, *The Light Behind Consciousness: Radical Self-Knowledge and the End of Seeking* (Salisbury, UK: Non-Duality Press, 2008), 3–4.

> Your fundamental position is prior to consciousness. From this non-conceptual source, which is what you are, arises initially the sense of conscious presence. This is also the sense of being, the experience that "I am", or the bare fact of knowing that you are. This is the first appearance upon your original state. Little can be said about your essential nature because it is clearly beyond all concepts and even prior to consciousness. Some pointers that have been used are: non-conceptual awareness, awareness unaware of itself, pure being (beyond being and non-being), the absolute, the unmanifest, noumenon, cognizing emptiness, no-thing-ness—to name a few.[81]

Finally, John Wheeler seals the deal by stating that we cannot know our real self *as an object*, because it is the knowing subject. The language comes to its very limit at this point, the subject and object coalesce. Like the eye cannot see itself, like the finger cannot scratch itself, we cannot know ourselves as an object. However, can we ever doubt that we are? This subjective experience that *we are* and that *we know we are*, are the only two certainties:

> This non-conceptual essence is pure non-duality or unicity in which the notions of both subject and object are merged. Just as the sun does not know light because it is light, so you do not know your original nature (as an object) because you are that. It is forever beyond the grasp of concepts and subject-object knowledge. Yet it is entirely evident and inescapable as that which allows you to say with utter certitude "I am" and "I know that I am". Even when those words subside, you *are*. Even when the Consciousness that knows those words subsides, you *are*. Consciousness is the light of creation. But you are the primordial non-conceptual awareness, being or "no-thing-ness" in which Consciousness and all subsequent appearances come and go.[82]

We have provided this rather long extract from John Wheeler because it captures the entire gamut of teachings about the Self as our true nature that is prior to the arising of all thoughts, emotions, experiences, and the three states. During the dream state, the mind conjures up a "dream ego" and "dream world" with its own coordinates of time and space. In deep sleep, the mind subsides fully but still "I," the Self, continues to exist. Otherwise, how else would I be able to recall upon waking that "I slept well, I knew nothing," and so forth? It is everyone's own, undeniable intuitive experience that there is no "I am" in deep sleep. But upon waking, the experience of deep sleep is appropriated in the memory of having slept well.

What is the common factor in all the three states? It is the presence of the invariable Self, because of which one says, I am awake, I dreamt, I slept well. Obviously, I was present in the state of deep sleep as Pure Awareness, illumining the objectless, pure, subjective experience. The entity or the "ego" which appear in waking and dream is therefore not my real nature at all. My Real

[81] Ibid.
[82] Ibid.

Nature illumines the states, Itself unchanging, uninvolved, and untouched by their coming and going.

When sleep gives way to the waking state, the "me-notion" and the whole manifestation (with time, space, and causality) appear simultaneously. The waking state cancels out both the dream state and deep sleep state, with all their respective contents. But at no time can "I" be canceled out. I, the Self, continue to subsist in and through all states. Since, I am prior (*agrayam*) to the arising of the states, "I," the Self is not conditioned by the states. This realization is truly unique, liberating, and transformative, and represents the highest understanding regarding Self-knowledge.

An important Upaniṣadic verse captures the entire methodology of three states succinctly as follows:

> जाग्रत स्वपन शुषुप्ति आदि प्रपंच यत प्रकाशते ।
> तत ब्रह्म अहम् ज्ञात्वा, सर्व बन्धनाय विमुचते ॥
>
> *jāgrata svapana śuṣupti ādi prapaṁca yata prakāśate /*
> *tata brahma aham jñātvā, sarva bandhanāya vimucate //*
>
> That by virtue of which the waking, dream, and deep sleep states are illumined; "I am That Brahma"—knowing thus one becomes free from all bondage.

To conclude this section, we cite an important verse from the Kaṭha Upaniṣad that encapsulates the methodology and glory of cognizing the Self as follows:

> *svapnāntaṁ jāgaritāntaṁ cobhau yenānupaśyati /*
> *mahāntaṁ vibhumātmānaṁ matvā dhīro na śocati* //2.1.4//
>
> Knowing that great and all-pervading Self by which one sees the objects both in the sleep and the waking states, the wise do not grieve.[83]

The Bhagavad Gītā 2.11 begins with the message, "The wise do not grieve." The Gītā defines a wise person as the one who knows the Self and who has developed equanimity of mind (*samatvam*) and steadily abides in the wisdom of the Self (*sthitaprajña*).

The Uniqueness of Vedānta

Vedānta tells us that we are not what we take ourselves to be. We take ourselves to be limited, wanting, and mortal beings. Our experience also tells us that we are small, fragmented, limited beings. Essentially, all our pursuits are geared toward overcoming this sense of limitation and inadequacy. And we continue

[83] V. Panoli, trans., *Prasthanathraya Volume-II*, 242. [slightly modified].

chasing one object after another, never really getting fully satisfied, no matter what we get. This also proves our fundamental search for everlasting fullness, which is at the core of our being.

Vedānta distinctively tells us quite the opposite: that we are whole and limitless. If in fact we were limited beings, then no matter what we do, we will always remain limited, for limited actions cannot accomplish unlimited results. Vedānta tells us that we already *are* what we want to be—limitless, whole, and complete. Perhaps our conclusions about ourselves have been wrong all along. The ultimate aim of Vedānta is spiritual freedom through Self-knowledge. It is accomplished through experiential realization of the truth of the Self as Pure Consciousness, by oneself, in one's own experience. But Self-knowledge is no mere intellectual creed gleaned from reading books, for how can the Self be found in books? Sri Ramana Maharshi explains succinctly:

> As for reading books on Vedanta, you may go on reading any number of them. They can only tell you, "Realize the Self within you." The Self cannot be found in books. You have to find it out *for yourself, in yourself*.[84]

Elsewhere, Sri Ramana memorably explains that the Self *itself* is the best book to read to know the Self: "The Self is the real book. You can glance anywhere in that book; nobody can take it away from you. Whenever you are free, turn towards the Self. Thereafter you may read whatever you like."[85] Books at best are pointers to the Self. One is reminded of a Zen story in which a young monk approached a wise old teacher and asked him to explain the Diamond Sutra. The teacher asked the young monk to read out the sutras as he himself didn't know how to read. The young monk was surprised and asked how the old man could explain the meaning if he couldn't even read the text. The old teacher pointed to the full moon shining brightly in the sky and asked what it was. On being given the correct reply he said, "My finger pointed to the moon. But the finger itself is not the moon. In the same way the words in the text point to the truth. But they themselves are not the truth."[86] When we understand this, we do not get attached to the teachings.

Vedānta: The Art and Science of Harmonious Living

The key message of Vedānta is that Reality is One without a second (*ekamevādvitīyam*[87]). Postulating one single reality, Brahman, as the Absolute or Ultimate Truth of the world, Vedānta then equates this reality with the sole

[84] A. Devaraja Mudaliar, *Day by Day with Bhagavan* (Tiruvannamalai, India: Sri Ramanasramam, 2002), 1. [emphasis added].

[85] Sri Ramana Maharshi, *Abide in the Self*. Retrieved September 1, 2015: http://www.innerquest.org/Ramana_Abide.htm

[86] Author unknown.

[87] Chāndogya Upaniṣad 6.2.1.

reality of our own Self, called *Ātman*. This fundamental Reality, the inmost Self of all and everything, is of the nature of Pure Consciousness. The goal of Vedānta is to establish the absolute identity, oneness, of the truth of the individual (*ātman*) and the truth of the universe (*Brahman*). Humanity has not yet conceived a loftier conception of its position in the universe.

Vedānta promotes harmonious living by garnering a vision of oneness of all existence. Outwardly, various forms of life such as plants, animals, birds, and human beings seem to be different from one another, but their underlying life principle of Pure Awareness, *the Consciousness Principle*, is one and the same. From the spiritual standpoint, while interacting with the world and myriad beings, we must remember that they are all none but our own Self. If we perceive someone as different from us, we may have aversion or fear, but if we have the vision of oneness, we will see the other as our own Self, and fear or hatred will not arise.[88] This knowledge and awareness of Oneness should be retained in and through all our activities. This is the glory of the vision of Vedānta.

This understanding of the fundamental truth of oneness, that we are essentially One Limitless Consciousness, "strikes at the very root of narrow views based on selfishness and is the foundation of higher ethics. This higher Self is of the nature of Bliss, as displayed in our instinctive love of Self; and to recognize it in others is to bring social harmony, for no one will be inclined to harm himself. It paves the way for spiritual and moral perfection."[89] By helping us perceive unity in diversity, Vedānta thus fosters a universal outlook of understanding, harmony, and inclusiveness so essential for present times. Sri Ramana put is so well: "Your own Self-Realization is the greatest service you can render the world."[90]

Vedānta deals with one, and only one, subject: the absolute identity of the individual self with the universal Self (*ātma-brahma-aikyam*). According to Vedāntic philosophy, spiritual liberation is not possible without realizing this identity, *aikya,* between the *Ātman* and the Brahman: *brahmātmaikya bodhena mokśaḥ sidhyati nānyathā*, says Śrī Śaṅkarācārya in *Vivekacūḍāmaṇi* (56).[91]

[88] When to a man who understands that the Self has become all things, what sorrow, what delusion can there be to him who once beheld that unity? ~Īśā Upaniṣad verse 7.

[89] K. A. Krishanswamy Iyer, *Collected Works of K. A. Krishnaswamy Iyer* (Holenarasipur, India: Adhyatma Prakash Karyalaya, 1969/2006), 239.

[90] Munagala S. Venkataramaiah, compil., *Talks with Sri Ramana Maharshi* (Tiruvannamalai, India: Sri Ramanasaramam, 2000), 16.

[91] See: Pranipata Chaitanya, trans., and Satinder Dhiman, revised and edited with notes and an Introduction (2012). *Sri Sankara's Vivekachudamani: Devanāgari Text, Transliteration, Word-for-Word Meaning, and a Lucid English Translation* (Burbank, CA: House of Metta, 2012), 102. http://www.lulu.com/shop/pranipata-chaitanya-and-satinder-dhiman/sri-sankaras-vivekachudamani/paperback/product-20465360.html

The book is under revision currently. An e-book version of an earlier iteration can be accessed at: http://www.realization.org/down/sankara.vivekachudamani.chaitanya.pdf

In Vedānta, liberation means realizing Brahman as our own true self (*ātmā*): *Aham Brahma asmi*. Only those who know their self (as the Limitless Reality) transcend worldly sorrow, *tarati śokam ātamvit*: Chāndogya Upaniṣad, 7.1.3. Since the bondage, *bandhana*, is only due to Self-ignorance, *avidyā*; the spiritual freedom, *mokṣa*, does not entail the creation or attainment of something new through some special spiritual practice; it is recognition of an ever-existing/proven thing/fact, *nitya siddha vastu*. That is why it is spoken of as the attainment of the ever-attained (*prāptasya-prāpati*). It is a quest from *ignorance* to *recognition*, a journey from *here* to *here!*

Concluding Thoughts

Through powerful stories, anecdotes, vignettes, poems, and quotes, the chapter demonstrated that the key to abiding fulfillment lies in dis-covering our true Self. It pointed out the obvious but often overlooked fact that there is nothing more intimate and immediate than the Self. The knowledge of the Self is therefore most direct and intuitive, devoid of the subject-object dichotomy. Attaining the ever-attained Self-knowledge is not a new acquisition. As the Witness-Self of the proceedings of senses, mind, and the ego, it is always, already there as awareness-presence. To *know* the Self is to *be* the Self. And to *be the Self* is to *be fulfilled* forever. This, then, is the true fulfillment of the Delphic Oracle (*gnothi seauton*): get to know yourself!

Just as in the presence of sunlight and space, all actions take place, but both the sunlight and the space remain unaffected by them, even so, in the light of the Self, all actions take place while the Self (साक्षी चैतन्य, Witnessing-Consciousness Principle) remains unaffected (असंग). When this knowledge becomes a living experience, one is freed from the noose of actions (and their binding effects) and attains liberation. This knowledge is called Self-knowledge, the only direct path to spiritual freedom. Sages tell us that this knowledge is not possible until our heart is pure and our mind is free from wayward likes and dislikes (राग-द्वेष). All other spiritual practices purify the mind and prepare it to receive this knowledge.

There is no wealth equal to Self-knowledge in the whole of creation. Its glory is such that it makes people walk away from the kingdoms. The Buddha is a case in point. He was a prince. He gave it up all to discover the truth of his existence. Today, he is revered not because he was a king-to-be, but because he renounced the transient kinghood *without* and discovered the eternal kingdom *within*. What he found has inspired billions ever since. To know the Self is to realize that there is nothing "personal" about it—in the sense of "myself" or "yourself." Since the true Self is at-one-with the Absolute Reality, to know the Self is to realize our oneness with all that is. Self-knowledge confers upon us the wisdom to see all existence as the expression of our very own Self and spontaneously act for the wellbeing of all beings.

Selfless love and compassion naturally flow out of this understanding of the unity and oneness of all life. This is the flowering of Self-knowledge in the form of Self-transformation.

Swami Paramārthānanda shares the following Mullah Nasruddin story that beautifully sums up the entire gamut of Vedāntic path, the seeker, and the goal:

Drawing the Moon out of the Well!
The Mullah, on his travels, reached a village late at night and, passing a well, looked down into it. And he saw the moon. Jumping to the conclusion that the moon must have fallen down the well, he rushed to find a rope and hook so that he could pull it out. After many unsuccessful attempts, the hook finally caught, and he began to pull with all his strength. What had happened, of course, was that the hook had lodged under a heavy rock, but he firmly believed that he was now rescuing the moon. Unfortunately, the rock was too heavy for the rope and, after a final tremendous pull, the rope snapped, and the Mullah fell back onto the ground from where, looking up, he saw the moon now resting back in its usual place!

According to Swamiji, this story is a metaphor for the process of Self-knowledge leading to Self-transformation. We believe that we are limited and struggle through years of spiritual practice until, when the rope finally snaps, we discover it right where we are.[92] The root of all seeking and suffering is lack of knowledge of our true Self. Due to this, we take ourselves to be a limited, separate entity. However, when we look directly at our experience, we find that we are this abundant space of radiant awareness-presence which is ever-full and eternally fulfilled. Self-knowledge is only a matter of becoming aware of what you already are! Perhaps the greatest affirmation on the subject is found in the Chāndogya Upaniṣad 6.8.7: You are That! (*Tat Tvam Asi*: तत्त्वमसि). Self-transformation is the fruit of Self-knowledge.

There is one Ultimate Reality. The world is the manifestation of IT. That *art* Thou! This is the declaration, *udaghośha*, of Vedānta.

We conclude this chapter with the following poem on the self-revealing, self-shinning, self-evident glory of Self:

Already, Always the Self!

All states of mind come and go.
No such thing as "permanent" state of mind.
Mind *disappears* daily during deep sleep.

[92] Cited in Dennis Waite, *The Book of One: The Ancient Wisdom of Advaita* (Winchester, UK: O Chapters, 2011), 289.

Thankfully, you don't.
Therefore, YOU are *not* the mind!

When sleep gives way to the waking state,
"Me" and the "world" appear simultaneously.
The "me-notion" and the manifold-manifestation:
Appearances only within waking and dream states.

YOU are *prior* to these states.
In fact, you are *prior* to *all* the states!
The states are mere "appearances"
on YOU, of YOU, in YOU—
likes waves of the ocean.

YOU abide in and through the three states
of waking, dream, and deep sleep;
And yet *prior* to them and *beyond* them.
YOU are the very source of All and Everything!

Notions of time, space, and causality arise within the states.
Being *prior* to the states,
YOU are not bound by time and space.
Time and space are mere appearances within You!
How can YOU be bound by time and space?

Likewise, the ego appears and disappears,
with the appearing and disappearing of the states.
It is just a self-cherished thought which comes and goes.
YOU are not the ego you fondly take yourself to be.

How can that which comes and goes
be your real nature, your true Self?!!!

Not bound by time and space,
Your true nature is
Eternal and All-Pervading.

Cognize this fact within yourself by yourself!

Abide in the Glory of the Self—
The Infinite, the Eternal, and the Immutable.
Be Free, which YOU are
Already, always![93]

[93] Satinder Dhiman, *Songs of the Self* (September 27, 2016). From the author's collection of unpublished poems. Dedicated to all my teachers in Vedānta who taught me how to get out of my own way. They showed me how the metaphor of the path is misleading. *One is so close to oneself that there is no room for a path.* Rumi put it so well: "Why struggle to open a door between us when the whole wall is an illusion?"

Song of the Self!

Your Self is already here, always.
It does not come and go.
You cannot take it, you cannot leave it.
That which is true is always with you![94]

The Sages remind us that life is short and can end anytime.
Therefore, one should first resolve the fundamental question—
"Who Am I?"—within oneself, by oneself.[95]
Bon voyage and Godspeed.

[94] "That which is true is always with you." A Song composed and sung by John Wheeler.

[95] Satinder Dhiman, *Songs of the Self.* From the author's collection of unpublished poems. The single line "That which is true is always with you" is from John Wheeler, as stated in the preceding note.

CHAPTER 5

Karma Yoga: The Path of Enlightened Action

Introduction

This is my secret; I don't mind what happens. That is the essence of inner freedom. It is a timeless spiritual truth: release attachment to outcomes, and—deep inside yourself—you'll feel good, no matter what.[1]

In this opening quote, J. Krishnamurti captures the essence of the discipline of *karma yoga*: Performing actions without attachment to outcomes leads to inner freedom. This is the alchemy of attaining freedom from the binding effect inherent in all actions. This chapter presents the teachings of the Bhagavad Gītā regarding the path of *karma yoga*, the path of enlightened action, and their application to leadership. Many scholars and practitioners believe that the philosophy of disinterested selfless action, *niṣkāma karma*,[2] is the most distinctive contribution of the Gītā to the domain of practical spirituality. It is perhaps true that nowhere else is the doctrine of disciplined action enunciated with such clarity and granularity as it is in the Bhagavad Gītā.

The universality and pervasiveness of action in human life is a veritable fact—nobody can remain action-less even for a moment. Indian philosophy postulates that all actions performed with the desire for self-referent results cause bondage. If we cannot remain without performing actions and self-

[1] In a 1977 lecture in California, writes Jim Dreaver, who was present at the talk, "Part-way through this particular talk Krishnamurti suddenly paused, leaned forward and said, surprisingly, 'Do you want to know what my secret is?' There was a silence. Then he said in a soft, almost shy voice: 'You see, I don't mind what happens.'" See Jim Dreaver, A Krishnamurti Story, "Do you want to know what my secret is?"—Release Attachment to Outcomes. Emphasis added. Retrieved September 3, 2017: https://scottfree2b.wordpress.com/category/j-krishnamurti/

Krishnamurti is pointing out a deep psychological truth: Problems are problems because thinking—*minding*—makes it so. Freedom lies in *choosing* not to mind the mind.

[2] Surprisingly, the most popular expression regarding karma yoga—"*niṣkāma karma*"—does not occur in the Gītā.

S. Dhiman, *Bhagavad Gītā and Leadership*,
Palgrave Studies in Workplace Spirituality and Fulfillment,
https://doi.org/10.1007/978-3-319-67573-2_5

centered actions lead to bondage, is there a way out of this relentless cycle of action and reaction? This chapter presents the Gītā's well-ascertained answer to this enigmatic question. It also discusses some key elements of the law of karma as necessary concomitants to understanding the philosophy of *karma yoga*.

Given its subject matter, this chapter has the most natural and direct application to leadership, especially servant leadership.[3] In this chapter, we will focus on the path of detached action (*karma yoga*) as a framework for performing selfless service. As a practical teaching, *karma yoga* furnishes the best set of guidelines to put *service before self* and to perform actions for the wellbeing of all beings. Regarding the Gītā's efficacy in this regard, we have the highest testimony of Mahatma Gandhi, who confirmed its teachings in every sphere of his life with great success. He called the Bhagavad Gītā the "Gospel of Selfless Action"[4] and referred to it as his "spiritual dictionary."[5] As Gandhi himself tells us in his autobiography and other writings, the Gītā's emphasis on Self-realization and selfless service were the primary sources of inspiration for his life and leadership.[6]

Understanding Karma Yoga, Properly!

In its most popular version, *karma yoga* is presented as follows: Perform your actions without expecting any results. That is, perform actions selflessly, *niṣkāma karma*,[7] unattached to the results. This has caused much confusion: How can one perform any action without expecting any results? Why perform any action at all if one were not to expect any results? This is not the intention of the Gītā, however, as we shall see.

Similar confusion exists regarding the meaning of the word yoga, as used in the Bhagavad Gītā. According to J. A. B. van Buitenen, "The word *yoga* and cognates of it occur close to 150 times in the Gītā, and it needs attention." It is also helpful to bear in mind that in the Gītā, *karman* (action) do not always equate with "karma yoga" and *jñāna* (knowledge) does not always signify "jñāna yoga." Secondly, the word "yoga" is used in several shades of meanings in the Gītā. The root meaning of the word is "union." However, at two places, Śrī Kṛṣṇa presents the word "yoga" in its truest meaning: BG 2:48 and BG 6:23. In BG 2:48, Śrī Kṛṣṇa states "*samatvaṃ yoga ucyate*"—"equipoise" or "equanimity" is called yoga. The second important sense in which the word

[3] See chapter entitled "Be the Change: The Making of a Servant Leader."

[4] M. K. Gandhi in John Strohmeier (Ed.), *The Bhagavad Gītā According to Gandhi* (Berkeley, CA: Berkeley Hills Books, 2000), 14.

[5] J. T. F. Jordens, "Gandhi and the Bhagavadgita," in Robert Neil Minor (Ed.), *Modern Indian Interpreters of the Bhagavad Gītā* (New York, NY: State University of New York Press), 88.

[6] See: M. K. Gandhi, *An Autobiography: The Story of My Experiments with Truth* (New York, NY: Dover Publications, 1983), 59, 60, 232, 233, 296–297; Y. P. Anand, *Mahatma Gandhi's Works and Interpretation of the Bhagavad Gītā* (New Delhi, India: Radha Publications, 2009). Also see: Ramesh S. Betai, *Gītā and Gandhi* (New Delhi, India: Gyan Publishing House/National Gandhi Museum, 2002).

[7] Any action performed without selfish motive is called *niṣkāma karma*.

"*yoga*" is used in the Gītā is in verse BG 6:23: *taṃ vidyādduḥkhasaṃyogaviyogaṃ yogasaṃjñitam*—freedom from contact with sorrow (of this body and material world) should be known as *yoga*. According to the Gītā, *the complete freedom from sorrow is possible only when one finds repose in the Supreme Self (Paramātman)*.

Some quote the phrase *yogaḥ karmasu kauśalam* (2.50) to explain that dexterity in action is yoga. Does that mean that proficiency in pickpocketing will make the pickpocket a *yogi*? This is not at all the intention of the Gītā, for that will be against the universal moral code (*dharma viruddha*). Recall that the first word of the Gītā is *dharmakṣetre* (1.1), the sphere of moral conduct, and the last word is *mama* (18.78), meaning "mine." Conjoined, literally, the first and last words of the Gītā signify: "my moral duty," my *svadharma*, as it is the *dharma* of fire to burn and of water to extinguish the fire.

Sri Krishna Prem, in his book *The Yoga of the Bhagavad Gītā*, explains the meaning of the word yoga as follows:

> By yoga is here meant not any special system called by that name, not jnana-yoga nor karma yoga, nor eightfold yoga of Patanjali, but just the Path by which man unites his finite self with the infinite being. It is the inner path of which these separate yogas are so many one-sided aspects.[8]

Karma yoga has two aspects, proper action and proper attitude:

1. Proper *Action*: Since we cannot remain without activity even for a moment, the first step on the spiritual journey is to perform *proper* or righteous actions. What makes an action a *proper* action? A proper action is that action which is *unopposed* to *dharma* (*dharma aviruddha*), the universal moral order—it is the *right* thing to do, in a *given* situation. The rightness of an action lies in its moral valence. When an action is good for one and good for all, it is called right action. Harmlessness of an action is one easy way to determine its righteousness. On the path of righteousness, tells the Gītā, one does not lose ever (BG 6.40).[9]

   The Gītā divides karma into several types. *Nitya naimita karma*: The obligatory duties—one should perform the obligatory duties such as sacrifice (*yajña*), charity (*dāna*), and austerities (*tapas*). These three types of actions, the Gītā says, are the purifiers of the wise: *yajñadānatapaḥkarma… pāvanāni manīṣiṇām* (18.5). These actions are performed with the attitude of duty that has to be done, for duty's sake. This leads to purification of the mind or the internal organ of perception (*antāhkaraṇa śuddhi*). Our daily duties done properly makes us fit to understand the subtle Self-knowledge. As S. K. Maitra has rightly observed, "it is only those who have gone through the drill of Karma properly that

[8] Sri Krihna Prem, *The Yoga of the Bhagavad Gītā*, xiv.

[9] न हि कल्याणकृत् कश्चित् दुर्गतिं तात गच्छति: One, who follows the path of goodness, there is no misery or misadventure, *durgati*, for him.

are entitled to receive Brahma-Vidyā [knowledge of the Absolute Reality or the Self-knowledge]."[10]

2. *Proper Attitude*: Proper attitude has two aspects:
   (a) *Īśvara arpaṇa buddhi*: Attitude of offering all actions to *Īśvara*, the Lord.
   (b) *Īśvara prasāda buddhi*: Considering the fruits of action as *Īśvara*'s grace.

A *karmayogi* should have an attitude of being a mere instrument in the hands of *Īśvara*, *nimita-mātra* (11.33). This then is the skill in action, the art of *karma yoga*: do *right* actions as an *offering* to the Lord—as an instrument of the Divine, *Īśvara*, accepting all *results* as Lord's *grace.*

Then the actions will lose their binding effect. Hence, the skillfulness of this discipline, *yoga karmasu kauśalam* (2.50)!

The Path of Enlightened Action

All Actions Lead to Results That May Be Binding

Indian philosophy postulates that all actions are inherently binding in their effect. Selfish or desire-prompted actions bind people to their results and subject them to the recurring cycle of birth and death (*saṃsāra*). Depending upon the purity of our intentions and means employed, all actions motivated by selfish desire have three possible results that accrue to its doer in the future—good, bad, or mixed. This is their binding effect—*good or bad, actions necessitate future states of existence to bear out their consequences.* In other words, they perpetuate the unending round of future of births and deaths, called *saṃsāra* in Hindu philosophy. As the Gītā (18.12) explains: "Agreeable, disagreeable, and mixed—three-fold is the fruit of action that follows those who perform actions prompted by desire for the results. But those who relinquish the desire for the fruit of actions do not reap the fruit of their actions, here or hereafter." Karma yoga is the simplest solution provided by the Gītā to escape from the noose of *saṃsāra.*

These words, "karma" and "yoga," have become a regular part of the daily discourse in the West. In order to understand the true import of karma yoga, the path of selfless action, we need to take a short excursion into the realm of Indian philosophy—especially the system of *Advaita Vedānta.* This system takes the Ultimate Reality to be one only, without a second, and represents the end or culmination of Vedas, the sacred books of knowledge. A proper understanding of

[10] S. K. Maitra, *The Spirit of Indian Philosophy* (Benares, India: Published by the Author; printed at The Indian Press Limited, Allahabad, 1947), 25.

karma yoga also assumes a clear grasp of the operation of the law of *karma* as conceived within the framework of the Indian spiritual paradigm. This section is presented as a self-contained, complete module and assumes no prior knowledge of Indian philosophy on the part of the reader.

All systems of Indian philosophy take it as axiomatic that the primary cause of our bondage (in the form of suffering or misery) is due to a special type of ignorance (*avidyā*). This ignorance does not denote lack of information or knowledge in any general sense. The ignorance that is referred to here is actually the ignorance of our essential nature, that is, self-ignorance. A person may be highly literate or educated but may still be operating under the spell of self-ignorance. Therefore, the *summum bonum* of all Indian philosophy is to eradicate this ignorance, root and branch, through Self-knowledge—the knowledge of our true nature.

Advaita Vedānta[11] is the most widely known system of Indian philosophy, both in the East and the West. It presents perhaps the clearest formulation of the human predicament and the means to address it. The be-all and end-all of *Advaita* (non-duality) is the absolute non-difference of the individual self (*Ātman*) and the Ultimate Reality (*Brahman*). It starts with the rather lofty assertion that the absolute (*Brahman*) alone is real, and the individual self is none other than the absolute. The Ultimate Reality is called *Brahman* because it is all-pervasive. *Brahman* is undifferentiated pure consciousness, devoid of parts, attributes, forms, changes, or limitations. It is self-luminous and non-dual—one only, without a second. It is the source and substratum of all and everything.

Vedānta postulates that at no time ever is our individual self not one with the Absolute Reality (Brahman). Due to metaphysical ignorance (*avidyā*), however, we do not realize our true oneness with the Brahman. When this ignorance is removed through the realization of our true Self—which is ever identical with the absolute—we attain liberation from the bonds of our conditioned existence. To achieve freedom from this bondage—the illusion of separation—through various disciplines is the goal of all systems of Indian philosophy. Since the bondage is due to self-ignorance, Vedānta presents the most natural solution to remove it through Self-knowledge. Karma yoga serves as a preamble to Self-knowledge through self-renunciation.

Vedānta philosophy makes it clear that karma yoga purifies the mind and prepares it to receive the wisdom of Self-knowledge, which alone directly leads to spiritual freedom. In the following section, the law of karma is presented in detail to facilitate the understanding of karma yoga.

[11] Please refer to Chapter 4, entitled "Advaita Vedānta: The Science of Reality." I am deeply indebted to Sri Ramana Maharshi, Swami Dayananda Saraswati, Swami Tejomayananda, Swami Paramarthananda, Swami Akhandanand Mahrajshri, Swami Brahmatmanand Saraswati, and Pujya Sri Sreenivasa Murthyji for their profound teachings of Advaita Vedānta.

Law of Karma: Our Moral Balance Sheet?

What Is Karma?

Etymologically speaking, the word *karma* is derived from a Sanskrit word, *karman*, which means *action* or *deed*. As a moral principle, *karma* means at once the *deed* and the *result* of deed. The doctrine of *karma* states that "whatever action is done by an individual leaves behind it some sort of potency which has the power to ordain for him joy or sorrow in the future according as it is good or bad."[12] The moment an action is performed, the universal law of karma takes over and processes it according to its moral quality. Underscoring the value of the law of karma, S. Radhakrishnan, a preeminent Hindu scholar, writes:

> There is no doctrine so valuable in life and conduct as Karma theory. Whatever happens to us in this life, we have to submit in meek resignation, for it is a result of our past doings. Yet the future is in our power, and we can work with hope and confidence. Karma inspires hope for the future and resignation to the past. It makes men feel that the things of the world, its fortune and failures, do not touch the dignity of the Soul. Virtue alone is good, not rank or riches, not race or nationality. Nothing but goodness is good.[13]

Humphreys, an eminent Buddhist writer, explains the nature of the law of karma in the following manner:

> It may be viewed exoterically, from the material point of view, in which case it is merely the law of causation, the balance of cause and effect, the fact known in every science laboratory that actions and reactions are equal and opposite. Esoterically, from the spiritual point of view, Karma is the law of moral retribution, whereby not only does every cause have an effect, but he who puts the cause in action suffers the effect.[14]

Karma: Is It Destiny?

A question is often asked, "Does the law of karma imply fatalism?" Is our fate a sealed book, once and for all, inevitable and unalterable? According to the Gītā, the answer is indeed no. Karma is not an arbitrary external agency dictating our affairs from above, but a self-created destiny that is constantly being created and recreated. In other words, karma is not a fixed fate waiting to unfold inexorably, but "a perpetual becoming in which the future is not only

[12] Surendranath Dasgupta, *History of Indian Philosophy*, vol. 1 (Cambridge, MA: Cambridge University Press, 1963), 71.

[13] S. Radhakrishanan, *Indian Philosophy*, vol. 1 (London, UK: Allen & Unwin Ltd., 1949), 249.

[14] Christmas Humphreys, *Karma and Rebirth* (London, UK: John Murray, 1976), 15.

shaped by the past, but is being modified by the present." Thus, according to this law, nothing is chaotic or capricious in the moral realm.

As we sow, so we reap: Sow a thought to reap an act. Sow an act and reap a habit. Sow a habit and reap a character. Sow a character and reap a destiny. Put simply, what goes around comes around. "A man becomes good by good deeds," says the *Bṛhadāraṅyaka Upaniṣad* (4.4.5), "and bad by bad deeds." Thus, karma becomes at once the law of cause and effect and also nature's way to restore lost harmony.

Types of Karma

Indian philosophy divides all *karmas* into three types: *sanchita*, *āgāmī*, and *prārabdha*.[15] This is a most useful classification to understand the workings of the law of karma. *Sanchita* is karma accumulated in the past—the vast store of accumulated works done in the past, the fruits of which have not yet been reaped; *āgāmī* is karma to be worked out in the future; and *prārabdha* is karma that has begun to fructify in the present lifetime. The *prārabdha* is a part of the *sanchita* karma, since this also is action done in the past. But the difference between the two is that, whereas the *sanchita* karma is not yet operative, the *prārabdha* has already begun to yield fruit. The fruit of all karmas must be reaped by oneself, the character and circumstances of one's life is determined by one's *prārabdha* karma.

The *prārabdha* karma cannot be avoided in any way. The attainment of Self-knowledge may enable one to abstain from future fruit-bearing action (*āgāmī karma*) or to avoid the consequences of the accumulated action that has not yet begun to operate (*sanchita karma*); but the *prārabdha*, which has begun to bear fruit, must be reaped. The person endowed with Self-knowledge may not actually suffer from the result, however, because such a person is detached from [identification with] the body and the sense-organs.[16]

Thus, all actions as normally undertaken entail results or outcomes that have a binding effect; that is, they bind the doer with their results, good or bad. Karma yoga—the *yoga* of selfless action—is the enlightened art of performing actions in such a way that actions *lose* their binding power. This is accomplished through performing actions with the spirit of self-renunciation and by way of submission to the divine will so that one remains unattached inwardly while being fully engaged in actions outwardly. This is the alchemy of karma yoga.

It is when one can so restrain oneself as to only perform actions in the spirit of self-renunciation that one ceases to accumulate any new karma for fresh

[15] J. C. Chatterji, *India's Outlook on Life* (New York, NY: Kailas Press, 1931), 71.

[16] See: Swami Nikhilananda, *Self-Knowledge: Atmabodha* (New York, NY: Ramakrishna-Vivekananda Center, 1987), 30.

results. One only has to experience the results of one's previous karma that have ripened for giving fruits. If, in the meantime, one attains true knowledge of one's real Self, all past accumulated actions are destroyed. In sum, once certain actions have become fit for fruition, these can't be avoided—like an arrow that has already been shot toward the target. However, those actions that have not yet matured are annulled once and for all if the person attains Self-knowledge in the meanwhile, as advocated by the Bhagavad Gītā.

Does Karma Teach Passive Resignation?

Some critics remark that the doctrine of Karma is fatalistic. So that such teachings are not misconstrued as a doctrine of passive resignation—and a license for laziness—the sages have always advised seekers to first do their part diligently and then trust in God. The following Sufi story illustrates this point admirably[17]:

Doing Our Rightful Share First and Then Trusting in God

Once, a novice seeker paid a visit to a Sufi master to learn something about the art of living. The master lived in a small tent in a remote part of the desert. The young seeker entered the tent intently and, after paying his respects, took his place among the select audience seated quietly around the Sufi.

The Sufi greeted the young man with a smile and asked him how he got there. The young man said that he had come riding on a camel.

"Where is your camel now?" asked the Sufi. "I left it outside under Allah's care," replied the young man, trying to impress the master.

"Go tie your camel first and then trust in Allah," replied the master.

This story also demonstrates that the strength of a teacher lies in using mundane occasions of life to illustrate the deeper lessons of life.

Karma Implies *Dynamic* Freewill Not *Static* Determinism!

Determinism and free will are two of the knottiest problems in philosophy, just as the wave and particle are the two enigmas of quantum physics. And, as the potter forms objects on his potter's wheel, even so, each and every person forms—out of his thoughts, deeds, and his way of being—that which we call fate. This law of cause and effect is called the law of karma. It states that we are the captains of our ship and the architects of our destiny:

[17] For an alternative version, see Fadiman and Frager, *Essential Sufism*, 75.

सुखस्य दुःखस्य न कोऽपि दाता परो ददातीति कुबुद्धिरेषा ।
अहं करोमीति वृथाभिमानः स्वकर्मसूत्रग्रथितो हि लोकः ॥ ६॥

sukhasya duḥkhasya na ko'pi dātā paro dadātīti kubuddhireṣā /
ahaṁ karomīti vṛthābhimānaḥ svakarmasūtragrathito hi lokaḥ // (*Adhyātma Rāmāyaṇa*: 2-6-6)

There is none external to oneself causing one happiness and misery. It is a perverted intelligence that attributes these experiences as caused by another. It is vain pride that makes one think "I am doing" such and such act. The world is stung, as it were, on the thread of one's own action.[18]

The law is completely impersonal and there is nothing capricious about it. There is nothing unjust or unfair about it either. Looked at objectively, we suffer not *for* our sins, but *by* our sins. Karma is less about *retribution* and more about *attribution.*

Our *present* is *determined* by the exercising of our *freewill* in the *past.* We remain totally free to determine our future by our thoughts and actions in the present. Thus, contrary to the popular belief, the law of karma implies dynamic freewill and not static determinism. We may not choose our cards; however, we have complete freedom as to how we choose to play them. And that is what really determines our success or failure in life. But, what about the killings of many innocent people during random shootings and wars, deaths during plane crashes, and myriad, unexplained sufferings of countless human beings and other creatures? How does the law of karma explain all that?

The law of karma is meant to help us comprehend life events in our own life so that we can live a life of understanding, without bitterness and revulsion. *There is nothing that should prevent us from helping others who are in need due to the suffering caused by unexplained events.* Instead of decrying the doctrine of karma, the right thing to do is go out and actually help those in need. Thus, the right understanding of the law of karma leads to compassion. If it makes us angry or bitter, we have missed the whole point about karma.

Paraphrasing Bṛhadāraṇyaka Upaniṣad (verse 4.4.5), "You are what your deep, driving desire is. As your desire is, so is your will. As your will is, so is your deed. As your deed is, so is your destiny." At another place in Vedic literature, Sage Vasishtha says, "Each thought is a link in an endless chain of causes and effects, each effect becoming a cause and each cause having been an effect; and each link in the endless chain is welded out of three components—desire, thought and activity. A desire stimulates a thought; a thought embodies itself as an act. Act constitutes the web of destiny."

[18] Swami Tapasyananda, trans., *Adhyātma Rāmāyaṇa* (Madras, India: Sri Ramakrishna Math, 2001), 81.

The following traditional tale splendidly illustrates the importance of changing our perspective when we cannot change our circumstances:

Stop Being a Glass. Become a Lake!
An aging master grew tired of his apprentice's complaints. One morning, he sent him to get some salt. When the apprentice returned, the master told him to mix a handful of salt in a glass of water and then drink it.

"How does it taste?" the master asked.

"Bitter," said the apprentice.

The master chuckled and then asked the young man to take the same handful of salt and put it in the lake. The two walked in silence to the nearby lake and once the apprentice swirled his handful of salt in the water, the old man said, "Now drink from the lake."

As the water dripped down the young man's chin, the master asked, "How does it taste?"

"Fresh," remarked the apprentice.

"Do you taste the salt?" asked the master.

"No," said the young man. At this the master sat beside this serious young man, and explained softly,

"The pain of life is pure salt; no more, no less. The amount of pain in life remains exactly the same. However, the amount of bitterness we taste depends on the container we put the pain in. Therefore, when you are in pain, the only thing you can do is to enlarge your sense of things. Stop being a glass. Become a lake."

Bhagavad Gītā and Human Freedom to Act

The Gītā does not deny human freedom. If it were so, there would not have been any need for the 18 chapters of the Gītā and for all the yogas presented therein. In fact, it expressly states that we are the authors of our actions and that we can lift ourselves by our own self: One should uplift oneself by one's own Self, so let one not weaken this Self. For this Self is the friend of oneself, and this Self is the enemy of oneself.[19] How can the Self be one's friend and foe at the same time? The Gītā provides a very rational answer to this question: The Self that has mastered the desires and passions is one's friend and the Self that is slave to one's desires and passions is one's enemy (BG 6.6). All the self-development systems of the world would agree on this vital point. This is probably the greatest lesson of Self-mastery that can be shared with all leaders aspiring for self-victory.

[19] *uddhared ātmanātmānaṃ nātmānam avasādayet /*
ātmaiva hy ātmano bandhur ātmaiva ripur ātmanaḥ //6.5//

Are we then the *ultimate* authors of our actions? Not really. Ramana Maharshi, the great Indian sage, once remarked that free will is nonexistent, that all our activities are predetermined, and that our only real choice is either to identify with the body that is performing the actions or with the underlying Self in which the body appears.[20]

As explained later in this chapter, the Gītā regards human agency as one of the several factors of actions and their results (18.14). Therefore, although there is freedom to act, we are not totally free. As S. K. Maitra explains:

> We are undoubtedly subject to cosmic purposes; but, subject to this limitation, we enjoy freedom. It should also be remembered that the freedom that the Gītā values is the…"rational freedom," the freedom which consists in being true to one's rational self and in mastering desires and passions. The desire for authorship (*kṛtṛtva*) is emphatically denounced as an *āsura* quality (16.14).[21]

In elucidating what is called the doctrine of selfless actions, the Gītā urges us to renounce selfish actions and fruits of actions. In the ultimate analysis, renunciation is an inner, mental act and should not be confused with outward tokens of abandonment. True renunciation is the renunciation of *kartāpan*—the deeply ingrained sense of doership. Only then, the actions do not bind a man: *na karma lipyate nare* (Īśā Upaniṣad, 2). Śaṅkara's great comment at the very outset of his commentary (BG 2.10) is particularly illuminating in this regard: "He who knows the truth does not think 'I act,' nor does he long for results."[22] Aṣṭāvakra Gītā declares: "Neither doer nor enjoyer—you are verily ever-free" (*Nā kartāsi nā bhōgtāsi, mukta evāsi sarvadā*, 1.6). This is the high art of "inaction in action and action in inaction" that the Gītā (4.18) declares to be the way of the wise ones (*brahma-jñānis*). Sri Ramana Maharshi once said: "An *ātma jñāni* alone can be a good *karma yogi*."[23]

[20] See: Daivd Godman (Ed.), *Annamalai Swami: Final Talks* (Tiruvannamalai, India: Annamalai Swami Ashram, 2000), 38.

[21] S. K. Maitra, *The Spirit of Indian Philosophy* (Benares, India: Published by the Author; printed at The Indian Press Limited, Allahabad, 1947), 48.

[22] Alladi M. Sastry, trans., *The Bhagavad Gītā with the Commentary of Sri Sankaracharya* (1897; reprint ed., Madras, India: Samta Books, 1995), 27.

[23] See: *Maharshi's Gospel: The Teachings of Sri Ramana* (Tiruvannamalai, India: Sri Ramanasaramam, 2003), 16. Michael James, the preeminent translator of some of Sri Ramana's most important books, once told this author that this is perhaps the most succinct and inspired collection of Sri Ramana's teachings. It is believed that Maurice Frydman, the gifted, self-effacing Polish humanitarian, is the compiler of *Maharshi's Gospel*. Frydman is also the compiler of another modern spiritual classic, *I Am That*. Everything Frydman did is touched with distinction.

Law of Karma: Our Moral Balance Sheet or Sure Path to Sagehood?

Indian philosophy explains that the doctrine of karma is very useful in explaining the experiences of life: it is seen as a law of moral harmony. It provides a highly plausible explanation of glaring inequities in life, and thus removes the cause of envy and jealousy and consequent ill will (e.g., our neighbor is more fortunate because he or she has *earned* it). It also seems to remove impatience (e.g., whatever is mine shall come to me sooner or later). It must be noted that the doctrine of karma does not negate the idea of personal freedom. Though our present seems to be largely determined by our own past, the future seems to be largely dependent on the propriety of our present actions.

In the words of Sir Radhakrishnan, "The cards in the game of life are given to us. We do not select them. They are traced to our past *Karma*, but we can call as we please, lead what suit we will, and, as we play, we gain or lose. And there is freedom."[24] It has been observed that life is a stage with one entrance and many exits. The nature of the "entrance" and "exits," however, seems to depend upon how well we play our part in the cosmic drama of life.

Reflecting on the question of the extent of "freedom" and "determinism" in our lives, Mysore Hiriyanna, notes that:

> Every deed that we do leads to a double result. It not only produces what may be termed as its direct result—the pain or pleasure following from it according to the nature of the deed done; it also establishes in us a tendency to repeat the same deed in the future. The necessity involved in the Karma doctrine is only in so far as the former of these results, viz., the pain or pleasure, is concerned. As regards the latter, viz. the tendencies, they are entirely under our control.[25]

In Indian philosophy, the law of karma is used to explain the cause of human bondage as well as the means to attain liberation from bondage. When actions are performed with a selfish motive, they bind; when actions are performed without any selfish desire for personal gain—and *by way of submission to divine will*—they liberate. Performance of actions selflessly purifies the mind and renders it worthy of receiving liberating spiritual wisdom. Ethics is thus considered a necessary prelude to spiritual freedom. According to a well-known Indian dictum, "Scriptures do not cleanse the ethically unworthy."

According to the principles of karma yoga, it is not what one does, but the *motive* or *intention* behind the act that produces the binding effect of karma.

[24] Sarvepalli Radhakrishnan, *Hindu View of Life* (London, UK: George Allen and Unwin, 1927), 75.

[25] Mysore Hiriyanna, *The Essentials of Indian Philosophy* (London, UK: Allen & Unwin, 1949), 49.

"God cares more for adverbs than for verbs."[26] Accordingly, it is not necessary to renounce any activity. All that is needed is to act with the pure intention of unselfishness. In the following sections, this path of enlightened action is explored in greater depth as the alchemy of sage-hood—the realization of one's highest self.

Newton's third law of motion states that for every action, there is an equal and opposite reaction. The law of karma says the reaction is never equal, but usually much more than the original action, depending upon the moral valence of the action. The reaction(s) may bring both visible and invisible results—*drishta* and *adrishta phala*. When we act for the wellbeing of all beings, the *adrishta phala* comes in the form of purification and subtlety of mind. When we work for ourselves alone, we work alone. When we work for the universe, the universe works with us! This is the algorithm of life. How is selfless action (*niṣkām karma*) a blessing? Because it bestows purity of mind. Self-knowledge can only dawn in a pure mind, a mind that is free from the taint of self-centeredness.

Besides, the reaction(s) of our action may be delayed. It may sometimes take a lifetime or life times for the reactions of the actions to manifest. Karma says do not look at life in a piecemeal manner; take a long-term, holistic view of life. The universe is never in a hurry and karma never loses an address!

The Gītā and the Key Teachings of Karma Yoga

The Bhagavad Gītā starts with Arjuna's admittance of his confusion regarding what is "right" (*śreya*) and what is "pleasant" (*preya*) in life (2.7). This is the basic human dilemma—the conflict between duty and desire. Arjuna admits that he is confused about the right thing to do, surrenders to the Supreme, and humbly asks for the guidance on the path (2.7).

The teachings regarding *karma yoga* are presented throughout the Gītā, although Chapters 2, 3, 4, and 5 of the Gītā specifically deal with it. Chapter 3 of the Gītā is explicitly called *karma yoga*, the discipline or path of action. Śrī Kṛṣṇa provides an important clue about this path, starting with the most important verse in the Gītā on the philosophy of *karma yoga*, as follows:

> Your right is to work only, but never to its results. Let not the fruit of action be your motive, nor let your attachment be to inaction. (2.47)

Śrī Kṛṣṇa presents all the foundational elements of *karma yoga* in this seminal verse. It has four parts: (1) your right is to work only; (2) your right is never to the results of your actions; (3) desire for the fruit of your actions must never be your motive for actions; and (4) never give way to inaction, either.

[26] S. C. Gould (Ed.), *Notes and Queries and Historical Magazine* 18 (Manchester, NH: S.C. and L.M. Gould, 1900), 241.

The first part states that our right is only to act. The second part presents an existential fact: we have no control over the results of our actions. This is true whether we are talking about actions in the secular or the sacred sense. Even our control over our actions per se is very limited, if at all, given that all actions are performed, impelled by our nature (3.27).[27] This crucial point is also elaborated upon later in chapters 3 (e.g., 3.28) and 5 (e.g., 5.8–10) of the Gītā. So that we do not therefore resign ourselves to inaction, the above verse (2.47) clarifies that the teaching here is about the *renunciation of results* and *not the renunciation of actions* themselves, that is, renunciation *in* action and not *of* action.

There is nothing metaphysical about the teachings of the Gītā regarding focusing on the actions and not being concerned about their results or outcomes. The outcome of every action is dependent on a variety of factors: (1) one's own efforts, (2) the efforts of others, (3) the attendant conditions and circumstances, (4) the individual *karma* of everyone involved as well as the group *karma*, and (5) the grace of the Lord. The only factor that one can really control is one's own effort and that too is restricted by one's ability and capacity. There are so many hidden unknown factors and so many other known but uncontrollable factors. Hence, the Gītā enjoins the focusing of one's efforts on the action, the process, and not the result thereof or the outcomes—that is, diligently performing actions and letting the universe work out the results.

This understanding has a far-reaching implication for leaders, and everyone else in the organization. Too often, leaders focus compulsively on the results disregarding the process or the means. This proves counterproductive and creates undue confusion, uncertainty, and stress for everyone in the organization. Instead, if the leaders duly focus on the process, the outcomes may very well take care of themselves.

The Gītā further tells us that the actions should be performed diligently and equanimously:

> Do your duty to the best of your ability, O Arjuna, with your mind steadfast in equanimity, abandoning worry and selfish attachment to the results, and remaining equanimous in both success and failure. This equanimity of mind is called yoga. (2.48)

Verse 2.48 exhorts us to perform our actions to the best of our capacities, abandoning any concern for their results, remaining equanimous in both success and failure. This *evenness of mind* in both success and failure is called *yoga*.

[27] Recent findings from neuroscience point out that the bacteria in our gut significantly affects our thoughts (*The Scientific American*, April 19, 2011). And the effect of our thoughts on our actions is a well-known fact. If that is the case, then we seem to have very little control even over actions, let alone over their results. So, what are we really relinquishing? Perhaps, only our false sense of doership! This point will become clearer as the chapter unfolds.

However, remaining unconcerned about the results is not a license for sloppiness. One has to perform one's actions remaining steadfast in the *yoga* of equanimity. This *yoga* (equanimity) is in fact the dexterity *(kauślam)* in the performance of actions (2.50). This dexterity works in two ways: it frees actions from their inherent binding power, while at the same time transforming actions into effective means of spiritual freedom. The *yogis* perform actions, says the Gītā 5.11, unattached, for the purification of their mind: *yoginaḥ karma kurvanti saṅgaṃ tyaktvātmaśuddhaye.*

Chapter 3 of the Gītā, titled the path of action (*karma yoga*), begins with a clarification that there are two paths: the path of knowledge for the contemplative and the path of works for the active (3.3). It adds, however, that no one attains perfection merely by giving up actions (3.4) *without* possessing Self-knowledge. Act we must, until the Self-knowledge dawns. After all, no one can remain without action even for a moment; everyone is driven to action by nature (3.5). One cannot even maintain one's body without action (3.8); therefore, one attains the supreme by performing proper actions effectively, *without attachment*, as a *matter of duty* (3.19). Only actions in the spirit of renunciation do not bind (3.9). The wise (the knowers of the Self) act for the unification of the world at large (*lokasaṃgraham* 3.20, 3.25).

Then come two verses that provide perhaps the greatest *raison d'etre* of all actions performed by the force of inherent qualities:

> All actions are performed by *guṇas* [qualities] of primordial nature [*Pakṛti*]. One whose mind is deluded by egoism thinks, "I am the doer."
> But one, with true insight into the respective domains of *guṇas* and action, knowing that *guṇās* as senses merely move among *guṇas* as objects, does not become attached. (3.27–28)[28]

These verses state that we perform all actions prompted by the energies of three qualities (*guṇas*)—purity (*satvic*), activity (*rajasic*), and inertia (*tamasic*). Being acted upon by the *guṇas* via senses, and deluded by our ego sense (*ahaṁkāra*), we take ourselves to be the doers. But those who understand the respective domains of these *guṇas* and their actions do not get attached to them:

> The knower of Truth, [being] centered [in the Self] should think, "I do nothing at all"—though seeing, hearing, touching, smelling, eating, going, sleeping, breathing, speaking, letting go, holding, opening and closing the eyes—convinced that it is the senses that move among sense objects.[29] (5.8–9)

[28] *Guṇa* means "quality" or "attribute" of material nature (*Prakṛti*). According to the *Sāṅkhya* philosophy, nature is constituted of three *guṇas*: purity (*Sattva*), activity (*Rajas*), and inertia (*Tamas*). *Guṇa* also means *rope*, or that which *binds*.

[29] Swami Swarupananda, trans., *Srimad Bhagavad Gītā* (1909; repr., Calcutta, India: Advaita Ashrama, 1996), 125.

The above verses state that the seer of reality (*tattva-vit*) is firm (*yukto*) in his or her belief (*manyeta*) that "I do nothing at all" (*na eva kinchit karom iti*), realizing that the senses are moving among the sense objects. Ādi Śaṅkarācārya (788–820 AD), the greatest Indian philosopher, explains in his commentary that one who has the knowledge of the actionless Self sees inaction in action (4.18), for he or she realizes that, in all actions, the senses operate upon objects (sense objects), while the Self remains immutably inactive.

The Bhagavad Gītā tells us that "for one who knows the self, who rejoices solely in the Self, who is satisfied with the Self, and who is content in the Self alone,—for him there is nothing more left to do" (3.17). In other words, the Self is ever actionless, as action in nature (*Prakṛti's guṇas*) is inaction in the Self (*Ātman*). Ultimately, the Self is beyond both action and inaction for, as we do with action, we also incorrectly attribute inaction to the Self; as we see, for example, in the phrase, "Quiet and doing nothing, I sit happy."[30]

A question may be asked here: If, for the knower of the Self, nothing remains to be done, then how do we explain the apparent actions of the enlightened ones? In his commentary on the Bhagavad Gītā, Ādi Śaṅkara presents at least four explanations. The sages act:

1. with a view to set an example to the masses, so the unwary do not go astray (3.26)
2. for the unification of the world at large (*lokasaṃgraham*: 3.20, 3.25)
3. for the welfare of the world at large (*sarvabhūtahite* 5.25, 12.4), and
4. for the purification of the mind (*ātmaśuddhaye*: 5.11)

In verses 5.25 and 12.4, a liberated person is described as "most naturally and intently engaged in seeking and promoting the welfare of all beings" (*sarvabhūtahite ratāḥ*). They have nothing left to accomplish for themselves, personally. Therefore, all their actions are prompted by the wellbeing of all beings, for the common good. Śrī Kṛṣṇa, using himself as an example of a liberated being, tells Arjuna, "there is nothing in all the three worlds for me to do, nor is there anything worth attaining unattained by me, yet I continue to work" (3.22). Then, in verse 3.25, we find the clearest practical advice to live by: "As the unwise act *with* attachment, so should the wise, seeking maintenance of the world order, act *without* attachment." This is perhaps the greatest lesson that the enlightened leaders can learn from the Gītā.

In sum, the seers act selflessly for the wellbeing of all beings (*sarvabhūtahite* 5.25, 12.4) and for the unification of the world (*lokasaṃgraham evāpi sampaśyan kartum arhasi*, 3.20, 3.25). At the highest level, they spontaneously embody the virtues of universal morality, such as selflessness, compassion, desirelessness, forbearance, peace, and harmony. This is the culmination of karma yoga. This is also the summit of servant leadership!

[30] Alladi M. Sastry, trans., *The Bhagavad Gītā with the Commentary of Sri Sankaracharya* (1897; repr., Madras, India: Samta Books, 1995), 131.

Bhagavad Gītā and Knowledge of the Actionless-Self: "I Am Not the Doer!"

The theme of actionless-Self—"The Self does nothing at all"—occurs directly during at least six key verses of the Bhagavad Gītā (BG): 3. 27 & 28; 5.8–9; 13.29; and 14.19. It is also indirectly indicated in BG 5.14, BG 7.14, and BG 18.46. Finally, this theme culminates in verses 49 and 50 of chapter 18, where the understanding of the ever-actionless state of Self or Brahman is referred to as *naiṣkarmyasiddhiṃ*, that is, (perfection of) achievement of the state of remaining established in one's own real nature as the actionless-Self and is called the "supreme consummation of Knowledge" (18.50)—the state of immediate Liberation.

Conducting Our Affairs Without the Tag of Doership

The alchemy of selfless action, *niṣkāma karma,* lies in neutralizing the binding power of *karma*. When an action is performed with an egoistic feeling, the pride of doership, then the *karma* binds us in two ways. First, it reinforces our false sense of ego, thus making the egoic grooves deeper. Second, it sows the seeds of reaping the good or bad results of our actions. From the absolute standpoint, it makes little difference whether the so-called results of our actions are good or bad since both are ultimately binding in the sense that both will require the agent—the ego entity—to be there to experience the results. It will create more occasions for further *karma* to be generated, which is precisely what conditioned existence (*saṃsāra*) entails—the cyclic rounds of endless births and deaths. This does not, therefore, involve complete spiritual freedom (*Mukti*) from all phenomenal existence, once and for all—the *summum bonum* of all spiritual pursuits. Viewed in the light of the Indian doctrine of *Mukti*, all of our selfish actions suffer from the defect of tainted results (*viprīta dōṣa*); that is, they lead to bondage. Only selfless actions purify the soul and prepare it to receive the spiritual wisdom that alone leads to liberation in due course of time.

The Bhagavad Gītā verse 13.29 clarifies that he who sees that all actions are performed in every way by the threefold qualities of the material nature (*tṛguṇātmika Prakṛti*), and the Self as the non-doer, alone truly sees:

> *prakṛtyaiva ca karmāṇi kriyamāṇāni sarvaśaḥ /*
> *yaḥ paśyati tathātmānam akartāraṃ sa paśyati* //13.29//

This is then the gist of *karma yoga*: perform all actions as offerings (*arpaṇa*) to the Supreme and accept all results as graceful gifts (*prasāda*) from the Supreme, that is, performing all actions unattached in the spirit of service to the Lord (*Īśvara arpaṇa bhāvanā*) and accepting all results as gracious gifts from the Lord (*Īśvara prasāda bhāvanā*).[31]

[31] The author is indebted to Swami Paramarthananda for his profound teachings on the Bhagavad Gītā.

The following story[32] clearly illustrates how one can discharge one's duties most diligently without any sense of personal agency.

Source of Our Misery and Sorrow: False Sense of Ownership

Once, a king decided to celebrate his birthday in an unusually generous manner. He announced that, on his birthday, he would organize an exhibition in which traders from far and wide would be invited to display their goods for sale. However, on the day of his birthday, anyone could come to the exhibition and get anything they wanted for free. This was the best deal ever. So people rushed from everywhere to get things for free on the day of the king's birthday.

Toward the evening, a sage was seen walking through the stalls. He did not seem to be interested in anything that was displayed. Instead, he had been asking for the whereabouts of the king who organized the unusual exhibition. Some people surmised that he might have a special wish that he wanted to express directly to the king.

He was soon directed to the king's court. As the sage walked into the court, the king greeted him respectfully and asked him if he found anything worth getting from the stalls in the exhibition. The sage indicated what he wanted was not available in the exhibition. The king readily agreed that he would be most happy to give him anything he wished for. "Anything?" asked the sage, just to make sure. The king replied, "Yes, I would be happy to give anything that you would like to have."

The sage said, "Actually, I want your kingdom!"

At first, the king was very surprised at the sage's unusual request. Then, being true to his word, the king said, "I will be happy to fulfill your wish. You can have my kingdom and everything that goes with it. It is all yours. Kindly come forward and be seated on the throne." Everyone in the court was stunned to hear this, and there was dead silence for several minutes. They had never seen or heard something like this before.

Everyone present was even more surprised when they heard the sage address the king, thusly: "I am very pleased with your generous sense of renunciation. However, I have no desire to claim this or any other throne. I am a forest-dweller and have no attraction for such worldly things. I ask you only this. From now onward, please rule your kingdom as before but with the understanding that it really belongs to me; you are just a caretaker. This way, you will be able to conduct all its affairs without your usual sense of "me and mine." Above all, you will always be happy and content because all worries and misery come from our false sense of ownership and undue attachment to things that are ultimately transient and subject to change."

The sage left the court.

The king's perspective on life and leadership had been changed forever!

[32] Traditional tale transcribed into English by the author.

Freedom from the Commanding Ego

The knower of Self has achieved complete freedom from the shackles of egoism, that is, from the false sense of ownership and doership. In a most telling verse, the sage Aṣṭāvakra analyzes the malady of egoism and prescribes the fitting medicine: "Do you who have been bitten by the great black serpent of egoism 'I am the doer,' drink the nectar of the faith 'I am not the doer,' and be happy" (Aṣṭāvakra Gītā 1.8).

Finally, we present a story that crystallizes the burden of false ego in a powerful manner. This story was first told by Swāmī Śrī Brahmātmānand Saraswati of Rishikesh, my root Vedānta teacher[33]:

The Irony of Carrying the Deadweight of Imposter Ego
A man was travelling in a train. He was alone in the train compartment. He was enjoying the moving scenery outside until another passenger got into the compartment and took the seat right in front of him. Outwardly, this passenger looked rather wealthy and was carrying a big long suitcase—a heavy trunk made of iron—that he put right beside himself. Because of its heavy weight, he could not put it up on the berth. The first passenger was watching it rather intently wondering what could be in the suitcase. He mused that this fellow seemed very wealthy (judging from the clothes, the golden watch, etc. that he was wearing); he must have something really precious in the suitcase, like gold bricks or diamonds. That is why probably he did not even put it up on the berth! Such thoughts were racing through his brain like crazy as he was watching very carefully every gesture of the mystery passenger.

The train stopped at the next railway station and the mystery passenger asked the first passenger: "I am going to get a cup of coffee for myself. Do you want me to get you something? Would you kindly watch my luggage until I come back?" "Sure, I will be happy to," said the first passenger. As the mystery passenger got off the train to get a cup of coffee, the first passenger's mind started working in a turbo mode, wildly imagining all sorts of things that could be in the suitcase.

In the meanwhile, the train started! Anxiously, he got up to look for the mystery passenger through the window. The mystery passenger was not to be seen anywhere. The first passenger thought that, may be, the mystery passenger got in to another train compartment due to the train departing so quickly. So, he waited for him till the next train stop. But the mystery passenger did not come back.

Now, his greedy mind again started spinning all sorts of thoughts about the contents of the suitcase. And then he suddenly saw the ticket

(*continued*)

[33] Transcribed into English by the author.

(continued)
collector—called the "Guard" in India—get in the train compartment to check tickets. He asked this passenger: "Whose suitcase is this and why is it placed on the seat and not placed on the berth?" A million thoughts raced through this passenger's mind: "The ticket collector does not know anything about the mystery passenger…what if I say this suitcase is mine…and then I can have it when he leaves and be rich for the rest of my life" so on and so forth.

The ticket collector asked him again: "Whose suitcase is this?" "It is mine, sir!" "And why did you put it on the seat?" asked the ticket collector. "Because it is a bit heavy and I did not have the strength to put it up on the berth. Besides the compartment was all empty; no one was here besides me so I thought it is okay to leave it on the seat." "Okay, so what is in it?" asked the ticket collector. The passenger was not ready for this question. Trying to look genuine, he immediately blurted: "Just the clothes, shoes, utensils—the usual house hold stuff." "Can you please open it for me? I want to see what is in it," asked the ticket collector. "Sure!" said the passenger, confused, anxious, and a bit worried but still trying to maintain a false look of confidence.

As the passenger opened the suitcase for the ticket collector to see, he was stunned to find out that there was a dead body inside!

The ticket collector asked the passenger: "What is this and who is this person?" The passenger, who was still in a state of complete shock, tried to explain that he did not know anything about the dead body and that the suitcase did not in fact belong to him. But the ticket collector told this person that he had been lying and arrested him on the spot and put him in prison for a crime that he did not really commit.[34]

Swāmī Śrī Brahmātmānand Saraswati's comment on this story is noteworthy:

> This is the common plight of man. All his life, man carries the burden (dead weight) of the imposter ego, which he falsely calls his own. And because of this false attribution/identification, he remains in bondage (prison), so to speak, and suffers all his life.

The story of course is symbolic, and has subtle layers of meaning. The mystery passenger in the story is a metaphor for *jīvanmukta*—a being who is liberated while living—who has abandoned the dead weight of the false ego and has been awakened to the reality of the pure, actionless Self. The false identification with body, mind, and senses—and becoming a doer-enjoyer (*kartā-bhōgtā*) as

[34] A traditional Hindu tale transcribed by the author.

a result, is what is called ignorance (*ajñāna*) in *Advaita Vedānta*. The realization that "I am not doer"—since all actions are performed by qualities (*guṇas*) borne of Nature (*Prakṛti*), the Divine Illusion (*Māyā*)—is called Knowledge (*jñāna*). In the Vedantic scheme of things, this is the final end and purpose, the *summum bonum*, of human existence.

The Gift of Selfless Service

Under the guise of the Darwinian struggle for survival, we frequently discern that self-interest is placed before service in the relentless race to accumulate wealth, possessions, power, and fame—all geared entirely toward personal benefit alone. This unbridled pursuit of self-gratification inevitably leads to excessive greed, competition, and materialism that reign supreme in the world today. As an antidote to rampant self-centeredness, selfless service is absolutely paramount, individually and collectively, without which there can be no real progress or harmony in society.

It has been observed that life is like the game of tennis; in order to win, we have to be good at service. Our desire to serve must be pure; it should emanate from the sheer joy of service without expecting any reward, self-recognition, or self-gratification. When service emanates from a self-centered motive, it ceases to be service and becomes a business transaction. Selfless service to others can be offered in numerous ways, ranging from financial assistance to physical help. Real self-growth depends upon transcending the ego, ennobling the spirit, and revering all life, expressed in actions guided by selfless service without any thought or expectation of reward whatsoever—always working selflessly in the spirit of oneness for the common good. In fine, service is a way of being where one approaches life as an offering rather than viewing it from the standpoint of entitlement.

The lives of moral leaders, such as Mahatma Gandhi and Mother Teresa, bear ample testimony to the power of selfless service. Gandhi devoted all his life in serving his country and its people and found deepest fulfillment through serving. According to Gandhi, "The best way to find yourself is to lose yourself in the service of others." His life serves as a beacon of light to all humanity. Likewise, Mother Teresa was a prime example of selfless service. Her entire life revolved around helping others in need—the poorest of the poor. As a result, she experienced a great deal of affection and self-fulfillment in her life.

Karma Yoga, Selfless Service and Servant Leadership

I don't know what your destiny will be, but one thing I know: the only ones among you who will be really happy are those who will have sought and found how to serve. (Albert Schweitzer)

In this quote, Albert Schweitzer underscores the role of service in happiness. Happiness is a by-product of serving a cause greater than oneself. This mindset has a great application in the realm of leadership. First and foremost, leadership is a responsibility—a call to serve—and not a position to wield power or influence. The power that is bestowed upon the leader by the followers is of the nature of trust and good faith. In other words, it is a fiduciary relationship. Viewed in this manner, the only reason a leader exists is to enable and empower the followers. Great leaders approach their work as a contribution, as a service, without any sense of entitlement whatsoever. They are more concerned that the work gets done than about who gets the credit.

Practicing servant leadership is deceptively simple: One is led by the deep desire to serve others. It is also about putting others' interest first. History is a testimony to the fact that true leaders, above all, are servant leaders. Servant leaders do their work silently without raising a flag. When all is said and done, there is no human ideal higher than the gift of selfless service. For, in serving others, we find our true joy and fulfillment.

The Gītā garners a view of the leader as an "enlightened sage" who operates from a higher stance of being anchored in authentic Self, doing actions in a spirit of offering to the Supreme for the good of all. According to the Gītā, all virtues obtain in a mind that has cultivated equanimity.

The Gītā extolls *samatā* as the highest spiritual attainment as follows:

> *ihaiva tairjitaḥ sargo yeṣāṃ sāmye sthitaṃ manaḥ /*
> *nirdoṣaṃ hi samaṃ brahma tasmād brahmaṇi te sthitāḥ* //5.19//
>
> Here in this world itself, they have conquered the entire worldliness, those who establish their mind in equanimity. Brahman is taintless and equal. Therefore, by their attainment, they remain established in Brahman.

Whatever the spiritual practice, says the Gītā, if evenness of mind (*samatā*) is not attained, the goal is still far away. It represents the culmination of *wisdom in action*, informed by Self-knowledge and guided by selfless service.

Self-knowledge transforms our motivation and liberates us from the narrow confines of self-centered action to the freedom of serving others. Self-knowledge enables one to act in the world with a deep sense of peace and inner fulfillment. Such leaders work selflessly for the wellbeing of all beings and attain the highest felicity of Self-realization, the supreme goal of the Gītā.[35]

The question is not how to live longer; the question is how to live well longer. The Gītā answers the question with a counter-question: how can I serve the world with my gifts? That's all, says the Gītā, you need to know to live well.

[35] See: Gītā 5.25 & 12.4. *labhante brahmanirvāṇam…sarvabhūtahite ratāḥ:* 5.25: working for the wellbeing of all beings, sages attain liberation in the Absolute. We have Gandhi's testimony inspired by the teachings of the Gītā: "What I want to achieve,—and what I have been striving and pining to achieve these thirty years,—is self-realization, to see God face to face, to attain *Moksha*. I live and move and have my being in pursuit of this goal. All that I do by way of speaking and writing and all my ventures in the political field are directed to this same end." See: M. K. Gandhi, *An Autobiography: The Story of My Experiments with Truth* (New York, NY: Dover Publications, 1983), viii.

Concluding Remarks

In this chapter, we approached the gift of selfless service as a discipline of *karma yoga*, as presented in the Bhagavad Gītā. It is important to realize the true import of these teachings. The most striking feature of our human existence is the sense of doership, the feeling of "me, my, and mine" in all that we undertake. These teachings strike at the very root of our fundamental existential illusion, namely, the false sense of doership. It invites us to consider a revolutionary viewpoint. Since all actions are performed by the three modes of nature, they do not really originate as deliberate acts of volition in our mind. This understanding frees us from the clutches of imposter ego and paves the way for the realization of our true self. For as long as we operate within the false paradigm of "me, my, and mine," real Self-knowledge will elude us.

In elucidating what is called the doctrine of selfless action (*niṣkāma karma*), the Bhagavad Gītā urges us to renounce selfish actions and the fruits of actions. In the ultimate analysis, renunciation is an inner, mental act and should not be confused with outward tokens of relinquishment. It is about renunciation of results and not renunciation of actions themselves. That is, renunciation *in* action and not *of* actions. True renunciation is the renunciation of *kartāpan*—the deeply ingrained sense of doership. In one word, the alchemy of *karma yoga* lies in performing actions without the tag of doership. This is the master key!

Commenting on *karma yoga* as enunciated in the Bhagavad Gītā, Mysore Hiriyanna explains, "The object of the Gītā is to discover a golden mean between the two ideals...of action and contemplation...preserving the excellence of both. *Karma-Yoga* is such a mean....[It] stands not for renunciation *of* action, but for renunciation *in* action."[36] When actions are performed with the spirit of self-renunciation and by way of submission to the Divine will so that one remains unattached inwardly while being fully engaged in actions outwardly, they serve as harbingers of sagehood—the realization of one's highest Self.

It has been observed that life is a stage with one entrance and many exits. The nature of the "entrance" and "exits," however, seems to depend upon how well we play our part in the cosmic drama of life—for *karma never loses an address*! Mother Teresa once said, "I alone cannot change the world, but I can cast a stone across the waters to create many ripples." The Gītā says, cast the pebble of your good karma in the river of life, and let the Divinity work out the ripples for you.

[36] Mysore Hiriyanna, *Essentials of Indian Philosophy* (London, UK: Allen and Unwin, 1949), 120–121.

CHAPTER 6

Being-Centered Leadership: Leader as an Enlightened Sage

Introduction

Leadership's first commandment: Know thyself.[1]

Ever since Socrates uttered these two famous words, Know Thyself, humanity has used this refrain in its perennial quest for Self-knowledge. It has now become a staple of all leadership development programs, albeit leadership's first commandment. If all true leadership is an expression of who we are, the journey must begin with Self-knowledge. This chapter takes as axiomatic that leadership is a voyage of inner discovery and that Self-knowledge is the key to leading from within. This journey begins with knowing oneself and culminates in living one's deepest values at the personal, team, and organizational level. This chapter presents a unique conception of the leader as an enlightened sage who operates from a higher stance of being, effortlessly anchored in Self-knowledge and self-mastery. It starts with self-awareness, which ultimately depends upon Self-knowledge (Gītā 2.55–72; 13.7–11).[2]

Self-awareness born of Self-knowledge is the hallmark of all authentic leaders, since it helps those in leadership positions to lead from their true Self. In its wake, it bestows the gift of genuine humility, paving the way for selfless service and, finally, for servant leadership. As leaders, when we are in touch with our deeper authentic self, we are also able to connect with the authentic self of others.

"Leadership's First Commandment," states a *Harvard Business Review* editorial, is to "Know Thyself....No tool can help a leader who lacks

[1] Harris Collingwood, Leadership's first commandment: Know thyself. *Harvard Business Review*, December 2001, 79 (11). Special Issue.

[2] All quoted verses are stated in this manner: chapter number and verse number. Therefore, the number "1.1" denotes chapter 1, verse 1 of the Gītā. All translations of the quoted Sanskrit words or (partial) verses are by the author, unless otherwise stated.

S. Dhiman, *Bhagavad Gītā and Leadership*,
Palgrave Studies in Workplace Spirituality and Fulfillment,
https://doi.org/10.1007/978-3-319-67573-2_6

self-knowledge."[3] According to the Gītā, Self-knowledge means the knowledge of one's true self at the "soul-level"—beyond the senses, mind, and intellect. Self-knowledge, as the knowledge of our true nature, is a self-evident, self-established fact. The Self is of the nature of Pure Consciousness (*chaitanya-svarūpa*). It is the witnessing principle (*sākṣī-tattva*) in us and illumines all our thoughts, emotions, and perceptions.

The *leitmotif* of the Bhagavad Gītā is the vision of a sage who is pure in heart and steady in mind, and who, having cast off all self-centered desires, moves about free from personal likes and dislikes (*rāga-dveṣa*), established in the Oneness of all existence,[4] even-minded in success and failure.[5] Having attained the highest knowledge of the Supreme Self (*brahma-vidyā*), such a person has "accomplished all that has to be accomplished" (*kṛtakṛtya* 15.20).[6] The Gītā boldly declares that this Self-knowledge (*ātma-jñāna*) or the knowledge of the Ultimate Reality (*tattva-jñāna*) is so special that having known it, nothing else remains to be known here in this world (*yaj jñātvā neha bhūyo'anyaj jñātavyam avaśiṣyate* 7.2).[7] Having nothing here left to be achieved for oneself, such a person works concertedly for the wellbeing of all beings (*sarvabhūtahite ratāḥ*: 5.25; 12.4) and revels in harnessing the coherence of the world order by bringing the world communities together (*lokasaṃgraham* 3.20, 3.25).

We discover that this conception of an *engaged* sage lies at the heart of all wisdom traditions of the world as well. In the first chapter of his masterly work *A Short History of Chinese Philosophy*, Dr. Yu-Lan Fang describes the character of the Chinese sage as that of "sageliness *within* and kingliness *without*." [Emphasis added] Similarly, we find the same theme in Plato's conception of the philosopher-king, who, having cultivated the wisdom, is *fit* to rule.

According to Plato, unless leaders become wise (kings become philosophers), there can be no cessation of evil for the humanity. This is the final verdict of Plato, perhaps the greatest philosopher of the entire Western world: *only the wise can truly sustain the world.* Plato also said that if wise refrain from Government, unwise will

[3] Harris Collingwood, Leadership's first commandment: Know thyself. *Harvard Business Review*, December 2001, 79 (11). Special Issue.

[4] Īśa Upaniṣad declares, "What sorrow or delusion for the one who is established in universal Oneness?" तत्र को मोहः कः शोक एकत्वमनुपश्यतः ॥ ७ ॥ *tatra ko mohaḥ kaḥ śoka ekatvamanupaśyataḥ //7//.*

[5] What can be favorable or unfavorable for the wise? The wise welcome all situations and experiences as opportunities for self-learning and growth.

[6] Verse 14.3 of *Pañcadaśi*, a philosophical sub-text of Vedānta, declares, "A Self-realized person is ever-blissful on four counts—absence of sorrow (*duḥkhābhāvaś*), the fulfillment of all desires (*kāmāptiḥ*), the satisfaction of having done all that was to be done (*kṛta-kṛtyo*) and the satisfaction of having achieved all that was to be achieved (*prāpta-prāpyo*)." See: H. P. Shastri, trans, *Panchadashi: A Treatise on Advaita Metaphysics by Swami Vidyaranya* (London, UK: Shanti Sadan, 1982, reprint edition), 448.

[7] See also BG 6.22:

yaṃ labdhvā cāparaṃ lābhaṃ manyate nādhikaṃ tataḥ /
yasmin sthito na duḥkhena guruṇāpi vicālyate //

Having attained which, one does not reckon any gain greater than that, and established in which one is not affected by even a great sorrow.

rule over them and everyone has to suffer the consequences of it, exactly as it is happening in many parts of the world right now.

In the Gītā's view, only those who know themselves are truly wise (*paṇḍitāḥ*). Hence, only those who have Self-Knowledge should lead. Only then, humanity may have happy individuals and harmonious society. Self-knowledge (wisdom) brings a certain measure of "integration" in human personality. Only a well-integrated (*yoga-yukta*) person can be an effective leader. An unexamined life, said Socrates, is not worth living. This self-examination is called discernment, the art of living attentively. The Buddha's last words were: "Act without inattention."[8]

As we shall see, the Gītā's conception of personal mastery of an ideal sage mostly centers on emotional maturity—the ability to manage emotional disturbances and reactions calmly. This evokes the image of a lotus leaf that never gets wet even though it always remains in water.[9] It symbolizes the enlightened sage (*jñāni*) who remains ever steadfast and essentially unaffected even though fully engaged in the proceedings of the world—even so, while paddling like crazy underwater, the duck remains unruffled and calm above water. As a prelude to the conception of a sage steady in the wisdom of the Self (*sthitaprajña*), the following section highlights the meaning, the need, importance, and the practice of Self-knowledge. Self-knowledge is also essential for leading a fulfilled life. Since happiness is sought for the sake of the self, it stands to reason that the quest for fulfillment should begin with knowing the Self.

What Is Self-Knowledge?

Simply put, Self-knowledge refers to the knowledge of the Self, the knowledge of our true nature.[10] Our true nature is the felt sense of being conscious and present. Every type of experience—sensations, thoughts, feelings, and so on—presupposes our own awareness-presence. While all other types of knowledge pertain to knowing everything that can be objectified externally as the knowable, Self-knowledge is about *knowing* the "Knower" *without* subject-object dichotomy. However, being the knower, the innermost Self (*pratyak ātmā*) cannot be an object of knowledge.[11] Our knowledge of the world *appears* to be

[8] *Digha Nikāya* II. 156. Cited in Roberto Calasso, *Kā: Stories of the Mind and Gods of India* (New York, NY: Alfred A. Knopf, 1999), 396.

[9] *brahmaṇy ādhāya karmāṇi saṅgaṃ tyaktvā karoti yaḥ /*
lipyate na sa pāpena padmapatram ivāmbhasā //5.10//

He who acts, abandoning attachment, dedicating his deeds to Brahman, the Absolute, is untainted by sin, as a lotus leaf by water. Ādī Śaṇkara, the preeminent Indian philosopher, singles out this verse (along with verse 5.11) in his introduction to his commentary on the Bhagavad Gītā.

[10] Śrī Śaṅkara, in his commentary to Brahma Sutra 1.1.6, states that "*ātmā hi nāma svarūpam*" आत्मा हि नाम स्वरूपम्: What is meant by the word "Self" is one's own nature. See V. Panoli, trans., *Prasthanathraya, Volume VI—Brahmasutra* (Kozhikode, India: Mathrubhumi Printing & Publishing Co. Ltd., 2011), 75.

[11] येनेदं सर्वं विजानाति, तं केन विजानीयात्। "Through what should one know That owing to which all this is known!" [*Bṛhadāraṇyaka Upaniṣad* 4.5.15] See also: Swami Satprakashananda, *Methods of Knowledge: According to Advaita Vedanta* (London, UK: George Allen and Unwin Ltd.), 230. This book presents the most succinct, lucid, and comprehensive exposition of some highly intricate

direct but, in reality, it is only a *mediated* knowledge, experienced through the medium of the five senses and the mind. Self-knowledge, the knowledge of one's own existence—being of the very nature of Consciousness itself—alone is direct and *im-mediate* intuitional experience (*sākṣādaparokṣād*).[12] There is no path to Self-knowledge. What path does one need to reach oneself?[13] Actually, the image of the path is misleading. This is the most essential point to grasp in approaching the question "who am I." As the undeniable truth of our being, the Self is already and always there as our conscious presence. The quest for Self-knowledge, therefore, is *not a journey* but *a homecoming*.

What we usually call "knowledge" is information *about* objects—about the things other than our Self. As such, *objective* knowledge is at best "indirect" and "mediate." Self-knowledge, being the knowledge of one's own self, is "direct" and "*im*-mediate." It is a self-evident fact. We know we *exist* and we are *aware* of our existence (*sadevachid, chidevasat*). Put differently, Self-knowledge is the knowledge of the knower, the very subject—the pure witnessing Consciousness (*sākṣhi chaitanyam*)—that illumines all knowledge. The question of questions is, while one uses perception and inference to know the external world, by what means should one know the knower—the knowing Self? The wisdom traditions of the world recommend several methods that can serve as good catalysts for Self-knowledge, such as self-awareness, self-remembering, and self-inquiry. This chapter will focus on Self-inquiry as the key method to know the Self.

As the following story illustrates, without Self-knowledge, one can overlook one's essential reality, even when completely *immersed* in it.[14]

What the Hell Is Water?

Two young fish were swimming one day and they happened to meet an older fish swimming the other way. The older fish nodded at them and said, "Morning, guys, how's the water?"

And the two young fish swum on for a bit, and then one of them looked over at the other and asked, "What the hell is water?"

concepts regarding the epistemology of Advaita Vedānta. Perhaps the best single volume presentation on this topic in the English language.

[12] यदेव साक्षादपरोक्षाद् ब्रह्म, य आत्मा सर्वान्तरः "The Brahman that is immediate and direct—the self that is within all." "This is your self that is within all." See: Swāmi Mādhavānanda, trans., *The Bṛhadāraṇyaka Upaniṣad with the commentary of Śaṅkarācārya* (Mayavati, Almora, Himalayas: Advaita Ashrama, 1934/2008), 330.

[13] Consider the following exchange between a Zen master and a student:

Student: What is the way to Enlightenment?
Master: What *path* do you need to *reach yourself*?
Student: So, practice does not help?
Master: No, it does help.
Student: How so?
Master: Enlightenment is an accident. Practice makes you more accident-prone!
Student: Then what is the cause of un-enlightenment?
Master: *Seeking enlightenment*! (Source: Unknown)

[14] This story was told in a commencement speech by David Foster Wallace to the 2005 graduating class at Kenyon College.

This is an excellent example of missing out on reality due to Self-ignorance. How can we explain the enigma of Self-ignorance when the Self is ever-present and self-evident? It is our common experience that, when we want to know or perceive something, there has to be some distance between us and the thing to be perceived. While all other types of knowledge pertain to external, objective phenomena, Self-knowledge is the knowledge of the Knower, the very subject, the Self. For example, we are not able to *see* a book if it is held too close to our eyes. Since our Self is closest to us, perhaps that is why we tend to overlook it. It requires a certain measure of detached objectivity and alert awareness to know oneself. Lao Tzu was right: "To know others is intelligence; to know oneself is wisdom." Hence, the importance of Self-knowledge in discovering the truth of our being!

That we exist is the only fact we know beyond any shadow of doubt, for no one can ever deny or doubt their own existence.[15] To say that "I do not exist" is illogical, for it presupposes my existence in order to claim that I do not exist! This understanding reverses the popular Cartesian logic of "*cogito, ergo sum*"—"I think, therefore I am"—into "*sum, ergo cogito*"—"I am, therefore I think."[16] After all, "I am" is *prior* to thinking and my being does not depend upon my thinking. *I do not need to think in order to be.* My true nature is presence-awareness: "I *am*" and I *know* I am. Though aware of our own existence, we are not aware of our real nature. It is with reference to our real nature that Socrates gave the instruction, "Know Thyself." "It is enigmatic," says a modern Vedānta teacher, "that man with all his pretensions to knowledge does not know himself. Nay, he knows himself wrong."[17] Hence, the need and importance to know one's true nature.

As Sri Ramana Maharshi has observed, "To the ignorant, 'I' is the self limited to body. To the wise, 'I' is the Infinite Self."[18] Through Self-inquiry, when we realize our true nature as the limitless Self, it puts an end to relentless seeking, suffering, fears, worries, and desperation. In Self-knowledge, we discover the source of supreme peace and freedom. We discover inner joy that is our own true nature. This joy is *not experiential* in that it does not depend upon external props. This is evident from the fact that everyone loves themselves the most. Our self must be the unconditional source of joy, for no one can love that which is the source of distress. This understanding brings about transformation in the form of freedom from fear, insecurity, and worry—once and for all.[19]

[15] Śri Śaṅkara, in his commentary to Brahma Sutra 2.3.7, states, "Being the basis of all proof and disproof, the self is established prior to them….What is extraneous can be denied, but not the self. For, he who denies that is the Self." Satprakashananda, *Methods of Knowledge*, 231. Also see, V. Panoli, trans., *Prasthanathraya, Volume VI—Bramasutra,* 669.

[16] It is not that "I think, therefore I am"; rather, "I am, therefore I think!" How can our *being* depend upon *thoughts* which come and go?

[17] Satprakashananda, *Methods of Knowledge*, 232.

[18] Cited in Swami Rajeswarananda (Ed.), *Thus Spake Ramana* (Tiruvannamalai, India: Sri Ramanasaramam, 1995), 21.

[19] The knower of Self crosses over sorrow (*tarati śokamātmavid*), declares Chāndogya Upaniṣad 7.1.3.

One recognizes oneself to be forever free, whole, and complete (*puraṇa*). All seeking and doubts—that I am a small, separate, limited entity—are conclusively resolved, once the fullness (*puraṇatvam*) of the Self is realized.

The Need for Self-Knowledge

Thousands of occasions for joy,
Thousands of occasions for sadness—
The ignorant are their victims,
The wise remain unmoved.[20]

The need for Self-knowledge in the personal transformation of a leader can hardly be overemphasized. The following story[21] shines light on the need for Self-knowledge before undertaking any journey of self-discovery:

Who Is Lost?
A tale is told of a tourist who went to an exotic travel gift shop to buy some maps for the city he wanted to visit. He saw an item on display that looked like a compass. The compass had a lid, the inside of which contained a mirror. A little surprised over the combination of compass and mirror in one product, the tourist asked the owner about the rationale behind such an unusual product.

The owner explained, "The compass helps to find out ***where*** *one is lost, while the mirror helps to determine* ***who*** *is lost!"*

In a famous dialog that occurs in the most important Upaniṣad, *Bṛhadāraṇyaka Upaniṣad* (4.5.6), the sage Yājñavalkya tells his wife, Maitreyī: *ātmanastu kāmāya sarvaṁ priyaṁ bhavati*: "It is for the sake of Self, everything becomes dear." The great sage is not glorifying selfishness but pointing out a most profound psychological fact: Self is always loved unconditionally by everyone. In addition, everything else is dear for the sake of Self alone. That being so, one should know the Self, since it is for the sake of Self alone that everything is sought. The sage wanted to awaken the yearning for Self-knowledge.[22]

Self-knowledge puts an end to a life of relentless *becoming* by revealing a Self that is at once whole, full, and complete (*puraṇa*). Anchored in Self-knowledge, fulfillment becomes more a matter of *being* than *having*, more a matter of

[20] P. Lal, *The Mahabharata of Vyasa: Condensed from Sanskrit and Transcribed into English* (Lake Gardens, Kolkata: Writers Workshop, 2010), 370.

[21] A traditional tale transcribed by the author.

[22] This dialog occurs twice in the *Bṛhadāraṇyaka Upaniṣad*: 2.4.5 and 4.5.6. For this famous dialog on the importance of (and the means to) Self-knowledge, See Swāmi Mādhavānanda, trans., *The Bṛhadāraṇyaka Upaniṣad with the commentary of Śaṅkarācārya* (Mayavati, Almora, Himalayas: Advaita Ashrama, 1934/2008), 246–247 and 538–539.

belonging than *belongings*, more a matter of *values* than *valuables*. True happiness is not experiential; it lies *within*, to be discovered as limitless Consciousness and bliss supreme. "Inside you," reminds Hermann Hesse, "there is a stillness and a sanctuary to which you can retreat at any time and be yourself....Few people have that capacity and *yet everyone* could have it."[23] This is then the greatest of all paradoxes: *chasing all around to get back to yourself*! It is perhaps due to the utter simplicity of the fact of Self-knowledge that it is said that millions seek, thousands teach, only a few realize.[24]

The Importance of Self-Knowledge

All wisdom traditions of the world have upheld the importance of Self-knowledge as a prelude to every pursuit of happiness and fulfillment. Śri Ramakrishna, a modern Indian saint, said, "Know yourself and you shall then know God."[25] It is said that, "one who knows oneself knows God."[26] An important Indian wisdom text, the Muṇḍaka Upaniṣad 3.2.9, goes a step further: Anyone who knows that supreme Brahman becomes Brahman indeed (ब्रह्म वेद ब्रह्मैव भवति)![27] The Bhagavad Gītā, the Hindu wisdom text par excellence, describes it as "That which is to be known and by knowing which immortality is reached."[28] The Upaniṣads, the primary Hindu treatises on Self-knowledge, extol that "there is nothing higher than the attainment of the Self";[29] "the knower of Self reaches the Supreme Felicity";[30] "Self-knowledge is the harbinger of liberation while living";[31] and "the knower of Self crosses over sorrow."[32]

The Keṇa Upaniṣad warns, "By not knowing the True Self, one is at a great loss."[33] Similarly, in the Greek wisdom tradition, Socrates succinctly framed it as the highest principle of wisdom to "Know Thyself."[34] He did not mince

[23] Hermann Hesse, *Siddhartha*, translated by Hilda Rosner (New York, NY: Bantam, 1982), 69.

[24] See the Bhagavad Gītā 7.3: Hardly one among thousands strives for perfection; of those striving, and attaining perfection, hardly one knows Me in truth. In the Bhagavad Gītā, wherever Śrī Kṛṣṇa says "me" (*mama*), it signifies the universal Self, *Paramātman*.

[25] Swami Satprakashananda, *Methods of Knowledge: According to Advaita Vedanta* (London, UK: George Allen and Unwin Ltd.), 232.

[26] Paraphrasing an important *Hadith*, "*man 'arafa nafsahu faqad 'arafa Rabbahu*": "Know yourself and you shall then know God," says Śri Ramakrishna. Cited in Swami Satprakashananda, *Methods of Knowledge*, 232. Muṇḍaka Upaniṣad 3.2.9 goes a step further: Whomsoever knows Brahman becomes Brahman: ब्रह्म वेद ब्रह्मैव भवति.

[27] See: Swāmī Gambhīrānanda, *Eight Upaniṣads with Commentary of Śaṅkarācārya*, vol. 1 (Calcutta, India: Advaita Ashrama, 1957/1991), 163.

[28] *yaj jñātvāmṛtam aśnute* ...यत् ज्ञात्वामृतम् अश्नुते / BG 13.12.

[29] "*ātmalābhānna paraṁ vidyate*: आत्मलाभान्न परं विद्यते".

[30] *Brahmavidāpnoti param* // ब्रह्मविदाप्नोति परम् ॥ [Taittirīya Upaniṣad 2.1.1]. In the Upaniṣads, the words Ātman (Self) and Brahman (Absolute) are used interchangeably, denoting the oneness of the individual Self and the universal Self.

[31] Brahma Sutra Bhāshya 1.1.12.

[32] *Tarati śokam ātmavit*: तरति शोकम् आत्मवित् ~ Chāndogya Upanisad (7.1.3).

[33] *na cedihāvedīnmahatī vinaṣṭi*: न चेदिहावेदीन्महती विनष्टि: Kena Up. 2.5.

[34] *gnōthi seautón* ("Know Thyself") is an ancient Greek aphorism and one of the two most famous Delphic maxims, the other being "nothing in excess."

words when he said, "The unexamined life is not worth living."[35] However, Socrates has left no self-help manual for us beyond such pithy dicta. His student, Plato, points out that "the essence of knowledge is Self-knowledge."[36]

The following story alludes to the power of knowledge and its relation to peace and security:

A certain billboard pictured a dog and a cat looking at each other.

The ferocious dog was trying to pounce at the cat, yet the cat seemed unperturbed and even amused, sitting quietly in front of the dog.

The caption simply read: The Power of Knowledge!

The dog was on a leash. The cat was aware of this fact.

This knowledge gave the cat the freedom to enjoy the moment with great peace of mind.[37]

Such is the power of knowledge!

If mere knowledge of our surroundings confers such security, imagine what level of security Self-knowledge can engender. It is here that we are told that there are no recipes, no formulas, and no quick, royal road to Self-knowledge.

Self-knowledge does not bestow any obvious advantages in the practical sense. It is not needed to be proficient in any discipline of knowledge—for which all one needs is five senses supported by the mind. Thus, one can be an expert in any number of fields and still continue to be ignorant about one's own true nature. Similarly, one may be the most *well-known* person in the world and still *unknown* to oneself. Since Self-knowledge is not really required to function well in the world, one may remain blissfully ignorant of oneself, even though outwardly being very knowledgeable and successful. To see this point *clearly* is a great step on the path to Self-knowledge.

If Self-knowledge does not bestow any special advantage, then why should one know oneself at all? A little reflection will show that our "self" is the only constant factor underlying all our experiences, perceptions, thoughts, and emotions. Wherever we go, there we are. Some people speak about finding oneself as if one can ever lose oneself! And no matter how far we travel, we cannot really get away from ourselves. The following exchange highlights the need and importance of Self-knowledge.

Why Should We Seek Self-Knowledge?

Once, a successful executive of a Fortune 500 company was travelling with a Swāmi, an Indian spiritual teacher. They happen to be sitting next to each other. After a while, the executive turned towards the Swāmi and asked, "What do you teach, Swamīji?"

[35] Plato, *Apology*, 38a.

[36] Plato, *Phaedrus*, 230a, H. and C., p. 478.

[37] This vignette is based on a discourse of Swami Paramārthānanda, a contemporary teacher of Vedānta. The pious teachings of the saints, *Gurubani*, likewise points out that, without Self-knowledge, the fog of delusion does not disappear: *Jan Nanak binu āpā chīnai mitae na bhram kī kāī //2//1//* ਜਨ ਨਾਨਕ ਬਿਨੁ ਆਪਾ ਚੀਨੈ ਮਿਟੈ ਨ ਭ੍ਰਮ ਕੀ ਕਾਈ ॥੨॥੧॥: (SGGS 684).

"Self-knowledge," replied the Swāmi.

"How is Self-knowledge *relevant* to my life?" the executive asked.

"Are *you* relevant to your life?" asked the Swāmi.

Still undaunted, the executive countered, "Well, why should I seek Self-knowledge? I am highly successful in what I do. I am blessed with good health, wealth, family, friends, power and all that. I am happy with my life as is?"

The Swāmi smiled and said, "I am happy that you are happy! However, with Self-knowledge, you will be '*happier!*' Moreover, now your happiness is dependent upon your position, possessions, circumstances, things, etc. You never know: Anything can change tomorrow. It is not that Self-knowledge will make everything go well. But it will give you that objectivity, detached inner freedom, to deal with any surprises life will bring in its wake for you. It will give you the inner security which is not dependent upon external circumstances and things. Above all, with Self-knowledge you will come to realize that the most important things in life are not 'things.' And, finally, since happiness is sought for the sake of Self, it stands to reason that the journey of fulfillment should begin with knowing the Self."[38]

This could be our common story. We may take the passing attractions of the "finite" world of things, objects, and experiences to be all that there is to our mortal life. Like the executive in the story, we may even ruminate that wealth, power, success, and so on, are the supreme goals of human life, without ever realizing their obvious limitations and their tantalizing transience. Life, in its infinite bounty and compassion, may still arrange an impromptu encounter with Truth, as in the case of our dear executive in the story—*albeit silently and in the manner of "To whom May It concern!"*

It has been observed that "philosophy bakes no bread, but without it no bread would ever have been baked." Likewise, Self-knowledge does not bestow any practical advantage per se. But without it, nothing makes sense really. The following story further illustrates the seminal role of Self-knowledge[39]:

The Case of the 18th Horse!

A father left a large inheritance of land, money, gold, and 17 horses to be divided as 1/2, 1/3, 1/9 among three children. Everything else got divided easily but they were confused as to how to divide the horses.

In desperation, they contacted an old friend of their father. He came riding on his horse and offered to add his to the herd, to make the total =18 in all.

Now they could easily divide it in 1/2, 1/3, 1/9, as (9+6+2) =17.

And the family friend still had his horse.

Self-knowledge is like the 18th horse in the story, without which the calculus of life makes no sense.

[38] Adapted from Swami Tejomayanandaji's discourses on the Bhagavad Gītā and Kenopaniṣad.

[39] As cited in Berthold Madhukar Thompson, *The Odyssey of Enlightenment: Rare Interviews with Enlightened Teachers of Our Time* (New York, NY: Origins Press, 2002), 282.

Modus Operandi of Self-Knowledge

Be as you are.[40]

This terse quote by Sri Ramana Maharshi is probably the most precise instruction that can be given on the path of Self-knowledge. Be what you are also means to cease to be what you are not. Therefore, a good place to start the journey of self-discovery is to realize that we often have false ideas about ourselves. We are not what we normally take ourselves to be. What does it really mean to know oneself? To know oneself at what level—at the body/physical level or at the mind/intellectual level? Or is there something more lurking behind these intuitively obvious categories? In our common usage, we tend to refer to these as "my body," "my mind," and "my intellect." We do not say "I-body," "I-mind," "I-intellect." This is not just a linguistic contrivance or convenience, but a fundamental distinction that goes to the very root of who we are. To refer to our body as "my" body and our mind as "my" mind is to say that I am *not* my body, *nor* my mind. For example, we are used to saying "my body is strong/weak" or "my mind is sharp/clear," et cetera. In other words, "I" and "my body/mind" are two separate things. After all, I "experience" my body and mind. It is a basic rule that "I am different from whatever I experience." Ontologically and epistemologically, the subject is different from the object (s).

When the senses perceive external objects, they act as the subject to the myriad objects. When the mind perceives senses or emotions—for example, when I say "my eyesight is weak" or "I am feeling happy,"—the mind acts as the subject and senses and emotions act as the objects. Similarly, when I say, "my mind is confused," my intellect is objectifying my mind. When I say "I want to think about this matter," my ego is objectifying my intellect. When I say, "I have low self-esteem," "I," the subject, is objectifying the ego, the seat of self-esteem. However, "I" the subject can never be objectified, for "I" is the ultimate subject.[41] This is what is referred to as our "being." This knowledge of our being, our true Self, is not an intellectual concept. It is prior to even the mind and the intellect. Before the next thought arises, we are there, ever-present as conscious-awareness. This intuiting of separation between "I" and my "body-mind-senses" apparatus is sometimes referred to as the awareness of "I-Amness," the awareness of our innermost being or felt presence. Come to think of it, this feeling of "I-Amness" is our only true capital. Everything else is either borrowed or construed knowledge/information.

Essentially, the process of discovering our true nature is largely a process of elimination[42]—finding out what you are not leads to the knowledge of what

[40] David Godman (Ed.), *Be as You Are: The Teachings of Sri Ramana Maharshi* (New York, NY: Arkana Penguin Chapters, 1985).

[41] This methodology, *prakriya*, is called *Dṛg-Dṛśya-Viveka*, the seer-seen discrimination.

[42] This approach called via *negativa* नेति नेति: *neti*, *neti*—not this, not this. *sa eṣa neti netyātmā*: स एष नेति नेत्यात्मा: This self is that which has been described as "Not this, not this." See: Swāmi Mādhavānanda, trans., *The Bṛhadāraṇyaka Upaniṣad*, mantra 4.2.4, 413–414. It should be noted that the methodology of *neti neti*—not this, not this—negates the reality of the objective world from the

you are: I am not this body, I am not these emotions or thoughts, and so on. On the path of Self-knowledge, one does not gain anything. Only Self-ignorance is lost. This is called arriving at the Self (*ātmā*) by negating the non-self (*anātmā*). This is a key methodology of arriving at Self-knowledge and is referred to as *ātmā anātmā viveka*—discrimination between the Self and non-Self. As Sri Nisargadatta Maharaj, a modern Vedānta teacher, succinctly put it:

> To know what you are, you must first investigate and know what you are not. The clearer you understand that on the level of mind you can be described in negative terms only, the quicker you will come to the end of your search and realize your limitless being.[43]

Once one has negated the non-Self, what remains is the Self, the natural state of the conscious Witness, the transcendent Self that is described as "Not this, not this."[44] However, it is equally important to emphasize the positive side of the equation of who we *are*: the unchanging conscious witnessing-principle that illumines the senses, emotions, thoughts, memory, and the "me-notion." This silent witness is our true nature. Recognizing this Conscious Eternal Witness principle in and through all our experiences is called Self-knowledge.

Kena Upaniṣad verse 2.4 describes a simple methodology regarding *how* the Self is known: "Self is known through each and every cognition."[45] Śrī Śaṅkara's comment on this verse is categorical: "*There is no other way to attain the knowledge of the inner Self.*"[46] Bṛhadāraṇyaka Upaniṣad 3.4.2 further clarifies: "Self is the Seer of vision, the Hearer of hearing, the Thinker of the thought, the Knower of knowledge."[47] In sum, Self is the illumining principle of the senses and the proceedings of the mind. This knowledge, avers Kena Upaniṣad 2.4, bestows immortality.

Who Am I? The Alpha and Omega of Spiritual Quest

There is no such thing as a healthy ego any more than there is a thing called healthy disease.[48] (Sri H. W. L. Poonja ji)

absolute standpoint. It does not—nay, cannot—deny the witnessing Self, which is the conscious-principle, the ultimate Subject. This approach is called via *positiva*, *eti*, *eti*—this, verily this indeed.

[43] Stephen Wingate, cited in John Wheeler, *The Light Behind Consciousness: Radical Self-knowledge and the End of Seeking* (Salisbury, UK: Non-Duality Press, 2002), v.

[44] See Swāmi Mādhavānanda, trans., *The Bṛhadāraṇyaka Upaniṣad*, 414. [Saṅkara's commentary on *mantra* 4.2.4.].

[45] Kena Upaniṣad 2.4: pratibodhaviditaṁ matamamṛtatvaṁ hi vindate: प्रतिबोधविदितं मतममृतत्वं हि विन्दते। The Self, which is self-evident, is recognized in every cognition. As consciousness, it is present as the *invariable truth* of all experience.

[46] *nānyaddvāramantarātmano vijñānāya*: नान्यद्द्वारमन्तरात्मनो विज्ञानाय: V. Panoli, trans., *Prasthanathraya Volume-II: Isa, Kena, Katha, Mandukya with the Karika of Gaudapada* (Kozhikode, India: Mathrubhumi Printing & Publishing Co. Ltd., 2006), 114.

[47] Cited Swāmī Gambhīrānanda, *Eight Upaniṣads with Commentary of Śaṅkarācārya*, vol. 1 (Calcutta, India: Advaita Ashrama, 1957/1991), 67.

[48] Cited in Dennis Waite, *The Chapter of One: The Ancient Wisdom of Advaita* (Winchester, UK: O Chapters, 2011), 23.

Poonja ji's satire is subtle: enlightened self-interest is a self-contradiction. Similarly, the quest for enlightenment is misplaced. Who wants to get enlightened? If enlightenment means the complete annihilation of ego, then the question of questions is who wants to get enlightened? Hence, the dire importance of Self-knowledge in life and leadership.

The Gītā teaches us that the spiritual quest starts and ends with Self-knowledge—asking and answering the question "Who Am I?" This simple process of self-exploration is called Self-inquiry and is considered to be the chief means to awaken to Self-knowledge. According to Sri Ramana Maharshi, "Self-inquiry is the one, infallible means, the only direct one, to realize the unconditioned, Absolute Being that you really are."[49]

Sri Ramana used to say that the very inquiry "Who am I?" will lead us to *realize* the Self, if consistently pursued. By conducting the "Seer-Seen discrimination," *dṛg-dṛśya viveka*, I can realize that all that is seen—from the world of objects up to my own mind—cannot be I, the Seer. We do not notice this because our attention is generally focused on the objects outside. The practice of this inquiry into the nature of the Self will slowly turn our attention inward—first to the mind, and then from the mind to the "I-thought," and finally from the "I-thought" to the Self. As Swami Sivananda explains beautifully:

> The Upanishads declare that the Atman [Self] is the unseen seer, the unheard hearer, the unknown knower. One cannot see the seer of seeing, one cannot hear the hearer of hearing, one cannot know the knower of knowing. The Atman [Self] has neither a subject nor an object. The subject and the object are both comprehended in the Atman [Self] in which all divisions appear and which is raised above them all.[50]

When we ask "Who Am I," we are basically inquiring about the essential nature of the Self. Upaniṣads tell us that the Self, *ātmā*, is of the nature of pure Consciousness (*shuddha chaitanya-svarūpa*) or of the nature of pure Knowledge (*shuddha jñāna-svarūpa*). Swami Paramārthānanda, a modern Vedānta teacher, explains the nature of the Self, *ātmā*, as follows[51]:

1. The Self is not a part, property or product of the body.
2. The Self is an independent conscious principle that pervades and enlivens the body.

[49] See: *Maharshi's Gospel: The Teachings of Sri Ramana* (Tiruvannamalai, India: Sri Ramanasaramam, 2003), 38. Michael James, the preeminent translator of some of Sri Ramana's most important books, once told this author that this is perhaps the most succinct and inspired collection of Sri Ramana's teachings. It is believed that Maurice Frydman, the gifted, self-effacing Polish humanitarian, is the compiler of *Maharshi's Gospel.* Frydman is also the compiler of another modern spiritual classic, *I Am That.* Everything Frydman did is touched with distinction.

[50] Swami Sivananda, *Essence of Vedanta* (Rishikesh, India: The Divine Life Society, 2009), 148.

[51] Swami Paramārthānanda, *The Essence of Vedanta*-Part 1 and 2. General Talks.

3. The Self is not limited by the boundaries of the body. It is all-pervading, like space.[52]
4. The Self is unborn and eternal and does not die with the death of the body.

Self-Knowledge: An Already Accomplished Fact

In the Vedāntic scheme of things, there is no difference between Self-knowledge and Self-realization, for, to *know* the Self is to *realize* the Self. As Afdal al-Din Kashani (c. 12th century C.E.) puts it succinctly, "To know oneself is to know the everlasting reality that is Consciousness, and to *know* it is to *be* it."[53] When one *knows* that the fire burns, one does not have to put one's hand in the fire to *realize* this fact. Put differently, in the realm of Self-knowledge, ***knowing is being and being is knowing***. Unlike things that are separated from us by time and space—for which we have to do something to attain them—Self-knowledge does not involve doing something new or attaining something afresh.

Therefore, in Vedānta, quest for Self-realization is regarded as "accomplishing an already accomplished fact" or, as Swami Dayananda Saraswati puts it, "the achievement of that which is already achieved, *prāpatasya prāpati*"[54]—it is only a matter of recognizing, rediscovering an already existing fact, attaining the already attained. It is because our "Self" is not separated from us in time or space. It is always present as our being. The only thing that is self-evident and ever-present is the Self—the *felt* awareness of our *being* or *presence*. Everything else becomes evident through the Self, which is of the nature of pure awareness or Consciousness. Sri Ramana Maharshi explains succinctly:

> "I exist" is the only permanent, self-evident experience of everyone. Nothing else is so self-evident (*pratyaksha*) as "I am". What people call "self-evident" viz., the experience they get through the senses, is far from self-evident. The Self alone is that. *Pratyaksha* is another name for the Self. So, to do Self-analysis and be "I am" is the only thing to do. "*I am*" is reality. I am *this* or *that* is unreal.[55]

Our whole existential experience can be reduced to two basic entities: "I" and "not-I." There is this "I" and everything else is "not-I." "I" refers to "I-am," the conscious principle, the "locus" of all experience and every emotion and thought. When Moses saw the blazing light of God on the Mount Sinai and, in awe, asked for God's name, we are told, the Light responded: "YHWH"—"I am That I am."[56] "I am" remains the most unique, the most exclusive, singular epithet to refer to oneself, as if partaking of the Divine Reality.

[52] Being all-pervading and limitless, it is known by two names: *ātmā* and *Brahma*. *Ātmā: Āpnōti sarvam*: It pervades all over. Brahma: *Brahmanāt bṛhad samastavāt*: It is the biggest one.

[53] William Chittick, *BĀBĀ AFŻAL-AL-DĪN, Poet and Author of Philosophical Works in Persian*. Retrieved August 30, 2015: http://www.iranicaonline.org/articles/baba-afzal-al-din

[54] Dayananda Saraswati, *Introduction to Vedanta: Understanding the Fundamental Problem* (New Delhi, India: Vision Books Pvt. Ltd., 2009), 39.

[55] A. Devaraja Mudaliar, *Day by Day with Bhagavan*, 182. [emphasis in the original].

[56] Sri Ramana Maharshi used to say that the whole of Vedānta is contained in the two Biblical statements: "I am that I AM" and "Be still and know that I am God." See *Talks with Sri Ramana Maharshi* (Tiruvannamalai, India: Sri Ramanasramam, 2000), 320.

This is also evidently how pronouns work in all languages. The second and third person pronouns, You, They, He, She, IT can be used to refer to any person or thing. But the first person pronoun, "I" can only be used to refer to one and only one person—namely, "you."[57] There is only one person that is referred to when anyone refers to himself or herself as "I am." There is only one person in the whole creation that is like you, and that is you. You are the sole actor/director of your life's drama. It is a one act play, a monolog. And it is so for every single person![58]

Little wonder, then, that we have transitioned from a "me culture" to a "*selfie* culture." Ever wonder about the secret of Apple's success? Apple Inc. chose their logo very well, all the way: First, at the dawn of creation, it was the apple that was offered by Eve to Adam. Perhaps the same apple fell on Newton's head, changing the nature of knowledge as the world knew it. And we are told that "an apple a day keeps the doctor away." Apple Inc. names its products ingeniously: *i*mac, *i*pod, *i*phone, *i*pad. Notice the prominence given to the "I." Hence, their success.

If Self-knowledge is a self-evident fact, how come we are told, as in the opening quote, that to know one's own self is the most difficult thing? How do we reconcile these two divergent viewpoints—that Self-knowledge is the most difficult thing and that Self-knowledge is the most naturally self-evident and an already accomplished fact? If Self-knowledge is an already accomplished fact, we may ask, why do we need all these reminders, such as "Know Thyself" (Socrates)? If by its very nature the Self is the most self-evident fact, why do we need any teaching at all to know ourselves? The sages point out that although we know ourselves in a general way—we are *conscious* that we exist—we do not know our true nature.

It can be explained in this manner: "I am" is a self-evident fact. "Who am I" is a *discovery*. And this discovery needs a specialized means to proceed. It is because, even if we have eyes, we still need a mirror to see our face. Vedānta—the science of truth about our existence—acts as a mirror to reveal "who am I." I know *I am*, but I do not know that *I am Brahman*. The Gītā says you are not the limited "body-mind-senses" complex that you take yourself to be. You are the Self that is whole, limitless Consciousness. Know yourself to be so and be happy. Whenever we feel sorrowful, we are missing something; for, all sorrow is born of some sense of limitation—physical or psychological. All seeking essentially involves a desire to be free from limitations. We are all seeking *puraṇatvam*, the fullness of our being. The Gītā says that you are already *puraṇa*, whole and complete: Reclaim your true status—as limitless Consciousness—and be free.

[57] Sri Ramana Maharshi has frequently emphasized this point in his writings: "It is only after the first personal pronoun arises that the second and third personal pronouns appear. Without the first person, the second and third persons cannot exist." See his famous essay: *Who Am I?* Retrieved October 15, 2016: http://www.davidgodman.org/gen2/p/ramana/who-am-i/who-am-i.html

[58] Remember, you are a completely unique and distinct person. Just like everyone else. ~ Anon.

The Sage Steadfast in Wisdom

At the heart of the Gītā, there is this conception of a sage steadfast in wisdom.[59] The last 18 verses of chapter 2 magnificently describe the marks of the sage steadfast in wisdom—*sthitaprajña*—which are "unparalleled in the spiritual literature of the world."[60] This is the central archetype of the Gītā—a person of steady wisdom, who has so conquered his carnal desires, subdued his senses, disciplined his mind, purified his heart, and attained the highest levels of virtuous living that there is no trace whatsoever of the ego left behind. Steadfast in the wisdom of the self, such a person functions in life spontaneously and equanimously, free from the tug of the warring pairs of opposites such as success and failure, good and bad, happiness and sorrow, gain and loss.

This conception of a sage has direct bearing on cultivating what has come to be known as authentic leadership. Defining the process of becoming a leader in terms of authenticity and self-mastery, Warren Bennis, the preeminent leadership expert, equates it with becoming yourself, which is not as simple as it sounds. He provides a succinct characterization of exemplary leadership in an interview to *Fast Company*:

> The process of becoming a leader is, if not identical, certainly similar to the process of becoming a fully integrated human being. It's got to do with authenticity, it's got to do with candor, it's got to do with the fact that one cannot truly lead unless one is an expert in self-management.[61]

Leadership qualities, Bennis maintains, can only emerge from an "integrated self." For this development, humility is a supreme virtue. Howard Schultz, the founder and chairman of the Starbucks chain of coffee shops, says that Bennis once told him that to become a great leader, you have to develop "your ability to leave your own ego at the door, and to recognize the skills and traits that you need in order to build a world-class organization."[62]

This goes on to show that humility is an essential ingredient of effective leadership. Jim Collins, the author of *Good to Great*, fully concurs and regards *compelling humility* to be one of the two hallmarks of level 5 leaders, the other being *fierce professional will*.[63]

[59] Śri Śaṅkara, in his legendary commentary on the Gītā (*Gītā Bhāṣyam*), defines *sthitāprajñaḥ*, a person established in steady wisdom, as follows: "*sthitā pratiṣṭhitā 'ahamasmi paraṁ brahma' iti prajñā yasya saḥ sthitaprajñaḥ*": He is a person of steady wisdom who has a firm conviction/awareness, "I am the Supreme Brahman." [author's rendition].

[60] Eknath Easwaran, cited in Louis Fischer (Ed.), *The Essential Gandhi* (New York, NY: Vintage Books, 2002), xvi.

[61] Warren Bennis, Interview: "Have the requirements for being a good leader changed?" Fast Company: Leadership Hall of Fame, December 26, 2011. (F. Company, Interviewer). Retrieved June 4, 2018: https://www.fastcompany.com/1786824/leadership-hall-fame-warren-bennis-author-becoming-leader

[62] Tim Hindle, *Guide to Management Ideas and Gurus* (The Economist) (London, UK: Profile Books Ltd., 2009), 218.

[63] Jim Collins, *Good to Great: Why Some Companies Make the Leap…and Others Don't* (New York, NY: HarperBusiness, 2001).

Bill George, the exemplary former head of Medtronic, who popularized the concept of authentic leadership, includes humility along with purpose, transparency, and integrity to define authentic leaders.[64] Humility is also a precondition for serving others for, without it, even service could be but an inflation of ego. Therefore, in learning as in leading, humility constitutes the key ingredient of living a profoundly significant life.

The Gītā's formulation of personal mastery of a Self-aware sage largely centers on emotional maturity—the ability to manage emotional disturbances and reactions calmly. It symbolizes the enlightened sage (*jñāni*) who remains ever steadfast and essentially unaffected by the ebb and flow of life even though fully engaged in the proceedings of the world. This is the wisdom we need in life and leadership during these turbulent times.

Let us first look closer at these 18 magnificent verses (2.55–2.72)[65] in order to understand their true import for Self-knowledge and Self-realization. In these verses, the marks of a sage established in wisdom (*sthitaprajña*) are described as follows:

> When one completely casts off all selfish desires of the mind, finding contentment by the Self in the Self alone; neither agitated by sorrow nor hankering after the sense pleasures; free from lust, fear, and anger; free from attachment; neither elated by good fortune nor depressed by bad; with senses subdued and mind ever absorbed in the Divine within—such a person is truly wise.[66]

In this part of the description of the traits of a person of steady wisdom, we notice three main things: freedom from self-centered desire (and the resultant anger, greed, and attachment: the triple gates of hell, according to the Gītā), an attitude of equanimity, and absorption in the wisdom of the Self or Divine. Then, the Gītā goes on to explain the psychology of anger and the glory of a person who has gone beyond self-interest and egotism:

> Brooding on sense objects leads to attachment; from attachment comes desire; and from (unfulfilled) desire ensues anger. Anger clouds judgment and leads to loss of reason; and loss of reason brings utter ruin....One who has given up all desires and moves about free from longing, without self-interest and egotism, such a person attains peace. Attaining this state even at the time of death, one passes from death to immortality.[67]

[64] Bill George, *Discover Your True North* (San Francisco, CA: Jossey-Bass; Expanded and Updated edition, 2015), 122, 126, 251, 259.

[65] As we shall see in a later chapter, Gandhi regarded these verses as representing the essence of the Gītā: "If the rest of the scripture were lost, these verses alone will be enough to teach a complete way of life." See: Easwaran, trans., *The Bhagavad Gītā*, 59.

[66] Ibid., xvi.

[67] Adapted from Eknath Easwaran, trans., *The Bhagavad Gītā* (New York, NY: Vintage Spiritual Classics, 2000), 67–69; Franklin Edgerton, trans., *The Bhagavad Gītā* (New York, NY: Harper & Row Publishers, 1964), 15–17; Dhiman, *Sahaja-Gītā: The Essential Gītā*, 36–39; See also, Strohmeier (Ed.), *The Bhagavad Gītā According to Gandhi*; Hingorani, *Gandhi for 21st Century*. Also see, Betai, *Gītā and Gandhi*.

It is important to note that the description of a person of steady wisdom starts and ends with casting off all the selfish desires of the mind. *Yogavāsiṣtha Mahāramāyaṇa* also states succinctly: "Wisdom proceeds from the curtailing of desires."[68]

There are at least four places where the characteristics of a perfected sage are presented in the Gītā from different perspectives: 2.55–72; 12.13–20; 14.21–27; and 18.49–56 (in addition, we also find reaffirmation of the same theme in selected verses of two other chapters: 13.7–11 and 16.1–3). For example, chapter 12 (verses 13–20) describes the marks of a devotee (*bhakta*); these marks have a striking similarity to the qualities of a person who has transcended the sway of three modes of material nature—*guṇātīta* (14.21–27), which in turn bear a great similarity to the characteristics of a person steadfast in wisdom (*sthitaprajña*), as described in chapter 2 (verses 55–72) as follows:

> That person is dear to me who is free from ill-will, friendly and compassionate; free from the sense of "I" and "mine"; equanimous in joy and sorrow, forgiving, ever-content, firm in faith with his mind ever united with Me; who has subdued his mind, senses, and body; and has surrendered heart and mind to Me. … Not agitating the world, nor agitated by it, above the sway of delight, envy, desire, and fear; who regards equally friend and foe, praise and blame, pain and pleasure, free from selfish attachments; quiet, ever-content, in harmony everywhere, firm in faith—such a person is dear to Me.[69]

What is noteworthy in the above-quoted verses is that almost all of these qualities of an ideal sage more or less focus on emotional maturity—the ability to manage emotional disturbances and reactions calmly. Cultivating these qualities is important for everyone, in both personal and professional arenas. For example, being friendly and compassionate and free from malice (*adveṣṭāsarva bhūtānāṃmaitraḥkaruṇa*: 12.13), being free from attachment, fear, and anger (*vītarāgabhayakrodhaḥ*: 2.56, 4.10), and neither being a source of annoyance to fellow-beings nor feeling vexed with them (*yasmānnodvijatelokolokānnodvij atecayaḥ*: 12.15)—all these are signs of emotional stability, which is the key to harmony in personal and professional relationships.

This is a tall order of personal qualities for any leader to cultivate and requires years and years of dedication, commitment, and perseverance. These qualities represent the highest level of emotional maturity, self-awareness, and self-discipline, equanimity, and detachment that may appear to be unattainable by any leader according to modern standards.

Have there been leaders who have demonstrated these qualities? Better yet, are there any contemporary leaders who embody the Gītā's ideals of self-awareness, Self-knowledge, selflessness, humility, and emotional maturity?

[68] Vihari-Lala Mitra, trans., *Vālmīki's Yoga-vāsiṣṭha-mahārāmāyaṇa*. Online edition, Retrieved February 10, 2015: http://www.wisdomlib.org/hinduism/book/yoga-vasistha-volume-2-part-ii/d/doc118202.html

[69] Easwaran, cited in Fischer, *The Essential Gandhi*, xvii [author's adaptation].

In Easwaran's estimation—who was present at one of the prayer meetings that Gandhi regularly held—Gandhi "fulfilled every condition that the Gītā lays down."[70] Exemplar leaders like Gandhi act as a "witness" of high moral leadership, and without them the limits of higher human possibilities will neither be known nor sustained.

We briefly present the examples of three leaders—whose leadership development was influenced, directly or indirectly, by the teachings of the Gītā: Steve Jobs, Nelson Mandela, and Gandhi.

Gītā and the Spiritual Quest of Steve Jobs

He wasn't a saint. I am not saying that. None of us are. But it's emphatically untrue that he wasn't a great human being.[71]

This quote from Tim Cook, Apple CEO, shows us that spiritual leadership is not about *being a saint*; it is about *becoming a great human being*. In their recent book on the evolution of Steve Jobs as a visionary leader, Brent Schlender and Rick Tetzeli quote Tim Cook, who tells the untold story of his friendship with Steve jobs. According to Cook, Steve was a passionate person, a caring leader, and a genuine human being. Tim believes that Walter Isaacson's biography[72] did Steve a tremendous disservice by unfairly portraying him as a sort of greedy, selfish egomaniac. It didn't capture his *humane side*—Steve Jobs, the person.

Tim recalls that when he offered his liver to Steve, Steve refused, stating, "No, 'I'll never let you do that. I'll never do that!" "Somebody that's selfish," Cook recounts, "doesn't reply like that."[73] According to Tim Cook, Steve cared. He cared deeply about things. Yes, he was very passionate about things, and he wanted things to be perfect. And that was what was great about him. He wanted everyone to do their best....A lot of people mistook that passion for arrogance.[74]

Many believe that the inner clarity and conviction that Steve Jobs attained was the result of his deep explorations into his spiritual Self. It is well known that Steve was mystified by Eastern philosophies. He went to India during the 1970s as teenager before he co-founded Apple. It proved to be a life changing experience and a great turning point in the real spiritual sense.

[70] Ibid., xvii.

[71] Brent Schlender & Rick Tetzeli, *Becoming Steve Jobs: The Evolution of a Reckless Upstart into a Visionary Leader* (New York, NY: Crown Business, 2015), 392.

[72] Walter Isaacson, *Steve Jobs* (New York, NY: Simon & Schuster, 2011), 43; 447.

[73] Brent Schlender & Rick Tetzeli, *Becoming Steve Jobs: The Evolution of a Reckless Upstart into a Visionary Leader* (New York, NY: Crown Business, 2015), 392.

[74] Ibid.

Steve Jobs' Spiritual Quest Begins

After reading Harvard professor Ram Das's *Be Here Now* and Paramahansa Yogananda's *Autobiography of a Yogi*, Steve Jobs traveled to India in 1974 with a friend, Dan Kottke—who later became Apple's first employee. His trip to India was disappointing and revelatory at once, as he himself realized and recounted: "We weren't going to find a place where we could go for a month to be enlightened."[75] Yet, in a far more important sense, during his short flings with various Indian *āshrams*, Steve picked up the importance of cultivating inner centeredness and composure and "looking at the world from the inside out." This orientation seemed to have served him well throughout his life as a leader of Apple.

His interest in Eastern spirituality was solidified later when he dabbled in Zen Buddhism at the Los Altos Zendo. Steve's credo "Actualize yourself" seems to have come directly out of Yogananda's philosophy of Self-realization based on the Bhagavad Gītā.[76] Jobs' affinity for Hindu spirituality dates back to his college days, as he noted in his Stanford commencement address in 2005:

> It wasn't all romantic. I didn't have a dorm room, so I slept on the floor in friends' rooms, I returned coke bottles for the 5¢ deposits to buy food with, and I would walk the 7 miles across town every Sunday night to get one good meal a week at the Hare Krishna temple. I loved it.

Life is short, art is long. Follow your heart and intuition, as Jobs recounts in his legendary 2005 Stanford commencement address:

> Your time is limited, so don't waste it living someone else's life. Don't be trapped by dogma—which is living with the results of other people's thinking. Don't let the noise of others' opinions drown out your own inner voice. And most important, have the courage to follow your heart and intuition. They somehow already know what you truly want to become. Everything else is secondary.[77]

ISKCON or International Society for Krishna Consciousness, notes Subhamoy Das, stoked Jobs' interest in Eastern spirituality. In 1973, he traveled

[75] Anthony Imbimbo, *Steve Jobs: The Brilliant Mind Behind Apple* (Life Portraits) (New York: Gareth Stevens Publishing, 2009), 42.

[76] See: Paramahansa Yogananda, *God Talks with Arjuna, The Bhagavad Gītā: Royal Science of God-Realization* (The Immortal Dialog between soul and Spirit: A new translation and commentary) (Los Angeles, CA: Self-Realization Fellowship, 1995); also see Paramahansa Yogananda, *Autobiography of a Yogi* (New York, NY: The Philosophical Society, 1955). This classic spiritual autobiography inspired Jobs throughout his life.

[77] "You've got to find what you love," Jobs says. Text of the Commencement address delivered by Steve Jobs, CEO of Apple Computer and of Pixar Animation Studios, on June 12, 2005. Stanford News. Retrieved May 29, 2018: https://news.stanford.edu/2005/06/14/jobs-061505/

to India to study Hindu philosophy under the popular guru Neem Karoli Baba.[78] As Harsimran Julka wrote in *The Ecomonic Times*:[79]

> Steve Paul Jobs traversed the loopy roads of Uttarakhand and ended up at the ashram of Baba Neeb Karori, near Ranikhet. The mystic saint had just died. Jobs never got the enlightenment he was looking for, but did return to California in Indian clothes, and a Buddhist.

The greatest influence on Steve Jobs, however, was the book *Autobiography of a Yogi*—"the guide to meditation and spirituality that he had first read as a teenager," his biographer, Walter Isaacson, tells us, "then re-read in India and had read once a year ever since." It was the *only* book, Isaacson notes, that Steve downloaded on his personal ipad2.[80] Yogananda's book, which deals with Self-realization and the *Kriya Yoga* system of meditation, remained Steve's spiritual succor throughout his life.

It has recently come to be known that copies of Paramahansa Yogananda's classic autobiography were handed out at Steve Jobs's memorial, as reported by Marc Benioff, CEO and Co-Founder of Salesforce.Com, in a Tech Crunch Disrupt SF 2013 conference interview with CNET.com.[81] Marc shares his story of opening the brown box that was given to every guest at Steve Job's memorial service. Steve Jobs had apparently arranged to gift Paramahansa Yogananda's *Autobiography of a Yogi* in his own memorial service as a last gift to the attendees![82] Benioff, who regarded Jobs a mentor, further notes, "He had the incredible realization that his intuition was his greatest gift and he needed to look at the world from the inside out. Steve was a very spiritual person. In many ways he was a guru."[83]

Reading Isaacson's biography of Steve Jobs, it becomes clear that Jobs' involvement with Eastern spirituality was much more than a passing fad:

> Jobs's engagement with Eastern spirituality, and especially Zen Buddhism, was not just some passing fancy or youthful dabbling. He embraced it with his typical intensity, and it became deeply ingrained in his personality.[84]

[78] Subhamoy Das, Steve Jobs and Hinduism. *ThoughtCo*, September 11, 2017. Retrieved May 28, 2018: https://www.thoughtco.com/steve-jobs-and-hinduism-1770109

[79] Harsimran Julka, Steve Jobs resignation: India didn't offer enlightenment but changed his outlook. *The Economic Times*, August 26, 2011. Retrieved May 28, 2018: https://economictimes.indiatimes.com/news/international/steve-jobs-resignation-india-didnt-offer-enlightenment-but-changed-his-outlook/articleshow/9739049.cms

[80] Walter Isaacson, *Steve Jobs* (New York, NY: Simon & Schuster, 2011), 527.

[81] Marc Benioff on the Invisible Hand of Steve Jobs | *Disrupt SF* 2013. Interview Retrieved May 29, 2018 https://www.youtube.com/watch?v=4rO_Vs4M29k

[82] Walter Isaacson in his biography, *Steve Jobs*, lists a number of books that influenced Steve Jobs: William Shakespeare's *King Lear*, Plato, Clayton Christensen's *Innovator's Dilemma*, Shunryu Suzuki's *Zen Mind, Beginner's Mind*, Chogyam Trungpa's *Cutting Through Spiritual Materialism*, Paramahansa Yogananda's *Autobiography of a Yogi*, and Herman Melville's *Moby Dick*. See: Isaacson, *Steve Jobs*, 35.

[83] Yoga Journal Editors, Steve Jobs Studied Yoga, *Yoga Journal*, September 11, 2013. Retrieved June 2, 2018: https://www.yogajournal.com/blog/steve-jobs-studied-yoga

[84] Ibid., 35.

Was Steve Jobs a saint? Steve jobs had his share of human failings. He never pretended to be a saint. His 2005 Stanford Commencement Address shows him to be searching for deep spiritual answers to the perennial questions of life. In him we find a curious integration of Jim Collins's level five leader, marked by a paradoxical combination of compelling humility ("*stay hungry, stay foolish*") and fierce professional will ("*making a ding in the universe*"). A popular "Steve Jobs in heaven" cartoon has St. Peter introduce Jobs to Moses with the caption: "Moses, meet Steve. He's gonna upgrade your tablets"[85] That he arranged to gift *Autobiography of a Yogi* in his own memorial service as a last gift to the attendees tells a lot about what was on his mind during the final period of his life.[86]

Steve Jobs: Karma Yoga Lessons

Some say that Jobs' statement "I was worth over $1,000,000 when I was 23, and over $10,000,000 when I was 24, and over $100,000,000 when I was 25, and it wasn't that important because *I never did it for the money*," was directly inspired by this passage from the holy Indian scripture *Bhagavad Gītā*: "Relinquishing attachment to the fruits of work, always contented, independent (of material rewards), the wise do not perform any (binding) action even in the midst of activities."[87] This is verse 20 from chapter 4 of the Bhagavad Gītā, quoted from Paramahansa Yogananda's translation.[88] It presents the alchemy of *Karmayoga*,[89] the discipline of performing disinterested actions that are not binding on the doer. Jobs' assertion that "it (money) wasn't that important because *I never did it for the money*," represents his intention of doing his work "independent of material rewards."

The sages call that person wise, the Gītā 4.19 tells us, whose all undertakings are free from selfish desire and will, and whose actions are burnt in the fire of knowledge. The expression "fire of knowledge" needs some elaboration.

[85] Retrieved May 31, 2018: http://maypalo.com/2011/10/09/top-5-best-steve-jobs-in-heaven-comics/

[86] The Salesforce.com CEO admonishes Apple, as well as the movies and books about Steve Jobs' life, for failing to understand and honor the spiritual aspect of Jobs' personality. See: Dan Farber, Marc Benioff explains Steve Jobs' spirituality and chides Apple, September 10, 2013, *CNET Tech Industry News*. Retrieved June 2, 2018: https://www.cnet.com/news/marc-benioff-explains-steve-jobs-spirituality-and-chides-apple/

[87] James Morcan and Lance Morcan, *GENIUS INTELLIGENCE: Secret Techniques and Technologies to Increase IQ* (The Underground Knowledge Series) (Volume 1) (New York: Sterling Gate Books, 2016), 131. [emphasis added].

[88] Paramahansa Yogananda, *God Talks with Arjuna, The Bhagavad Gītā*, 472. See: Marco Pino's fine blog entry, Karma Yoga Lessons from Steve Jobs, September 12, 2011. This article was published, Marco Pino tells us, three weeks before Steve Jobs' death, October 5, 2011. Retrieved June 3, 2018: https://www.path2yoga.net/2011/09/karma-yoga-lessons-from-steve-jobs.html

[89] Karmayoga is the discipline of union (*yoga*) of the self with the Self through actions (*karma*) performed with a certain frame of mind—unprompted by the desire for self-centered material rewards.

The knowledge spoken of here—as well as throughout the Gītā—is the knowledge of the higher Self. The Gītā calls only that person as wise (*paṇḍitāḥ*) who has attained Self-knowledge (2.11). For such a person, all actions are understood to be performed by the interplay of the threefold constituents (*guṇas*) of material nature (*prakṛti*), as explained in the Gītā 3.27. Such a person, says the Gītā 3.28, is not bound by the actions, knowing that the *guṇas* (in the shape of senses, mind, etc.) express themselves in the *guṇas* (objects of perceptions). This "fire of knowledge" burns the binding effects of all actions, as stated in the Gītā 4.19.

One may ask, "How can one perform actions without expecting any reward since reward is the very motive for performing any action in the first place?" Moreover, why would one perform any action in the absence of any desire for results, as the Gītā is recommending? The Gītā says that wise perform actions to purify their mind (of attachment and aversion), without attachment to the results as an offering to the Divine (BG 5.10; 5.11). Steve Jobs tells us that he did what he did for the sheer love of it, and not for money; perhaps, as a matter of duty for duty's sake? While Apple Inc.'s goal may not be as exalted as the Gītā expects, however, the company has become successful doing what they love to do.

Since all actions have binding effect, the only way to free oneself from their effects is by forsaking [attachment to] their fruits (*karmaphalatyāga*):

> O Arjuna, remaining steadfast in Yoga, perform all actions, abandoning attachment (to their fruits), and remaining equanimous in success and failure. This mental evenness (*samatvaṃ*) is called Yoga. (BG 2.48)

In the final chapter, the Gītā tells us, "The three-fold results of actions—undesirable, desirable, and a mixture—exists after death for the nonrenunciates, but never for the renunciates."[90] Additionally, "O Arjuna, when dutiful action is performed solely because it should be done, forsaking attachment to it and its fruit, that renunciation is considered *sāttvic*."[91]

Whether Jobs achieved this level of perfection in *Karmayoga* is a matter of anyone's conjecture. There is a little doubt, however, that he "actualized himself" as he envisioned it.

Nelson Mandela and the Gītā: The Leader Who Spent 10,000 Days in Jail!

Of all the three leaders featured in this chapter, Nelson Mandela may at first seem to be the least likely candidate to be influenced by the teachings of the Gītā. However, we are told that Nelson Mandela had a very good knowledge

[90] Swami Dayananda Saraswati, *Śrīmad Bhagavad Gītā* (Text with Roman transliteration and English translation) (Chennai, India: Arsha Vidya Research and Publication Trust, 2007), 218.

[91] Paramahansa Yogananda, *God Talks with Arjuna, The Bhagavad Gītā*, 1022.

of the Gītā, that he learned from a fellow prisoner, who happened to be Indian, during his stay on Robben Island. In fact, he came several times to ISKCON's Ratha Yatra[92] in South Africa while he was president of the nation.

Sipho Kings of *Mail & Guardian*, a South African weekly newspaper, reports:

> Mandela had an intimate knowledge of the *Bhagavad Gītā* thanks to his time in prison. During his one visit to a temple he joined in conversation with its Swami, who quoted excerpts from the religion's founding text. Mandela finished his quotes, and challenged him to try find a part he did not know. Upon being asked, Mandela said that the apartheid government had tried to break the prisoners on Robben Island by giving them mindless labour and creating a monotonous routine. An Indian lawyer among the prisoners taught them verses of the text, and the group would quote and discuss it at length while they were working.[93]

"He was a caring man, a spiritual leader," notes Kesava Krishna dasa. "He accepted his shortcomings." This is why people were so willing to follow Madiba, because they immediately respected him and saw his humanity.[94]

Nelson Mandela certainly fulfils one of the Gītā's most important requirements to be a leader: selfless service. Familiar with the Gītā's verses, he probably was also aware of the alchemy of *karmayoga*: doing one's duty for duty's sake without the expectation of rewards (BG 3.19, 20). Even more so, Mandela concertedly worked for the wellbeing of his people (*sarva bhuta hitae* BG 5.25; 12.4) and for bringing the communities together (*lokasaṃgraham* BG 3.20). The Gītā mentions humility (*amānitvam*: 13.7) as a precondition to learning and forgiveness (*kṣamā*: 16.3) as one of the divine, *daivī*, qualities. In his ripe years, Mandela embodied engaged humility and forgiveness: two qualities that the Gītā exalts as essential in life and service.

It has been said that the function of leadership is to produce more leaders, not more followers. What is the alchemy of producing more leaders? Most of the time, it is about leading from behind. In his autobiography entitled *Long Walk to Freedom*, Nelson Mandela, equated a great leader with a shepherd: "A leader…is like a shepherd. He stays behind the flock, letting the most nimble go

[92] ISKCON stands for International Society for Krishna consciousness. Ratha Yatra (literally, chariot voyage) is an ancient celebratory parade/procession that originated 5000 years ago in India, on the East Coast state of Orrisa, in a city called Jagannatha Puri. For the festivities, there are three chariots, one for each of the three deities: Lord Jagannatha, Lord Balarama, and Lady Subhadra. The canopied chariots are decorated with flowers and balloons and are pulled with long, thick ropes by hundreds of people who ecstatically dance while chanting the sacred names of the Lord and sacred mantras. Retrieved June 1, 2018: http://festivalofchariots.com/

[93] Sipho Kings, Madiba and the Bhagavad Gītā. *Mail & Guardian*, December 8, 2013. Retrieved May 29, 2018: https://mg.co.za/article/2013-12-08-madiba-and-the-bhagavad-gita

[94] Ibid.

out ahead, whereupon the others follow, not realizing that all along they are being directed from behind."[95]

Elsewhere, Mandela states that "It is better to lead from behind and to put others in front, especially when you celebrate victory when nice things occur. You take the front line when there is danger. Then people will appreciate your leadership."[96] Within the short compass of these two quotes, Mandela encapsulates the leadership lessons he learnt having spent 10,000 days in jail over a period of 50 years of struggle (1944–1994) for ending bondage. Leading from behind is a leadership style whose time has come. It is a style that puts followers at the forefront of the leadership line. However, it requires supreme humility.

Was Nelson Mandela a saint-like figure? Although many viewed Mandela as such, citing qualities such as humility and forgiveness, yet there were "dissenting voices," says Hitendra Wadhwa, Professor of Practice at Columbia Business School and founder of the Institute for Personal Leadership (IPL). Professor Wadhwa quotes Mandela's staunch adversary, F.W. de Klerk, the last apartheid-era leader of South Africa, who said, "I do not subscribe to the general hagiography surrounding Mandela. He was by no means the avuncular and saint-like figure so widely depicted today."[97] Although F.W. de Klerk shared the Nobel Prize with Mandela for their work in ending apartheid, it is no secret that both were "fierce opponents." However, on the point of his own sainthood, notes Professor Wadhwa, Mandela actually agreed with de Klerk: "I was not a messiah, but an ordinary man who had become a leader because of extraordinary circumstances."[98]

Like all great leaders, Mandela approached universe as a university and life as a school. Professor Wadhwa narrates the following touching story:

> *Once, when he [Mandela] was in hiding at a friend's estate prior to his arrest and imprisonment, he shot and killed a sparrow with an air rifle in a prideful display of his firearms skills. As he turned to boast, his friend's five-year-old son turned to him with tears in his eyes and said, "Why did you kill that bird? Its mother will be sad." Mandela reflected, "I felt that this small boy had far more humanity than me. It was an odd sensation for a man who was the leader of a nascent guerrilla army."*[99]

John Carlin, the author of *Knowing Mandela* and *Playing the Enemy: Nelson Mandela and the Game that Made a Nation*, which was the basis for the film *Invictus*, once asked Archbishop Desmond Tutu, a Nobel peace prize winner

[95] Nelson Mandela, *Long Walk to Freedom: The Autobiography of Nelson Mandela* (New York, NY: Little, Brown and Company, 1995), 22.

[96] As quoted in Ryan Lizza, Leading from Behind. *New Yorker*, April 26, 2011. Retrieved May 31, 2018: http://www.newyorker.com/news/news-desk/leading-from-behind

[97] Hitendra Wadhwa, Nelson Mandela and the evolution of great leaders. *Fortune Magazine*, December 6, 2013. Retrieved July 16, 2017: http://fortune.com/2013/12/06/nelson-mandela-and-the-evolution-of-great-leaders/

[98] Ibid.

[99] Ibid.

like Mandela and one of the people who knew him most intimately, if he could define Mandela's greatest quality. Tutu thought for a moment and then—triumphantly—uttered one word: magnanimity. "Yes," he repeated, more solemnly the second time, almost in a whisper. "Magnanimity!"[100]

Adds Carlin: "There is no better word to define Mandela. No leader more big-hearted, more regal, more generously wise. Not now and, quite possibly, not ever."

In the opening verse of chapter 9 of the Bhagavad Gītā, we find "magnanimity" (*anasūyave*) as the qualification to receive higher knowledge. Mandela was free from the defect of calumny or carping spirit, which made him eminently qualified to understand the profound mystery of oneness of all humanity—an ideal to which he devoted 50 years of his life.

The Bhagavad Gītā: Spiritual Dictionary of Gandhi

It is well-known that the Bhagavad Gītā was Gandhi's moral and spiritual anchorage. He regarded the Gītā as his "dictionary of daily conduct"[101] and turned to it throughout his life for guidance and solace during moments of doubts, difficulties, and gloom. He translated the Gītā into his native *Gujarati* and pondered over it incessantly until its message got inscribed on the tablet of his heart.

Soon, the Gītā became "an infallible guide of conduct"[102] for Gandhi and he began to pattern his whole life on its lofty teachings. To put into practice the concepts that he gleaned from the Gītā, such as *aprigraha* (non-possession) and *samabhāva* (equanimity), became his constant challenge: "How was one to divest oneself of all possessions? Was not the body itself possession enough? Was I to give up all I had and follow Him?" As he wrestled with such questions, straight came the answer in the form of inner renunciation: "I could not follow Him unless I gave up all I had."[103] He allowed his insurance policy to lapse and gave all he had saved up to that moment to his brother and pledged all future savings, if any, to "be utilized for the benefit of community."[104] Such was the sincerity of this pilgrim of the soul who gave up all that was inessential and extra on the journey to the Divine.

Where did Gandhi get the certitude of his moral conviction? What were the sources of his moral and spiritual anchorage? We believe that it was indeed the Bhagavad Gītā! "At the back of my reading of Gītā," writes Gandhi, "there is the claim of an endeavor to enforce the meaning in my own conduct for an

[100] John Carlin, Nelson Mandela: The freedom fighter who embraced his enemies. *The Guardian*, December 7, 2013. Retrieved July 16, 2107: https://www.theguardian.com/world/2013/dec/07/nelson-mandela-freedom-fighter-john-carlin

[101] M. K. Gandhi, *An Autobiography: The Story of My Experiments with Truth* (New York, NY: Dover Publications, 1983), 233.

[102] Ibid.

[103] Ibid.

[104] Ibid.

unbroken period of forty years."[105] Gandhi interpreted the Gītā as the "Gospel of Selfless Action" (*Anāsaktiyoga*).[106] The key Gandhian concepts such as selfless actions (*niṣkāmakarma*), nonviolence (*ahiṁsā*), steadfastness in truth (*sthitaprajñatā*), and non-possession (*aparigraha*) proceed directly from his unique interpretation of the Gītā. By reflecting deeply on the import of the Gītā's teachings, it became clear to Gandhi that his path is the path of Self-realization through service to humanity and he made efforts and experiments at every moment of his life to come closer to this goal.

The Gītā's goal of Self-realization and its doctrine of selfless action (*niṣkāma karma*) defined Gandhi's *modus operandi*: choose the right goal (common good) and follow the right means (nonviolence) and be detached from the results (by dedicating them to the Supreme Lord). Gandhi once eloquently paraphrased this formula when he replied to an English Quaker who was complaining about being ignored by the media, "Throw the right stone into the right pond, let the ripples take care of themselves."[107] Gandhi defined "right" in terms of "harmlessness" or "nonviolence," which provided the foundation for his core strategy—*Satyagraha*. He took quite an expansive view of nonviolence to denote not just non-injury, but a positive force of love and compassion.

This greater regard for the right means above desired ends served as a moral compass for Gandhi throughout his life and defined all and everything that he undertook in his personal and political life, which to him constituted one undivided whole. Nevertheless, Gandhi did not regard the Gītā as a book only for the learned; he found its message to be eminently *practical* and meant to be *lived*. It has been rightly observed that the Gītā is "catholic in its message, comprehensive in its outlook, and concrete in its suggestions."[108] Gandhi believed that its teachings can be easily understood and put into practice by all, to whatever race or religion, time or clime they may belong.

The most distinctive spiritual tenet Gandhi learned from the Gītā was perhaps the truth of One Reality that pervades all and everything in the universe. This non-dual Reality is called Brahman (the Absolute) and is the very Self (Ātman) of everyone and everything. He who perceives the one Divine principle dwelling in all beings as their very Self cannot harm another, for the Self cannot harm itself. This provided the ontological support for Gandhi's categorical adherence to nonviolence and selfless service. This understanding in turn paved the way to strive for spiritual and moral perfection, the twin preconditions to Self-realization, signifying the summum bonum for Gandhi. Gandhi once said, "Our greatness lies not so much in being able to *remake the*

[105] M. K. Gandhi in John Strohmeier (Ed.), *The Bhagavad Gītā According to Gandhi* (Berkeley, CA: Berkeley Hills Books, 2000), 16.

[106] Ibid., 14.

[107] Michael N. Nagler, *Gītā Theory of Action*. Retrieved June 8, 2018: https://mettacenter.org/definitions/gloss-concepts/gita-theory-of-action/

[108] P. Nagaraja Rao, *Introduction to Vedanta* (Bombay, India: Bharatiya Vidya Bhavan, 1966), 102.

world as being able to *remake ourselves*."[109] It is only through internalizing Self-knowledge that leaders are able to truly "remake" themselves and fulfill their mission.

The greatest lesson that Gandhi learned from his lifetime study of the Gītā was karma yoga—a discipline he lived his life by: *use the right means for a just cause and leave the results in hands of God.*[110]

Concluding Thoughts

What kind of lamp can I light
for the one who has lit
the sky with stars?
O Nanak…
Light the lamp within!

This translation of an important verse from Guru Nanak Dev ji underscores the importance of lighting the lamp of Self-knowledge within. With it shining, everything in the world shines. Self-knowledge deals with who and what we truly are. It is the unchanging, ever-present awareness of our own being. Self-knowledge is not a journey of *becoming*; it is a state of *being*. It is a journey from unreal "me" to the real "I." In the final reckoning, Self-knowledge is the harbinger of all that is true, beautiful, and good in our life and work—the hallmarks of fulfillment and flourishing. Self-awareness born of Self-knowledge is the hallmark of all authentic leaders, since it helps those in leadership positions lead from their true self. In its wake, it bestows the gift of genuine humility, paving the way for selfless service and, finally, for servant leadership. As leaders, when we are in touch with our deeper authentic self, we are also able to connect with the authentic self of others.

Only when we find higher meaning and purpose and seek to live in accord with moral and spiritual principles will we find true happiness, peace, and fulfillment. The unbridled worship of individualism, greed, pride, fame, and consumerism are contrary to the virtues of truth, love and justice. Developing moral and spiritual virtues can help us transcend self-centeredness and create a caring, compassionate society built on the values of truth, love and justice. By seeking perennially who we truly are and serving selflessly, we may redeem our existence and be fulfilled. "The mark of the immature man," said J.D. Salinger, "is that he wants to die nobly for a cause, while the mark of the mature man is that he wants to live humbly for one."[111] The leaders whom we call good and great lived as well as died for the causes they believed in. There is no calling

[109] Eknath Easwaran, *The Compassionate Universe: The Power of the Individual to Heal the Environment* (Tomales, CA: Nilgiri Press, 1989), 20 (emphasis added).

[110] For detailed information on how the Gītā permeated Gandhi's life and leadership, refer to the chapter titled "Be the Change: The Making of a Servant Leader."

[111] J. D. Salinger, *Catcher in the Rye* (New York, NY: Little, Brown and Company, 1991), 224.

higher than living humbly for a noble cause. It is the path of loving service and altruistic love. This is the hallmark of all great leaders. A fulfilled life is gratifying consequence of selfless service.

The lives of great leaders such as Mother Teresa, Nelson Mandela, Martin Luther King, Jr., and Mahatma Gandhi bear testimony to the fact that the greatest fulfillment in life comes from serving others. Gandhi devoted all his life to serving his country and its people and found deepest fulfillment through serving. His life serves as a beacon of light to all humanity. Likewise, Mother Teresa was a prime example of selfless service. Her entire life revolved around helping others in need—the poorest of the poor. As a result, she experienced a great deal of affection and self-fulfillment in her life. As a US Marine who handed out food and blankets to tsunami victims in 2004 said, "I have been serving my country for 34 years and this is the first day I've gotten any fulfillment out of it."

Lao Tzu, the great Chinese sage, stated so well, "A leader is best when people barely know he exists, when his work is done, his aim fulfilled, they will say: we did it ourselves." He recognized the importance of humility as the key ingredient of leadership for only the humble can truly serve a cause higher than themselves.

As human beings, we seem to be eternally caught in the vicious cycle of becoming. There is this desire for "being" and the struggle for "becoming." The world of becoming lies outside and is teeming with competition, comparison, aggression, and acquisition. It is a path without any final destination and a race with no visible finish line. The world of being lies within us and is paved with Self-knowledge, contentment, contemplation, and understanding. It is already within our reach and ever-attained. Struggle for becoming brings unstable anchors and invariably leads to unhappiness, anxiety, stress, and strife. Being is the road that verily leads to happiness, peace, serenity, and fulfillment. Being-centered leadership is the fulfillment of operating from our true authentic self, from the core of our being.

The Gītā's formulation of personal mastery of a Self-aware sage largely centers on emotional maturity—the ability to manage emotional disturbances and reactions calmly. It symbolizes the enlightened sage (*jñāni*), who remains ever steadfast and essentially unaffected by the ebb and flow of life, even though fully engaged in the proceedings of the world. This is the wisdom we need in life and leadership during these turbulent times.

We conclude this chapter with a quote from Einstein that urges us to free ourselves from the optical illusion of separation by widening our circle of compassion, and anticipates the essence of *jñāna yoga*:

> A human being is a part of the whole, called by us "Universe," a part limited in time and space. He experiences himself, his thoughts and feelings as something separated from the rest—a kind of optical delusion of his consciousness. This delusion is a kind of prison for us, restricting us to our personal desires and to affection for a few persons nearest to us. Our task must be to free ourselves from

this prison by widening our circle of compassion to embrace all living creatures and the whole of nature in its beauty. Nobody is able to achieve this completely, but the striving for such achievement is in itself a part of the liberation and a foundation for inner security.[112]

[112] Letter of 1950, as quoted in *The New York Times* (March 29, 1972) and *The New York Post* (November 28, 1972). The New Quotable Einstein by Alice Calaprice (Princeton University Press, 2005: ISBN 0691120749), 206, has a slightly different and presumably more accurate version of this letter, which she dates to February 12, 1950 and describes as "a letter to a distraught father who had lost his young son and had asked Einstein for some comforting words":

> A human being is a part of the whole, called by us "Universe," a part limited in time and space. He experiences himself, his thoughts and feelings as something separate from the rest—a kind of optical delusion of his consciousness. The striving to free oneself from this delusion is the one issue of true religion. Not to nourish it but to try to overcome it is the way to reach the attainable measure of peace of mind.

CHAPTER 7

Bhakti Yoga: Love and Faith in Leadership

INTRODUCTION[1]

This chapter presents the path of divine love and devotion (*bhakti yoga*) as a means of yoking the mind to the highest principle, being, or intelligence. A person who treads this path is called a devotee, a *bhakta*, one who has given all his heart and all his mind to the Divine within. It is a path of humility, service, faith,[2] and devotion. In Hinduism, as in some other major world religions, the *bhakti yoga* is a spiritual path of loving devotion to a personal God. The Gītā postulates two main paths to spiritual freedom—*karma yoga*: the pursuit of enlightened action and *jñāna yoga*, the pursuit of Self-knowledge (BG 3.3). Bhakti yoga is considered a necessary concomitant to both *karma yoga* and *jñāna yoga*, for without loving devotion to the ideal of action or knowledge, it is not possible to succeed in either the pursuit of action or Self-knowledge.

One of the most important applications of *bhakti yoga* is by way of treating everything as sacred invested with intrinsic goodness and meaning. *Bhakti yoga* bestows the perspective that everyone and everything has a purpose. Essentially, it means a feeling of oneness (at-one-ment) with the whole of existence

[1] In presenting the path of *bhakti yoga* in this chapter, we will be primarily guided by Swāmī Shrī Rāmsukhdāsjī's interpretations, as stated in his two main commentarial works in *Hindi* on the Gītā, namely, "*Sādhaka-Sañjīvanī*" and "*Gītā Prabōdhani.*" Swāmī Rāmsukhdāsjī was a unique (*vilakṣana*) saint. He was actually saints' saint! He ceaselessly devoted all his waking hours (of 100+ years of his life) pondering over the deep mysteries of the Gītā. The Gītā permeated in every atom of his body, mind, and soul. In our humble opinion, this kind of dedication to a single scripture has seldom been seen before! And this is what makes Swāmījī's observations supremely authentic and precious.

[2] The use of the word "faith" here requires some clarification. It is not used in the sense of "blind" faith in the form of some religious dogma. It means initial belief in some teaching, pending verification. It means "religious spirit" or loving devotion to an ideal. The proper Sanskrit term for faith is *śradhā*.

S. Dhiman, *Bhagavad Gītā and Leadership*,
Palgrave Studies in Workplace Spirituality and Fulfillment,
https://doi.org/10.1007/978-3-319-67573-2_7

(*sarvātmabhāva*) and seeing God in everything and everything in God. This understanding lends a certain sanctity to all of our activities and helps foster an environment of empathy, kinship, and solidarity. This reclaiming of the sacred dimension of life is sorely needed in the present-day world plagued by distrust, disengagement, and disharmony. The chapter will conclude with leadership lessons based on the path of loving devotion.

What is the essence of bhakti yoga according to the Gītā? According to Swāmī Shrī Rāmsukhdāsjī, who devoted his whole life to pondering over the deep mysteries of the Gītā, "Taking refuge in the Lord (*śarṇāgati*) is the quintessence of the entire message of the Gītā." S. K. Maitra concurs: "the final instruction is: surrender."[3] In surrendering to the Lord lies the culmination of the Gītā's teachings. The devotee who has taken refuge in the Lord accepts firmly the belief that "I am God's and God is mine." Then the devotee becomes forever free from the pangs of fear, sorrow, worry, and so on. This is the glory of the path of devotion: a life free from sorrow, fear, and worry. It is precisely in bestowing such freedom that the value of the path of divine love, *bhakti yoga*, lies in life and leadership.

Paths to Attaining Spiritual Freedom: True Message of the Gītā?

Of the two preeminent classical commentators on the Gītā—Śaṅkarācārya and Rāmānujācārya—Śaṅkarā considered the path of knowledge (*jñāna yoga*) to be the most important discipline to reach spiritual liberation or *mokṣa*. The liberating knowledge according to Śaṅkarā consists of realizing one's identity with the Ultimate Reality. Śaṅkarā categorically states in his Vedantic classic, *Vivekacūḍāmaṇi*, the Crest Jewel of Wisdom, "Without the realization of one's identity with the Brahman, the Self, there shall be no liberation for the individual, not even in the life times of hundred Brahmas put together."[4] In the same text, he says that, among the means of attaining liberation, *bhakti* (devotion) reigns supreme. He defines *bhakti* in a very special manner, as follows: "A constant contemplation of one's own Real Nature is called devotion."[5]

[3] S. K. Maitra, *The Spirit of Indian Philosophy* (Allahabad, India: The Indian Press, 1947), 103.

[4] आत्मैक्यबोधेन विनापि मुक्तिः
न सिध्यति ब्रह्मशतान्तरेऽपि ॥ ६॥

See: Pranipata Chaitanya and Satinder Dhiman, translated by Chaitanya & edited with notes and an introducation by Dhiman, *Śrī Śaṅkarā's Vivekacūḍāmaṇi: Devanāgari Text, Transliteration, Word-for-Word Meaning, Notes, and a Lucid Translation* (Burbank, CA: House of Metta, An Imprint of ASPEX, 2012), 54.

[5] Ibid., 82.

मोक्षकारणसामग्र्यां भक्तिरेव गरीयसी ।
स्वस्वरूपानुसन्धानं भक्तिरित्यभिधीयते ॥ ३१॥

For Rāmānuja, service (*upāsana*) to Śrī Kṛṣṇa Vasudeva, the Supreme Being, in the form of devotion (*Bhakti*) is the most important discipline. R.C. Zaehner, an impartial and objective scholar who served as a Spalding Professor of Eastern Religions and Ethics at the University of Oxford during the 1950s, finds Rāmānuja's interpretation to be "nearer in spirit to the Gītā."[6] In Zaehner's estimate, Rāmānuja comes nearest to the mind of the author of the Gītā. "In his commentary as elsewhere," notes Zaehner, "Rāmānuja is concerned with establishing the absolute supremacy of the personal God (Śrī Kṛṣṇa) not only over the phenomenal world but also over the impersonal Absolute, Brahman."[7]

Zaehner finds the Gītā to be a far more unitary work than most modern scholars had been prepared to admit; and it was this realization that impelled him to prepare an edition of his own. Zaehner decries that "most recent translations of the Gītā (particularly the more popular ones) have not been accurate at all, and by both being inaccurate and theologically biased, a very false view of what the Gītā actually says has been passed off on an unsuspecting public."[8]

Describing his own growing familiarity with the text, Zaehner further notes that "as he grew more familiar with the text, it became evermore insistently clear to me that here was a text the whole purpose of which seemed to me to demonstrate that love of a personal God, so far from being *only* a convenient preparation for the grand unitary experience of spiritual 'liberation' (the *mokṣa* or mukti of the Upaniṣads and the *vimutti* of the Buddhists), was also the crown of this experience itself which, without it, must remain imperfect."[9] To support his position, Zaehner quotes a celebrated French interpreter of the Gītā, Lamotte, who writes, "Contrary to what one might suppose, the return of the soul into Brahman is not yet the final stage (*térme definitif*) or at least the exact expression of perfect deliverance. Śrī Kṛṣṇa who has supplanted the Brahman both in theodicy and in cosmology now surpasses it in eschatology too: it is union with Śrī Kṛṣṇa, the Bhagavat, which is the ultimate and final stage of deliverance."[10]

The Gītā is a scripture of small size. Its Sanskrit is simple. However, its meaning is very deep and profound. In describing various spiritual disciplines, in making their meanings abundantly clear, and in restating every single discipline in various ways, it spares no elaboration. Yet, the size of this scripture has not become too voluminous. There is perhaps no other such scripture that is so *brief in its details*!

[6] R. C. Zaehner, *The Bhagavad-Gītā with a Commentary Based on Original Sources* (London, Great Britain: Oxford University Press, 1973), 3.

[7] Ibid., 8.

[8] Ibid., 2.

[9] Ibid., 3.

[10] Ibid., 3.

Universality of the Gītā's Teachings[11]

The message of the Gītā is for everyone who is interested in attaining their spiritual freedom. The sole purpose of the Gītā is the salvation of all of humankind. Regardless of one's race, religion, or philosophical orientation, one can attain one's spiritual welfare by following its teachings. In the following paragraphs, we will explain how one can practice the universal teachings of the Gītā while following one's own religious tradition or belief system.

The Gītā teaches us that every human being can realize the Divine in every life-situation; verily, God-realization is every human being's birthright. One can attain one's spiritual welfare even amidst an extreme situation like a war. In this manner, the Gītā teaches the great art of seeking the highest spiritual good in ordinary, practical matters (व्यवहार में परमार्थ की कला *vyavahār mein paramārath ki kalā*). We have not come across another scripture of its kind that shows the path for the salvation of all of humankind.

Some people say that the Gītā's teachings were imparted to prod Arjuna to engage in the war. However, this is not so in reality. The Lord did not prompt Arjuna to war, but made him aware of his righteous duty. Besides, given that Arjuna was from the warrior class, war was his rightful duty anyway. It was Arjuna's own idea after all to engage in the war (BG 1.20–22); he himself became inclined to the war—that is why he himself invited the Lord to war. But Arjuna became disinclined to war due to the sorrow and delusion (*śōka-mōha*)—aroused by filial piety—and was retreating from fulfilling his prescribed duty (as a member of the warrior class).

After seeing his kinsmen, Arjuna became confused and entertained the thought, "I will not fight"—"*na yotsya*" (Gītā 2.9). After listening to the message of the Lord, Arjuna did *not* say, "Okay, I will fight now." Rather, he said, "I will do as You command"—"*kariṣye vacanaṃ tava*" (Gītā 18.73); that is, "I will fulfill my duty." From these words of Arjuna, it becomes evident that Śrī Kṛṣṇa did not prompt Arjuna to war, but only made him aware of his natural duty.[12]

Like all theistic systems, the Gītā also postulates a simple threefold structure of reality to which every discerning person can relate: the world (*jagat*), the individual self (*jīva*), and God (*Paramātmā*—i.e., Supreme Being/Consciousness); besides these three, there is no other entity. Regarding these three subjects, there are divergent opinions and different schools of thoughts that have given rise to heated debates and discussions. It is beyond the scope of this chapter to recount all of them here. The Gītā stays clear of all such controversies and states

[11] Partially based on an essay entitled "*Gītā kā Tātprya*" from Swāmī Rāmsukhdāsjī's Hindi book जित देखूँ तित तू "*Jit Deikhun Tit Tu.*"

[12] After presenting the entire teachings of the Gītā, Śrī Kṛṣṇā points out, "Thus has this wisdom, more mysterious than the mystery itself, been imparted to you by Me. Fully pondering over it, *do as you like.*" (BG 18.63).

in a straightforward manner that whatever we see right in front of our own eyes is the world: we all have a vivid experience of the world characterized by activities and objects (*kriya aur padāratha*). Similarly, everyone has a vivid experience of their being or existence or self by way of a sense of "I-am-ness." We do not need the testimony of any scripture to know that the "world exists" *out there* and that "we exist" *in here*. This is a law that, at the root of every creation, there is some creator. The common creator of us all, the Lord of all and everything—the sentient and the insentient creation—is *Īśvara* (God).

In this tri-partite structure of reality, the Gītā introduces a unique viewpoint, in that if someone does not believe in God, they too can seek their highest spiritual welfare by following the teachings of the Gītā! It teaches the great art of seeking the highest spiritual good amidst the ordinary practical matters. It teaches us to perform our dutiful actions, with the spirit of sacrifice (*yajña*), for the supreme wellbeing of each other. By cherishing each other in this manner, we will attain our supreme good (BG 3.11). It further assures us that "by properly performing one's duty, everyone attains perfection" (BG 18.45). While many scriptures enjoin the renunciation of the world to attain God, the Gītā teaches us that one can attain perfection by worshiping God (who is the source of all creation and is all pervading) *through* the performance of one's ordained duties—*svakarmaṇā tam abhyarcya siddhiṃ vindati mānavaḥ* (BG 18.46).

The Gītā teaches us how to attain the highest spiritual good while interacting with the world. When we fulfill all our duties selflessly, remaining equanimous in success and failure, we attain the same goal (God-realization) that has been attained by sages and seers by undergoing years and years of spiritual regimen. In a seminal verse of the Gītā (2.48), Arjuna is advised to perform actions, renounce attachment, and remain steadfast in equanimity. According to the Gītā, this equanimity or even-mindedness is called *yoga*. This discipline of equanimity, the supreme *yoga* of the Gītā, is equally available to all seekers under all circumstances.

We experience the world in the form of actions, objects, and situations. Experience and observation soon bring about the realization that, to the making of actions and objects, there is no end. Therefore, in order to realize the highest principle or God-essence, one has to sever one's identification with actions and objects. The Gītā explains the technique to sever our affinity with actions and objects through the threefold discipline of the path of action (*karma yoga*), the path of knowledge (*jñāna yoga*), and the path of devotion (*bhakti yoga*). For example, the *karma yogi* renounces attachment to actions and objects by applying them for the welfare of others (BG 5.25; 12.4); the *jñāna yogi* attains freedom by remaining unattached to actions and objects (3.28; 5.8; 13.29); and the *bhakti yogi* surrenders actions and objects to God (BG 11.55; 18.62, 18.65). According to the teachings of the Gītā, by surrendering all actions and objects to God, one easily attains salvation by becoming free from the sorrow and delusion of the conditioned existence (BG 18.66).

Swāmī Rāmsukhdāsjī, a saint who devoted all his life to pondering over the profound mysteries of the Bhagavad Gītā, used to say that the word *yoga* (union) should more properly be used in the context of *karma yoga* because, with regards to the paths of knowledge (*jñāna yoga*) and devotion (*bhakti yoga*), the "union" is quite natural. The seer, after realizing that God is all, remains naturally established in the experience of Oneness; and the devotee likewise constantly experiences reverential union with the Lord by keeping the mind and the thoughts fixed on God. It is because the path of actions is marred by selfish desire and attachment to results that we need to "attain union"—*yoga*—through *karma yoga*.

Thus, through equanimity, service, detachment, and surrender, the Gītā teaches the art of spirituality while being deeply engaged in the worldly conduct.

Three Disciplines: Yogas for Salvation

There are only three disciplines or paths for the salvation of human beings—the path of action (*karma yoga*), the path of knowledge (*jñāna yoga*), and the path of devotion (*bhakti yoga*). Besides these three, there is no other path for salvation—"*nopāyo 'nyo 'sti kutracit*" (*Śrīmad Bhāgavatam* 11.20.6). All other disciplines are included within these three. It is because the human beings are endowed with three powers—the power to do, the power to know, and the power to accept (or believe). For the proper use of these powers, human beings are endowed with a physical body to "do," an intellect to "know," and a heart to "believe." *Karma yoga* is meant for the proper use of the power to "do"; *jñāna yoga* for the proper use of the power to "know"; and *bhakti yoga* is meant for the proper use of the power to "accept" or "believe." A person with a penchant for actions is fit for *karma yoga*; a person with a penchant for discrimination is fit for *jñāna yoga*; and a person with a penchant for feelings is fit for *bhakti yoga*.

As stated earlier, there are verily three entities—the world (*jagat*), the self or the soul (*ātmā*), and God (*Paramātmā*). *Karma yoga* belongs to the world, *jñāna yoga* belongs to the self, and *bhakti yoga* belongs to God. Devoting what we have received from the world—such as our physical body, and so on—in the service of the world without expecting anything in return is called *karma yoga* (Gītā 3.11; 4.23; 18.45). To sever one's affinity with the objects that are transitory and fleeting by not identifying with them with a sense of "I" or "mine" is called *jñāna yoga* (Gītā 3.27). Considering only God as one's own and dedicating all undertakings and objects to God—and taking complete refuge in God—is called *bhakti yoga* (Gītā 7.26–27; 18.66). The follower of the path of action (*karma yogi*) severs their relationship with the world through service; the *jñāna yogi* severs relations with world through renunciation (of doership); and the *bhakti yogi* severs affinity with the world by establishing a relationship with, and surrendering to, the Lord, whose veritable part the embodied soul is.

Through *karma yoga* and *jñāna yoga*, one attains salvation; and through *bhakti yoga*, one attains the Love Supreme. If one is free from insistence on (and bias about) one's own spiritual discipline and one does not condemn other spiritual disciplines, then one verily attains perfection in *all* the three paths by following *any one* of the three *yogas*. Because, after one has attained abidance in one's self or after salvation (*mokṣa*), a fragment (*aṁśa*) naturally develops attraction (love) toward the totality (*aṁśī*) or God. *In the attainment of that Love Supreme lies the fulfillment of human life!*

The Gītā is a universally respected scripture. It is neither interested in supporting or rejecting a particular philosophy or viewpoint. That is why we find numerous commentaries on it by the followers of various spiritual traditions. The Lord has said, "*Gītā mei hṛdayaṁ Pārtha*: O Pārtha, the Gītā is my very heart." It is gem of a scripture, in which we can find the complete essence of the path of action (*karma yoga*), the path of knowledge (*jñāna yoga*), and the path of devotion (*bhakti yoga*). In it, Śrī Kṛṣṇā has revealed the innermost spiritual secrets to his dearest friend and devotee, Arjuna. Such matters are not meant to be revealed to all and sundry. It is an endearing dialog between two friends. It is a supremely mysterious scripture.

Essentials of Bhakti Yoga: The Path of Loving Devotion

To underscore the Divine glories of the Lord and present a systematic methodology of attaining *bhakti* (loving devotion) of the Lord, we provide select extracts from chapters 7–12 and 15[13]:

Śrī Bhagavān said—"O Conqueror of Wealth (Arjuna)! There is no being higher than I am in this whole universe; that is, the whole creation is strung on Me like a row of beads threaded on a string. I am the source and the root-cause of all that is visible in the world. O son of *Kuntī*, I am the 'taste' of water, the 'light' of the all the *Vedas*; I am the 'sound' in space, 'manliness' in men, sacred 'fragrance' in earth, and 'brilliance' in fire. I am also the life-giving principle—the '*prāṇaśaktī*' in all living beings, and I am the 'penance' of all ascetics. O Pārtha! I am the eternal (indestructible) 'seed' of all beings." (BG 7.7–10)

"O Best among Bhāratas! Of the brave, I am the 'strength' devoid of desire and attachment; and in living beings, I am virtuous 'desire.' What more can I say, whatever emanations (qualities, objects, and activities) there are, born of *sattva* (goodness/purity), *rajas* (activity/passion), and *tamas* (inertia/dullness), know them all to have evolved (or proceeding) from Me alone. But neither do I exist in them, nor do they (*guṇas*) exist in Me. It means that these modes (*guṇas*) have no independent existence apart from me—that is, I alone am everything. Therefore, the mind of the aspirant should be directed toward Me and not toward the three modes. However, accepting the independent existence of the objects evolved from these three modes (*guṇas*), the individual

[13] See: Satinder Dhiman, trans., *Sahaja Gītā* (chapters 7–11).

self (*jīva*) gets attached to them, and consequently, becomes subject to repeated births and deaths. That is why the *jīva* does not know Me as the Eternal One, standing beyond these three *guṇas*, and does not turn toward Me." (BG 7.11–13)

Śrī Bhagavān said—"Although it is extremely difficult to break free from this Divine Veil (*Māyā*) of Mine, consisting of *sattva, rajas,* and *tamas guṇas*, yet those, who take refuge in Me alone, are able to cross over this *Māyā*. There are four types of righteous people who worship Me: the distressed (*ārta*), the seeker of security and pleasure (*arthārthī*), the one who desires to know Me (*jijñāsur*), and the one who knows Me (*jñānī*). All these are exalted indeed; however, the wise person (*jñānī*—those who know me as their very Self) is myself alone. In the very last of all the births, namely, in this human form, one who has experientially realized the truth '*vāsudevaḥ sarvam*'—that is, everything is verily God—only that devotee is truly wise and great (7:19). For such a devotee, there is no reality apart from one God—this is the divine refuge (*śarṇāgati*) for him. Such a great-souled devotee (*bhakta*) is very rare indeed to find in this world." (BG 7.14–19)

In chapter 8, Śrī Bhagavān explains the process of fixing one's thoughts on the Lord at the time of death—"One who has not been able to attain Me while living, at the time of death, leaves the body thinking of Me, attains to Me alone; regarding this, there is no doubt. It is a law that the thoughts at the time of death determine the future of the soul. Depending upon the thoughts at the end, the 'mental body' (*mānsīka śarīra*) is formed, and one attains another body based on the mental body. The end-time can come upon anytime, for there is no such time when the end-time (death) cannot befall. Therefore, if you want to attain Me by remembering me at the time of death, then dwell on Me constantly at all times, and fight the battle of life. Surrendering your mind and intellect to Me, by not identifying with them, you will always dwell on Me only. As a result, you will undoubtedly attain to Me only." (BG 8.5–7)

Śrī Bhagavān now explains the process of attaining the attributeless and formless Brahman—"I shall now briefly (and clearly) describe for you That Ultimate Reality, the attributeless and formless ('*Nirguṇa-Nirākār*') Supreme State described by the knowers of the *Vedas* as the Imperishable, which ascetics free from passion achieve, and, desiring to attain which, the aspirants lead a life of celibacy (*brahmacārya*). Having closed all the doors of senses, having resolved the mind in the heart, having restrained the life-breath in the head (tenth gate—*dasam dwār*), and remaining steadfastly established in the *yogic* concentration, the aspirant (*sādhaka*) who leaves the body mentally uttering the One Imperishable OM, and remembering the attributeless and formless, attains the Supreme Goal of realizing the Absolute (the attributeless and the formless, Brahman)." (BG 8.11–13)

"O Pārtha! It is very difficult for everyone to attain to the *Nirguṇa-Nirākār* (Brahman) as described above. But it is very easy to attain to My '*Saguṇa-Sākār*'

Svarupa (with attributes and with form). I am easily attainable (*sulabhaḥ*)[14] by the ever-steadfast *yogī*, who, thinking of none else except Me, remembers Me constantly (from now till death and from waking till falling sleep deeply). Having attained Me, by being fully established in supreme devotion (*param-prem*), the great souls are no longer subject to rebirth in this world, which is the abode of sorrow, and is constantly subject to change. O Son of Kuntī (Arjuna)! All the worlds extending from the earth to the realm of Brahmā are subject to rebirth; having gone there, the embodied soul (*jīva*) has to come back again to *saṅsāra* (the mortal world, the realm of unending cyclic existence). But, O Son of Kuntī! After attaining Me, there is no return to the mortal world or rebirth again. O Arjuna! You too, at all times, be motiveless and be steadfast in the *yoga* of equanimity." (BG 8.14–16)

"The *yogī* who understands (the essence of) the subject matter of this chapter, does not get entangled in the worldly enjoyments, and becomes steadfast in My devotion. Therefore, such a *yogī*, transcending all the rewards of meritorious deeds assigned to the study of the *Vedas*, pious sacrifices (*yajñās*), austerities and charities, attains to the Supreme Primal Abode." (BG 8.27–28).

In chapter 9, continuing the theme of *Bhakti*, Śrī Bhagavān explains the yoga of royal mystic knowledge, thus—"This whole universe is pervaded by My unmanifest form or Divinity (*Nirākār-rupa*). All beings exist in Me, but in *reality* I do not exist in them nor do they exist in Me. This is My divine mystery! Though I am the source of all things and support of all beings, yet, I do not dwell in them—that is, I am ever-devoid of any attachment (to them). As the mighty wind, blowing everywhere ever abides in the space, and cannot exist apart from the space, even so all beings roaming in various life-forms and worlds, abide in Me and cannot exist apart from Me. Accept this truth with a steadfast mind." (BG 9.4–6)

Then, Śrī Bhagavān explains the relative simplicity of performing His worship—"My worship is very easy also as compared to that of the deities. Whosoever makes an offering to Me, with devotion, of any object (that is spontaneously received) such as a leaf, a flower, a fruit or (even) water, I gladly accept that devout offering of the pure in heart, because I value the sentiment (*bhāva*) and not the object. Therefore, O Son of Kuntī! Whatever you do, whatever you eat, whatever you give as donation, whatever you offer as sacrifice, and whatever austerities you perform, do that as an offering unto Me. By offering all objects and activities to Me, you will become free from

[14] According to Swami Ramsukhdasji, the word "*sulabhaḥ*" (easily) is used by the Lord *only once* in the context of spiritual practices to attain God. In all the 574 *ślokas* spoken by Bhagavān Śrī Kṛṣṇa, the word "*sulabhaḥ*" occurs only once in the entire Gītā! Hence, its great importance. The great-souled devotee (*bhakta*) who has experientially realized the truth "*vāsudevaḥ sarvam*" is very "*durlabhaḥ*," or rare indeed, to find in this world (BG 7.19). The implications of these two verses (BG 7.19 and 8.14) are highly profound: the Lord Himself is *easy* to attain through devotion; the Lord's great-souled devotees are *very hard* to come by indeed!

the bondage of actions and from the pleasurable and the sorrowful results of good and bad actions performed during countless births. By offering everything, including yourself, to Me, you will become free from all bondage and will thereby come to Me....O son of Kuntī! Know this for certain that 'My devotee never perishes.'...Having gained this world, which is impermanent (*anityam*) and of little happiness (*asukhaṃ*), may you seek Me. Therefore, be My devotee—regard Me as yours in this manner: 'I am only God's'—fix your mind on Me, worship Me with all your activities, and bow to Me in reverence. That is, be happy in each Dispensation/Providence (*vidhān*) of Mine. Having thus made your heart steadfast in Me, and regarding Me as the Supreme Goal, you will verily come to Me." (BG 9.26–28, 31, 33, 34[15])

Description of Divine Glories: As the devotee never feels content listening to the glories of the Lord, even so, the Lord never feels content sharing His heart's desire with His dear devotee, Arjuna. Thus, Śrī Bhagavān, even without having been asked by Arjuna, graciously started telling Arjuna on His own—"O mighty-armed, Arjuna! Hear once more My supreme word, which I will tell you for your spiritual welfare since you are so greatly devoted to Me. Neither the gods nor the great sages know the mystery of My origin in full for I am the source of the gods and the great sages in every way. He who knows Me as the unborn, the beginning-less, and the Supreme Lord of all the worlds—that is, *accepts* Me without any doubt—he, among mortals is undeluded and liberated from all sins." (BG 10.1–4)

"Intelligence, knowledge, non-delusion, patience, truth, self-control, calmness, pleasure and pain, birth, death, fear and fearlessness; nonviolence, equanimity, contentment, austerity, charity, fame and ill-fame—all these twenty different qualities of being proceed from Me alone. I am at the very root of all these qualities. I alone am the prime source of all; from Me the whole creation proceeds. Knowing this, the wise devotees worship Me with all their heart. With their thoughts fixed on Me, their vital breath surrendered to Me, enlightening one another about Me, ever conversing of my divine qualities, influence, divine play, and so on, such devotees remain constantly contented and rejoicing in Me alone. To them, ever-devout, worshiping Me with whole-souled love constantly, I grant that *yoga* of wisdom (*buddhī-yoga*) by which they come to Me. Out of pure compassion for these devotees, dwelling in their heart, I destroy the darkness born of ignorance by the luminous lamp of wisdom—that is, I accord them the knowledge of the essential Reality (*tattva-jñāna*). It

[15] मन्मना भव मद्भक्तो मदयाजी मां नमस्कुरु।
मामेवैष्यसि युक्त्वैवमात्मानं मत्परायणः॥9.34॥

manmanā bhava madbhakto madyājī māṃ namaskuru /
mām evaiṣyasi yuktvaivam ātmānaṃ matparāyaṇaḥ //9.34//

This *śloka* (BG 9.34) occurs in essentially the same form in chapter 18 (18.65). Many consider it the summit of *bhakti yoga* in the Gītā.

means that to devotees who rely on Me, bestowing My grace on them, I myself grant both the *karma yoga* in the form of equanimity (*samatā*) and the *jñāna yoga* in the form of knowledge of Reality (*tattva-jñāna*), so that they do not feel any lack whatsoever." (BG 10.4–5, 7–11)

Thus, Śrī Bhagavān described His 82 glories (*vibhūtīs*) in chapter 10. Whatever distinctiveness, uniqueness, greatness, prominence is seen, it is not of itself but of God's, and has stemmed from God. Therefore, wherever any special quality is observed in the universe, instead of viewing it as the personal quality of the object, person, and so on, it should be seen as God's glory and should direct our attention toward God. Really speaking, the purpose of describing the glories (of the Lord) is to do away with (the attraction of) the (assumed) reality, significance, and dearness of the world so as to help us experience the reality of "*vāsudevaḥ sarvam*" (God is all there is), which is the main goal of the Gītā.

Then, finally, Śrī Bhagavān said—"O Arjuna! There is no end to my Divine glories. Whatever I have told you by way of my glories is but a brief indication by way of mere examples of the extent of My glory. Whatever opulence, brilliance, or strength is seen in any object or person in the entire universe—know all that to have sprung from but a spark of My *Yogīc* Splendor. What need is there to know all this, when I, who support the entire creation (infinite universes) pervading it with a single fraction of Myself, am sitting right in front of you?"

Thus, in chapters 7 through 10, Arjuna is progressively led to the knowledge of the mysteries and the glories of the Divine Being—Bhagavān Śrī Kṛṣṇa—and now Arjuna is ready to behold the Lord's Universal Form—*viśva-rūpa-darśana*. The Lord bestows Arjuna with divine vision (*divya-driṣṭi*) to enable him to witness the universal form. Arjuna is scared upon seeing the dreadful form and prays to the Lord to kindly "assume Your same four-armed shape (of Viṣnu)." (BG 11.45–46)

Śrī Bhagavān said—"O Arjuna! Do not be afraid. Pleased with you I have shown to you, through My own *Yogīc* power, this Supreme, effulgent, primeval, infinite, universal Form of Mine, which none other than you has ever seen before. "Extremely difficult indeed it is to see this Form of Mine that you have seen. Even the gods are ever eager to see this Form. Neither by the study of the *Vedas*, nor by penances, nor by charities, nor by (sacred) sacrifices can I be seen in this Form (with four-arms). O Scorcher of Foes (Arjuna)! But by unswerving devotion (*ananyā bhakti*) alone it is possible to know Me in this (*sākār*) form, to realize Me in very truth, and so to enter into Me. Seeing such an awe-inspiring Form of Mine, you should not be afraid or bewildered. Now with a fearless and cheerful (tranquil) mind, behold again the same four-armed Form of Mine." (BG 11.47–49)

Finally, Śrī Bhagavān uttered the most special verse on *bhakti yoga*—"He who does work for My sake (pleasure) only, he who looks upon Me as the Supreme Goal, who lovingly worships Me, who is free from attachment (to worldly things) and from enmity to all beings, that devotee verily comes to Me." (BG 11.55)[16]

Then, in chapter 12 entitled "*Bhakti Yoga*: The Yoga of Devotion," Śrī Bhagavān further explains—"Those who fixing their mind on Me, with the thought that 'I am verily God's and God alone is mine'—who are constantly devoted to me; who, with supreme faith (*śraddhā*), continuously worship Me (as *saguṇa-sākār*), I consider them to be the most perfect *yogīs* (devotees). Those who are delightfully devoted to the welfare of all beings, even-minded toward all, with senses subdued, worship the Imperishable, the Ineffable, the Unmanifest, the Omnipresent, the Unthinkable, the Unchangeable, the Immutable, the Constant, and the Eternal—they also come to Me indeed. Because the attributeless and the formless are verily My Form only; they are not any different from My Integral Form in its entirety. But devotees who lack dispassion and have body-conceit (*dehābhimān*) are not able to merge their minds in the Attributeless-Essence (*nirguṇa-tattva*). Such devotees find it difficult to worship the Attributeless." (BG 12.2–4)

"But O Arjuna, those who worship Me, renouncing all actions in Me, rely exclusively on Me as the Supreme Goal, meditate on Me with single-minded devotion—to them, whose minds are thus absorbed in Me, I Myself deliver swiftly from the death-fraught ocean of the world. Therefore, fix your mind on Me only, let your thoughts rest on Me alone; then in Me alone you will live thereafter. Of this there is no doubt." (BG 12.7–8)

Then, Śrī Bhagavān describes four means to spiritual welfare for human beings—(1) Surrender Yoga, (2) Abhyāsa Yoga, (3) Performing actions for God's sake, and (4) Renunciation of the fruits of action (*karmaphalatyāga*). Depending upon one's interest, faith, and competence, one can seek one's spiritual welfare by following any one of these four practices. Now, Śrī Bhagavān describes the characteristics of devotees perfected by all these four methods in the following five sub-sections:

(*First Section*—) "My devotee who sees Me in all beings has no ill-will toward any being. Rather, such a person has a feeling of friendliness and compassion toward all beings. He is free from the feelings of "I and mine," even-minded in pleasure and pain, and is forgiving. He is ever content under all circumstances and constantly experiences oneness with Me. His body, mind, and intellect remain naturally under his control. He is of firm conviction in Me alone and has dedicated his mind and intellect to Me. Such devotee of Mine is dear to Me."

(*Second Section*—) "My devotee does not cause agitation to anyone and is not agitated by anyone. He is always free from such feelings as joy and anger,

[16]This concluding verse of chapter 11 (11:55) represents the essence of *Bhakti* and is declared to be the very heart, the quintessence of the whole teaching of the Gītā, by Hindu commentators.

fear and anxiety. When, in one's view, there is no Reality besides Me, then who would one feel anxious, envious, and afraid of and why. Such devotee of Mine is dear to Me."

(*Third Section*—) "He who has no expectations for any object, person, and so on; who is pure in body and mind; who has accomplished what is worth accomplishing (i.e., has realized God); who is unconcerned and unattached in all circumstances; whose mind in untroubled by pain, worry, sorrow, and so on; and who does not initiate any new undertaking for the sake of sense-gratification and hoarding—such a devotee is dear to Me."

(*Fourth Section*—) "He who is ever free from four *vikāras* (mental modifications)—attachment/attraction (*rāga*), aversion (*dveṣa*), joy (*harṣa*), and sorrow (*śoka*)—and has no attachment to good actions and aversion to evil actions—such a devotee is dear to Me."

(*Fifth Section*—) "He who is alike to friend and foe; equanimous in honor and dishonor, in pleasant and unpleasant, joy and sorrow; who is free from attachment whatsoever (to persons and objects); who regards praise and blame alike; who constantly contemplates on My essential nature; who is ever content with whatever way body's sustenance comes about or not; who is free from the sense of ownership and attachment with regard to his body and his dwelling-place; and whose mind is steadfast in My Devotion—such a devotee is dear to Me." (BG 12.13–19)

The reason for describing different characteristics of devotees over five sections is that, due to differences in the modes of practice, circumstances, and so on, there is also some variation in the nature of devotees. Even then, as far as relinquishing the relationship with the world and love for God is concerned, all devotees are verily alike.

Śrī Bhagavān concludes his teachings in chapter 12 as follows—"But those who have full faith (*śraddhā*) in Me, who regard Me as the Supreme Goal, and who diligently follow the qualities of perfected devotees as described above—such aspirant-devotees are exceedingly dear to Me. It is because, despite having not attained Me yet, they still have full faith in Me and are exclusively devoted to Me." (BG 12.20)

Then comes the most special chapter of all, chapter 15, entitled "*Puruṣottamayoga:* The Yoga of the Supreme Person." The Gītā presents the tenet that Śrī Kṛṣṇa is the Supreme Person (*Puruṣottama*) and *Avatār* of the Absolute in the world of humans. The Gītā affirms the reality of a personal God (*Bhagavān Śrī Kṛṣṇa*), the ground and goal of human existence. Underscoring the unique importance of this chapter, Krishna Warrier, presents Śaṅkara's commentary on the final verse of this chapter (15.20), thus: "Though the entire Gītā is held to be a *'Śāstra,'* this chapter by itself is here styled *'Śāstra'* by way of eulogy. This is clear from the context, because the import of the entire Gītā has been briefly set forth here. Not only the import of the Gītā, but also the entire import of the *Veda* has been given here in summary."[17] Given its great importance, we present below representative selections from this chapter.

The chapter begins with an analogy of the eternal tree that signifies *saṅsāra*, the ever-changing, mundane world of impermanence. Śrī Bhagavān said—"They speak of the eternal *aśvattham* (*Pīpal*) tree with its roots above and branches below. The Supreme Spirit (God) is indeed the root (support, cause) of this cosmic tree; and Brahmāji is verily its principal branch (stem) from which several branches have sprung forth in the form of cosmic creation. Since it does not endure till the next day, it is called '*aśvattha*.' Since no one knows the beginning or end of this cosmic tree—and being of the nature of an eternal flow—it is called 'immutable.' Actions prompted by selfish motive as described in the *Vedas* are called its leaves. One who knows this cosmic tree in its essential reality is the knower of the truth of the *Vedas*." (BG 15.1)

"Nourished by the three *guṇas—sattva, rajas*, and *tamas*—the branches of this cosmic tree (in the form of creation) extend widely in all lower, middle, and higher regions. The apparent form of this cosmic tree—as *true, beautiful, and pleasing*—does not turn out to be so in reality upon mature reasoning. For, from the standpoint of time and place, this tree neither has a beginning, nor an end; nor any independent reality of its own. The aspirant should first cut asunder the roots of this tree—characterized by identification, attachment, and desire—with the strong weapon of non-attachment (*asaṅgaśastreṇa*). That is, the aspirant should first sever affinity with this mundane world. After that, the aspirant should set about to seek that Supreme Self, the very root of this comic tree—which is the Supreme Abode and the Supreme Architect of this universe—attaining which, there is no more return to this mortal world. For this, the aspirant should take refuge in that Primal Being from whom this eternal cosmic process has streamed forth." (BG 15.2–4)

"The aspirants who have surrendered to the Lord become free from delusion and pride (honor and dishonor of the physical body). Being free from attachment, they are able to overcome flaws born of false attachment such as the 'sense of mine,' and so on. They abide constantly and always in the Supreme Self; they become free from all worldly desires, and from the dualities such as pleasure and pain. Such devotee-aspirants, freed from pride and delusion, desires and attachments, attain to the Imperishable, Highest Abode of the Supreme Being (*Avınāśī, Paramapada Paramātmā*). That Supreme Abode is illumined neither by the sun, nor the moon, nor fire. For the sun, the moon and fire, and so on, illumine the physical universe by receiving the illumination from that Supreme Abode only. That is My Abode Supreme, after reaching which one never returns to the mortal world." (BG 15.5–6)

We are indeed a fragment of God. Therefore, the abode of the Supreme Self is verily our true abode. That is why, attaining that abode, one does not return

[17] A. G. Krishna Warrier, trans., *Śrīmad Bhagavad Gītā Bhāṣya of Ādi Śaṅkarācārya* (Madras, India: Śrī Ramakrishna Math, 1983), 509–510.

to the world of conditioned existence (*saṅsāra*). Until we attain that Abode, until then, like a traveler, we will keep drifting in myriad lifeforms and various regions, and will not find repose. For this whole world is a foreign land and is not our homeland. This is someone else's home (*parāyā ghar*) and not our home. Our drifting in various life forms and regions will come to an end only when we will reach our true home.

"Having become the embodied soul (*jīva*) in this world of living beings, this *jīva* is eternally a fragment of My very own Self. That means, it essentially remains ever-established in Me and can never be separated from Me. But mistakenly turning away from Me, it considers mind and five senses (born of *prakṛti*, the material nature) to be its own and establishes its relationship with them. Just as the wind carries the fragrance from its source, even so the embodied soul, as the controller of the body, carries the five senses and mind (subtle and causal body) from one body to another. Identifying with the mind, the embodied soul, through its five senses, namely, ear, skin, eyes, tongue, and nose, enjoys, indulgingly, the sense-objects, namely, sound, touch, sight, taste, and smell. In this manner, despite its being identified with the *guṇas* and enjoying the sense pleasures while living in or leaving the present body or residing in another body, *the embodied soul remains essentially unattached*. The ignorant ones do not know this mystery; rather, it is known to the discerning individuals endowed with the eye of wisdom. The *jñāna-yogīs* striving steadfastly realize this Supreme Self as residing within themselves. But those whose mind is not pure—that is, those in whose mind worldly enjoyments and hoarding (*bhōga-saṅgraha*) are important—such irrational individuals, despite being engaged in spiritual practices, are not able to realize this essential truth." (BG 15.7–11)

"The splendor that proceeds from the sun and illumines the entire world, the same brilliance that is in the moon and fire, know that radiance to be Mine. Shinning as the luminosity in the sun, the moon and the fire, I verily illuminate the entire universe. Entering the earth, I sustain all living beings through my vital energy; and becoming the watery *soma* (moon), I nourish all plants and herbs. Abiding in the bodies of all living beings as the digestive fire of life (*vaiśvānara*), and associated with *prāna* (inhaling) and *apāna* (exhaling), I digest the four kinds of foods (that are chewed, swallowed, sucked, and licked). I dwell in the hearts of all creatures in a special way. From Me arise memory, wisdom, and reasoning (to dispel doubts, delusion, etc.) as well as their loss. I am indeed He who is to be known by all the *Vedas*. I am the deciding authority of the true essence of the *Vedas* and I am the knower of the *Vedas* too." (BG 15.12–15)

"There are two types of *Puruṣas* in this world—the Perishable (inert) and the Imperishable (conscious principle). The bodies of all creatures are called 'perishable' while the embodied soul (*jīvātman*) is called 'imperishable.' But there is yet another Being, the Highest, called the Supreme Person (*Puruṣottama*), who, as the Imperishable Lord, pervades and sustains all the three worlds. I am verily the Supreme Personality of Godhead (manifested in the personal form as *Śrī Kṛṣṇa*). I am beyond the perishable and also higher even than the imperishable. In the scriptures such *Purāṇas*, *Smṛtis*, and so on, and also in the *Vedas*, I am celebrated as the '*Puruṣottma*' (Supreme Person).[18] O Bhārata! The wise devotee, who, knows me as the 'Supreme Person,' and turns toward Me, for such a devotee there remains nothing else here to be known. That person worships Me in every way with all his being (in all states of mind and activities), for in his view there is verily no one else other than Me and higher than Me." (BG 15.16–19)

"O Blameless One (Arjuna)! Thus, the utmost secret *Śāstra* (scriptural doctrine), the most profound of all in the entire sacred lore, has now been revealed by Me. Understanding this, a person becomes truly enlightened. For such a person, there remains nothing else here whatsoever to be known, to be done, or to be attained. *His human birth becomes fulfilled for he has achieved the Highest Goal of human life.*" (BG 15.20)

We conclude this section on *bhakti yoga* by summarizing seven culminating verses or *carma ślokas* of chapter 18: 18.54, 18.55, 18.56, 18.57, 18.62, 18.65, and 18.66:

> Having become one with the Ultimate Reality, such an aspirant (*sādhaka*) neither grieves nor desires. Alike to all beings, he attains supreme devotion to Me. By virtue of My devotion supreme, he comes to know Me, what My measure is and who I am in essence. Knowing Me thus in very truth and essence, he enters into Me straightway. A devotee who has taken refuge in Me with exclusive and unswerving devotion, even while performing all ordained actions, by My Grace, attains to the Eternal, Imperishable Abode (*mat-prasādāt avāpnoti śāśvataṁ padam avyayam*). Therefore, mentally dedicating all actions to Me, regarding Me as the Supreme Goal, and resorting to the *yoga* of equanimity—that is, by severing affinity with the world—fix your mind and thoughts constantly on Me. By being constantly absorbed in Me, you will, by My Grace, overcome all difficulties. O Bhārata (Arjuna)! Seek refuge in Him alone, surrendering your whole being (*sarvabhāvena*). By His Grace you shall attain Supreme Peace and the Eternal Abode. (18.54, 18.55, 18.56, 18.57, 18.62)

The final two verses conclude the teachings on *bhakti yoga* as follows:

> *manmanā bhava madbhakto madyājī māṃ namaskuru /*
> *mām evaiṣyasi satyaṃ te pratijāne priyosi me* //18.65//
>
> Fix your mind on Me—that is, accept Me as your very own; worship Me with all your actions; and bow to Me with reverence—that is, be completely surrendered to Me. By turning completely towards Me in this manner, you will verily attain to Me—This is my sincere pledge to you because you are dear to Me.
>
> *sarvadharmān parityajya mām ekaṃ śaraṇaṃ vraja /*
> *ahaṃ tvā sarvapāpebhyo mokṣyayiṣyāmi mā śucaḥ* //18.66//
>
> Relinquishing all *dharmas* take refuge in Me alone. I will release you from all sins. Do not grieve.

[18] See: Muṇḍaka Upaniṣad, II.i.2: *hyakṣarātparataḥ paraḥ puruṣaḥ*: the Supreme Being is higher than that which is even higher than the Imperishable.

According to Swāmī Shrī Rāmsukhdāsjī, "Taking refuge in the Lord (*śaraṇāgati*) is the quintessence of the entire message of the Gītā." S. K. Maitra concurs: "the final instruction is: surrender."[19] In surrendering to the Lord lies the culmination of the Gītā's teachings. The devotee who has taken refuge in the Lord accepts firmly the belief that "I am God's and God is mine." Then the devotee becomes forever free from the pangs of fear, sorrow, worry, and so on.[20]

With this key verse, we have come full circle in the teachings of the Bhagavad Gītā: Śrī Kṛṣṇa started the teaching declaring that "the wise do not grieve" (2.11: *nānuśocanti paṇḍitāḥ*) and concludes it with an assurance "do not grieve" (18.66: *mā śucaḥ*). So, if you want to overcome the sorrow, attain to the liberating wisdom. What is this liberating wisdom? Just this: Perform your actions as an offering to the Supreme (*Ishvara-arpanabhāvanā*), perform your duties without the expectation of any reward. Be an instrument of the Divine in all that you do.

Let all your actions be for the wellbeing of all beings (*sarvabhūtahite ratāḥ*: 5.25); be a role model for the bringing together of the world communities and the maintenance of the world order (*lokasaṃgraham evāpi saṃpaśyan kartum arhasi*: 3.20). Above all, accept the results of your actions with graceful equanimity, as the Grace of the Lord (*Ishvara-prasādabhāvanā*). Then, your actions will never taint you. Attain the highest pure knowledge by which the One Imperishable Being is seen in all the existences, undivided in the divided (18.20). In this manner, with Divine Grace, you will attain the communion of the individual self with the Supreme Self.

Thus concludes this manual for transformational living and leadership.

Bhakti Yoga and the Art and Science of Leadership

Through equanimity, service, detachment, and surrender, the Gītā teaches the art of spirituality while being deeply engaged in the worldly conduct. One of the most important applications of *bhakti yoga* is by way of treating everything as sacred and invested with intrinsic goodness and meaning. *Bhakti yoga* bestows the perspective that everyone and everything has a purpose. Essentially, it means a feeling of oneness (at-one-ment) with the whole of existence (*sarvātmabhāva*) and seeing God in everything and everything in God. This understanding lends a certain sanctity to all of our activities and helps foster an environment of empathy, kinship, and solidarity. This reclaiming of the sacred dimension of life is sorely needed in the present-day world plagued by distrust, disengagement, and disharmony.

We present below some lessons from *bhakti yoga* with application to workplace spirituality and leadership.

[19] S. K. Maitra, *The Spirit of Indian Philosophy* (Allahabad, India: The Indian Press, 1947), 103.
[20] See: Dhiman, trans., *Sahaja Gītā*, 172.

1. *Work is Worship*. Perhaps the greatest life and leadership lesson the *bhakti yoga* mindset teaches us is to approach our work as worship. They say that life is 10% what you *make* of it, and 90% how you *take* it. It is all about the attitude that we bring to it. Work is not a 9-to-5 thing meant primarily to pay our bills. It is our offering to the universe, a creative sacrifice, a *yajña*. Regarding our work as sacred spiritualizes life and lends certain sanctity to our daily economic grind. Leaders that regard their work as an offering can serve selflessly the cause of the organization in a more effective and engaged way. Approached in this manner, work assumes a greater dignity and life becomes more worthwhile and meaningful. *Bhakti yoga* teaches us that our work is our way of worshiping the Divine, the inner guide that inspires all actions and undertakings.
2. *Making the Lord the mainstay of our Life and Lifework*. Arjuna made Śrī Kṛṣṇa his sole guide in the battlefield. He had unswerving faith in Śrī Kṛṣṇa. He surrendered to the Divine. That made all the difference in the outcome of the war. As W. D. P. Hill has observed about the key message of the Gītā, "One who works with [Self-] knowledge and devotion, and without desire, wins liberation."[21] Śrī Kṛṣṇa tells Arjuna at several places in the Gītā that for any devotee who worships the Lord with sincere devotion, the Lord provides for what is lacking and preserves what has been provided (*yogakṣemaṃ vahāmy aham*: 9.22).

   As I write this, I recall-watching a video of a 34-year-old aerialist, Nik Wallenda, walking on the tightrope across a gorge near the Grand Canyon. Wallenda didn't wear a harness and stepped slowly and steadily throughout, murmuring prayers to Jesus almost constantly along the way.[22] This is the incomparable power of making God the mainstay of one's life. Make no mistake, this is an extremely risky adventure: you walk across, you live; you fall, you die. In 1978, Karl Wallenda fell to his death while attempting to walk a cable strung between two hotel towers in San Juan, Puerto Rico.[23]
3. *Seeing the Lord in All, and All in the Lord*. Perhaps one of the greatest benefits of the path of devotion (*bhakti yoga*) is that it confers a perspective whereby one is able to approach life and its myriad relationships in a new light. One is no longer stuck in the quagmire of narrow thinking of a limited entity, feverishly devoted to protecting and promoting the personal agenda of a "skin-encapsulated" ego, to use a felicitous phrase coined by Alan Watts. We present two important verses that splendidly encapsulate all the essential teachings on this theme, providing the path as well the culmination of *bhakti yoga*:

[21] W. D. P. Hill, *The Bhagavad Gītā: A Translation and Commentary* (Madras, India: Oxford University Press, 1928/1953), 62.

[22] Nik Wallenda completes tightrope walk across gorge near Grand Canyon https://www.cbsnews.com/news/nik-wallenda-completes-tightrope-walk-across-gorge-near-grand-canyon/

[23] See: The rich, tragic history of daredevil Wallendas: https://www.cbsnews.com/news/the-rich-tragic-history-of-daredevil-wallendas/

yo māṃ paśyati sarvatra sarvaṃ ca mayi paśyati /
tasyāhaṃ na praṇaśyāmi sa ca me na praṇaśyati //6.30//

The one who sees Me in all beings and all beings in Me, to such a person I am never lost (invisible), nor is he (or she) ever lost to Me.

ātmaupamyena sarvatra samaṃ paśyati yorjuna /
sukhaṃ vā yadi vā duḥkhaṃ sa yogī paramo mataḥ //6.32//

Arjuna, that *yogī* is considered to be the best among all *yogīs* who judges what is happiness and sorrow in all beings, by the *same* standard as he would apply to himself.[24]

He looks at the joy and sorrow of all with the same eyes, because he feels the pleasure and pain in others the same way that he feels pleasure and pain in himself—since he has realized the oneness of all existence. Although the word *yogī* occurs 15 times in the Bhagavad Gītā, Śrī Kṛṣṇa has used the word "*paramaḥ*" (supreme) along with the word *yogī* only once in this very verse. Hence, the utmost importance of this unique verse!

4. *Bhakti Yoga bestows the gift of Equanimity—Samatā.* Cultivating loving devotion toward the Lord helps in garnering equanimity. This also follows from seeing sameness everywhere, as the following verse indicates:

sarvabhūtastham ātmānaṃ sarvabhūtāni cātmani /
īkṣate yogayuktātmā sarvatra samadarśanaḥ //6.29//

One who meditates on his Self (*ātmā*) existence perfectly and uniformly everywhere beholds the Self as present in all beings and all beings as present in the Self.

When our mind has become pure and our intellect "*sama*"—"balanced and equanimous"—we have attained oneness with the highest principle of existence. Such is the supreme importance of *samatā*.

The value of cultivating equanimity for today's leaders and managers can hardly be overemphasized. Its importance is evident in every action, every decision a leader makes. Without the evenness of mind, self-awareness and emotional intelligence—two markers of success in leading oneself and others—remain a distant goal.

[24] Swami Gambhirananda, *Bhagavad Gītā with the Commentary of Sri Shankaracharya* (Calcutta, India: Advaita Ashrama, 1984), 302.

Concluding Thoughts

The message of the Gītā is for everyone who is interested in attaining spiritual freedom. The sole purpose of the Gītā is the salvation of all of humankind. Regardless of one's race, religion, or philosophical orientation, everyone can attain their spiritual welfare by following its simple teachings. The Gītā teaches the great art of seeking the highest good in ordinary practical matters *(vyavahār mein paramārath ki kalā)*. It teaches us to perform our duties, in the spirit of detachment and sacrifice *(yajña),* for the mutual benefit of each other and for the welfare of the world (*lokasaṃgraham*: 3:20; 3:25). By cherishing each other in this manner, we will attain the Supreme good (3:11). It further assures us that "by properly performing one's duty, one attains perfection" (18:45). While many scriptures enjoin the renunciation of the world to attain God, the Gītā states that one can attain perfection by surrendering to God (who is the source of all creation and is all pervading) through the performance of one's prescribed duty—*svakarmaṇā tam abhyarcya siddhiṃ vindati mānavaḥ* (18:46).

When we fulfill all our allotted duties selflessly, remaining equanimous in success and failure, we attain the same goal (God-realization) that has been attained by the sages and the seers by undergoing years and years of spiritual regimen. In a seminal verse of the Gītā (2:48), Arjuna is advised to perform actions, renouncing attachment, by remaining steadfast in equanimity. This equanimity or even-mindedness is called *yoga*. This discipline of equanimity, the supreme *yoga* of the Gītā, is equally available to all seekers. Thus, through equanimity, service, detachment, and surrender (to the Supreme), the Gītā teaches the art of spirituality while being deeply engaged in worldly conduct.

At the conclusion of chapter 6, the Gītā especially extols the Path of Devotion (6.47), even while presenting the outcome of the discipline of meditation. Thus, in chapters 7–10, Arjuna is progressively led to the knowledge of the mysteries and the glories of the Divine Being—Bhagavān Śrī Kṛṣṇa—and now, Arjuna is ready to behold the Lord's Universal Form—*viśva-rupā-darṣanaṁ,* which forms the subject matter of chapter 11. The Lord bestows Arjuna with the divine vision (*divya-driṣṭi*) to enable him to witness the Universal Form. Śrī Kṛṣṇa presents the quintessence of the path of devotion in the culminating verse of chapter 11—"He who does work for My sake (pleasure) only, he who looks upon Me as the Supreme Goal, who lovingly worships Me, who is free from attachment (to worldly things) and from enmity to all beings, that devotee verily comes to Me" (11.55).

This concluding verse of chapter 11 (11:55) represents the essence of *bhakti* and is declared to be the very heart, the quintessence, of the whole body of teachings of the Gītā—by Hindu commentators. The great commentator, Śaṅkarā, calls it "the essence of the whole Gītā."[25] Paraphrasing BG 11.55,

[25] See: W. D. P. Hill, *The Bhagavad Gītā: A Translation and Commentary* (Madras, India: Oxford University Press, 1928/1953), 167. See also: *The Bhagavad Gītā*, Translated and Interpreted by Franklin Edgerton (New York, NY: Harvard University Press, 1944), 176.

Dr. Rādhākrishnan states, "we must carry our duties directing the spirit to God and with detachment from all interest in the things of the world and free from enmity towards any living being."[26]

This is the essence of *bhakti yoga*: Perform your duties as an offering to God, beholding the Divine in all and all in the Divine, free from attachment and ill will toward anyone. Then, your feet will be firmly planted on the path that leads to joy, harmony, and fulfillment.

[26] S. Rādhākrishnan, *The Bhagavad Gītā: With an Introductory Essay, Sanskrit Text, English Translation and Notes* (London, UK: George Allen & Unwin Ltd., 1958), 289.

CHAPTER 8

Mind: A Leader's Greatest Friend and Foe

Introduction

The Gītā is a practical manual of Self-knowledge, Self-mastery, and Self-awareness. It places great emphasis on self-restraint and mental discipline. The outcome of an unrestrained mind is a life given to selfish desire, anger, and greed leading to disempowering culture. Given the need and importance of meditation during these stressful times, this chapter will also present the teachings of the Gītā on the art and science of stilling the mind. This chapter presents the teachings of the Gītā on understanding and restraining the mind and emotions. It is common knowledge that mental strength and determination are the keys to leadership success; leaders who are emotionally weak and wayward cannot achieve a durable and consistent organizational vision or mission.

The Gītā reminds us characteristically that an unruly mind is our greatest foe, and a stable mind our greatest friend (6.5). It places great emphasis on self-restraint and mental discipline. This is a mature understanding based on self-responsibility and not on blaming others. The outcome of an unrestrained mind is a life given to selfish desire, anger, and greed leading to disempowering culture. Such toxic cultures lead to apathy, distrust, and disengagement that play havoc with the integrity of organizational flourishing and wellbeing. The Gītā fosters workplace wellbeing by suggesting practical strategies for managing negative emotions such as anger, greed, and hatred.

Buddhist psychology also warns of three mental traps or unwholesome roots of mind: greed, hatred, and ignorance. If our attention emanates from any of these three unwholesome roots, then it is not appropriate and will not give us the knowledge of reality as it truly is. Moreover, a leader's first job is to have an accurate knowledge of the current reality.

If leadership is an extension of who we are, then leaders first need to manage themselves before they can aspire to lead others. Underscoring the importance of self-leadership, the Bhagavad Gītā further stresses that, when facing a crisis,

S. Dhiman, *Bhagavad Gītā and Leadership*,
Palgrave Studies in Workplace Spirituality and Fulfillment,
https://doi.org/10.1007/978-3-319-67573-2_8

leaders must elevate themselves by self-effort (*uddharedātmanātmānaṃ*: 6.5). This requires a deep understanding of the workings of the mind. For those who have conquered their mind, the mind is the best of friends; but for those who have failed to control their mind, the mind will be their greatest enemy (*ātmaiva hy ātmano bandhur ātmaiva ripur ātmanaḥ*: 6.5). Without self-victory *ātma jayaha* or Self-mastery, one cannot attain success in any field. Essentially, it points out that an un-mastered self is the biggest enemy of the individual; in fact, Śrī Kṛṣṇa goes one step further, it is not the greatest enemy, but the only enemy of a human being!

Dhyānayoga: The Path of Meditation

It is important to note that although the Gītā recognizes two primary spiritual disciplines (3:2)—*jñāna yoga* (the path of Self-knowledge) and *karma yoga* (the path of action); yet, at various points, the Gītā also presents other disciplines such as *bhakti yoga* (the path of devotion) and *dhyāna yoga* (the path of meditation) as equally viable paths or aids to enlightenment. Besides, in the Gītā, the path of meditation or concentration serves as a necessary concomitant to all other paths, since a certain measure of calm concentration is verily required to practice the path of action, knowledge, and devotion in a proper manner. The Gītā takes an integral view of the spiritual disciplines and often extols other disciplines while discussing a particular path as preeminent.

In chapter 6, entitled *Ātmasaṁyamayogaḥ*: The Yoga of Self-Discipline, we find the most detailed instructions on the discipline of meditation that culminates in *bhakti yoga—śraddhāvān bhajate yo māṃ sa me yuktatamo mataḥ:* the *yogīn* who worships Me devoutly with his inmost self abiding in Me, is considered by Me to be the best of the *yogīns* (6:47).

As a prelude to the discipline of meditation, we are told in chapter 6 that responsibility for one's spiritual welfare and downfall rests with oneself and no one else. Therefore, one should uplift oneself by one's own self (efforts)—and not degrade oneself; for one's own self alone is one's friend, and one's own self alone is one's enemy (6.5). At the very outset of chapter 6, as the path as well as the goal, Śrī Kṛṣṇa presents the following marks of a *yogīn* steadfast in equanimity: "When one does not get attached to sense-objects or to actions, and has renounced all purposes *(sarvasaṃkalpasaṃnyāsī)*, then, he is said to have ascended the heights of *yoga (yogārūḍha)*."

According to the Gītā, "Success in this *Yoga* of meditation is neither attained by one who either eats too much or does not eat at all, nor by one who either sleeps too much or does not sleep at all. This *Yoga* (of meditation), which destroys sorrows, is accomplished only by him who is temperate in diet and recreation, who is disciplined (and detached) in the performance of actions, and is temperate in sleep and waking." As Franklin Edgerton has noted, "This is one of the points of contact between the Gītā and Buddhism, for Buddhism too makes much of the doctrine of 'golden mean,' opposing the extreme of self-torture as well as the extreme of worldliness."[1]

The Gītā is fully aware that the mind is restless and hard to control. It maintains that the mind can be controlled by constant practice and detachment (or dispassion). The following two verses provide the preliminary instructions on meditation:

saṅkalpaprabhavān kāmāṃs tyaktvā sarvān aśeṣataḥ /
manasaivendriyagrāmaṃ viniyamya samantataḥ //6.24//

śanaiḥ śanair uparamed buddhyā dhṛtigṛhītayā /
ātmasaṃsthaṃ manaḥ kṛtvā na kiṃcid api cintayet //6.25//

Renouncing entirely all desires, and withdrawing, by strength of mind, all senses from their respective objects, the meditator should, with an unhurried intellect set in firmness, gradually become detached (*uparām*) from the world. *He should then abide his mind in the Self and should not think of anything else whatsoever.*

PATAÑJALI'S AṢṬĀṄGA YOGA: THE EIGHTFOLD PATH

In the yoga tradition, Patañjali is a revered name, the famous author of *Yoga Sūtras* consisting of 196 aphorisms, on the theory and practice of yoga. He presents a progressive yoga system comprising eight steps called Raja Yoga, which are briefly described as follows[2]:

1. Yama

The five *yamas* (fivefold abstentions) constitute step one (*Yoga Sūtra* 2.30) of the eight well-known steps that Patañjali states in the *Yoga Sūtras*, his user-manual on meditation. They are:

1. Nonviolence (अहिंसा *ahiṃsā*)
2. Truth (सत्य *satya*)
3. Non-stealing (अस्तेय *asteya*)
4. Self-discipline or celibacy (ब्रह्मचर्य *brahmacārya*)
5. Non-possession (अपरिग्रहः *aparigraha*)

2. Niyama

Niyamas, according to Patañjali, constitute five observances that prepare the mind for spiritual freedom (*Yoga Sūtra* 2.32). The five *niyamas* (fivefold disciplines) represent the following virtues:

[1] Franklin Edgerton, *The Bhagavad Gītā* (Cambridge, MA: Harvard University Press, 1944), 68.
[2] See: Swami Prabhavananda & Christopher Isherwood, *How to Know God: The Yoga Aphorisms of Patanjali* (Hollywood, CA: Vedanta Society, 1953/2007), 96–164.

1. Purity (शौच *śauca*)
2. Contentment (सन्तोष *santoṣa*)
3. Austerity (तपस् *tapas*)
4. Spiritual study (स्वाध्याय *svādhyāya*)
5. Surrender to God (ईश्वरप्रणिधान *Īśvarapraṇidhāna*)

3. Āsana

The third step is physical posture—*āsana*. Patanjali provides a touchstone about *āsana* as follows: स्थिरसुखमासनम्॥४६॥ *sthirasukhamāsanam//46//*—the posture is what is steady and pleasant. In other words, for meditation, the posture should be such that one is able to sit still in a comfortable manner for a good length of time.

4. Prāṇāyāma

The next step is about consciously regulating the breath—consciously changing the time/length of the breath (inhalation and exhalation). Almost all systems of meditation use breath to control the mind, since the mind is intimately connected to the breath. When we are calm, our breath is relaxed. When we are agitated, we breathe fast. There is a highly develop science of *prāṇāyāma*. Six most important types of *prāṇāyāma* are frequently practiced by the skilled meditators. However, the technique of *prāṇāyāma* should be properly learned under a competent teacher. One should not attempt it on one's own by reading a book or watching a video. It can have severely adverse effects if practiced incorrectly. Regulating breath is the first step to turn the mind inward for contemplation and directing the *prāṇa-śakti* or energy toward its source.

5. Pratyāhāra

Pratyāhāra is the fifth step and signifies "interiorization of the mind." Once the mind has been stabilized, one should try to *interiorize* one's consciousness so that thoughts do not wander ceaselessly in all directions externally. This marks the first step of unhinging the awareness from outside and hinging it to the inside world.

6. Dhāranā

Dhāranā means concentration or one-pointedness of the mind. The mind is made to focus on a mantra, or object, to regulate one's breath so that it does not drift from the subject or object of concentration.

7. Dhyāna

Dhyāna literally means meditation or absorption or contemplation of an object. Whatever we meditate upon gets stronger. If we meditate on our faults, they become stronger. However, if we meditate on virtues, we develop a virtuous mind.

8. Samādhi

Samādhi is oneness with the object of meditation. It is a state of oneness, when there is no separation between the meditator, the act of mediation, and the subject of mediation. All three fuse into one. Only oneness reigns supreme in *Samādhi*. This is the culmination of Patañjali's yoga system.

Meditation, Yoga Sūtras of Patañjali, and the Gītā

According to Patañjali, *yoga* is defined as "stilling or inhibiting the modification of the mind": योग: चित्त-वृत्ति निरोध: (*yogaś citta vṛtti nirodhaḥ*): *Yoga Sutra* 1.2. Patañjali continues to state the result of quietening the mind in sutra 1:3: *tadā draṣṭuḥ sva-rūpe'vasthānam*: The seer then abides in its very own nature. Both the *Yoga Sutras* can be combined as follows: When the modifications of the mind cease, the seer then abides in its own very nature.

Tangentially, it may seem that Patañjali is advocating the same methodology as Advaita Vedānta, especially when we consider *Yoga Sutra* 1.3. However, there is a vital difference between the metaphysics of Patañjali and that of Advaita Vedānta. Patañjali's metaphysics is based on the dualistic system of the Sāṃkhya School that conceptualizes two different realities of *Puruṣa* (consciousness) and *Prakṛti* (matter). The *yamas*, *niyamas*, and *guṇas* furnish the ethical theory of Pajanjali's yoga system. Advaita Vedānta admits no such dualistic view of two independent entities of *Puruṣa* and *Prakṛti* as such. *Puruṣa* as consciousness is all there is and *prakṛti* is its potency, its creative energy. This distinction is reconciled in chapter 15 of the Bhagavad Gītā by the transcending principle of *Puruṣottma*.

There is another important distinction regarding basic methodology, *prakriyā*, employed by Patañjali's Yoga Sūtras and Advaita Vedānta. Patañjali presents a graded system of eight steps, *Aṣṭāṅga Yoga*, starting with ethical do's and don'ts, culminating in the deep meditative absorption called *Samādhi*. Since *Samādhi* is a *state* attained through effort on the part of the meditator, it cannot be permanent. When the meditator comes out of *Samādhi*, the mind emerges again, with all its myriad modifications.

In Vedānta, the goal is to know one's true Self (*ātman*) as the Absolute Reality (*Brahman*). Our true Self is already one with the Reality; it is due to self-ignorance that we think otherwise. The ignorance is not some general lack of information. It is a metaphysical ignorance due to which we take our body-mind-sense complex to be our true nature. Vedānta recommends self-inquiry as the choice methodology to intuit our true nature. When, through proper self-inquiry, the mind abides in the Self, it loses its mind-ness, so to speak. Only the Self remains, which has been there all along. The Gītā 6.25 provides the key practice: आत्मसंस्थं मनः कृत्वा: establishing the mind in the Self.

In the modern times, Śrī Ramana Maharshi laid exclusive emphasis on this method. He called it *ātma-vicāra*, a Sanskrit word, which simply means, Self-inquiry. This method transcends the need for the graded eight-step system of

Patañjali by directly establishing the seeker in the Self. It is the *jñāna-mārga*, the path of knowledge, which is considered the highest of the *yogas*, as it can directly lead to Self-realization or liberation. When asked about breath control, pranayama, Ramana replied, "This vichara brings about the desired result. For one not so advanced as to engage in it, regulation of breath is prescribed for making the mind quiescent. Quiescence lasts only so long as the breath is controlled. So it is transient."[3] When asked about the efficacy of bhakti, Sri Bhagavan said: "So long as there is *vibhakti*, there must be *bhakti*. So long as there is *viyoga*, there must be *yoga*."[4]

In Advaita Vedānta, Self-knowledge (*ātma-jñāna*) refers to discrimination (*viveka*) between the Self, *ātma*, and the mind (*citta*), and to know their nature as they truly are (*yathārtha-jñāna*). Let us look at how the Bhagavad Gītā approaches this topic. The most definitive instructions are provided in chapter 6, verse 25, as follows:

शनैः शनैरुपरमेद्बुद्ध्या धृतिगृहीतया ।
आत्मसंस्थं मनः कृत्वा न किञ्चिदपि चिन्तयेत् ॥ २५ ॥

śanaiḥ śanairuparamedbuddhyā dhṛtigṛhītayā /
ātmasaṁsthaṁ manaḥ kṛtvā na kiñcidapi cintayet //6.25//

One should attain tranquility through gradual practice; *establishing the mind in the Self through steadfast intellect*, one should not think of anything else.

Therefore, this is the long and short of meditation according to the Gītā: आत्मसंस्थं मनः कृत्वा: establishing the mind in the Self. Śaṅkara's well-ascertained view on this verse is as follows:

आत्मसंस्थम् आत्मनि संस्थितम् 'आत्मैव सर्वं न ततोऽन्यत् किञ्चिदस्ति' इत्येवमात्मसंस्थं मनः कृत्वा न किञ्चिदपि चिन्तयेत् ।
एष योगस्य परमो विधिः ॥

ātmasaṁstham ātmani saṁsthitam 'ātmaiva sarvaṁ na tato'nyat kiñcidasti' ityevamātmasaṁsthaṁ manaḥ kṛtvā na kiñcidapi cintayet /
eṣa yogasya paramo vidhiḥ // [Śaṅkara commentary, *bhāṣya*, on verse 6.25]

One should make the mind constantly abide in the Self, bearing in mind that the Self is all (सर्वं) and that nothing else exists. This[5] is the highest form of yoga.[6]

Thus, the focus of Patānjali's yoga is on controlling the changing states, the modifications or the *vṛttis* of the mind, whereas Vedānta's focus is on cognizing the unchanging Seer (Witnessing Principle) of the *vṛttis* of the mind.

[3] Munagala Venkataramiah, *Talks with Ramana Maharshi* (Tiruvannamala, India: Sri Ramanasramam, 2013), 137.

[4] Ibid.

[5] Anandgiri's gloss: "This" denotes "the steadiness of the mind (in the Self)."

[6] Alladi M. Sastri, *The Bhagavad Gītā with Commentary of Sri Sankaracharya* (Madras, India: Samata Books, 1897/1995), 196. [emphasis added].

This fundamental distinction should never be forgotten. It is also important to remember that all meditative states (including the highest meditative absorption, called *nirvikalpa samādhi*) are subject to appearance and disappearance; they come and go, *āgamāpāyino'nitya* (BG 2.14). Whereas the Self, *ātma*, is an ever-attained, *nitya-prāpta-vastu*, and does not come and go. This is also the basic difference between the Buddhist view of consciousness as momentary (*kṣanika*) and the Vedāntic understanding of eternal pure consciousness, *nitya-shuddha chaitanyam*. Logically speaking, there has to be a conscious, changeless principle to register the changes. And that changeless principle is our true nature according to the Gītā and Advaita Vedānta.

From the foregoing, the following further corollaries can be drawn:

1. Advaita Vedānta, or its goal (*sādhya*) the Self, is *vastu-tantra* (the science of cognizing the Reality, the *vastu*, as is). It does not depend upon the whims and fancies of the knower or the so-called meditator.
2. Meditation, as commonly understood and practiced, is *kratru-tantra* (a state or something to be "attained" or "created" or "accomplished").
3. Put differently, cognizing/realizing the Self in Vedānta is a *karaṇ-nirpekṣa-sādhan* (independent of action and means of action), whereas Patānjali yoga and all forms of meditation are *karaṇ-sāpekṣa-sādhan*—means that are dependent upon action for their accomplishment.
4. Anything "created" can never be eternal. It will be subject to the laws and limitations of time and space and causality (*deśa-kāla-vastu-parichinna*). Muṇḍaka Upaniṣad clearly states that "the eternal cannot be created through action": *nāstyakṛtaḥ kṛtena* (1.2.12).
5. My true nature (Self) has to be/is eternal and ever-attained. It is my very *svarūpa*, essential nature. It is direct and immediate, *sākṣādaparokṣād*.

   One has to listen to It from a teacher (*gurur-mukhārvinda*) who has realized It in his/her *anubhava, direct experience. One-on-one, sitting at the feet of the master.* One cannot "get it" on one's own, just by reading books or surfing the internet.

How can the Self be found in the books, in meditation or outside? It is *aprameyam* (cannot be objectified). It is the very subject. It is our true nature. *Tat Tvam Asi.* That YOU are. My Vedānta teacher once explained to me the simplicity of knowing the Self, thusly, "It is like going home. Why should it be complicated?" He then added, "But it is subtle. It requires सूक्ष्म बुद्धि *sukṣma-buddhi*, subtle intellect, not so much sharp intellect, तीक्ष्ण बुद्धि *tīkṣna-buddhi*."

To Meditate or Not to Meditate? That Is the Question!

People resort to meditation for a variety of reasons. Some like to meditate just for fun, others for relaxation, while a few others meditate to go with the flow. Still some curious ones want to try myriad forms of meditation, having done some quick "window-shopping" on the internet. There are actually quite a variety of meditation forms out there to choose from: namely, [Om] Mantra Meditation, Chakra Meditation, Kundalini Meditation; then there is Zazen, Vipassana, Mindfulness Meditation, Transcendental Meditation, Taoistic Meditation, Qigong Meditation.

And if that is not already enough, and one wants more peppered, nuanced, and customized variety, one may still go for guided imagery, creative visualization, lucent dreaming, nada yoga, kriya yoga, third-eye meditation, navel gazing, and so forth. Or else try the ubiquitous stress reduction, the count/watch-your-breath sort. Then there is also the option of eyes fully closed, half-closed or fully open—to say nothing about the sitting, walking, lying down, and swimming meditation varieties.

The following story humorously illustrates the state of happy confusion that surrounds the world of meditation these days:

Once a person was meditating with his eyes tightly closed.
He was also repeating an unintelligible mantra.
His wife noticed it and the following exchange ensued:
(questions by the wife, answers by "you know who")
What are you doing?
I am meditating.
Why are you meditating?
To release my stress!
What stress? I am the one who does all the work:
shopping, cooking, laundry, paying the bills.
Why are you *stressed?*
I am just stressed.
And what is this thing that you are uttering, slowly?
It is a mantra. It is a very precious mantra.
[...coming to the real question, *the wife asks...]*
How much did you pay for it?
500 dollars.
500 dollars?!!
Last month, when we wanted to buy a vacuum cleaner,
you said, "Honey, let's buy a used one.
We are on a limited budget!"
And you spent 500 dollars on this trivial thing! I can't believe it.
What is this mantra?
I cannot tell you. My guru told me not to tell it to anybody.
What??!!! Not even to me? I am your wife!
Sorry, honey, I cannot. I really cannot.
I took a vow of secrecy.
How can you keep secrets from your wife?
Sorry. I cannot. I really *can't.*
That's it! I have had it. I am leaving right now!!!!
Saying this, his wife left him for good.
The man opened his eyes and joyously exclaimed:
"This mantra thing really *works!"*

There you have it! Without knowing what we want, we will not know the difference between what we want to *get* and what we want to *get rid of*. Knowing one's purpose is as pivotal in meditation as in any other serious pursuit. Buyers *beware*: Mantras do work, albeit in some mysterious ways. Above all, do stay clear from "quick-fix-it-all," "enlightenment-in-sixty-seconds" variety deals.

As stated before, the Bhagavad Gītā provides succinct guidelines about the "how to" of meditation in chapter 6. We quote the following quintessential verse on the means and the end of meditation:

> शनैः शनैरुपरमेद् बुद्ध्या धृतिगृहीतया ।
> आत्मसंस्थं मनः कृत्वा न किञ्चिदपि चिन्तयेत् ॥ ६.२५ ॥
>
> *śanaiḥ śanair uparamed buddhyā dhṛtigṛhītayā /*
> *ātmasaṃsthaṃ manaḥ kṛtvā na kiṃcid api cintayet //6.25//*
>
> By the intellect held in firmness, may one slowly resolve the mind in the Self (*ātman*). Keeping the mind established in the Self, may one not think of anything else.

Let us see what people generally want to get out of meditation. Most people *want* peace of mind, the "calming effect."

Some want to *gain* concentration; while others *want* greater clarity and sharper memory. A few others want to cure their headache or migraine through meditation. While all such reasons may have their relative legitimacy, we should remember that the "wanting attitude" or the "gaining mindset" could actually be greatly counterproductive to the very spirit of meditation. Meditation accords the greatest avenue to get in touch with our deepest self, for the profoundest secrets of the Self are revealed only in the stillness of mind, in the silence of soul. If we approach meditation practice with the mindset of "acquiring something" or a "what-is-in-it-for-me" attitude, it may turn out to be just another mundane activity or mind-game. The following popular version of an ancient Buddhist parable points out the irony in pursuing things with a "wanting/gaining mindset":

> *A man said to Gautama Buddha, "I want happiness."*
> *The Buddha said, "First remove 'I,' that's ego; then remove 'want,' that's desire.*
> *See, now you are left with only 'Happiness'." (Sayings of Buddha)*[7]

Perhaps, it is not what we *gain* but, rather, what we *lose* that may determine the true value of a mediation practice, as the following story splendidly illustrates:

> *The Buddha was once asked, "What have you* gained *from meditation."*
> *"Nothing," he replied.*
> *However, the Buddha added, let me tell you what I* lost: *anger, anxiety, depression, insecurity, fear of old age, and death.*

[7] These are probably not the exact words of the Buddha. Given that the quote talks about overcoming ego and desire, it is likely that the Buddha might have said something similar on the subject of wanting happiness.

Mastering the Path of Meditation[8]

In this section, we present detailed instructions about mediation as stated in chapter 6. As will be seen in the following paragraphs, in chapter 6, titled *Ātmasaṁyamayogaḥ*: The Yoga of Self-Discipline, we find the most detailed instructions on the discipline of meditation that culminates in *bhakti yoga—śraddhāvān bhajate yo māṃ sa me yuktatamo mataḥ*: the *yogi*[9] who worships Me devoutly with his innermost self abiding in Me, is considered by Me to be the best of the *yogis* (6:47). Besides, in the Gītā, the path of meditation or concentration serves as a necessary concomitant to all other paths, since a certain measure of calm concentration is required to practice the path of action, knowledge, and devotion in an effective manner.

No one can become any type of *yogi* without giving up *saṅkalpa* (subtle hankerings and self-centered purposes) or without the cultivation of a detached mind free from attachments, hopes, and expectations. A wise *yogi* attains *yoga* (*samatā*—equanimity) only by performing allotted duties in a detached manner. Because without performing dutiful deeds—that is, without dedicating the objects received from the world in the service of the world—one cannot be established in *yoga* (discipline of *samatā*). The equanimity or evenness of mind (*samatā—samabuddhi*) that is attained through *karma yoga* is the very same equanimity that is also attained through the *yoga* of meditation (*dhyāna yoga*).

As a prelude to the discipline of meditation, we are told in chapter 6 that responsibility for one's spiritual welfare and downfall lies within oneself and no one else. Therefore, one should uplift oneself by one's own self (efforts) and not degrade oneself; for one's own self alone is one's friend, and one's own self alone is one's enemy. One who has conquered oneself by oneself—that is, one who relies solely on oneself and has forsaken all dependence on perishable objects—such a person is one's own friend. But one who has not conquered oneself—that is, one who feels the need for perishable things—is one's own enemy.

At the very outset of chapter 6, by way of the path as well as the goal, Śrī Kṛṣṇa presents the following marks of a *yogi* steadfast in equanimity: "When one does not get attached to sense-objects or to actions, and has renounced all purposes *(saṅkalpas)*, then, he is said to have ascended the heights of *yoga (yogārudha)*. One who has achieved mastery over oneself and who remains untainted and equanimous while experiencing favorableness and unfavorableness, joy and sorrow, honor and dishonor, such a person should be considered to have attained the Supreme Self. One who is content, who is steady and has control over the senses, and for whom a lump of clay, stone, and gold are the same (i.e., perishable), such a person is said to be established in *yoga* (*samatā*). He who looks with equal regard (and with the same sense of wellbeing) toward

[8] For details, see: Satinder Dhiman, trans., *Sahaja-Gītā: The Essential Gītā—Simplified* (Gorakhpur, India: Gītā Prakāshan, 2013), 30–34.

[9] A *yogi* is a practitioner who has achieved a certain measure of success in yoga.

all—a well-wisher, a friend, a foe, an indifferent person, a mediator, the hateful (detrimental to others), relatives, the virtuous and the sinful—such a person is indeed the most excellent of all."

Śrī Kṛṣṇa then explains the necessary preliminaries of meditation as follows: "An aspirant-meditator (*Dhyānayogi*) should constantly engage his mind and thoughts in meditation upon God, living alone in seclusion, having subdued his mind and body, and having got rid of the fetters of desires and possessions for personal enjoyment. Its technique is as follows—On a clean and pure land, place a seat (*āsana*) and cover it with *kuśa*-grass first, then cover it with a deer skin and place a soft cotton cloth on the top. The seat should be firm and stable and should neither be too high nor too low. While seated on it, restraining the activities of the mind and senses and concentrating the mind, the aspirant should engage in the practice of *yoga* of meditation for the purpose of self-purification (i.e., only for the purpose of God-realization).

For meditation, one should hold the body, head, and neck straight and still—sitting motionless like a portrait—fixing the gaze on the tip of the nose, without looking in any other direction. With a serene mind, free from likes and dislikes (*rāga-dveṣa*), fearless, with life that is disciplined and chaste, such a vigilant *dhyāna yogi* should sit with the mind exclusively fixed and absorbed in Me alone, as the Supreme Goal. Thus always keeping the mind steadfast on Me, the *dhyāna yogi* of disciplined mind attains everlasting Peace, the Supreme Bliss abiding in Me—attaining which there is nothing more that remains here to be attained."

According to the Gītā, "Success in this *Yoga* of meditation is neither attained by one who either eats too much or does not eat at all, nor by one who either sleeps too much or does not sleep at all. This *Yoga* (of meditation), which destroys sorrows, is accomplished only by him who is temperate in diet and recreation, who is disciplined (and detached) in the performance of actions, and is temperate in sleep and waking."

Description of Meditation on the Self [*Svarūpa*]—When the mind is absorbed in the Self alone, completely free from longing for worldly objects and desires, then one is said to be "really" steadfast in the *Yoga* (of meditation). As the flame of a lamp that is placed in a spot sheltered from wind does not flicker even slightly, even so the disciplined mind of the one who practices the *Yoga* of meditation remains established in the Self (*svarūpa*) and does not think about anything other than the Self. When the mind of the *dhyāna yogi* becomes indifferent even toward the profound meditative absorption (*Nirbīja-Samādhi*: trance without seed)—that is, when the *yogi* does not revel even in the bliss of deep meditative absorption—in that state the *yogi* remains content within the self by realizing the Self within his *swarūpa*. There is no bliss greater than the bliss experienced by the *dhyāna yogi* in which he beholds the Self through the self and rejoices in the Self, and wherein established the *yogi* is not shaken even by the greatest sorrow. This bliss is not dependent upon the senses, and, in this bliss, the intellect remains fully awake (and alert). It means that this bliss (*sukha*) is utterly distinct from *sāttvika*, *rājasika* and *tāmasika sukha*—all three types of happiness.[10] Established in such bliss, the *dhyāna yogi* never deviates from it. To have attained this bliss is the touchstone (litmus test) of all spiritual practices—a sure proof of Spiritual Plenitude.

According to the Gītā, the state in which there is forever severance (*viyoga*) of an assumed connection with pain (the sorrowful world) is the only state that should verily be known by the name of "*Yoga*" (6:23). This state of permanent severance from worldly sorrow, along with the state of equanimity (*samatvaṃ* 2:48), is true *yoga* (communion with the Supreme). This *yoga* must be practiced with determination and with an undistracted mind. "The devotee who sees Me everywhere at all times, in all objects, persons, and so on, and sees everything (places, objects, persons, etc.) in Me, to him I am never lost (invisible), nor is he ever lost to Me. It is because such a perfected devotee has become one (*abhinna*) with Me and perceives all world verily as My Being (*Svarūpa*) only."

"Established in the unity of all existence, a *yogi* who adores Me as present in all beings, verily abides in Me—in whatever condition he may be. O Arjuna! As an ordinary person seeks the wellbeing of all parts of his body equally, even so a devotee, who sees God in all beings equally, seeks the wellbeing of all beings equally. As an ordinary person acts quite naturally to eradicate the pain in his body (and to seek his pleasure); even so, the devotee acts quite naturally to eradicate the pain of others and to provide them pleasure. Such a devotee is deemed to be the supreme *yogi* in my estimation."

"All desires arise from *saṅkalpa*—subtle hankerings and self-centered purposes of the world. Renouncing entirely all such desires, and withdrawing, by strength of mind, all senses from their respective objects, the aspirant should, with an unhurried intellect set in firmness, gradually become detached (*uparām*) from the world. The aspirant (*sādhaka*) should then focus his mind on the Supreme Self (*Paramātman*). That is, the aspirant should firmly resolve that 'everywhere there is only One all-pervading Supreme Spirit (God), and there is nothing else except God.' Having determined thus, he should think of nothing else whatsoever—neither of the world nor of God. If the aspirant is not able to practice this 'silent method' (*chup-sādhan*), then he should bring his unsteady and wavering mind back, wherever it wanders, and practice concentrating it on God properly. An aspirant whose sins have been destroyed through this spiritual practice, whose *rajoguṇa* (passion that promotes activity/movement) and its modes (tendencies) have become still, and whose mind has become forever peaceful and pure, such a *dhyāna yogi*, whose very self has merged with Brahman, certainly attains to the *sāttvika-sukha* (pure bliss). Abiding constantly in this manner in the Supreme Spirit, the *yogi*, who is free from all sins, peacefully experiences the infinite bliss of the attainment of Brahman."

(*Experience of the aspirant who meditates on the Real Self* [*Svarūpa*]—) The *dhyāna yogi* who meditates on his Self (*svarūpa* or *ātman*) existent perfectly

[10] *Prakṛti* or Primordial Nature is constituted of three strands or modes or qualities or *Guṇas: Sattva* (light or radiance or equilibrium or purity or goodness), *Rajas* (energy or passion or activity), and *Tamas* (dullness or inertia). The "three types of happiness" referred to here signify the three different types of pleasure arising from these *guṇas*.

and uniformly everywhere, beholds the Self as present in all beings and all beings as present in the Self.

(*Experience of the aspirant who meditates on the One with Form and Attributes* [*Saguṇa-Sākār*]—) The devotee who sees Me everywhere at all times, in all objects, persons, and so on, and sees everything (places, objects, persons, etc.) in Me, to him I am never lost (invisible), nor is he ever lost to Me. It is because such a perfected devotee has become one (*abhinna*) with Me and perceives all world verily as My Being (*Svarūpa*) only. Established in the unity of all existence, a *yogi* who adores Me as present in all beings, verily abides in Me—in whatever condition he may be. O Arjuna! As an ordinary person seeks the wellbeing of all parts of his body equally, even so a devotee, who sees God in all beings equally, seeks the wellbeing of all beings equally. As an ordinary person acts quite naturally to eradicate the pain in his body (and to seek his pleasure); even so, the devotee acts quite naturally to eradicate the pain of others and to provide them pleasure. Such a devotee is deemed to be the supreme *yogi* in my estimation.

How to Control the Mind

After hearing about attaining equanimity by the *yoga* of meditation, Arjuna said, "O slayer of Madhu, due to a wavering mind, I find it very difficult to attain perfection in equanimity through *dhyāna yoga*. O Śrī Kṛṣṇa! The mind is verily restless, turbulent, unyielding, and strong. I regard it quite as hard to achieve its control as capturing the wind in the palm of hand."

After listening to Arjuna's viewpoint, Śrī Bhagavān said, "O Mighty Armed! You are very right: The mind is restless and hard to control. O Son of Kuntī! It can be controlled by constant practice and detachment (or dispassion). However, I am of the conviction that this *yoga* is very difficult to attain by one whose mind is not fully under his control (i.e., whose mind is attracted or attached to sense-objects or pleasures). It is because in the perfection of *yoga*, the restlessness of mind is not as great a hindrance as an uncontrolled mind. Therefore, one, who strives steadfastly in the *yoga* of meditation and whose mind is under control, is able to attain success in the *yoga* (of equanimity).

Those who undergo various types of severe austerities to attain *siddhis* are called ascetics. The *yogi* is superior to the ascetics and even to a scholar of scriptures. The *yogi* is also superior to those who engage in sacrifice (*yajñā*), donation, pilgrimage, and so on, with interested motive. This is my conviction. Therefore, O Arjuna! You too be a *yogi*."

The Gītā and Self-Mastery: The Life Worth Leading

What the caterpillar calls the end of the world, the master calls a butterfly. (Richard Bach)

Self-mastery is essentially a transformative process, a metamorphosis, a progression involving a series of stages. It is a journey of many steps. At every stage, we may feel that we have lost something that we had prior to it. But it is actually a "graded" process in which every successive step builds on all the steps preceding it. Nothing is lost. What is the end of the limiting world from a caterpillar's standpoint is the beginning of the life of freedom of a butterfly. Perspective is all.

Warren Bennis, a preeminent leadership scholar, has observed, "Leaders are people who do the right thing; managers are people who do things right."[11] While this may be a bit of an oversimplification—*since both leaders and managers need to do things right as well as do the right thing*—doing the right thing remains the perennial leadership challenge. But doing the right thing presupposes knowledge of what the right thing is in the first place. *This is exactly the point where the Gītā begins.* What is the utmost right thing to do in any given situation? Surely, the answer to this enigmatic question holds the key to many a management conundrum. By helping us focus on the highest good in all we do, the Gītā unfolds as an extended ode to the attainment of the ultimate good (*nisśreyas*)—the knowledge of our oneness with the Ultimate Reality.

Mind: A Leader's Greatest Friend and Foe

The Gītā presents an inside-out leadership development approach based on Self-knowledge and self-mastery, the two main qualities of authentic self-leadership. Peter Senge, one of the key management thinkers of our time, has quoted the Gītā in two of his celebrated books, *The Fifth Discipline* and *Presence.*[12] Although traditionally interpreted as a religious-spiritual text, the Gītā encompasses great practical life lessons for modern times. Its message fosters the holistic development of human personality in all its dimensions (physical-psychological, emotional, intellectual, and spiritual) by providing guidance on the three essential spiritual practices: "training the mind," "transforming the passions," and "guarding the heart."[13] The Gītā unfolds as an infallible guide for those higher-order individuals who *externally* live a life of full engagement with the world, while *internally* always remaining steadfastly anchored in the wisdom of their Higher Self.

[11] Warren Bennis, *An Invented Life: Reflections on Leadership and Change* (New York, NY: Perseus Books Group, 1994), 78.

[12] See Peter M. Senge, *The Fifth Discipline: The Art & Practice of The Learning Organization* (New York, NY: Doubleday, Revised and updated edition, 2006), 76. Peter M. Senge, C. Otto Scharmer, & Joseph Jaworski, *Presence: Human Purpose and the Field of the Future* (New York, NY: Crown Books, 2008), 92.

[13] In his fine preface to *The Essential Gandhi* (New York, NY: Vintage Books, 2002), Eknath Easwaran calls these three practices "the essence of the spiritual life." These conform to the threefold disciplines enunciated in various Indian wisdom texts—the path of knowledge (*jñāna yoga*), the path of action (*karma yoga*), and the path of devotion (*bhakti yoga*).

The Gītā reminds us that an unruly mind is our greatest foe, and a stable mind our greatest friend. It places great emphasis on self-restraint and mental discipline. It is common knowledge that mental strength and determination are the keys to leadership success; leaders who are mentally weak and wayward cannot achieve a durable and consistent organizational vision or mission. The outcome of an unrestrained mind is a life given to selfish desire, anger, and greed. Buddhist psychology also warns of three mental traps or unwholesome roots of mind: greed, hatred, and ignorance. If our attention emanates from any of these three unwholesome roots, then it is not appropriate and will not give us the knowledge of reality as it truly is. And a leader's first job is to have an accurate knowledge of the current reality.

If leadership is an extension of who we are, then leaders first need to manage themselves before they can aspire to lead others. Underscoring the importance of self-leadership, the Bhagavad Gītā further stresses that, when facing a crisis, leaders must elevate themselves by self-effort (*uddharedātmanātmānaṃ*: 6.5). This requires a deep understanding of the workings of the mind. For those who have conquered their mind, the mind is the best of friends; but for those who have failed to control their mind, the mind will be their greatest enemy (*ātma ivahyātmanobandhurātmaivaripurātmanaḥ*: 6.5). Without self-victory *ātma jayaha* or Self- mastery, one cannot attain success in any field. Essentially, it points out that an un-mastered self is the biggest enemy of the individual; in fact, Śrī Kṛṣṇa goes one step further, it is not only the greatest enemy, but the *only* enemy of a human being!

An unrestrained and untrained mind is very weak and unstable and cannot carry out any task, let alone lead. Arjuna tells Śrī Kṛṣṇa that his mind is unsteady, restless, and yet very powerful, and as difficult to control as the wind. Śrī Kṛṣṇa agrees that the mind is not easy to control; however, he says that it is possible to control the mind by constant practice and detachment or dispassion (*abhyāsena…vairāgyeṇaca*: 6.35).

Enlightened leaders need to employ their intellect effectively to direct their mind. In this regard, another Indian wisdom text, *Kaṭhopaniṣad* 1.3.3–4, likens the human body to a chariot (*rathakalpanā*) to describe the position of the individual self (*ātmā*) vis-à-vis the senses (*indriya*), mind (*manas*), and intellect (*buddhi*). The mind represents the reins and the five senses are the horses. The objects perceived by the senses chart the chariot's path. The intellect is the driver and the self as the passenger acts as the enjoyer or sufferer in the association of the mind and senses.[14] Whereas an ordinary leader is constantly driven by a wayward mind and unruly desires for sense objects, a wise leader uses the power of intelligence to discern between what is pleasant (*preyas*) and what is right (*śreyas*).

[14]The chariot metaphor occurs during *mantras* three and four in chapter 1, section three of *Kaṭhopaniṣad*, an *Upaniṣad* that has a few verses in common with the Bhagavad Gītā. Plato also uses the chariot allegory in his dialog *Phaedrus* to explain the journey of the human soul toward enlightenment.

Psychology and Tyranny of Wants!

At times, we experience ourselves as limited, inadequate, and incomplete. This gnawing sense of lack is felt as something wanting, something missing. Then our mind, which cannot endure this state of inadequacy for too long, "makes up" something to fill the void. This "something" can be in the form of an object, a person, or a situation. Having postulated thus, our mind then jumps on the craving bandwagon to attain the desired object, person, or experience—it starts positively seeking them out. This creates agitation in our mind and we become restless.

When, finally we are able to attain the desired thing, our restlessness goes away and our mind feels peaceful momentarily. Soon, the wanting state returns and our mind starts hankering after another set of objects or experiences all over again. This is the psychology, albeit tyranny, of wants. There is an intimate connection between "wanting" (meaning, something lacking) and "wants."

In fact, it is not that attaining the desired or wanted object, person, or experience brought us happiness, joy, or peace; it is the cessation of agitation or restlessness of mind that brought fleeting moments of happiness. Temporarily free from mental restlessness caused by wanting, we felt at peace upon the attainment of our desired object. The peace did not reside in the object or experience, but in the quietude, stillness of the mind. Free from mental restlessness, we felt the fullness of our being. If the peace in fact resided in the objects or experiences, we would not ever get bored with them or look for other haunts of happiness constantly.

This is the alchemy of fulfillment and the approach to free oneself from the unending servitude of wanting-having-wanting vicious cycle.

The Buddha story presented earlier in this chapter is a good reminder about the tyranny of wants.

Curbing Desire, Anger, and Greed: Managing Negative Emotions

All wisdom traditions of the world are in agreement that self-centered desire is the source of all sorrow and evil. The Gītā calls desire, anger, and greed the triple gates of hell, which bring about one's downfall (*trividhaṃnarakasyedaṃ dvāraṃnāśanamātmanah*: 16.21). It clarifies that (unsatisfied) desire is the cause of greed as well as anger. The Gītā says that, to control anger, we first need to pay attention to its root cause. Anger arises when someone stands in the way of our desired object—that is, anger ensues from (unfulfilled) desire. And attachment to things, ideas, and opinions lie at the root of desire. Basically, to control anger, we should first guard and calm our mind. If our mind remains in a state of calm, then no negative emotions can provoke it. The easiest way to be peaceful in mind is to let our mind rest content within its own inner sanctuary rather than constantly hankering after the worldly objects outside.

The Gītā categorically states:

śaknotīhaivayaḥsoḍhuṃprākśarīravimokṣaṇāt /
kāmakrodhodbhavaṃvegaṃsayuktaḥsasukhīnaraḥ //5.23//

Only those who are able to withstand the impulses of lust and anger arising in the body are integrated (*yuktaḥ*) and live in joy.

The reason the Gītā lays so much importance on curtailing one's desires is because all evil proceeds from self-centered desires. A selfish person cannot serve others; in fact, such a person becomes a bane to society. Therefore, according to the Gītā, a leader must first conquer desire if he or she is to serve others. The three traps (excessive desire, anger, and greed) are present in every dysfunctional organization, manifested to the highest degree in its leaders. Elsewhere in the Gītā, Śrī Kṛṣṇa explains that attachment breeds desire, and from desire (unfulfilled) ensues anger; anger clouds judgment, and when judgment is clouded, one's powers of reasoning are lost; and with the loss of reasoning, one falls from one's status as a human being (2.62–63).

Therefore, leaders should manage their anger well and should not let anger gain control over them. Mastering the emotion of anger is a not an easy task, as many sages of the past and present have reminded us. Aristotle expressed it deftly: "Anybody can become angry, that is easy; but to be angry with the right person, and to the right degree, and at the right time, for the right purpose, and in the right way, that is not within everybody's power and is not easy."[15] A most practical method for controlling anger and other negative emotions is expressed by the acronym F.I.R, denoting the first letters of the words frequency, intensity, and recovery. We should try to first reduce the frequency of the occurrence of these negative emotions, then curb their intensity, and finally reduce their recovery period.[16]

David J. Pollay, a syndicated columnist and business consultant, and author of the book *The Law of Garbage Truck*[17] tells an interesting story about his experience about managing negative emotions (such as anger, resentment, frustration, and disappointment). Twenty years ago, while riding in a New York City taxi, David narrowly escaped a life-threatening car crash. The driver who almost caused the accident started yelling at the cab driver, who remarkably just smiled, waved, and wished him well. Pollay asked how the cab driver could remain so calm, and his response sparked the defining principle of The Law of the Garbage Truck (and the said book):

Many people are like garbage trucks. They run around full of garbage, full of frustration, full of anger, and full of disappointment. And when the garbage piles up, they need a place to dump it on. And if you let them, they'll dump it on you.

[15] Quoted in Edith M. Leonard, Lillian E. Miles, & Catherine S. Van der Kar, *The Child: At Home and School* (New York, NY: American Book Co., 1944), 203.

[16] The F.I.R strategy of controlling anger was shared by Swami Paramarthananda in one of his discourses on the Gītā.

[17] David J. Pollay, *The Law of the Garbage Truck: How to Stop People from Dumping on You* (New York, NY: Sterling Publishing Co., 2012).

> So when someone wants to dump on you, don't take it personally. Just smile, wave, wish them well, and move on. Don't let their garbage spread to people at work, at home or on the streets. You love those who treat you right; you pray for those who don't. Life is 10% what you make it. The other 90% is how you take it.[18]

David provides a simple strategy to deal with the negativity around us that can be stated in three refrains: (1) Don't let others dump their garbage on you; (2) don't dump it on yourself, and (3) don't dump it on others. In this manner, we can help others and ourselves.

Life Marked by Sacrifice, Charity, and Austerity

The Gītā (18.5) mandates a threefold act of sacrifice (*yajña*), charity (*dānaṃ*), and austerity (*tapas*) and considers these as the "purifiers of the wise." "*Yajña*" literally means a creative sacrifice or an offering. The highest form of offering is living a life of sincerity—a life led by being good and doing good. A sincere life is characterized by doing what we love and loving what we have to do. "*Dānaṃ*" means charity and denotes much more than writing a check to a favorite cause or organization. At the deepest level, it means the gift of "expressed love." "*Tapas*" means austerity or discipline. The Gītā talks about several kinds of discipline. The most important is "*vāk tapas*"—"discipline of speech."

There are five such disciplines of speech that the Gītā recommends:

> *anudvegakaraṃvākyaṃsatyaṃpriyahitaṃcayat* /
> *svādhyāyābhyasanaṃcaivavānmayaṃ tapa ucyate* //17.15//
>
> That speech which causes no mental anguish (disturbance) to anyone, which is truthful, agreeable, and beneficial, as well as the practice of study of the sacred books, is considered to be the discipline of speech.

It is said that the Greek philosopher Socrates used to recommend a triple test for the discipline of speech: "before you speak, let your words pass through three gates: 1. Is it true; 2. Is it necessary; and 3. Is it kind?" According to the Gītā 6.32, that person "is considered best who judges happiness and sorrow in all beings, by the same standard as he would apply to himself."[19] Holistic leaders apply this proverbial golden rule in all spheres of their life. This is the key to their moral self-mastery. The Gītā states that the wise leader acts to set an example to the masses; so that the unwary do not go astray (3.26); they work for the unification of the world at large (*lokasaṃgraham*: 3.20, 3.25); for the welfare of all beings (*sarvabhūtahite*: 5.25); and for the purification of the self (*ātmaśuddhaye*: 5.11). These four goals together furnish a touchstone for leadership success in any setting.

[18] People Are Like Garbage Trucks! A YouTube video: https://www.youtube.com/watch?v=H4NW-Cqh308

[19] See Swami Gambhīrānanda, trans., *Bhagavad Gītā with the Commentary of Śaṅkarācārya* (Calcutta, India: Advaita Ashrama, 1984), 302.

The Gītā and Subduing the Imposter Ego

One of the key dimensions of personal mastery is understanding (and subduing) the workings of the imposter ego. Misplaced ego has dire personal and professional consequences: it is the greatest enemy of workplace amity and harmony. Most psychological and emotional stress is caused by our excessive self-centeredness. Understanding the workings of the imposter ego and thereby rendering it ineffective is the first step on the path of wisdom. In chapter 13 of the Bhagavad Gītā, where Śrī Kṛṣṇa begins to describe the marks or means of true knowledge, we see "absence of self-pride" (13.7) listed as the very first mark. In the next verse (13.8), Śrī Kṛṣṇa again states: "and absence of egotism also" (*anahaṁkāra eva ca*). Note the word "also" after the word "egotism." Of the 20 marks of true knowledge listed in verses 13.7–11, the word "also" is appended only to egotism/self-pride (*ahaṁkāra*). Something to take serious note of and ponder over deeply!

As long as one harbors a sense of distinction/superiority, regardless of the reason—justified or unjustified—one will labor in vain, not much unlike the ox that turns the oil-press by going back and forth. When God is all there is, where is the need for entertaining any feelings of distinction or superiority—no matter what the justification may be? Those who are truly awakened become aware of the fact that "God is all there is"—and that God includes all, even the ones who may not be as superior as oneself, in one's estimation! This knowledge fosters amity, understanding, and harmony in all settings and removes the conflict inherent in the "game of one-up-ness" that plagues most human interaction.

This feeling of false pride springs from a mistaken sense of inadequacy about oneself and leads to a false projection of superiority and need for constant seeking of external validation. The proper resolution of this problem is found in understanding oneself, through self-inquiry and contemplation, to be the full and complete self (*ātman*). Such knowledge enables one to act in the world with a deep sense of peace and inner fulfillment. This is what is meant by being *ātmavān* (2.45), possessing the real self, or being unitively self-possessed.

According to the Gītā, no action is genuine unless it is performed in the full wakefulness of Self-knowledge. Self-knowledge transforms our motivation and liberates us from the narrow confines of self-centered action to the freedom of serving others. Through this rediscovery of our intrinsic freedom, we are also able to experience the calm bliss of the fullness of our real self and intuit the harmonious oneness of all existence. When the false divisions and distinctions based on our narrow personal likes and dislikes disappear, we are able to extend our benevolence without preference or prejudice in all directions, and our existence benefits the whole universe. Our very existence then becomes an offering to the Supreme, a celebration of the Whole. And our feet get firmly planted on the path that leads to peace, happiness, and liberation.

Ego seems to be the root of all problems अनर्थ—greed, anger, hatred, and so forth. Any spiritual practice undertaken while the imposter ego is in place, leads us nowhere. Ego can never be liberated any more than the water in a mirage can quench our thirst. It is the little "me" that wants to be liberated, not the "pure being," which is ever-liberated. There is no liberation *for* the ego; liberation is freedom *from* the notion of ego—freedom from the limited being we mistakenly take our self to be. This freedom is available to all of us, right here right now. It is a hard cash and not a promissory note.

Personal Mastery According to the Gītā

In the last 18 verses (2.55–2.72) of chapter 2, the Gītā presents the highest ideal of personal mastery through the conception of a sage steadfast in the wisdom of the higher Self. Let us first look closer at these magnificent verses in order to understand their true import for Self-knowledge and Self-realization. In these verses, the marks of a sage established in the wisdom of the self (*sthitaprajña*) are described as follows:

> When one completely casts off all selfish desires of the mind, finding contentment by the Self in the Self alone; neither agitated by sorrow nor hankering after the sense pleasures; free from lust, fear, and anger; free from attachment; neither elated by good fortune nor depressed by bad; with senses subdued and mind ever absorbed in the Divine within—such a person is truly wise.[20]

In this part of the description of the traits of a person of steady wisdom, we notice three main things: freedom from self-centered desire (and the resultant anger, greed, and attachment: the triple gates of hell), an attitude of equanimity, and absorption in the wisdom of the Self or Divine. Then, the Gītā goes on to explain the psychology of anger and the glory of a person who has gone beyond self-interest and egotism:

> Brooding on sense objects leads to attachment; from attachment comes desire; and from (unfulfilled) desire ensues anger. Anger clouds judgment and leads to loss of reason; and loss of reason brings utter ruin....One who has given up all desires and moves about free from longing, without self-interest and egotism, such a person attains peace. Attaining this state even at the time of death, one passes from death to immortality.[21]

[20] Eknath Easwaran, cited in Louis Fischer (Ed.), *The Essential Gandhi* (New York, NY: Vintage Books, 2002), xvi.

[21] Adapted from Eknath Easwaran, trans., *The Bhagavad Gītā* (New York, NY: Vintage Spiritual Classics, 2000), 68–69; Franklin Edgerton, trans., *The Bhagavad Gītā* (New York, NY: Harper & Row Publishers, 1964), 15–17; S. Radhākrishnan, *The Bhagavad Gītā: With an Introductory Essay, Sanskrit Text, English Translation, and Notes* (London, UK: George Allen and Unwin, 1958), 296–299; and Satinder Dhiman, trans., *Sahaja-Gītā: The Essential Gītā* [Selection and Compilation, Rajendra Kumar Dhawan]. Based on Paramśraddheya Swāmījī Shrī Rāmsukhdāsjī Mahārāj's commentary on Śrīmad Bhagavad Gītā, titled *Sādhaka-Sañjivanī* (Gorakhpur, India: Gītā Prakāshan, 2013), 125.

It is important to note that the description of a person steady in wisdom starts and ends with casting off all the selfish desires the mind. The *Yogavāsiṣṭha Mahāramāyaṇa* also states succinctly, "Wisdom proceeds from the curtailing of desires."[22]

There are at least four places where the characteristics of an ideal sage are presented in the Gītā from different perspectives: 2.55–72; 12.13–20; 14.21–27; and 18.49–56 (in addition, we also find reaffirmation of the same theme in selected verses of two other chapters: 13.7–11 and 16.1–3). For example, chapter 12 (verses 13–20) describes the marks of a devotee (*bhakta*); these have a striking similarity to the qualities of a person who has transcended the sway of three modes of material nature *triguṇātīta* (14.21–27), which in turn bear a great similarity to the characteristics of a person steadfast in wisdom (*sthitaprajña*) as described in chapter 2 (verses 55–72) as follows:

> That person is dear to me who is free from ill-will, friendly and compassionate; free from the sense of "I" and "mine"; equanimous in joy and sorrow, forgiving, ever-content, firm in faith with his mind ever united with Me; who has subdued his mind, senses, and body; and has surrendered heart and mind to Me....Not agitating the world, nor agitated by it, above the sway of delight, envy, desire, and fear; who regards equally friend and foe, praise and blame, pain and pleasure, free from selfish attachments; quiet, ever-content, in harmony everywhere, firm in faith—such a person is dear to Me.[23]

What is noteworthy in the above-quoted verses is that almost all of these qualities of an ideal sage more or less focus on emotional maturity—*the ability to manage emotional disturbances and reactions calmly.* Cultivating these qualities is important for everyone, in both personal and professional arenas. For example, being friendly and compassionate and free from malice (*adveṣṭāsarvabhūt ānāṃmaitraḥkaruṇa*: 12.13), being free from attachment, fear, and anger (*vītarāgabhayakrodhaḥ*: 2.56, 4.10), and neither being a source of annoyance to fellow-beings nor feeling vexed with them (*yasmānnodvijatelokolokānnodvij atecayaḥ*: 12.15)—all these are signs of emotional stability, which is the key to harmony in personal and professional relationships.

This is a tall order of personal qualities for any leader to cultivate and requires years and years of dedication, commitment, and perseverance. These qualities represent the highest level of emotional maturity, self-awareness, self-discipline, equanimity, and detachment that may appear to be unattainable by any leader according to modern standards. Enlightened leaders act as a "witness" of high moral leadership, without which the limits of higher human possibilities would neither be known nor sustained.

[22] Vihari-Lala Mitra, trans., *Vālmīki's Yoga-vāsiṣṭha-mahārāmāyaṇa*. Online edition, Retrieved January 25, 2016, http://www.wisdomlib.org/hinduism/book/yoga-vasistha-volume-2-part-ii/d/doc118202.html

[23] Easwaran, cited in Fischer, *The Essential Gandhi*, xvii [author's adaptation].

It is important to understand that the key to life's fulfillment, according to the Gītā, lies in Self-realization through Self-knowledge. Self-realization is the means as well as the end. This is the desideratum and the *summum bonum* of all human aspiration and quest.

The Gītā and Passion for Excellence

Greek thinkers of yore have defined happiness as the exercising of human faculties along the lines of excellence. In the same manner, the Bhagavad Gītā defines yoga as skillfulness, dexterity, or excellence in action (*yogaḥ karmasu kauśalam*: 2.50). Does that mean that skillfulness in *any* action is yoga? The Gītā clarifies that only that state of mastery leads to *yoga*, a higher communion, which is not opposed to *dharma*, the moral order. A sniper's or thief's skillfulness, for example, will not qualify as yoga since it is does not spring from wholesome intention.

It is common to experience a feeling of soaring spirit when we are doing excellent work. The converse is also true. It has been observed that the best way to kill human motivation is to expect and accept mediocre performance from others. Expecting less than excellent work is the greatest disservice we can do to ourselves and to others. We owe excellence to ourselves, as much as we owe it to the society. No mere ideology, this passion for excellence has far-reaching implications for holistic leaders and for workplace performance. Nobody comes to work to put in a shoddy performance. Everyone is looking for creative self-expression. And when we create opportunities for meaningful self-expression, we help build a workplace where people act with self-fulfillment and not merely work for it. Creating such a liberating work environment is the real job of an enlightened leader.

Aristotle's Theory of Golden Mean and Personal Mastery

According to Aristotle, good moral behavior is the desirable mean between two extremes—one of excess and the other of deficiency. The key to acting morally lies in finding a moderate position between those two extremes. For example, courage is a virtue, but if taken to excess it would appear as recklessness and, in deficiency, as cowardice. In his work titled *Nicomachean Ethics*, Aristotle explains the development of virtues essential for achieving the ultimate goal, happiness. It must be noted that the golden mean is not the exact arithmetic mean; it depends on the situation. There is no universal middle that would apply to every situation. Different degrees may be needed for different situations.

In the Gītā's estimation, to be able to focus the mind is no big deal. The big deal, according to the Gītā, is the evenness of mind or the equanimity (*samatā*)—to remain *unperturbed* and *unattached* through steadiness of mind. If a person is able to attain equanimity—regardless of other virtues—that person is a *siddha* (perfected being) or *sthitaprajñā* (established in steady wisdom) according to the Gītā. The Gītā does not regard that person a *siddha* who has cultivated all other qualities but lacks the essential equanimity!

Samatā: The Harbinger of Emotional Maturity

The Gītā regards "equanimity" or "evenness of mind" to be the *yoga* (2:48). And the finest teaching on this topic is provided in the Gītā as follows:

> *yogasthaḥ kuru karmāṇi saṅgaṃ tyaktvā dhanañjaya /*
> *siddhyasiddhyoḥ samo bhūtvā samatvaṃ yoga ucyate //2.48//*
>
> Abiding in equanimity, abandoning attachment, perform actions, O Arjuna, viewing with equanimous mind success and failure. Evenness of mind (*samatvaṃ*) is *Yoga*.

Samatā (equanimity) is the "fulcrum" around which the entire teachings of the Gītā revolve. Wherever the Lord has mentioned the highest peaks of the paths of action, knowledge, and devotion, He has very carefully interspersed "*samatā*" in their consummation (2.48, 53, 57; 5.6, 18–20; 12.13–19; 14.24, 25; 18.10, 26). So, in the Gītā's estimation, *samatā* is the litmus test of perfection (*siddhi*) in all the paths to God-realization. Whatever the spiritual practice, if *samatā* is not there, the goal is still far away.

Attaining Equanimity Through the Path of Action (Karma Yoga)

The Gītā teaches us how to act *without attachment* to the outcomes. The attachment to outcomes, desiring a specific result, sets the stage for anxiety. One gets elated by favorable results and feels dejected when the results are unfavorable. This is to live a life of perpetual emotional roller-coaster. When we release ourselves from the attachment to outcomes, we develop certain mental equipoise (*samatā*) to deal with "the slings and arrows of outrageous fortune."

In practicing the path of action, Arjuna is advised to perform actions as an offering to the Supreme, renouncing attachment to actions and their results, remaining steadfast in equanimity. The Gītā tells us that equanimity *(samatā)* can be attained both through the path of knowledge *(jñāna yoga)* as well as through the path of (selfless) action *(karma yoga)*. After having explained the *yoga* of equanimity according to the path of knowledge (involving discriminating reasoning regarding the body and the soul) [2:11–2:30], the Lord now explains equanimity *(samatā)* from the standpoint of the path of (selfless) action *(karma yoga)* [2:39–53], following which one completely overcomes the fetters of *karma*. This equanimity has four qualities:

1. Performing actions while established in equanimity, a person does not get entangled in the shackles of *karma*.

2. There is no loss (forfeiture) of efforts directed toward attaining this equanimity.
3. There is no fear of adverse results due to any omission in following this path.
4. Even a little observance of this practice saves one from the great fear (caused by the unending wheel of birth and death). In other words, even a little practice of this virtue of selfless actions grants liberation.

Then comes one of the most popular verses about *karma yoga* (2:47): Your right is only to perform your allotted duty; that is, your right is for action alone. But you have no right whatsoever to the results thereof; that is, you are not free in this regard. Therefore, let not the fruits of action be your motive, that is, do not become the cause of the fruit of your actions through attachment (with the instruments of actions, such as body); nor become attached to inaction (indifference, laziness, etc.). It means that "doing" is under our control; "happening" is under the purview of *prārabdha* (our earned destiny). To paraphrase Swami Sharnanandji's wisdom, *one should be "careful" about what one "does" and be "happy" with whatever "happens."*

In fact, the need for *yoga* (equanimity) is paramount in the performance of actions because the path of action is marred by selfish desire and attachment. In order to act as "free-agents," we need the discipline of "equanimity"—*yoga*—in the form of *karma yoga*. While in regards to the paths of knowledge and devotion, the "*yoga*" (communion) is quite natural. The seer, after realizing "All is God" (*Vāsudevaḥ Sarvam,* 7.19), remains naturally established in the experience of Oneness; and the devotee likewise constantly experiences reverential communion with the Lord. Therefore, In the Gītā, the word yoga *especially* signifies *karma yoga.*[24]

All undertakings, all actions, are tainted with some blemish—this means that all actions are inherently "binding" *in effect*, as they lead to good, bad, or mixed results (18.3; 18.12). But when the actions are performed with pure motives or intentions—that is, as an offering to the Supreme, without attachment to actions or fruits thereof—they become free from the blemish. This is the secret of *karma yoga*. And the finest teaching on this is provided in the Gītā as follows:

> *brahmaṇy ādhāya karmāṇi saṅgaṃ tyaktvā karoti yaḥ /*
> *lipyate na sa pāpena padmapatram ivāmbhasā* //5.10//
>
> He who acts offering all actions to the Lord, renouncing all attachment, remains untouched by the sin, as the lotus leaf by water.

[24]Swami Rāmsukhdāsjī, *Śrīmad Bhagavad Gītā: Sādhaka-Sañjivanī,* (Gorakhpur, India: Gītā Press, 2007), 5.

Karma yoga is the secret of becoming free from the effects of karma. Purification of mind is limit as far as the attainment of the Karma Yoga is concerned.

Samatā (Equanimity) and Kauśalta (Excellence) and Yogas of the Gītā

As stated before, the paradigmatic term "*samatvaṁ*," equanimity, is introduced in the second chapter of the Bhagavad Gītā as the *meaning* of yoga: *samatvaṁ yoga ucyate* (Gītā 2.48): Equanimity or evenness of mind is called yoga. It occurs throughout the Gītā in various forms and contexts: as *samaḥ*, evenness of mind: 2.48, 4.22, 9.29, 12.18, 18.54; as *samaṃ*, equanimous: 5.19, 6.13 & 32, 13.27 & 28; *samadarśanaḥ,* seeing the same Self in all: 5.18, 6.29; *samabuddhir*, impartial: 6.9; 12.4, and so forth. The glory of *samatā* is such that wherever in the Gītā the perfection in any of the three yogas is stated, it is expressed through the attainment of *samatvam*.

This yoga of even-mindedness in actions is an art in itself. That is, to remain even-minded both in success and failure of actions and the resultant detachment toward the outcome, is the skillfulness (*kauśalam*) in actions—the wisdom in actions. Actions are not important per se; only the yoga (*samatā*) in actions is important. Hence, the Gītā declares that evenness of mind *is* the skillfulness in action. This is the essence of karma yoga.

In its broader sense, *Samatā* or equanimity is the harmony that is there among all things—*samatva*—the equanimous, integrative, cooperative feature operating between one and another, thus fortifying all particularities or individualities into a sort of cosmic universal whole. This is the suggestion of the second chapter when it says: *Samatvaṁ yoga ucyate* (Gītā 2.48): Equanimity is yoga, balance is yoga, harmony is yoga, cooperation is yoga—*not* competition, *not* strive, *not* war, *not* exploitation, *not* animosity, *not* hatred. Hence, the necessity of maintaining a *balanced* attitude of mind while performing actions excellently.[25]

In this balance, the *dialectical tension* between self-centeredness and selflessness gets harmonized elegantly. In the Gītā, all the three *yogas* are essentially at par. This parity is brought out through a dialectic of inaction in actions (4.18) in *karma yoga*, seeing the Self in all and all in the Self (6.29) in *jñāna yoga*, and seeing the Lord *everywhere* and *everyone* in the Lord (6.30) in *bhakti yoga*—repose, Self, and the Lord being one and the same thing.[26]

[25] Swami Krishnananda, *The Teachings of the Bhagavadgita*. Retrieved November 14: http://www.swami-krishnananda.org/bhagavad/bhagavad_03.html

[26] Swami Ramsukhdasji, *Gītā Darpaṇ* (Gorakhpur, India: Gītā Press, 2005), 133. This quote is translated from Hindi by the author.

The evenness of mind, *samatā*, is the touchstone of all the three *yogas* in the Gītā. If one has not attained *samatā*, the spiritual goal of steady abidance in wisdom (*stithaprajña*: BG 2.555–72) is still far away.

Concluding Thoughts

Only that person is fit to contemplate the Divine light who is slave to nothing, not even to his virtues. (Ruysbroeck)

Meditation is essentially an art of attaining freedom from our inveterate attachments. One should not cling to anything, including the highest states and virtues. Ruysbroeck is right: In order to meditate upon the Divine Light within, we need to free ourselves from all attachments, however exalted they may be. The same lesson is conveyed by the Buddha's parable of the raft: when you have crossed over, you do not carry the raft with you. You leave it right there on the shore, and move on.

What is the methodology for meditation recommended by the Gītā? In short, direct your attention to the ever-changeless principle within you. This is the only spiritual practice, *sādhanā*, required. The Gītā calls it steadying the mind in the Self (*ātmasaṃsthaṃ manaḥ kṛtvā*: 6.25). This brings tranquility. This is the long and short of the *dhyāna yoga*, the path of meditation, according to the Gītā.

Intrinsically, our mind is pure and calm. It is only when we sit down to meditate that it starts becoming restless! The only purpose of meditation is to allow the mind to be restored to its pristine intrinsic purity. Then, like a bright crystal, it reveals our true nature in a spontaneous, *sahaja*, manner. The equanimous state of mind, *samatvam*, taught in both the Gītā and Buddhism, allows us to respond to all of life's emotional disturbances and fluctuations in such a way that we are, as Buddhist scholar Peter Harvey describes it, the opposite of the way James Bond likes his martini: *stirred* but *not shaken.*[27]

What is the litmus test that meditation is working in our lives? One can gauge one's progress on the path of meditation through a simple test. Ask yourself: *In the post-meditation period…*

> Am I becoming more calm, humble, peaceful, considerate, generous, grateful, tolerant, forgiving, cheerful, understanding, accepting, responsible, life-affirming, celebrative, loving, joyous, kind and compassionate? Am I growing in goodness?

[27] Cited in Frank Jude Boccio, Calm Within, *Yoga Journal Yoga 101*, August 9, 2010. Retrieved February 27, 2017: http://www.yogajournal.com/article/yoga-101/calm-within/

[It was in the 1964 film Goldfinger that Connery utters the words: "A Martini. Shaken, not stirred."].

Love, joy, and compassion are signs of being awake.
Anger, hatred, and greed are signs of being asleep.

Awakening to our true nature—
the sole purpose of all spiritual practice.[28]

Bon Voyage and Godspeed.

[28] Satinder Dhiman, *Songs of the Self.* Unpublished collection of poems by the author.

CHAPTER 9

Doing the Right Thing: Leaders' Moral and Spiritual Anchorage

Introduction: Understanding the Fundamental Human Problem

The fundamental seeking of all human beings is security, peace/happiness, and liberation. All human pursuits can be essentially reduced to these three basic endeavors. More often, we tend to search for these goals among external sources such as objects, people, and situations. However, we soon discover that no lasting peace and security can be found in external things because, in their ultimate bidding, they are unpredictable, unreliable, and subject to constant change. By gently pointing out that our whole problem is a *misdirected search due to self-ignorance*, the Gītā tells us that the only place where permanent and complete happiness and fulfillment can be found is within ourselves—in the fullness of our own being.

The Gītā further explains that it is the self-ignorance that covers our intrinsic fullness of being, and only Self-knowledge can lift the veil and lead us to the eternal fountain of abiding security, peace, and happiness that lies within us all. We finally make the pleasant discovery that searching for peace is like searching for one's glasses everywhere when they have been perched on our nose all along. Interestingly, we even tend to forget that we have been searching *for* them while unknowingly looking *through* them!

The Gītā teaches us that the fundamental human problem is the lack of Self-knowledge and the resultant extroverted-ness of our search for happiness and the mistaken way we relate to the world. In all our quests, we approach people, objects, and situations through the prism of our likes and dislikes (*rāga-dvēṣa*), which leads to attachment or aversion. Attachment leads to sorrow and sorrow leads to delusion which in turn compounds our misery. When the Self-knowledge (*ātma-jñāna*) dawns, we realize that whatever we have been seeking is already within us. It is in fact our own essential nature or Self. We are also able to experience the calm bliss of the fullness of our being and intuit the

S. Dhiman, *Bhagavad Gītā and Leadership*,
Palgrave Studies in Workplace Spirituality and Fulfillment,
https://doi.org/10.1007/978-3-319-67573-2_9

harmonious oneness of all existence. When the false divisions and distinctions based on our narrow personal likes and dislikes disappear, we are able to extend our benevolence without preference or prejudice in all directions, and our very existence benefits the whole universe. Our whole existence then becomes an offering to the Supreme. And our feet get firmly planted on the path that leads to peace, happiness, and liberation.[1]

Doing Good and Feeling Good Are Connected

Recent research on altruism shows that doing good and feeling good are closely related.[2] Matthieu Ricard, in his recent book titled *Altruism: The Power of Compassion to Change Yourself and the World*, presents a vision revealing how altruism can answer the key challenges of our times: economic inequality, life satisfaction, and environmental sustainability. With a rare combination of the mind of a scientist and the heart of a sage, he makes a robust case for cultivating altruism—*a caring concern for the wellbeing of others*—as the best means for simultaneously benefiting ourselves and our global society. The Gītā calls it *sarva bhūta hita*, wellbeing of all beings (BG 5.23; 12.4). This is the master key to happy individuals and harmonious society, the *summum bonum* of all ethical and spiritual leadership.

In the scheme of the Bhagavad Gītā, ethical conduct (*dharma*) furnishes the essential foundation for the quest for spiritual freedom. Conjoining the last word of the last verse of the Gītā (18.78) मम (*mama*) with the first word of the first verse of the Gītā (1.1), धर्म (*dharma*), we get "मम धर्म," signifying "my duty." Thus, the Gītā accords great importance to performing one's innate duty (*svadharma*) for the good of others, *without* expecting anything in return. And if we rearrange the first two words of the Gītā *dharmakṣetre kurukṣetre* "धर्मक्षेत्रे कुरुक्षेत्रे" as "क्षेत्रे क्षेत्रे धर्मम् कुरु:" (*kṣetre kṣetre dharmam kuruḥ*), we get the following meaning: In every sphere of life, do the *right* thing—in the full wakefulness of Self-knowledge. Doing the right thing brings one under the protective care of Dharma, the cosmic moral order. We have a Vedic injunction: धर्मो रक्षति रक्षिताः *Dharmo rakṣati rakṣitāḥa:* Dharma protects those who uphold Dharma. Hence, the *dharma* (innate moral duty or righteousness) is the province of the entire Gītā! In the Gītā's terminology, the performance of actions selflessly as a service to the Supreme purifies the mind and makes it a fit vessel for the reception of Self-knowledge which alone is the means to spiritual freedom. Śrī Kṛṣṇa, the teacher par excellence in the Gītā, does not merely want to make us philosophically learned, but wants to help us realize the Truth *experientially*—not to merely *instruct*, but to make us truly *wise* and *free*. After presenting the entire teachings of the Gītā, Śrī Kṛṣṇa points out, "Thus has this wisdom, more mysterious than the mystery itself, been imparted to you by Me. Fully pondering over it, *do as you like*." (18.63)

[1] These opening observations about our quest for happiness are inspired by Swāmī Paramārthānandajī's discourses on the Bhagavad Gītā. See: https://archive.org/details/BhagavadGītā_SwamiParamarthananda

[2] Matthieu Ricard, *Altruism: The Power of Compassion to Change Yourself and the World* (New York, NY: Little, Brown and Company, 2015).

Ethical and Spiritual Disciplines (Yogas) of the Gītā

The essential Idea in the reply which Krishna offered to Arjuna was that through the discharge of the duties of one's station without thought of fruit one was on the way to salvation.[3]

John McKenzie, in this quote, distils the essence of perfection that ensues following enlightened action according to one's station in life: right conduct and proper attitude. Do your duty diligently without attachment to or expectation of results. Then, your feet will be firmly set on the path that leads to freedom, joy, and harmony.

The Bhagavad Gītā presents several paths or disciplines (*yogas*) for attaining ethical purity and spiritual freedom. The word "yoga" is used in the Gītā in several different shades of meaning, although the basic meaning of the word "yoga" is union or yoking. It is derived from the Sanskrit root, *yuj,* meaning "to join" or "to unite." It is helpful to bear in mind that, in the Gītā, *karman* (action) do not always equate with "*karma yoga*" and *jñāna* (knowledge) does not always signify "*jñāna yoga*." Secondly, the word "*Yoga*" is used in several shades of meanings in the Gītā. However, at two places, Śrī Kṛṣṇa presents the word "*Yoga*" in its truest meaning: BG 2.48 and BG 6.23. In BG 2.48, Śrī Kṛṣṇa states "*samatvaṃ yoga ucyate*"—"equipoise" or "equanimity" is called *yoga*. The second important sense in which the word "*Yoga*" is used in the Gītā is in verse BG 6.23: *taṃ vidyād duḥkhasaṃyogaviyogaṃ yogasaṃjñitam*—freedom from contact with sorrow (of this body and material world) should be known as *yoga*. According to the Gītā, the complete freedom from sorrow is possible only when one is established in the Supreme Self *(Paramātman).*
Some quote the phrase *yogaḥ karmasu kauśalam* (2.50) to explain that *dexterity in action* is *yoga*. Does that mean that proficiency in pickpocketing will make the pickpocket a *yogi*? This is not at all the intention of the Gītā, for that would be against the universal moral code (*dharma viruddha*). Recall that the first word of the Gītā is *dharmakṣetre* (1.1), the sphere of moral conduct, and the last word is mama (18.78), meaning "mine." Conjoined, literally, the first and last words of the Gītā signify: "my moral duty," my *svadharma*, as it is the *dharma* of fire to burn and of water to extinguish the fire.

Sri Krishna Prem in his book titled *The Yoga of the Bhagavat Gītā* explains the meaning of the word yoga as follows:

> By yoga is here meant not any special system called by that name, not jnana-yoga nor karma yoga, nor eightfold yoga of Patanjali, but just the Path by which man unites his finite self with the infinite being. It is the inner path of which these separate yogas are so many one-sided aspects.[4]

[3] J. John McKenzie, *Hindu Ethics: A Historical and Critical Essay* (Oxford, UK: Oxford University, 1922), 125.

[4] Sri Krishna Prem, *The Yoga of the Bhagavat Gītā* (New York, NY: Penguin Books; Second edition, 1973), xiv.

Commenting on the key disciplines, *yogas*, in the Gītā, S. K. Maitra writes:

> Yoga means union with God, and this union can be effected in various ways. It can be effected through Karma, it can be effected through Jñāna, it can be effected through Dhyāna, it can be effected through Bhakti. It can also be effected in other ways. In fact, each of the 18 chapters of the Gītā is called a Yoga and shows the way in which the union with God is to be achieved.[5]

Three Paths to Liberation According to the Gītā

A sacred Hindu text tells us that there are only three disciplines or paths for the salvation of human beings—the path of action *(karma yogā)*, the path of knowledge *(jñāna yoga)*, and the path of devotion *(bhakti yoga)*. Besides these three, there is absolutely no other means of liberation—"*na upāyaḥ anyo asti kutracit.*" Śrīmad Bhāgavatam (11.20.6), an important sacred text, provides the following order of spiritual disciplines:

> *Yōgās trayo mayā proktā narrnām shreyo-vidhitsaya;*
> *Jñānam karma ca bhaktis ca na upāyaḥ anyo asti kutracit.* (Śrīmad Bhāgavatam 11.20.6)
>
> I have enunciated three paths for those who want to attain spiritual welfare—the Path of Knowledge (Jñāna yoga), the Path of Selfless Actions (Karma yoga), and the Path of Devotion (Bhakti yoga). Besides these three, there is absolutely no other path for the spiritual advancement of human beings.

According to Swāmī Rāmsukhdāsjī, "All these three *Yogas*-paths are independent means to God-realization. All other spiritual disciplines, such as *dhyānayoga*, etc., are also implicit within these three."[6] It is because human beings are endowed with three powers—power to do, power to know, and power to accept (or to believe). For the proper use of these powers, human beings are endowed with a physical body to "do," an intellect to "know," and a heart to "believe." *Karma yoga* is meant for the proper use of the power to "do"; *jñāna yoga* for the proper use of the power to "know"; and *bhakti yoga* is meant for the proper use of the power to "accept" or to "believe." A person with a penchant for actions is fit for *karma yoga*; a person with a penchant for discrimination is fit for *jñāna yoga*; and a person with a penchant for feelings is fit for *bhakti yoga*.

[5] S. K. Maitra, *The Spirit of Indian Philosophy* (Allahabad, India: The Indian Press, 1947), 28–29.

[6] Swami Rāmsukhdāsjī, *Śrīmad Bhagavad Gītā: Sādhaka-Sañjivanī* (Gorakhpur, India: Gītā Press, 2007), 20. See also: Satinder Dhiman, trans., *Sahaja-Gītā: The Essential Gītā*. [Selection & Compilation, Rajendra Kumar Dhawan]. Based on Paramśraddheya Swāmījī Shrī Rāmsukhdāsjī Mahārāj's commentary on *Śrīmad Bhagavad Gītā*, titled, "*Sādhaka-Sañjivanī*" (Gorakhpur, India: Gītā Prakashan, 2013); and Satinder Dhiman, trans., *Kripāmayi Bhagavad Gītā: The Benedictory Gītā*. [Selection & Compilation, Rajendra Kumar Dhawan]. Based on Paramśraddheya Swāmījī Shrī Rāmsukhdāsjī Mahārāj's Discourses. (Gorakhpur, India: Gītā Prakāshan, 2014).

There are verily three entities—the world *(jagat)*, the self or the soul *(ātman)*, and God *(Paramātman)*. *Karma yoga* pertains to the world, *jñāna yoga* pertains to the Self, and *Bhaktiyoga* pertains to God. Dedicating what we have received from the world—such as the physical body—in the service of the world without expecting anything in return, is called *karma yoga* (Gītā 3.11; 4.23; 18.45). To sever one's affinity with the objects that are transitory and fleeting by not identifying with them as "I" or "mine," is called *jñāna yoga* (Gītā 3.27). Considering only God as one's own and dedicating all undertakings and objects to God—and taking refuge in God—this is called *bhakti yoga* (Gītā 7.26–27; 18.66). *Karma yogī* severs relationship with the world through service; *jñāna yogī* severs relation with the world through renunciation (of doership); and *bhakti yogī* severs relation with the world by establishing relationship with, and surrendering to, the Supreme Lord.[7]

The skillfulness in actions lies in the wisdom of equanimity, dedicating them all to Vasudevaḥ, which is all there is. The whole art and science of karma yoga lies in just this understanding. In addition, this abidance in equanimity, *samatava-sthitiḥ,* is also the natural state, *sahaja avasthā*, of all saints and sages, the epitome of all spiritual realization.

Karma Yoga: The Path of Action

The universality and pervasiveness of action in human life is a veritable fact—nobody can remain action-less even for a moment. Indian philosophy postulates that all actions performed with the desire for self-referent results cause bondage. If we cannot remain without performing actions and self-centered actions lead to bondage, is there a way out of this relentless cycle of action and reaction? The Gītā's well-ascertained answer to this enigmatic question is the path of action, *karma yoga*. Given its emphasis on selfless service, *karma yoga* has the most natural and direct application to leadership, especially servant leadership. As a practical teaching, *karma yoga* furnishes the best set of guidelines to put *service before self* and to perform actions for the wellbeing of all beings. Regarding the Gītā's efficacy in this regard, we have the highest testimony of Mahatma Gandhi, who confirmed its teachings in every sphere of his life with great success.

In its most popular version, *karma yoga* is presented as follows: perform your actions without expecting any results. That is, do actions selflessly, *niṣkāma karma*,[8] unattached to the results. This has caused much confusion: How can one perform any action without expecting any results? Why perform any action at all if one were not to expect any results? This is not the intention of the Gītā, however, as we shall see.

[7] Swami Rāmsukhdāsjī, *Śrīmad Bhagavad Gītā: Sādhaka-Sañjivanī*; Also see: Satinder Dhiman, trans., *Sahaja-Gītā: The Essential Gītā*. [Selection & Compilation, Rajendra Kumar Dhawan]. Based on Paramśraddheya Swāmījī Shrī Rāmsukhdāsjī Mahārāj's commentary on *Śrīmad Bhagavad Gītā,* titled, "*Sādhaka-Sañjivanī*" (Gorakhpur, India: Gītā Prakashan, 2013); and Satinder Dhiman, trans., *Kripāmayi Bhagavad Gītā: The Benedictory Gītā*.

[8] Interestingly, the expression "*niṣkāma karma*" does not occur in the Gītā!

Karma yoga has two aspects: proper action and proper attitude:

1. *Proper Action*: Since we cannot remain without activity even for a moment, the first step on the spiritual journey is to perform *proper* or righteous actions. What makes an action a *proper* action? A proper action is that action which is *unopposed* to *dharma* (*dharma aviruddha*), the universal moral order—it is the *right* thing to do, in a *given* situation. The rightness of an action lies in its moral valence. When an action is good for one and good for all, it is called right action. Harmlessness of an action is one easy way to determine its righteousness. On the path of goodness, one does not ever lose (BG 6.40).[9] It is not just the *work ethic* that is important, for a serial killer may also have a good work ethic. It is the *work ethics* that matters the most.

   The Gītā divides karma into several types. *Nitya naimita karma*: The obligatory duties: one should perform the obligatory duties such as sacrifice (*yajña*), charity (*dāna*), and austerities (*tapas*). These three types of actions, the Gītā says, are the purifiers of the wise: *yajñadānatapaḥkarma… pāvanāni manīṣiṇām* (18.5). These actions are performed with the attitude of duty that has to be done for duty's sake. In life and leadership, doing one's duty for duty's sake purges our actions from self-centered willfulness and contributes to individual and social harmony. This leads to purification of the mind or the internal organ of perception (*antāhkaraṇa śuddhi*). Our daily duties done properly makes us fit to understand deeper, subtle Self-knowledge. As S. K. Maitra has rightly observed, "[I]t is only those who have gone through the drill of Karma properly that are entitled to receive Brahma-Vidyā [knowledge of the Absolute Reality or the Self-knowledge]."[10]
2. *Proper Attitude*: Proper attitude has two aspects:

   (a) *Īśvara arpaṇa buddhi*: Attitude of offering all actions to *Īśvara*, the Lord.
   (b) *Īśvara prasāda buddhi*: Considering fruits of action as *Īśvara*'s grace.

A *karma yogi* should have an attitude of being a mere instrument in the hands of *Īśvara*, *nimita-mātra* (11.33). This then is the skill in action, the art of *karma yoga*: do *right* actions as an *offering* to the Lord—as an instrument of the Divine, *Īśvara*, accepting all *results* as the Lord's *grace*. Then the actions will lose their binding effect. Hence, the skillfulness of this discipline, *yoga karmasu kauśalam* (2.50). It will also prepare the mind to receive the knowledge of the Self, *jñāna yoga*. The greatest practical lesson that the Gītā teaches us is karma yoga—the highest discipline to live by: *use the right means for a just cause and leave the results in hands of God.*

[9] न हि कल्याणकृत् कश्चित् दुर्गतिं तात गच्छति: To one, who follows the path of goodness, there is no misery or misadventure (*durgati*), for him.

[10] S. K. Maitra, *The Spirit of Indian Philosophy* (Benares, India: Published by the Author; printed at The Indian Press Limited, Allahabad, 1947), 25.

While in regards to the paths of knowledge and devotion, the "*yoga*" (communion) is quite natural. The seer, after realizing "All is God" (*vāsudevaḥ sarvam* 7:19), remains naturally established in the experience of Oneness; and the devotee likewise constantly experiences reverential communion with the Lord. Therefore, in the Gītā, the word "*yoga*" especially signifies *karma yoga*.[11] All undertakings, all actions, are tainted with some blemish—this means that all actions are inherently "binding" *in effect* as they lead to good, bad, or mixed results. But when the actions are performed with pure motive or intentions—that is, without attachment to actions or the fruits thereof—they become free from blemish. This is the alchemy of *karma yoga*.

Jñāna Yoga: The Path of Knowledge

The definite conclusion of the Gītā is that
Liberation is attained only through the knowledge of Reality.[12]

This quote summarizes the final position of the Gītā on the question of the means to liberation. Liberation, says the Gītā, is achieved only through the essential knowledge of the reality of our Self. All spiritual traditions postulate that there is Ultimate Reality or Value worth experiencing. It is experienced as our own self, as the unchanging witnessing consciousness illumining all thoughts, perceptions, and so on. To know that we are that Reality is to be liberated. This is the path that the Gītā teaches.

The Gītā teaches us that there is a way to live in this world without being bound by it. It is called *jñāna yoga*, the path of Self-knowledge or the knowledge of Ultimate Reality. In the second chapter of the Gītā (verses 2.11–2.30), the knowledge of our true Self (*sāṅkhya yoga*) is expounded. The word *sāṅkhya* is used in the special sense here. It means knowing a thing completely, *samyakjñānaṃ* (*sam* = properly/fully/completely; *khyā* = knowing). Here it signifies knowing our true nature, the Self, completely. The Gītā follows a specialized methodology of teaching under which the highest teaching is given first, and elaborated upon later.[13] Accordingly, chapter 2 of the Gītā introduces all its essential teachings in summary form, which are later elaborated upon in the next 16 chapters. This is an important pointer to the understanding of the deeper import the Gītā.

The teachings of the Gītā start when Arjuna, confused about his proper duty, beseeches the Lord to instruct him in what is decidedly best for him (2:7). At this point, the sublime message of the Gītā begins as follows with the highest teachings of *Sāṅkhya* (2.11–30):

[11] Swami Rāmsukhdāsjī, *Śrīmad Bhagavad Gītā: Sādhaka-Sañjivanī*, 5.

[12] Swami Gambhirananda, *Bhagavad Gītā with the commentary of Sri Shankaracharya* (Calcutta, India: Advaita Ashrama, 1984), 44–45.

[13] I. Schepetin, The Traditional Method by which a Guru enlightens the student. *Les Cahiers Aditi*, 2018, 15.

The wise [who know the Self to be free from death and birth] do not grieve over the coming or going of people, objects, and situations. For the unreal has no existence whatsoever; and the real never ceases to be. The wise one to whom pain and pleasure are the same, and who is not tormented by these (unavoidable changing conditions), is fit for realizing the state of immortality or liberation (*mokṣa*).

Thereafter, in verses 2.12–25, 30, the Gītā describes the nature of the perennial Self (*ātmā*) as follows: The Self is *nitya* (ever-existent), *satya* (real), *avināśi* (indestructible), *nirvikāra* (immutable), *sarvagataḥ* (all-pervading), *aprameya* (not an object of thought), and ever indestructible (*nityam avadhyo*). Therefore, knowing the Self to be thus, there is no cause for grief. The Gītā (2.22) tells us that, "As a person discards old and worn out clothes and takes other new ones, even so the soul, casting off worn out bodies, enters other new ones." It is interesting to note that BG 12.3–4 describe the characteristics of the Supreme Self, *Paramātman*, as the unthinkable, omnipresent, indestructible, indefinable, eternal, immovable, unmanifest, and immutable Brahman. The striking similarity between the features of *Ātmā* and *Paramātmā* proves their essential oneness. To help us realize this oneness (of the individual self with the universal Self) is the ultimate goal of the Bhagavad Gītā, and the fruit of the path of knowledge, *jñāna yoga*.

At the heart of the Gītā, there is the conception of a sage steady in wisdom (*sthitaprajña*)—one who is incapable of ill-will, who is friendly and compassionate, and has conquered his selfish desires and attachments; who has purged himself of the sense of "I" and "mine" to such an extent that he sees himself in all and all in himself; free from lust, fear, and anger; who is self-controlled and tranquil-minded; who lives beyond the sway of the pair of opposites such as pleasure and pain, joy and sorrow, success and failure; who is self-controlled, patient, and firm in faith; contented and reposed in the Self; rejoicing in the Self alone; and who has given all his heart and all his mind to the Divine within.[14]

Essentially, *jñāna yoga* entails not identifying with the body and the objects as "I" or "mine" and realizing ourselves as pure, *action-less* Self. "He who knows the truth," says Śaṅkara, "does not think 'I act,' nor does he long for the results."[15] This understanding, promises the Gītā, leads to abiding peace and happiness. Through the knowledge of the Self, one realizes that what one is seeking is the very nature of the seeker and that happiness is not something to be gained from outside—it is the *very* nature of the Self:

vihāya kāmān yaḥ sarvān pumāṃś carati niḥspṛhaḥ /
nirmamo nirahaṃkāraḥ sa śāntim adhigacchhati //2.71//

[14] There are three places specifically where the Gītā explains the characteristics of a person steady in the wisdom of the Self (2.55–72), a person who has firm devotion to God (12.13–19) and one who has transcended the domain of three *guṇas* (14.21–27). See also: BG 13.7–11 (for qualities of the seeker for Self-knowledge); 16.1–3 (for noble traits of head and heart); and 18.49–56 (for characteristics of the one established in Ultimate Reality).

[15] Alladi M. Sastry, *The Bhagavad Gītā with Commentary of Sri Sankaracharya* (Madras, India: Samata Books, 1897/1995), 27.

> One who has given up all desires, free from longings and the sense of "I" and "mine," attains peace.

There is one more dimension of *jñāna yoga* that we need to cover to bring it full circle. It entails the understanding of the Self as *akartā* and *abhōgtā* (non-doer and non-enjoyer). The Gītā makes it very clear that all actions are performed by the threefold properties of the material nature (BG 3.27–28; 5.8–9; 13.29; 14.19. The following two verses provide perhaps the greatest *raison d'etre* that all actions are performed by force of inherent qualities:

> *prakṛteḥ kriyamāṇāni guṇaiḥ karmāṇi sarvaśaḥ /*
> *ahaṃkāravimūḍhātmā kartāham iti manyate* //3.27//
>
> *tattvavit tu mahābāho guṇakarmavibhāgayoḥ /*
> *guṇā guṇeṣu vartanta iti matvā na sajjate* //3.28//
>
> All actions are performed by *guṇas* [qualities] of primordial nature [*Prakṛti*]. One whose mind is deluded by egoism thinks, "I am the doer." But, one, with true insight into the respective domains of *guṇas* and their action, knowing that *guṇas* as senses merely move among *guṇas* as objects, does not become attached.

These verses state that all actions are performed by the interplay of three qualities (*guṇas*)—purity (*sattva*), activity (*rajas*), and inertia (*tamas*). Deluded by our ego sense (*ahaṃkāra*), we take ourselves to be the "doers." But those who understand the respective domains of these *guṇas* and their actions do not get attached to them: The knower of Truth, [being] centered [in the Self] should think, "I do nothing at all"—though seeing, hearing, touching, smelling, eating, going, sleeping, breathing, speaking, letting go, holding, opening and closing the eyes—*convinced that it is the senses that move among sense objects.* (5.8–9).

The Gītā clarifies that he who sees that all actions are performed in every way by nature (*Prakṛti*), and the Self as the non-doer, alone truly sees:

> *prakṛtyaiva ca karmāṇi kriyamāṇāni sarvaśaḥ /*
> *yaḥ paśyati tathātmānam akartāraṃ sa paśyati* //13.29//

The definite conclusion in the Gītā is that "Liberation is attained only through the knowledge of Reality."[16]

Three Guṇas and Their Transcendence

The Gītā (18.40) categorically declares that there is no being anywhere in the material world free from the qualities/properties/modes (*guṇas*) born of material nature (*Prakṛti*). Wherever there is name and form (*nāma-rupa*), there is *guṇa*. The individual self (*jīva*) feels itself in bondage on account of two things—due to *Prakṛti* (material nature) and due to the effects of *Prakṛti*

[16] Swami Gambhirananda, *Bhagavad Gītā with the commentary of Sri Shankaracharya* (Calcutta, India: Advaita Ashrama, 1984), 44–45.

in the form of the three modes (*guṇas*) of material nature, that is, *Sattva, Rajas, and Tamas. Prakṛti*, or nature, is constituted by three *guṇas*: *Sattva* (purity), *Rajas* (activity), and *Tamas* (inertia). *Sattvaguṇa* refers to qualities such as purity and goodness; *rajoguṇa* denotes such qualities as activity and passion; and *tamoguṇa* refers to qualities such as inertia and dullness.

Guṇa also means a rope—that which binds. All *guṇas* in some measure bind the individual soul or empirical self (*jīva*) to *saṃsāra* (the unending cycle of births and deaths). *Sattvaguṇa* binds through attachment to happiness and pride of knowledge (14.6); *Rajoguṇa* binds the individual soul (*jīva*) to *saṃsāra* through attachment to actions and their fruit (14.7); and *tamoguṇa* binds through heedlessness, sloth, and sleep (14.8). Hence, the Gītā extols the ideal of transcending the triad of *guṇas* (*guṇātita*) (2.45; 14.19, 14.22–26).

The Transcendent Sage of the Gītā: One Beyond the Sway of Three Guṇas of Prakṛti

The transcendent Sage of the Gītā is one who has gone beyond the three modes of nature (*guṇas* of *Prakṛti*)—who, by means of truth and goodness (*sattva*), overcomes compulsive activity (*rajas*) and confusion (*tamas*); and then gets beyond attachment to goodness (*sattva*) itself. In response to Arjuna's question, the Lord first describes the marks of the sage who has transcended the three modes of material nature and then describes how to go beyond the *guṇas*: "The transcendent sage behaves with equanimity (*samatā*). Alike in pleasure and in pain, who is ever established in the eternal Self, regarding a clod of earth, a stone, and a piece of gold as of equal worth (without any attraction or aversion—for they are perishable); who is equanimous in the success and failure of actions, the same in blame and praise, honor and dishonor; who is same to friend and foe; and who has abandoned all initiative of new undertakings prompted by selfish desire and attachment—such a person is called a transcendent sage." (14.24–26).

The Gītā draws upon the philosophy of *Sāṃkhya* in stating that all actions take place within the domain of the creative energy of material Nature, *Prakṛti* (3.27/28 and 5.8/9). It regards the *Prakṛti* as the mother of all the [three] *guṇas*—*sattva*, *raja*, and *tama*; and, therefore, *Prakṛti* alone is the agent, cause, and effect of all actions: *kāryakāraṇakartṛtve hetuḥ prakṛtirucyate* (BG 13.20). However, when a person assumes an "I am the doer" attitude (3.27), the "activities" of the *Prakṛti* become "actions" for him.[17]

The following verse succinctly captures the alchemy of actions performed by the strands of material nature and points out a right approach to understand the algorithm of *karma yoga*:

> *prakṛtyaiva ca karmāṇi kriyamāṇāni sarvaśaḥ /*
> *yaḥ paśyati tathātmānamakartāraṁ sa paśyati* //13.29//

[17] Swami Ramsukhdasji, *Gītā Darpaṇ* (Gorakhpur, India: Gītā Press, 2005), 143.

> They alone see truly who see that all actions are performed by *Prakṛti*, while the Self remains actionless.

The following verse quintessentially enlightens us about the art and the significance of transcending the *guṇas* while following any of the three spiritual disciplines (*Karma yoga, Jñāna yoga, Bhakti yoga*):

> *nānyaṃ guṇebhyaḥ kartāraṃ yadā draṣṭānupaśyati /*
> *guṇebhyaś ca paraṃ vetti madbhāvaṃ sodhigacchhati* //14.19//
>
> When the seer beholds no one as the doer other than the *guṇas* and knows That which is entirely beyond the *guṇas*, he enters into My being.

It is important to note that seldom in the Gītā is the glory of the outcome of a spiritual practice so explicitly stated as it is in this phrase—*madbhāvaṃ sodhigacchhati*: enters into My being! Essentially, this single verse presents the crux of all three main disciplines, *yogas*, in the Gītā: *karma yoga*, *jñāna yoga*, and *bhakti yoga*. Performing all actions with the understanding that all actions are performed by the interplay of the triad of material nature (*triguṇātmik prakṛti*) while the Self remains action-less brings one face to face with the One who is beyond the sway of these *guṇas*.

The wise clearly see that all actions are the work of the *guṇas* [the modes of nature, *prakṛti*]. Knowing that which *transcends* the *guṇas*, they enter into union with Me.

This verse (BG 14.19) then represents the essence of all the three *yogas*:

1. *Karma yoga*—the yoga of *right action*: Performing actions selflessly without any desire for or attachment to the results.
2. *Jñāna yoga*—the yoga of *right knowledge*: Performing actions without the tag of doership, with the understanding that all actions are performed by the *guṇas* of the *Prakṛti*. A person who performs actions with this understanding—*I am not the doer*—is the *Sāṃkhya yogi*.
3. *Bhakti yoga*—the yoga of *right devotion*: By performing right actions with correct understanding—that all actions are performed by the interplay of three *guṇas* of *prakṛti*, one attains union with the *Puruṣa*.

Thus, in all the three *yogas*, the spiritual aspirant remains merely an instrument in the hands of the Divine: *nimittamātraṁ* (11.33).

This is the right knowledge (*samyaka-jñānam*) according to the Gītā.

Dhyānayoga: The Path of Meditation

It is important to note that although the Gītā recognizes two primary spiritual disciplines (3:2)—*Jñānayoga* (the Path of Knowledge) and *Karmayoga* (the Path of Action)—yet, at various points, the Gītā also presents other disciplines, such as *Bhakti yoga* (the path of devotion) and *Dhyānayoga* (the path of meditation) as viable paths or aids to enlightenment. Besides, in the Gītā, the path of meditation or concentration serves as a necessary concomitant to all other paths, since a certain measure of calm concentration is verily required to practice the path of action, knowledge, and devotion in a proper manner. The Gītā takes an integral view of the spiritual disciplines and often extols other disciplines while discussing a particular path as preeminent.

In chapter 6, titled *Ātmasaṁyamayogaḥ*: The Yoga of Self-Discipline, we find the most detailed instructions on the discipline of meditation, which culminate in *Bhaktiyoga—śraddhāvān bhajate yo māṃ sa me yuktatamo mataḥ:* the *yogīn* who worships Me devoutly with his inmost self-abiding in Me, is considered by Me to be the best of the *yogīns* (6:47).

As a prelude to the discipline of meditation, we are told in chapter 6 that responsibility for one's spiritual welfare and downfall rests with oneself and no one else. Therefore, one should uplift oneself by one's own self (efforts)—and not degrade oneself; for one's own self alone is one's friend, and one's own self alone is one's enemy (6.5). At the very outset of chapter 6, by way of the path as well as the goal, Śrī Kṛṣṇa presents the following marks of a *yogīn* steadfast in equanimity: "When one does not get attached to sense-objects or to actions, and has renounced all purposes *(saṅkalpas)*, then, he is said to have ascended the heights of *yoga (yogārūḍha)*."

According to the Gītā, "Success in this *yoga* of meditation is neither attained by one who either eats too much or does not eat at all, nor by one who either sleeps too much or does not sleep at all. This *yoga* (of meditation), which destroys sorrows, is accomplished only by him who is temperate in diet and recreation, who is disciplined (and detached) in the performance of actions, and is temperate in sleep and waking." As Edgerton (1944, p. 68) has noted, "This is one of the points of contact between the Gītā and Buddhism, for Buddhism too makes much of the doctrine of 'golden mean,' opposing the extreme of self-torture as well as the extreme of worldliness."[18]

The Gītā is fully aware that the mind is restless and hard to control. It maintains that the mind can be controlled by constant practice and detachment (or dispassion). The following two verses provide the preliminary instructions on meditation:

> *saṅkalpaprabhavān kāmāṃs tyaktvā sarvān aśeṣataḥ /*
> *manasaivendriyagrāmaṃ viniyamya samantataḥ* //6.24//
>
> *śanaiḥ śanair uparamed buddhyā dhṛtigṛhītayā /*
> *ātmasasthaṃ manaḥ kṛtvā na kiṃcid api cintayet* //6.25//
>
> Renouncing entirely all desires, and withdrawing, by strength of mind, all senses from their respective objects, the meditator should, with an unhurried intellect set in firmness, gradually become detached (*uparām*) from the world. *He should then focus his mind on the Supreme Self (Paramātmā) and should not think of anything else whatsoever.*

[18] Franklin Edgerton, translated and Interpreted, *The Bhagavad Gītā* (New York, NY: Harvard University Press, 1944), 68.

In the chapter mainly devoted to the practice of meditation comes the final assurance about *bhakti yoga*: My devotee is superior to all possible types of *yogīs—karmayogī, jñānayogī, dhyāna yogī, haṭha yogī, laya yogī, rāja yogī*, and so on.

> *yogināṁ api sarveṣāṃ madgatenāntarātmanā /*
> *śraddhāvān bhajate yo māṃ sa me yuktatamo mataḥ* //6.47//
>
> Even among all the *yogīs*, he who worships Me devoutly with his inmost self abiding in Me, he is considered by Me to be the best of the *yogīs*.

This concluding verse of chapter 6 prepares the perfect ground for the next *shatkam* on *bhakti yoga* comprising chapters 7–12.

Bhakti Yoga: The Path of Loving Devotion

As stated above, at the conclusion of chapter 6, the Gītā especially extols the path of devotion (6.47) even while presenting the outcome of the discipline of meditation. Thus, in chapters 7–10, Arjuna is progressively led to the knowledge of the mysteries and the glories of the Divine Being—Bhagavān Śrī Kṛṣṇa—and now Arjuna is ready to behold the Lord's Universal Form—*viśva-rupā-darśanaṁ*, which forms the subject matter of chapter 11.55. The Lord bestows Arjuna with the divine vision (*divya-driṣṭi*) to enable him to witness the universal form. Śrī Kṛṣṇa presents the quintessence of the path of devotion in the culminating verse of chapter 11.55—"He who does work for My sake (pleasure) only, he who looks upon Me as the Supreme Goal, who lovingly worships Me, who is free from attachment (to worldly things) and from enmity to all beings, that devotee verily comes to Me."

This concluding verse of chapter 11 (11:55) represents the essence of *Bhakti* and is declared to be the very heart, the quintessence of the whole teaching of the Gītā, by Hindu commentators. The great commentator, Śaṅkarā, calls it "the essence of the whole Gītā."[19] Paraphrasing BG 11.55, Dr. Rādhākrishnan states that "we must carry our duties directing the spirit to God and with detachment from all interest in the things of the world and free from enmity towards any living being."[20]

We conclude this section on *bhakti yoga* by summarizing seven culminating verses or *carma ślokas* of chapter 18: 18.54, 18.55, 18.56, 18.57, 18.62, 18.65, and 18.66:

[19] W. D. P. Hill, *The Bhagavad Gītā: A Translation and Commentary* (Madras, India: Oxford University Press, 1928/1953), 167. See also: *The Bhagavad Gītā*, Translated and Interpreted by Franklin Edgerton (New York, NY: Harvard University Press, 1944), 176.

[20] S. Rādhākrishnan, *The Bhagavad Gītā: With an Introductory Essay, Sanskrit Text, English Translation and Notes*, (London, UK: George Allen & Unwin Ltd., 1958), 289.

Having become one with the Ultimate Reality, such an aspirant (*sādhaka*) neither grieves nor desires. Alike to all beings, he attains supreme devotion to Me. By virtue of My devotion supreme, he comes to know Me, what My measure is and who I am in essence. Knowing Me thus in very truth and essence, he enters into Me straightway. A devotee who has taken refuge in Me with exclusive and unswerving devotion, even while performing all ordained actions, by My Grace, attains to the Eternal, Imperishable Abode (*mat-prasādāt avāpnoti śāśvataṁ padam avyayam*). Therefore, mentally dedicating all actions to Me, regarding Me as the Supreme Goal, and resorting to the *Yoga* of equanimity—i.e., by severing affinity with the world—fix your mind and thoughts constantly on Me. By being constantly absorbed in Me, you will, by My Grace, overcome all difficulties. O Bhārata (Arjuna)! Seek refuge in Him alone, surrendering your whole being (*sarvabhāvena*). By His Grace you shall attain Supreme Peace and the Eternal Abode. (18.54, 18.55, 18.56, 18.57, 18.62)

The final two verses conclude the teachings as follows:

> *manmanā bhava madbhakto madyājī māṃ namaskuru /*
> *mām evaiṣyasi satyaṃ te pratijāne priyosi me* //18.65//
>
> "Fix your mind on Me—i.e., accept Me as your very own; worship Me with all your actions; and bow to Me with reverence—i.e., be completely surrendered to Me. By turning completely towards Me in this manner, you will verily attain to Me—This is my sincere pledge to you because you are dear to Me."
>
> *sarvadharmān parityajya mām ekaṃ śaraṇaṃ vraja /*
> *ahaṃ tvā sarvapāpebhyo mokṣayiṣyāmi mā śucaḥ* //18.66//
>
> Relinquishing all *dharmas* take refuge in Me alone. I will release you from all sins. Do not grieve.

According to Swāmī Shrī Rāmsukhdāsjī, "Taking refuge in the Lord (*śarnāgati*) is the quintessence of the entire message of the Gītā." S. K. Maitra concurs: "the final instruction is: surrender."[21] In surrendering to the Lord lies the culmination of the Gītā's teachings. "The devotee who has taken refuge in the Lord accepts firmly the belief that 'I am God's and God is mine.' Then the devotee becomes forever free from the pangs of fear, sorrow, worry, etc."[22]

With this key verse, we have come full circle in the teachings of the Bhagavad Gītā: Śrī Kṛṣṇa started the teaching declaring that "the wise do not grieve" (2.11: *nānuśocanti paṇḍitāḥ*) and concludes it with an assurance "do not grieve" (18.66: *mā śucaḥ*). So, if you want to overcome the sorrow, attain to the liberating wisdom. What is this liberating wisdom? Just this: Performing your actions as an offering to the Supreme (*īśvara arpaṇa bhāvanā*), performing your duties without the expectation of any reward. Be an instrument of the Divine in all that you do. Let all your actions be for the wellbeing of all beings (*sarvabhūtahite*

[21] S. K. Maitra, *The Spirit of Indian Philosophy* (Allahabad, India: The Indian Press, 1947), 103.
[22] See: Dhiman, trans., *Sahaja Gītā*, 172.

ratāḥ: 5.25); be a role model for the bringing together of the world communities and the maintenance of the world order (*lokasaṃgraham evāpi saṃpaśyan kartum arhasi*: 3.20). Above all, accept the results of your actions with graceful equanimity, as the Grace of the Lord (*īśvara-prasādabhāvanā*). Then, your actions will never taint you. Attain the highest pure knowledge by which the One Imperishable Being is seen in all the existences, undivided in the divided (18.20). In this manner, with the Divine Grace, you will attain the communion of the individual self with the Supreme Self.

Thus, concludes this manual for transformational living and leadership.

Understanding Dharma, *Ṛtaṃ*, the Cosmic Order

We are quintessentially integral with the universe.[23]

Dharma is the most important and pivotal concept in the spiritual tradition of India. Etymologically, the word *dharma* comes from the root *dhṛ*, which means "to bear, to support, to uphold,"—*dhārayate uddhāryateva iti dharma*—that which "supports, sustains, and uplifts" is *dharma*. We have a Vedic injunction: धर्मो रक्षति रक्षिताः *Dharmo rakṣati rakṣitāḥa*: Dharma protects those who uphold Dharma. There is another Vedic concept that is closely related to *dharma*, called *ṛta*. *Ṛta* is the *order* behind the manifest world, the harmony among all aspects of manifestation, each of which obeys its own truth. There is physical order, biological order, and psychological order.

Everything in the universe follows its own inner order, *ṛtaṃ*. Actually, *dharma* is conceived as an aspect of *Ṛta*. As John Warne explains in his editorial preface to Taittirīya Upaniṣad, "*Ṛta* is the universal norm identified with truth which, when brought to the level of humanity, become known as *dharma*, the righteous order here on earth."[24] Indian seers and sages prescribed that one should fulfill one's desires (*kāma*) or pursue wealth and security (*artha*) within the framework of *dharma*, which ensures the good of everyone.[25]

In Indian philosophy and religion, *dharma*[26] has multiple meanings, such as religion, duty, virtue, moral order, righteousness, law, intrinsic nature, cosmic

[23] Thomas Berry, *The Great Work: Our Way into the Future* (New York, NY: Harmony/Bell Tower, 1999), 32.

[24] See: *Taittiriya Upanisad* by Swami Dayananda Saraswati (Saylorsburg, PA: Arsha Vidya Gurukulum, 2005), transcribed and edited by John Warne, iv.

[25] Bangalore Kuppuswamy, *Dharma and Society: A Study in Social Values* (Columbia, MO: South Asia Books, 1977).

[26] There is no single word in any Western language that can capture the multiple shades and subtle nuances of the word *dharma*. Like the words *karma* and *yoga*, it has been left untranslated in this chapter for the most part, with their contextual meaning presented in parentheses where necessary. These words have found wide currency and familiarity in the Western culture. Similar confusion also exists regarding the meaning of the word *yoga*, as used in the Bhagavad Gītā. According to the preeminent Sanskrit scholar, J. A. B. van Buitenen, "The word *yoga* and cognates of it occur close to 150 times in the Gītā, and it needs attention." See: J. A. B. van Buitenen, ed. and trans., *The Bhagavad Gītā in the Mahābhārata: A Bilingual Edition* (Chicago, IL: University of Chicago Press, 1981), 17.

order, and nonviolence (*ahiṁsā paramo dharmaḥ*[27]). *Dharma* also means the invariable, intrinsic nature of a thing (*svadharma*) from which it cannot deviate, like there cannot be a cold fire. In the realm of ethics and spirituality, *dharma* denotes conduct that is in accord with the cosmic order, the order that makes life and creation possible. When our actions are in harmony with the cosmic order (*Ṛta*), and in accord with the dictates of inner law of our being (*dharma*), they are naturally and spontaneously good and sustaining. Alexander Pope was right: "He can't be wrong whose life is in the right."

The Bhagavad Gītā, the loftiest philosophical poem that forms a part of the epic of the Mahābhārata, is a well-known Indian spiritual and philosophical text and its message is universal and non-sectarian. Both the Gītā and the Vedas base their philosophy on the understanding that the whole of existence essentially forms one single unitary movement despite the apparent and variegated diversity. What universal vision of ethical conduct is presented by the Gītā and the Upaniṣads that fosters a sustainable lifestyle and growth? In the next section, we present some spiritual values and virtues, based on the teachings of the Gītā and Upaniṣads, which can contribute significantly to sustainable existence.

Vasudhaiva Kutumbakam: The Entire World as One Family

> *A human being is a part of the whole called by us universe, a part limited in time and space. He experiences himself, his thoughts and feeling as something separated from the rest, a kind of optical delusion of his consciousness. This delusion is a kind of prison for us, restricting us to our personal desires and to affection for a few persons nearest to us. Our task must be to free ourselves from this prison by widening our circle of compassion to embrace all living creatures and the whole of nature in its beauty.* (Albert Einstein)

Einstein's observation is perfectly in line with the Vedic philosophy of oneness. In the Vedic vision, for the magnanimous, the entire world constitutes

Etymologically, the word *yoga* comes from the Sanskrit root "*yuj*," which is cognate with the word "yoke." The *yoga*, "yoking," that is intended in the Gītā is the union of individual self, *jivātmā*, with the Supreme Self, *Paramātmā*.

[27] *ahiṁsā paramo dharmaḥ, ahiṁsā paramo tapaḥ /*
ahiṁsā paramo satyaṁ yato dharmaḥ pravartate //
ahiṁsā paramo dharmaḥ, ahiṁsā paramo damaḥ /
ahiṁsā parama dānaṁ, ahiṁsā parama tapaḥ //
ahiṁsā parama yajñaḥ ahiṁsā paramo phalam /
ahiṁsā paramaṁ mitraḥ ahiṁsā paramaṁ sukham // (*Mahābhārata/Anuśāsana Parva* (115-23/116-28-29))

but a single family (*udāracaritānām tu vasudhaiva kuṭumbakam*).[28] This vision is in stark contrast to viewing the world as a giant market place. Selfless love is the glue that holds the members of a family together while self-centered profit is the basis of a marketplace. This vision calls for a certain awareness and a worldview that is predicated on our understanding of the universe as a divine manifestation. The Bhagavad Gītā and the Upaniṣads, the oldest wisdom texts of the world, regard this entire world, *jagat*, as the manifestation of the Lord, *Īśvara*. This thinking invests all existence with a deeper moral basis and a higher spiritual purpose. And a new vision of the leader emerges. Under this new vision, a leader becomes a trustee, a caretaker of the Divine property.

We also find similar understanding in various other philosophical traditions of the world. The great Stoic philosopher and Roman Emperor, Marcus Aurelius, has this to say about the unity of all existence:

> Constantly regard the universe as one living being, having one substance and one soul; and observe how all things have reference to one perception, the perception of this one living being; and how all things act with one movement; and how all things are the cooperating causes of all things which exist; observe too the continuous spinning of the thread and the contexture of the web.[29]

When this vision dawns, we understand the true meaning of such terms as compassion, contribution, and harmony. When we see unity in diversity, it helps us develop a universal outlook to life, which is so essential sustaining the sanctity of our war-ravaged planet. By developing universal pity and compassion toward all and everything, one is then able to make peace with the world and feel at home in the universe. For this vision to become a reality, we have to understand that runaway economic growth is no longer an option. We either secure or discard our place in the biosphere. And this isn't some idealistic, romantic notion. It is preparation for a profounder life that is dramatically different from the one we are living now.

While we are "busy putting on our oxygen mask first," let's not forget that a larger system provided us with that oxygen mask to begin with. Let's seek and share the underlying truth of mutuality that does not lead to self-centeredness and unnatural differences and disharmony. That is the truth of our unity behind diversity—the essential oneness of all that exists. By seeking the truth that is equally good to all existence, we will be able to revere all life and truly redeem our human existence. Only then can we ensure equally the happiness and welfare of all beings—a necessary precondition to a state of "happy individuals and harmonious society."[30] That will be our true gift to the universe.

[28] *Mahōpaniṣad*—VI.73 (a). Alternative rendering: "For those who live magnanimously, the entire world constitutes but a family." See: Dr. A. G. Krishna Warrier, trans., *Maha Upanishad* (Chennai, India: The Theosophical Publishing House, n.d.). Accessed July 31, 2015: http://advaitam.net/upanishads/sama_veda/maha.html

[29] Marcus Aurelius, in *Meditations* (c. 161–180 CE), Book IV, 40.

[30] The expression "a happy individual and a harmonious society" is coined by Dr. Vemuri Ramesam, author of *Religion Mystified* and *Yogavasistha*. Dr. Vemuri runs a remarkable blog called Beyond Adviata: http://beyond-advaita.blogspot.com/

Turning the Wheel of Cosmic *Co*-creation: Our Life As an Offering, a Creative Sacrifice!

In order to grow spiritually, enjoin the Vedas, one has to convert one's whole life into an offering to the Divine, as a sort of cosmic sacrifice (*yajñārthāt karmaṇo*: BG 3.9). According to the Gītā (3.10–3.13), all beings are a part of the cosmic wheel of creation, sustained by the principle of mutual contribution and mutual maintenance. Therefore, every action should be performed in a spirit of sacrifice, *Yajña*, which sustains all beings, as an offering to the Universal Lord. They are great thieves, according to the Gītā, who do not help in the turning of this cosmic wheel of sacrifice (3.12). Thus, the Gītā does not stop at concern for humans alone, it is cosmic in its scope and universal in it view.

The Gītā (18.5) mandates threefold acts of sacrifice (*yajña*), charity (*dānaṃ*), and austerity (*tapas*), and considers these as the "purifiers of the wise" (*pāvanāni manīṣiṇām*). "*Yajña*" literally means a sacrifice or an offering. The highest form of offering is living a life of sincerity—a life led by being good and doing good. A sincere life is characterized by doing what we love and loving what we have to do. "*Dānaṃ*" means charity and denotes much more than writing a check to a favorite cause or organization. At the deepest level, it means the gift of "expressed love."

The Vedic philosophy of India has always emphasized the human connection with nature. The sacred literature of India—The Vedas, Upaniṣads, Purāṇas, Mahābhārata, Rāmāyaṇa, and the Bhagavad Gītā—contain some of the earliest teachings on ecological balance and harmony and the need for humanity's sustainable treatment of Mother Nature. The Vedic seers recognized that the universe is intelligently put together, which presupposes knowledge and intelligence. They underscored interdependence and harmony with nature and recognized that all natural elements hold divinity. They posit the Lord as the maker as well as the material of the world, thus investing all creation with divine significance. Vedas do not view creation as an *act* of "creation" per se, as many theologies postulate, but an *expression* or manifestation (*abhivyakti*) of what was unmanifest before.

The following excerpt from the Chāndogya Upaniṣad, one of the most important Upaniṣads, explains the process of creation in amazingly simple scientific terms, and places the irreducible minimum of spirituality based on this understanding within the compass of one short paragraph. By way of universal spirituality, it also represents its pinnacle:

> In the beginning, there was Existence alone—
> One only, without a second.
> It, the One, thought to Itself:
> "Let Me be many, let Me grow forth."
> *Thus, out of Itself, it projected the universe,*
> *and having projected the universe out of Itself,*
> *It entered into every being.*
> All that is has its self in It alone.

Of all things It is the subtle essence.
It is the truth. It is the Self.
And you are That! (Chāndogya Upaniṣad)[31]

The Gītā and the Art of Happiness

Observation and reflection make it evident that half of our unhappiness is caused by not appreciating what we have; the other half by pining for what we do not have. This is the enigma of unhappiness. This deceptively simple analysis shows that 100% of our unhappiness is caused by self-ignorance. Therefore, whether one is looking for material happiness or for supreme bliss, Self-knowledge seems to be the key. Self-knowledge by definition is an inner quest. The Bhagavad Gītā (2.55) starts the description of a person of steady wisdom (*sthitaprajñā*) as one who, casting off all the desires of the mind, is "content in the joy of the Self by the Self."

When one has found the *inner* font of peace and joy, then one acts *with* fulfillment and not *for* fulfillment! Recipes for happiness do not come any better than this.

The Bhagavad Gītā frees us from the syndrome of "more-ism"—wanting more and more of more and more in more and more ways—from the compulsive habit of, from the torment of, or the relentless pursuit of chasing after myriad objects compulsively. It also frees us from the "destination-addiction." It invites us to focus on the *process* rather than obsessing about the *goals*. Stress comes from misalignment between our actions and results. The Gītā says do your allotted duty conscientiously and leave the results to the workings of the Cosmic Order. It asks us to focus on the process and holds that the outcome will take care of itself. The Gītā teaches us that cultivating equanimity (*samatā*) is the best antidote to the "slings and arrows of outrageous fortune" (2.48).

The Gītā introduces us to the intrinsic fullness of our being, *puraṇattvam*. It teaches us that running after desires is a race without a finish line—it is like trying to put out the fire by adding oil to it! The Gītā says that our happiness will increase in proportion to the decrease in our desire for the objects. Only those who are content are happy.

The Gītā teaches us that the path of greed leads to unhappiness, as one can never have enough.

The Gītā teaches us that fulfillment of any particular desire does not free us from craving or greed because desire increases with enjoyment even as a fire grows stronger with the addition of fuel (3.39). It further states that a mind tormented by desires cannot find peace (2.66). The Gītā likens the mind of sage steadfast in wisdom (*sthitaprajña*) with the ocean that remains undisturbed despite the raging rivers of desires.

[31] Adapted from Eknath Easwaran, trans., *The Upanishads, Translated for the Modern Reader* (Berkeley, CA: Nilgiri Press, 1987) and Swami Nikhalananda, ed. and trans., *The Upanishads: A One-Volume Abridgement* (New York, NY: Harper & Row Publishers, 1964).

The Gītā teaches that "be good, do good" is all that one needs to "be" and "do" to foster happiness in oneself and others. Greek thinkers of yore have defined happiness as the exercising of human faculties along the lines of excellence. In the same manner, the Bhagavad Gītā defines yoga as dexterity or excellence in action (*yogaḥ karmasu kauśalam*: 2.50). It is common to experience a feeling of soaring spirit when we are doing excellent work. The converse is also true. It has been observed that the best way to kill human motivation is to expect and accept mediocre performance from others. Expecting less than excellent work is the greatest disservice we can do to ourselves and to others. We owe excellence to ourselves, as much as we owe it to the society.

No mere ideology, this passion for excellence has far-reaching implications for leaders and for workplace performance. Nobody comes to work to put in a shoddy performance. Everyone is looking for creative self-expression. And when we create opportunities for meaningful self-expression, we help build a workplace where people act with self-fulfillment and not merely work for it. Creating such a liberating work environment is the real job of a leader.

Five Practices That Lead to Security, Peace, and Liberation

The Alchemy of Karma Yoga: Renunciation in Action

As a practical teaching, karma yoga furnishes the best set of guidelines to put service before self and to perform actions for the wellbeing of all beings. Regarding its efficacy, we have the testimony of Mahatma Gandhi, who verified its teachings in every sphere of his life with great success. He called the Bhagavad Gītā the "Gospel of Selfless Action" and used to regard the Kurukṣhetra war as an allegory of the battle that is fought in the human heart.[32] As a matter of fact, the Bhagavad Gītā's emphasis on selfless service was the prime source of inspiration for his life and leadership. He considered selfless service as the path to self-discovery: "The best way to find yourself is to lose yourself in the service of others."

Karma yoga is performing the right actions with the right attitude. Right actions are those which help everyone and harm no one. Why should I do all good and do no harm, one may ask? The law of karma explains, "As you sow, so shall you reap." There is nothing chaotic or capricious about this law: We alone are responsible for everything we face in life. Thus, Karma becomes at once the motivation to do good (by invoking the inevitability of the law of cause and effect) and also nature's way to restore moral harmony. The right

[32] For further details on the contribution of the Gītā in the making of Gandhi as a servant leader, refer to Chapter 10 of this book. See also: Satinder Dhiman, *Gandhi and Leadership: New Horizons in Exemplary Leadership* (New York, NY: Palgrave Macmillan, 2015); and Satinder Dhiman, *Holistic Leadership: A New Paradigm for Today's Leaders* (New York, NY: Palgrave Macmillan, 2017).

attitude is toward actions and their results. Performance of one's "duty for duty's sake" is the right attitude toward actions. It is an experiential fact that we have no control over the results of our actions. Thus, renouncing the fruits of actions is the right attitude toward their results.

According to karma yoga, it is not what one does, but the motive or intention behind the act that produces the binding effect of karma. Someone has said that *God cares more for adverbs than for verbs*; that is, more for *how* a thing is done than for *what* is done. In Indian philosophy, the law of karma is used to explain the cause of human bondage as well as the means to attain liberation from bondage. When actions are performed with a selfish motive, they *bind*; when actions are performed with the spirit of self-renunciation—and by way of submission to Divine will—they *liberate*. Performance of actions selflessly purifies the mind and renders it worthy to receive the liberating spiritual wisdom. *Ethics is thus considered a necessary prelude to spiritual freedom.* According to a well-known Indian dictum, "Scriptures do not cleanse the ethically unworthy."

Thus, karma yoga furnishes the highest basis for acting ethically in the world. The law of karma tells us that *whatever we do to others is rendered unto us—manifold.* When we practice karma yoga in the right spirit, it fosters understanding, harmony, and mutual trust in the workplace environment. Performing duties selflessly purifies the mind and makes it a fit instrument to receive the higher teachings of Self-knowledge.

It is when one can so restrain oneself as to only perform actions in the spirit of self-renunciation that one ceases to accumulate any new karma for fresh results. One only has to experience the results of one's previous karma that has ripened for giving fruits. If, in the meantime, one attains true knowledge of one's real Self, all past accumulated actions are destroyed. In elucidating what is called the doctrine of selfless action *(niṣkāma karma)*, the Bhagavad Gītā urges us to renounce selfish actions and fruits of actions. Commenting on karma yoga as enunciated in the Bhagavad Gītā, Mysore Hiriyanna explains, "The object of the Gītā is to discover a golden mean between the two ideals… of action and contemplation…preserving the excellence of both. Karma-Yoga is such a mean….[It] stands not for renunciation *of* action, but for renunciation *in* action."[33] This is the alchemy of karma yoga.

In the ultimate analysis, renunciation is an inner, mental act and should not be confused with outward tokens of relinquishment. It is about renunciation of results and not renunciation of actions themselves. That is, renunciation *in* action and not *of* actions. True renunciation is the renunciation of *kartāpan*—the deeply ingrained *sense of doership.* The path of knowledge (*jñāna yoga*) furnishes the best *raison d'être* for relinquishing the sense of doership in our actions.

[33] Mysore Hiriyanna, *Essentials of Indian Philosophy* (London, UK: Allen and Unwin, 1949), 120–121.

Becoming a Person of Steady Wisdom and Attaining the Absolute

At the heart of the Gītā, there lies the conception of a sage of steady wisdom (*sthitaprajñā*), who has gone beyond the pair of opposites such as pleasure and pain, success and failure, virtue, and vice. According to the Bhagavad Gītā, that person of steady wisdom, whose mind is unperturbed in sorrow, who is free from longing for pleasure, and who has gone beyond attachment, fear, and anger (*duḥkheṣv anudvignamanāḥ sukheṣu vigataspṛhaḥ vītarāgabhayakrodhaḥ sthitadhīr munir ucyate,* 2.56)—that person attains liberation (*mokṣa*):

> One who rejoices only in the Self, who is satisfied with the Self, who is content in the Self alone—for such a person, there is nothing left to do. Such a person has nothing to gain from work done or left undone and no selfish dependence on any being for any object to serve any purpose. Therefore, remaining unattached, always perform actions which are obligatory; by performing action without attachment, one attains the Supreme. (3.17–19)

> Resting in the Absolute, with intellect steady and without delusion, the knower of Self neither rejoices in receiving what is pleasant nor grieves on receiving what is unpleasant. (5.20)

The inner autonomy described in the above verses is the blossoming of Self-knowledge that expresses itself in the threefold-virtues of security, peace, and freedom.

Such a person of steady wisdom acts naturally and spontaneously for the welfare of all and attains the Supreme Brahman: "The seers whose sins have been washed away, whose doubts have been cleared, whose disciplined mind is firmly established in God, and who are engaged in the welfare of all beings, attain Supreme Brahman" (BG 5.25).

Attaining True Wisdom and Rejoicing in the Self Alone

Steady in wisdom, the *sthitaprajñā* enjoys the constant bliss of the Self, regardless of the changing circumstances. Established in the Oneness of Self, unattached and unperturbed, the person of steady wisdom is at peace and ease with everything in all situations. Such a person attains to the Absolute: "The *yogi* who is happy within, who rejoices within the delight of the soul, and who is illumined within (by the light of the soul) attains liberation in Brahman, having become one with Brahman" (BG 5.24).

Understanding the workings of the imposter ego and thereby rendering it ineffective is the first step on the path of wisdom. In chapter 13 of the Bhagavad Gītā where Śrī Kṛṣṇa begins to describe the marks or means of True Knowledge (Gītā 13. 7–11), we see "absence of self-pride" (13.7) listed as the very first mark. In the very next verse (13.8), Śrī Kṛṣṇa again states,"...and absence of egotism also" (*anahaṃkāra eva ca*). Please note the word "also" after the word "egotism." Out of the 20 marks of true knowledge listed in verses 13. 7–11, the word "also" (*eva*) is appended only next to the absence of "self-pride" ("*ahaṃkāra*").[34] This is an important point to bear in mind.

The Gītā presents detailed instructions about attaining steady abidance in Self-knowledge. As long as one is harboring a sense of distinction/superiority, regardless of any reason—justified or unjustified—one is still belaboring in vain, not much unlike the ox that turns the oil press by going back and forth. When God is all there is (*Vasudevaḥ Sarvam:* Gītā 7.19), where is the need for entertaining any feelings of distinction or superiority—no matter what the justification may be?

Those who are truly awake become awake to the fact that "God is all there is"—*including* the ones who may not be yet awake, in their estimation! This knowledge fosters amity, understanding, and harmony in all settings and removes the conflict inherent in the "game of one-up-ness" that plagues most human interaction. Likewise, we come to realize that most psychological and emotional stress is caused by our excessive self-centeredness. Self-centeredness is a condition borne with a deeply ingrained sense of separateness, anchored in self-ignorance. Self-knowledge is freedom from self-ignorance; when self-ignorance transforms into Self-knowledge, our need to maintain our separateness is resolved into the fullness of our being. We no longer feel the gnawing sense of inadequacy, incompleteness, and insecurity. We have arrived at an unassailable stillness, blessed with the fullness of our essential nature. We have made peace with the universe.

Doing Our Work Without the Tag of Doership

The Gītā makes it clear that all actions are performed by the interplay of the qualities of material nature. Due to our identification with ego, we think we are the doers. This identification results in attachment and aversion, which affects the quality of our work and leads to bondage. The seer of reality (*tattva-vit*) is firm (*yukto*) in his or her belief (*manyate*) that "I do nothing at all" (*naiva kiṃcit karomīti*), realizing that the senses are moving among the sense objects. Śaṅkarā explains in his commentary that one who has the knowledge of the actionless-Self sees inaction in action (4.18) for he or she realizes that, in all actions, the senses operate upon objects (sense objects) while the Self remains immutably inactive. The Bhagavad Gītā tells us that "for one who knows the Self, who rejoices solely in the Self, who is satisfied with the Self, and who is content in the Self alone,—for him there is nothing more left to do" (3.17). In other words, the Self is ever actionless, as action in nature (*Prakṛti's guṇas*) is inaction in the Self (*Ātman*). This is the true understanding of a person of knowledge.

A question may be asked here: If, for the knower of the Self, nothing remains to be done, then how do we explain the apparent actions of the enlightened ones? In his commentary on the Bhagavad Gītā, Śaṅkara, the greatest Indian philosopher, presents at least four explanations. The sages act:

[34] Swami Maheshānandjī Girī, *Jñāna-Sādhanā* (Varanasi, India: Sri Dakshinamurti Math, 1989).

1. with a view to set an example to the masses, so the unwary do not go astray (3.26)
2. for the unification of the world at large (*lokasaṃgraham*, 3.20, 3.25)
3. for the welfare of the world at large (*sarvabhūtahite ratāḥ*, 5.25;12.4)
4. for the purification of the self (*ātmaśuddhaye*, 5.11)

These can serve as great motivators for leadership as well. Effective leaders model their behavior to set a standard; they act for the wellbeing of all beings, and for the purification of their mind through selfless service.

In verses 5.25 and 12.4, a liberated person is described as "most naturally and intently engaged in seeking and promoting the welfare of all beings." Śrī Kṛṣṇa, using himself as an example of a liberated being, tells Arjuna, "there is nothing in all the three worlds for me to do, nor is there anything worth attaining unattained by me, yet I continue to work" (3.22). Then, in verse 3.25, we find the clearest practical advice to live by: "*As the unwise act with attachment, so should the wise, seeking maintenance of the world order, act without attachment.*" In sum, the seers act for the wellbeing of all beings and for the unification of the world. At the highest level, they spontaneously embody the virtues of universal morality, such as selflessness, compassion, desirelessness, forbearance, peace, and harmony. This is the culmination of karma yoga.

Samatā and Sthitaprajñā: Supreme Goals of the Gītā

If there are two key virtues that the Gītā teaches above all, they are equanimity and steady wisdom. Two important verses in chapter 2 reveal the secret to this supreme goal, as well as the means to the attainment of the goal of *sthitaprajñā*, as follows:

> *prajahāti yadā kāmān sarvān pārtha manogatān /*
> *ātmany evātmanā tuṣṭaḥ sthitaprajñas tadocyate* //2.55//
> *vihāya kāmān yaḥ sarvān pumāṃś carati niḥspṛhaḥ /*
> *nirmamo nirahaṃkāraḥ sa śāntim adhigacchhati* //2.71//

> When one completely casts off all the desires of the mind, content in the Self alone, by [the joy of] the Self, then one is said to be established in steady wisdom.
> One who has given up all desires and moves about free from longings and the sense of "I" and "mine" attains peace.

All schools of Indian philosophy take it to be axiomatic that the fundamental human error is self-ignorance. Due to this error we are not able to experience our intrinsic perfection and take ourselves to be limited, inadequate, and incomplete beings. Since self-ignorance is the cause of our malady, only Self-knowledge can provide permanent solution to this gnawing sense of inadequacy.

A seminal verse captures both the means and the end of Self-knowledge, as follows:

> *ātmaupamyena sarvatra samaṃ paśyati yorjuna /*
> *sukhaṃ vā yadi vā duḥkhaṃ sa yogī paramo mataḥ* //6.32//
>
> O Arjuna, that *yogī* is considered to be the highest among all *yogīs* who judges what is happiness and sorrow in all, by the *same* standard as he would apply to himself.

He looks at the joy and sorrow of all with the same eye, because he feels the pleasure and pain in others same as the pleasure and pain in himself, since he has realized the oneness of all existence. Although the word *yogī* occurs 15 times in the Bhagavad Gītā, Śrī Kṛṣṇa has used the word "*paramaḥ*" (supreme) along with the word *yogī* only once in this very verse. Hence, the utmost importance of this unique verse!

When our mind has become pure and our intellect "*sama*"—"balanced and equanimous"—we have attained oneness with the highest principle of existence. Such is the supreme importance of *samatā*.

The value of cultivating equanimity for today's leaders and managers can hardly be overemphasized. Its importance is evident in every action, every decision a leader makes. Without the evenness of mind, self-awareness, and emotional intelligence—two markers of success in leading oneself and others—remain a distant goal.

Concluding Thoughts: The Universality of the Gītā's Teachings

The message of the Gītā is for everyone who is interested in attaining spiritual freedom. The sole purpose of the Gītā is the salvation of all of humankind. Regardless of one's race, religion, or philosophical orientation, everyone can attain their spiritual welfare by following its simple teachings. The Gītā teaches the unique art of attaining supreme fulfillment through secular conduct *(vyavahār mein paramārath ki kalā)*—by which one can, under every situation, performing all ordained actions, verily attain one's spiritual welfare. It teaches us that all actions and their results are material in nature. When performed selflessly, actions serve as purifying agents and prepare the mind to receive the Self-knowledge which alone is the means to the ultimate goal of liberation. One should always remember the final goal and never get carried away by other pursuits. According to the Gītā, the final goal is liberation (freedom from all limitations) and Self-knowledge is the only means to it. All other means are but a preparation for it.

The Gītā teaches us that the real security lies within us and comes only from Self-knowledge. You are already the complete being that you long to be. The Gītā accomplishes this by revealing to us the true nature of the Self. Life will always have its ups and downs. Learn to forebear and do not get carried away.

Always maintain *sattva-guṇa*—the quality of purity and truthfulness. It teaches us to perform our duties, in the spirit of detachment and sacrifice *(yajña)* and as an offering to the Supreme, for the mutual benefit of each other and for the welfare of the world (*lokasaṃgraham*: 3.20; 3.25). By cherishing each other in this manner, we will attain the Supreme Good (3.11). It further assures us that "by properly performing one's duty, one attains perfection" (18.45). While many scriptures enjoin one to renounce the world to attain God, the Gītā states that one can attain perfection by surrendering to God (who is the source of all creation and is all-pervading) through the performance of one's prescribed duty—*svakarmaṇā tam abhyarcya siddhiṃ vindati mānavaḥ* (18.46).

When Self-knowledge removes self-ignorance that was covering our natural state of limitlessness, we discover that happiness is not a state of *becoming*; rather, it is a state of *being*. And we can retreat in this inner sanctuary of stillness of our being anytime and *be* ourselves. When we have discovered our inner font of peace and joy, we act "with" fulfillment and not "for" fulfillment. Thus, through equanimity, service, detachment, and surrender (to the Supreme), the Gītā teaches the art of spirituality while being ethically engaged in the worldly pursuits. This is the path of Self-realization paved by selfless service which alone leads to inner peace, fulfillment, and freedom. Having realized this Self-knowledge, the Gītā assures us, one swiftly attains supreme peace (*jñānaṃ labdhvā parāṃ śāntim acireṇādhigacchati*: 4.39).

The law of karma places one's psycho-spiritual evolution in one's own hands. It inspires the leaders to evolve and help others evolve. The Gītā teaches renunciation *in* action, not renunciation *of* action. Renounce desire and attachment, not action, states the most important verse (2.47) on *karma yoga* in the Gītā. The sage outwardly does all activities like others, inwardly unattached. This is the essence of *karma yoga* of the Bhagavad Gītā. Wise leaders do everything without selfish motive, remaining equanimous in success and failure, pleasure and pain, joy and sorrow.

Wise leaders offer their work as a loving service to the Supreme. They work for the purification of their mind (*ātmaśuddhaye*: 5.11) and act with a view to set an example to the masses, so the unwary do not go astray (3.26). They work for the wellbeing of all beings (*sarvabhūtahite*: 5.25, 12.4) and for bringing the people together (*lokasaṃgraham*: 3.20, 3.25). This is the entire teachings of the Gītā on life and leadership. According to W. D. P. Hill,

> The Gītā's ultimate message in one sentence is: One who works with [Self-] knowledge and devotion, and without desire, wins liberation.[35]

This observation distils the essence of all three main *yogas* in the Gītā! Therefore, by all our seeking, let us seek Self-knowledge and work devotedly for the common good. This is the abiding foundation of all wise leadership.

This is the message leaders need during these turbulent times!

[35] W. D. P. Hill, *The Bhagavad Gītā: A Translation and Commentary* (Madras, India: Oxford University Press, 1928/1953), 62.

CHAPTER 10

Be the Change: The Making of a Servant Leader

Introduction

My life has been full of external tragedies—and if they have left no visible or indelible scar on me, I owe it all to the teaching of the Bhagavad Gītā.[1] (Gandhi)

It is evident from this opening quote that the Bhagavad Gītā served as a spiritual reference book for Gandhi throughout his life. He turned to it when the going got tough. He constantly drew spiritual solace from it. His gratitude for this gem of a scripture comes loud and clear from this testimony.

Among the key influences on Gandhi's life and thought, pride of place must go to the Bhagavad Gītā. It is well known that Gandhi modeled his life upon the teachings of the Gītā[2] and "constantly referred to it as his 'spiritual dictionary,' 'the mother who never let him down,' or his '*kāmdhenū*,' 'the cow that grants all wishes.'"[3] The Gītā played a pivotal role in guiding, shaping, and solidifying his beliefs and actions. Gandhi's firm and sustained belief in spiritual

[1] M. K. Gandhi, *Young India* (1925), 1078–1079.

[2] See: Ramesh S. Betai, *Gītā and Gandhi* (New Delhi, India: Gyan Publishing House/National Gandhi Museum, 2002).

[3] J. T. F. Jordens, Gandhi and the Bhagavadgita. In Robert Neil Minor (Ed.), *Modern Indian Interpreters of the Bhagavad Gītā* (New York, NY: State University of New York Press), 88. See: M. K. Gandhi, *An Autobiography: The Story of My Experiments with Truth* (New York, NY: Dover Publications, 1983), 59, 60, 232, 233, 296–297.

Partially based on the author's previously published book, *Gandhi and Leadership: New Horizons in Exemplary Leadership*, Palgrave Macmillan, New York, NY – September 2015.

S. Dhiman, *Bhagavad Gītā and Leadership*,
Palgrave Studies in Workplace Spirituality and Fulfillment,
https://doi.org/10.1007/978-3-319-67573-2_10

freedom (*mokṣa*[4]) and Self-realization was almost entirely shaped by the teachings of the Gītā. *Mokṣa* supplied the unifying force in and through all of Gandhi's activities, as he tells us in his autobiography,[5] and the Gītā's emphasis on Self-realization and selfless service were the primary sources of inspiration for his life and leadership.

Prominent world leaders such as Martin Luther King, Jr., Mother Teresa, the Dalai Lama, and Desmond Tutu have drawn abiding inspiration from their spiritual roots and moral convictions. Contemporary leadership writers and thinkers such as John H. Maxwell, Max De Pree, C. Michael Thompson, James A. Autry, and Stephen R. Covey, to name just a few, have also underscored the moral and spiritual dimensions of leadership. That Gandhi considered the spiritual dimension as primary is evident from his autobiography:

> What I want to achieve,—and what I have been striving and pining to achieve these thirty years,—is self-realization, to see God face to face, to attain *Moksha*. I live and move and have my being in pursuit of this goal. All that I do by way of speaking and writing and all my ventures in the political field are directed to this same end.[6]

Since spirituality without ethics and morals is of little value,[7] Gandhi further clarifies that the existential experiments with truth that he is going to describe "are spiritual, or rather moral, for the *essence of religion is morality*."[8] In this chapter, we focus on the core message of the Gītā—as viewed by Gandhi—and the practical lessons in leadership that he drew from his lifelong study of this timeless spiritual classic.

It is important to remember that though in its ultimate bidding the Gītā is essentially a manual for the attainment of spiritual freedom (*mokṣaśāstra*)—as Śaṅkarācārya, its greatest commentator and exponent, constantly reminds us—yet, in its practical aspect, it is also a great manual for living. The Gītā is not a world-abnegating esoteric treatise on spirituality. As A. Parthasarathy has rightly noted, "The Bhagavad Gītā is a technique, a skill for dynamic living, not a retirement plan."[9] It teaches us, here and now, how to live a life imbued with service, contribution, and meaning, free from the trammels of desire, anger, and greed: the great art of seeking the highest spiritual good amidst the ordinary practical matters—the alchemy of supreme spiritual fulfillment through secular behavior. There is no shying away from any responsibility or any effective action, as long as it is done with the right attitude and in the right manner.

[4] *Mokṣa* is a Sanskrit term for liberation, which means freedom from the servitude of sensual pleasures and equanimity toward favorable and unfavorable circumstances while living, and, ultimately, liberation from the conditioned existence—the cycles of birth and death.

[5] Gandhi, *An Autobiography*, viii.

[6] Ibid.

[7] According to a well-known Indian dictum, "Scriptures do not cleanse the ethically unworthy."

[8] Gandhi, *An Autobiography*, viii.

[9] A. Parthasarathy cited in Dennis Waite, *Back to the Truth: 5000 Years of Advaita* (Winchester, UK: John Hunt Publishing, 2007), 519.

At what point of one's life one should pursue the goal of *mokṣa* or Self-realization? Many believe that spiritual quest is something to be pursued during the last phase of one's life. Dispelling this popular "superstition" that Self-realization is to be attained only in the last stages of life, Gandhi tells us in his autobiography that people who defer it until then "attain not self-realization but old age amounting to a second and pitiable childhood, living as a burden on this earth."[10] This serves as a strong warning to those who think that spirituality is something to be pursued only at the end of one's life. "Seek ye the good things of the spirit," we are told; the rest will either not matter, we are told, or will be supplied to us.[11]

Gandhi Moment: A Warrior of Spirit, Spirit of a Warrior

Very early in his life, Gandhi realized that in order to serve a cause higher than himself, his own personal transformation was necessary. To become what is now widely known as a "servant leader," he realized that he needed to get his self out of the way, to get his ego out of the way, and put service before self. In the concluding section of his autobiography, he wrote, "I must reduce myself to zero."[12]

We think of warriors training themselves for battle and all the disciplines they must undergo by way of endurance training. From his autobiography and other writings, we gather that Gandhi had to undergo similar training and discipline to effect his spiritual transformation and become a peaceful warrior of spirit. And he had a great training manual to follow: the Bhagavad Gītā! The warrior metaphor is very appropriate here since the Gītā is a dialog between the warrior-prince, Arjuna, and Śrī Kṛṣṇa, the Lord within.

Effective leaders understand the vital difference between a fighter and a warrior. A fighter always thinks in terms of *ends*, namely, winning or losing; a warrior focuses on perfecting the *means*. At every failure, the fighter gets into the blame game and contemplates quitting; the warrior confronts the enemy within and doggedly perseveres. When a master archer fails to hit the target, she/he does not blame the target. She/he steps back, works more steadfastly on her/his technique, and comes back—doubly renewed.

[10] Gandhi, *An Autobiography*, 302.

[11] According to the Bible, "Seek ye first the kingdom of God, and his righteousness; and all these things shall be added unto you" (verse 33, King James Version).

[12] Gandhi, *An Autobiography*, 454.

Ethics: The Heart of Leadership

For Gandhi, the Gītā was a manual of exemplary moral conduct, a textbook of higher ethics. He knew the value of values and lived his life upholding the highest standards of ethical conduct. Throughout his life, Gandhi underwent austerities (*tapas*) to properly attune his spirit and to attain a certain purity of mind. His frequent fasts, long walks, and Spartan life style all contributed to making Gandhi a fit vessel to carry out his mission selflessly. The unity and purity of his thought, his firm commitment to truthfulness, and his uncompromising adherence to nonviolence were the mainstay of his leadership style.

Underscoring the role of ethics in life, the Gītā upholds a vital competency that is sorely needed in the modern world plagued by rampant financial frauds and inveterate moral ineptitude. It has been rightly observed that "ethics lies at the very heart of leadership."[13] When leaders forget this vital point, leadership regenerates into a narcissistic pursuit of self-aggrandizement, to the detriment of the society. In the final reckoning, "the only true leadership is values-based leadership."[14]

The spirituality of the Gītā is firmly rooted in ethical values. There is no progress on the path of spirituality if there is no harmony and unity between our *vicāra* (thought process) and *ācāra* (conduct). Without ethical purity, the true message of the Gītā will elude us.

Transforming Anger: The Gītā Way!

Many methods are recommended to control anger, with varying degrees of effectiveness. Most people recommend the "delay tactic"—not to respond at all in the heat of anger. That is effective only if one remembers this counsel of perfection before the onset of the fit of anger. The Gītā says that, to control anger, we first need to pay attention to its root cause—desire. Anger arises when someone stands in the way of our desired object—that is, anger ensues from (unfulfilled) desire. And attachment to things, ideas, and opinions lie at the root of desire. Basically, to control anger, we should first guard and calm our mind. If our mind remains in a state of calm, then no negative emotions can provoke it. The easiest way to be peaceful in mind is to let our mind rest content within its own inner sanctuary rather than constantly hankering after the worldly objects outside.

To manage anger effectively, we have to work patiently on reducing the frequency of the anger, its intensity, as well as the recovery period.[15] The Gītā categorically states:

[13] Joanne B. Ciulla (Ed.), *Ethics, The Heart of Leadership* (Westport, CT: Praeger, 2004, Second edition), xv.

[14] Harry M. Jansen Kraemer, Jr., *From Values to Action: The Four Principles of Values-Based Leadership* (San Francisco, CA: Jossey-Bass, April 2011). See also: James O'Toole, Notes toward a definition of values-based leadership. *The Journal of Values-Based Leadership*, 2008, 1 (1), 4, Article 10.

[15] Swāmī Paramārthānanda, "The Spiritual Journey: Guru Purnima Talk 2008." Retrieved October 5, 2014: http://www.vedanta.gr/wp-content/uploads/2013/03/SwParam_GP2008_Spiritual-Journey_ENA4.pdf

Also see: Swāmī Paramārthānanda, General Talks: Understanding Anger.

śaknotīhaivayaḥsoḍhuṃprākśarīravimokṣaṇāt /
kāmakrodhodbhavaṃvegaṃsayuktaḥsasukhīnaraḥ //5.23//

Only those who are able to withstand the impulses of lust and anger arising in the body are integrated (*yuktaḥ*) and live in joy.

Gandhi Moment: Transforming Anger into Light

The Gītā (16.21) calls anger one of the triple gates to hell—desire and greed being the other two. Gandhi knew from experience that anger conserved becomes compassion that can be harnessed in the service of others. "I have learnt through bitter experience," he tells us, "the one supreme lesson to conserve my anger, and as heat conserved is transmuted into energy, even so our anger controlled can be transmuted into a power which can move the world."[16]

Gandhi once told young Arun Gandhi, his grandson, that uncontrolled anger can be deadly, like lightning; however, when channeled properly, it can serve to illuminate our life like a lamp:

> Have I told you how anger is like electricity....Anger can strike like lightning, and split a living tree in two....Or it can be channeled, transformed. A switch can be flipped, and it can shed light like a lamp....Then anger can illuminate. It can turn the darkness into light.[17]

Gandhi Made His Life an Offering to the Divine

The Gītā is a practical manual of living. It lays down the guidelines for leading a meaningful life—a life marked by goodness and contribution. What makes our life purposeful and meaningful? What is the essence of being good and doing good? What does it mean to grow in goodness? How can one grow from being a consumer to becoming a contributor? The Gītā holds the keys to all these existential questions. It recommends that we approach life as a network of mutual interdependencies in which everyone has to contribute their allotted share. And the touchstone is not mere human welfare, but the welfare of all beings (*sarvabhūtahite*: 5.25; 12.4). Only then can we ensure the preservation of the universe. This understanding holds the key to a sustainable future for all.

In order to grow spiritually, one has to convert one's whole life into an offering to the Divine, as a cosmic sacrifice (*yajñārthātkarmaṇo*: 3.9). According to the Gītā (3.10–3.13), all beings are a part of the cosmic wheel of creation, sustained by the principle of mutual contribution and mutual maintenance. Therefore, every task should be performed in the spirit of sacrifice that

[16] *Young India*, September 15, 1920, 6.

[17] Arun Gandhi & Bethany Hegedus, *Grandfather Gandhi* (New York, NY: Antheneum Books for Young Readers, 2012), 32–33.

sustains all beings, in a spirit of offering to the Universal Lord. They are great thieves who do not help in the turning of this cosmic wheel of sacrifice (3.12).

The Gītā (18.5) mandates threefold acts of sacrifice (*yajña*), charity (*dānaṃ*), and austerity (*tapas*) and considers these as the "purifiers of the wise." "*Yajña*" literally means a sacrifice or an offering. The highest form of offering is living a life of sincerity—a life led by *being* good and *doing* good. A sincere life is characterized by doing what we love and loving what we have to do. "*Dānaṃ*" means charity and denotes much more than writing a check to a favorite cause or organization. At the deepest level, it means the gift of "expressed love." "*Tapas*" means austerity or discipline. The Gītā talks about several kinds of discipline. The most important is "*vāk tapas*"—"discipline of speech." There are five such disciplines of speech that the Gītā recommends:

> *anudvegakaraṃvākyaṃsatyaṃpriyahitaṃcayat /*
> *svādhyāyābhyasanaṃcaivavāṅmayaṃ tapa ucyate* //17.15//
>
> That speech which causes no mental anguish (disturbance) to anyone, which is truthful, agreeable, and beneficial, as well as the practice of study of the sacred books, is considered to be the discipline of speech.

Gandhi's whole life was defined by the threefold acts of sacrifice, charity, and austerity. He converted his whole life into an offering to the Divine, devoted all his time and energy to service, and led all his life in self-discipline and self-restraint. This inspired trust, faith, and hope in those he led. Gandhi's dedication to selfless service is one of the keys to understanding his influence as a leader.

Lead by Example: Hallmark of Gandhi's Leadership

Gandhi inspired emulation not so much by his professed set of values and beliefs as by the exemplary nature of his life and conduct. *He made his life his message*. This virtue of "being the change" that we wish to see in the world became a Gandhian hallmark—his most precious legacy for which he will be always remembered. He was a rare one who did what is most difficult: he practiced what he preached.

Śrī Kṛṣṇa tells Arjuna that those in leadership positions should act responsibly, since whatever standards or example the leader sets, people in general will follow (3.21). Leaders' actions do speak louder than their words. In essence, leaders are the brand ambassadors of their organizations. Humanity has yet to discover a more effective way to bring about change and lead others than by setting an example. All great leaders lead by example.

The Gītā states that the wise leader acts to set an example to the masses so that the unwary do not go astray (3.26); for the unification of the world at large (*lokasaṃgraham*: 3.20, 3.25); for the welfare of all beings (*sarvabhūtahite*: 5.25); and for the purification of the self (*ātmaśuddhaye*: 5.11). These four goals together furnish a touchstone for leadership success in any setting.

Leaders do their duty for duty's sake (cf. Kant's Duty Ethics), to set an example for others, to bring communities together, for the wellbeing of all; and above all, for the purification of the mind and the heart. No higher teaching on the sublimity of a leader's work ethic can be conceived.

In the ultimate analysis, leadership is not about changing outer conditions or others. More often than not, there is not much that we can do to change what is external to us. However, we have full control over our own conduct. "When we are no longer able to change a situation," writes psychotherapist Viktor E. Frankl, "we are challenged to change ourselves."[18] And when we are able to do that, in due course of time, we are also able to change the situation, unexpectedly. This is the alchemy of all social change.

The Gītā: A Dictionary of Daily Conduct for Gandhi

It is now well known that Gandhi regarded the Gītā as his primary go-to spiritual reference book, to which he constantly turned for daily guidance and solace.[19] Writing for his weekly journal *Young India* in 1925, he tells us:

> I find a solace in the *Bhagavad Gītā* that I miss even in the Sermon on the Mount. When disappointment stares me in the face and all alone I see not one ray of light, I go back to the *Bhagavad Gītā*. I find a verse here and a verse there, and I immediately begin to smile in the midst of overwhelming tragedies—and my life has been full of external tragedies—and if they have left no visible or indelible scar on me, I owe it all to the teaching of the *Bhagavad Gītā*.[20]

In no uncertain words, Gandhi describes how the Gītā has helped him in dealing with the "slings and arrows of outrageous fortune" of life, and establishes the practical utility of its teachings.

However, what is not generally known is that Gandhi not only wrote a verse-by-verse translation of the Gītā (*Anāsaktiyoga*), but also delivered 218 discourses on it, compiled a comprehensive glossary (giving meanings) of words and phrases in the Gītā (*Gītāpadārthakōṣa*), wrote 18 letters from jail on each chapter of the Gītā (*Gītābōdha*), and, above and beyond all this, referred to the study, teachings, and relevance of the Gītā (often citing specific verses) about 1200 times in his articles, letters, speeches, and discussions, as recorded in the *Collected Works of Mahātmā Gandhi*.[21]

[18] Viktor E. Frankl, *Man's Search for Meaning: An Introduction to Logotherapy* (New York, NY: A Touchstone Book, 1984, Third edition), 116.

[19] See note 2 above.

[20] M. K. Gandhi, *Young India* (1925), 1078–1079. Cited in S. Radhākrishnan, *The Bhagavad Gītā: With an Introductory Essay, Sanskrit Text, English Translation, and Notes* (London, UK: George Allen and Unwin, 1958), 10.

[21] Y. P. Anand as cited in Ramesh S. Betai, *Gītā and Gandhi* (New Delhi, India: Gyan Publishing House/National Gandhi Museum, 2002), xi. Dr. Y. P. Anand has done a wonderful job of bringing together all of Gandhi's works on the Gītā and its interpretation in a two-volume set. See: Y. P. Anand, *Mahatma Gandhi's Works and Interpretation of the Bhagavad Gītā* (New Delhi, India: Radha Publications, 2009).

Even at the time of his first acquaintance with the book, while he was still a law student in England in 1889, the Bhagavad Gītā struck him "as one of priceless worth."[22] It became for him, as he tells us in his autobiography, the "book par-excellence for the knowledge of Truth."[23] Gandhi's mother passed away shortly before his return to India from England in 1891. Later, he referred to the Gītā as his beneficent "mother": "The Gītā has been a mother to me ever since I became first acquainted with it in 1889. I turn to it for guidance in every difficulty, and the desired guidance has always been forthcoming."[24] He regarded the Gītā as his "dictionary of daily conduct"[25] and it never failed to provide him guidance and solace in moments of doubt, difficulty, or gloom. He translated the Gītā into his native Gujarati and pondered over it incessantly until its message became inscribed on the tablet of his heart.

Soon, the Gītā became "an infallible guide of conduct"[26] for Gandhi and he began to pattern his whole life on its lofty teachings. To put into practice the concepts that he gleaned from the Gītā—such as *aparigraha* (nonpossession) and *samabhāva* (equanimity)—became his constant challenge: "How was one to divest oneself of all possessions? Was not the body itself possession enough? Was I to give up all I had and follow Him?" As he wrestled with such questions, straight came the answer in the form of inner renunciation: "I could not follow Him unless I gave up all I had."[27] He let his insurance policy lapse, gave all he had saved up to that moment to his brother, and pledged all future savings, if any, to "be utilized for the benefit of community."[28] Such was the sincerity of this pilgrim of the soul who gave up all that was inessential and extra on the journey to the Divine.

Gandhi Moment: Knowledge to Conviction to Paradigm Shift
What is the process that transforms knowledge into conviction and finally leads to a shift in perspective? It starts with the acquisition of knowledge through listening, converting knowledge into firm conviction through reflection, and finally changing our perspective—a paradigm shift—through internalizing or assimilating the doubt-free knowledge made firm through constant reflection.

How did Gandhi come to this certainty of moral conviction and his goal of Self-realization? He tells us that he deeply pondered over the message of the Gītā constantly for 40 years! "It was characteristic of Gandhi," Narayan Desai informed this writer in a personal interview, "that he will

(*continued*)

[22] Gandhi, *An Autobiography*, 59.

[23] Ibid.

[24] Eknath Easwaran, *Gandhi the Man: The Story of His Transformation* (Tomales, CA: Nilgiri Press, 1997), 107.

[25] Gandhi, *An Autobiography*, 233.

[26] Ibid.

[27] Ibid.

[28] Ibid.

(continued)
strive hard to put into practice what he had learned....Once he has determined the moral worth of an idea, he will follow it unswervingly with a great courage of conviction....The most remarkable thing about Gandhi was that his life indeed was his message."[29] Through his understanding of the key teachings of the Gītā and by observing his spiritual role model, Raychand Bhai (a Jain jeweler), Gandhi set Self-realization and selfless service to be his supreme goals in life and devoted all his waking hours to achieving these goals. Everything he did—the *satyāgraha* in South Africa, or the Dandi Salt March, or his fasts for self-purification in India—was a part of his struggle for Self-realization, a facet of his soul searching.

Anāsakti Yoga: A Gospel of Selfless Action

Where did Gandhi get the courage of his moral conviction? What was the source of his spiritual strength? We believe that it was indeed the Bhagavad Gītā. "At the back of my reading of Gītā," writes Gandhi, "there is the claim of an endeavor to enforce the meaning in my own conduct for an unbroken period of forty years."[30] Gandhi interpreted the Gītā as the "Gospel of Selfless Action" (*Anāsaktiyoga*).[31] Key Gandhian concepts such as selfless action (*niṣkāma karma*), nonviolence (*ahiṁsā*), steadfastness in truth (*sthitaprajñatā*), and nonpossession (*aparigraha*) proceed directly from his unique interpretation of the Gītā. By reflecting deeply on the import of the Gītā's teachings, it became clear to Gandhi that his path was the path of Self-realization through service to humanity, and he made efforts and experiments at every moment of his life to come nearer to this goal.

The Gītā's goal of Self-realization and its doctrine of selfless action (*niṣkāma karma*) defined Gandhi's modus operandi: choose the right goal (common good) and follow the right means (nonviolence), and be detached from the results (by dedicating them to the Supreme Lord). Gandhi once eloquently paraphrased this formula when he replied to an English Quaker who was complaining about being ignored by the media, "Throw the right stone into the

[29] Conversations with Sriman Narayan Desai, unpublished interview transcripts. Narayan Desai, son of Mahatma Gandhi's personal secretary and biographer, Mahadev Desai, lived with Gandhi for 21 years since he was about one-year old. His magnum opus, *My Life Is My Message*, is the English translation of the epic four-volume biography in Gujarati, *Maru Jivan Ej Mari Vani*, and is hailed as one of the finest insights into the life of Gandhi. It brings alive Gandhi's several quests as one indivisible whole, in which the political is not outside the realm of the spiritual. The interviews with Narayan Desai took place in 2013 in Ahmedabad at his sister's house where he was staying at the time. Sriman Narayan Desai informed this author that for the last 68 years, he has studied and taught only one topic: Gandhi!

[30] M. K. Gandhi in John Strohmeier (Ed.), *The Bhagavad Gītā According to Gandhi* (Berkeley, CA: Berkeley Hills Books, 2000), 16.

[31] Ibid., 14.

right pond, let the ripples take care of themselves."[32] Gandhi defined "right" in terms of "harmlessness" or "nonviolence," which provided the foundation for his core strategy—*satyāgraha* or "truth force." He took an expansive view of nonviolence to denote not just non-injury, but a positive force of love and compassion.

This greater regard for the right means above desired ends served as a moral compass for Gandhi throughout his life and defined all that he undertook in his personal and political life—which to him constituted one undivided whole. He did not regard the Gītā as a book only for the learned; he found its message to be eminently *practical* and meant to be *lived*. It has been rightly observed that the Gītā is "catholic in its message, comprehensive in its outlook, and concrete in its suggestions."[33] Gandhi believed that its teachings could be easily understood and put into practice by all, to whatever race or religion, time or clime they might belong.

Gandhi Moment: The Secret of Servant Leadership

Gandhi extracted the idea of trusteeship from his reading of Snell's Maxims of Equity during his study of the Law in England. He discovered a whole new religion in it, interpreting it in the light of the teachings of the Gītā. Particularly appealing was the maxim that one should hold everything in trust on behalf of those who follow. What a brilliant idea to relate to our possessions!

Only by not regarding anything as our own can we truly devote ourselves, body and soul, to the selfless service of others. For, unless the mind is purged of personal desire and attachment, even service is but an inflation of the ego. When asked to sum up the meaning of life in three words or less, Gandhi responded cheerfully, "That's easy: Renounce and enjoy."[34] It was this spirit of renunciation that made Gandhi a paragon of servant leadership.

[32] Michael N. Nagler, *Gītā Theory of Action*. Retrieved: August 8, 2014: http://mettacenter.org/definitions/gloss-concepts/Gītā-theory-of-action/

[33] P. Nagaraja Rao, *Introduction to Vedanta* (Bombay, India: Bharatiya Vidya Bhavan, 1966), 102.

[34] Eknath Easwaran, trans., *The Upanishads, Translated for the Modern Reader* (Berkeley, CA: Nilgiri Press, 1987), 205. Gandhi was referring to the first verse of Iśā Upaniṣad here. He regarded it so highly that he is reported to have said that it contained the essence of Hinduism: "If all the Upanishads and all the other scriptures happened all of a sudden to be reduced to ashes, and if only the first verse in the Iśā Upaniṣad were left in the memory of the Hindus, Hinduism would live forever."

īśāvāsyamidaṃsarvaṃyatkiñcajagatyāṃjagat /
tenatyaktenabhuñjīthāmāgṛdhaḥkasyasviddhanam //

[Enveloped by the Lord must be This All—each thing that moves on earth.
With that renounced enjoy thyself. Covet no wealth of any man.]

Selfless Service and Servant Leadership

Selfless service, the cardinal doctrine of the Gītā that Gandhi lived by, has great applications in the realm of leadership. First and foremost, leadership is a responsibility—a call to serve—and not an opportunity to wield power or influence. The power that is bestowed upon the leader by the followers is of the nature of trust and good faith. In other words, leadership is a fiduciary relationship built upon mutual trust between the leader and the followers. Viewed in this manner, the only reason a leader exists is to enable and empower the followers. Great leaders approach their work as a contribution, as a service, without any sense of entitlement whatsoever. "Like the 'Guardians' of Plato's *Republic*," writes Al Gini, "leaders must see their office as a social responsibility, a trust, a duty, and not as a symbol of their personal identity, prestige, and lofty status."[35]

Servant leaders act as fiduciaries of trust in the service of their followers—the beneficiaries. They hold the resources of the organization as trustees for the common good and not for their personal use. Gandhi was a paragon of such servant leadership. He held everything life brought into his orbit in sacred trust and related to it in an utterly unselfish way. He treaded the planet lightly, but left his footprints and fingerprints on the sands of human consciousness; he was a true pilgrim of soul.

One key requirement of servant leadership is the ability to subordinate one's personal ambition for the common good. As long as one is belaboring under self-ignorance, even social service is but an inflation of ego. Only those who have freed themselves from the shackles of the imposter ego can truly serve. This then represents the essence of leadership: selfless devotion to a cause greater than oneself. Practicing servant leadership is deceptively simple: one is led by the deep desire to serve others. It is also about putting others' interests first. The Gītā teaches us that leaders should serve a common cause greater than their individual self (*lokasaṃgraha*), by becoming an instrument of the whole (*nimitamātra*) and by immersing themselves in the wellbeing of all (*sarvabhūtahite ratāḥ*). History is testimony to the fact that humanity's truest leaders were servant leaders. When all is said and done, there is no human ideal higher than the gift of selfless service. In giving of ourselves unconditionally and serving others selflessly, we truly redeem our existence.

Does the Gītā Advocate Violence?

Not too long ago, at the behest of the Russian Orthodox Church, a court in Siberia received a call to ban an edition of the Bhagavad Gītā because it advocated killing! This was a classic case of taking certain teachings out their context and labeling the book as "extremist." The Russian court finally dismissed the case, declaring the book legal.[36] A clear understanding of the text will reveal

[35] Al Gini, Moral leadership and business ethics. In Ciulla (Ed.), *Ethics, The Heart of Leadership*, 36.

[36] See: Russia court declares Hindu book Bhagavad Gītā legal. *BBC News*. December 28, 2011. Retrieved March 27, 2017: http://www.bbc.com/news/world-asia-india-16344615

that the only killing that the Gītā advocates is the killing of the self-ignorance! It is also important to bear in mind that the context of war is at best tangential for the central teachings of the Gītā. Beyond the first few chapters, there is no discussion about war in the Gītā. Arjuna was confused about his duty; he was not looking for a sermon on warfare.

The teachings of the Bhagavad Gītā take place amidst the battlefield with the impending historic war between two clans as the backdrop. A cursory reader may conclude that the Gītā instigates violence or promotes war. It is important to realize that the battlefield setting of the Bhagavad Gītā is vital and is infused with deepest significance. First, it conveys the message that in the battle of life, one has to constantly confront and choose between right and wrong. No one can escape this universal fact.

Secondly, the battlefield is a place where one's commitment to values is tested to its very core. The Gītā teaches that through proper understanding and discretion, one can adhere to the path of *dharma*, righteousness, even amidst the urgency of war. For example, one important verse (2.21) in the second chapter states the Gītā's perspective on violence, thusly: "How can one who knows that the Self is indestructible, eternal, free from birth and death, kill or cause others to kill?" It teaches that the Self is imperishable, permanent, eternal, and remains unaffected even when the body is slain. There is no birth or death for the Self.

The teaching of the eternality of Self is *not* a license to kill.

The Gītā teaches that the highest ethical ideal for the humankind is *lokasaṅgraham* (3.20, 3.25)—working for the welfare of the entire world. That in which the greatest good of all beings lies is the key characteristic of Truth.[37]

The wise perform actions for the wellbeing of all beings (*sarvabhutahitae* 5.25) and by remaining equanimous in victory or defeat, they uphold the order and regularity of the world by bringing its communities together.

Does the Gītā, a text that Mahatma Gandhi regarded his "dictionary of daily conduct,"[38] support war? In order to properly answer this question, it is important to bear in mind the overall setting of the Gītā as well as a few cardinal tenets of Hindu philosophy, such as the concept of *svadharma*—the specific duty of a specific individual in a specific situation.[39] Most importantly, the teachings of the Gītā should be viewed in the broader background of the war of Mahābhārata.

The teachings of the Gītā took place on the eve of the Mahābhārata war in the form of a dialog between the warrior prince, Arjuna, and the Lord in human form, Śrī Kṛṣṇa. It was Arjuna's bounden duty as a *kṣatriya* to engage

[37] यद् भूतहितं अत्यन्तं, ऐतद सत्यस्य लक्षणं *yad bhūtahitaṁ atyantaṁ, aitad satyasya lakṣaṇaṁ* Mahābhārata: Shanti Parva, Mokṣa Dharma, chapter 248, śloka 16.

[38] M. K. Gandhi, *An Autobiography: The Story of My Experiments with Truth* (New York, NY: Dover Publications, 1983), 233.

[39] For a balanced discussion on this topic, see Jeffery D. Long's fine essay, War and Non-violence in the Bhagavadgita, *Prabuddha Bharata*, October 2009. Retrieved March 27, 2017: http://www.esamskriti.com/essay-chapters/War-and-Non-violence-in-the-Bhagavadgita-1.aspx

in war. After viewing armies arrayed on both sides ready to fight, he became confused about his duty. He begged for knowledge that will dispel his confusion; he was not looking for a sermon on warfare.

At some places in the Gītā, we find Śrī Kṛṣṇa directing Arjuna to fight the just war, as his bounden duty (2.18; 2.31–33; 2.37; 8.7). Many may hastily think that Śrī Kṛṣṇa is goading Arjuna to war, reading such verses as 2.3: "Do not yield to unmanliness"; or as in 2.18: "The bodies are perishable while the soul is eternal; therefore, Arjuna, get up and fight."[40] Śrī Kṛṣṇa presents several arguments in the second chapter in favor of fighting the war. Finally, Arjuna is given the choice to decide for himself to fight or not to fight (18.63):

> *iti te jñānam ākhyātaṃ guhyād guhyataraṃ mayā /*
> *vimṛśyaitad aśeṣeṇa yathecchasi tathā kuru* //18.63//
>
> Thus has the wisdom, more secret than all that is secret, been declared to you by Me; reflect over it all and act as you please.[41]

In this regard, we have the highest testimony of one of the great Western Sanskrit scholars, Franklin Edgerton, who, analyzing the historical setting and doctrinal content of the poem, states:

> One positive feature of the Bhagavad-Gītā's morality deserves special mention. The metaphysical doctrine that the one universal Soul is in all creatures furnishes an admirable basis for a lofty type of morality. *Since one's own Self or Soul is really identical with Self or Soul of all other creatures, therefore one who injures others injures himself.* "For beholding the same Lord residing in all beings, a man does not harm himself (his own self and others) by himself." Thus one of the most striking and emphatic of the ethical doctrines of the Gītā is substantially that of the Golden Rule. Man must treat all creatures alike, from the highest to the lowest, namely like himself. The perfected man "delights in the welfare of all beings." This principle is usually regarded at as perhaps the highest formulation of practical ethics that any religion has attained. It is interesting to see how naturally and simply it follows from one of the most fundamental tenets of the Gītā's philosophy.[42]

Edgerton notes the pragmatic value of this understanding in realizing nonviolence: "A genuine application of this moral principle would seem almost inevitably to include avoidance of any violent injury to living beings….And we must not forget, either, that 'non-injury' is clearly implied in the Gītā's teachings on the subject of unselfishness and doing good to others. That is, to carry out these teachings in any real sense would necessarily involve doing no harm."[43] Edgerton recognizes that the Gītā does indeed include "harmlessness" or "nonviolence" in several of its lists of virtues (10.5; 13.7; 16.2; 17.14) but laments that the Gītā never "singles out" nonviolence (*ahiṁsā*) for "special emphasis" in a form such as "Thou shalt not kill."

[40] BG 2.18.
[41] Alladi Mahadeva Sastry, trans., *The Bhagavad Gītā with the commentary of Sri Shankaracharya*, 497.
[42] Franklin Edgerton, *The Bhagavad Gītā* (New York, NY: Harper & Row, 1964), 185.
[43] Ibid., 185–186.

Besides, the Mahābhārata was not an ordinary war about some dispute over land or kingdom between two families of cousins, the Pāṇdavas and the Kauravas. It was a war of ideologies, which became inevitable after all the means of peaceful negotiations had failed. Reading the Mahābhārata, we discover that both Pāṇdavas and Kauravas had weaknesses. However, in addition to their *weaknesses*, Kauravas also had *wickedness*. At the relative level, no absolute injunctions such as "Though shalt not kill" can be prescribed. For example, when all other means of cure have failed, surgery may be prescribed to save the patient. In some cases, one may have to cut the finger to save the arm, so to speak. For example, in case of a tumor, a surgeon has to remove it to save the patient. No one would call the actions of a surgeon violent—not even when the patient dies, for the intention is to heal the patient. In the same manner, soldiers who serve in the military have to sometimes engage in war as a call of duty to the nation. Likewise, Arjuna is also doing his allotted duty, *svadharma*, in fighting a righteous battle that is forced upon him as a last resort. In all such cases, it is not a violation of the principle of nonviolence. All such acts will be regarded as nonviolent. On the contrary, if a surgeon or a warrior does not follow their allotted duty, it will be considered a highest act of violence!

Śrī Kṛṣṇa did not tell Arjuna to fight; Arjuna was confused about his duty. Śrī Kṛṣṇa just made him aware of his duty, *svadharma*. After the entire teachings of the Gītā had been delivered, Śrī Kṛṣṇa tells Arjuna: "do as you wish" (*yathecchasi tathā kuru* 18.63). Be that as it may, in the final reckoning, the Gītā is a *mokṣa śāstra*—a treatise on liberation, and its primary purpose is to garner Self-knowledge and not to preach a certain set of values or to rank order them. The Gītā presents nonviolence (*ahiṁsā*) among other values for their role in purifying the mind—that is, for the mind to become a fit instrument to receive the Self-knowledge. When Self-knowledge dawns and one realizes a profound sense of the Oneness of all existence, one views *oneself in all* and *all in oneself*. Such a person has realized the unity imminent in all diversity and cannot harm another, for in his view, *there are no others*. For such a person, the practice of nonviolence is a spontaneous outcome of realizing his kinship with all beings. This transformation brings about a great change of vision both in terms of how we see the world and how we relate to the world.[44]

In short, the Gītā does not advocate war. It teaches how to perform one's duty under all circumstances, including war. To reiterate, the Gītā should be read in the context of the entire Mahābhārata. Suffice to say that the decision to engage in the war was as a last resort when all other means to have peaceful outcome had been duly tried and failed.

[44] The change of vision is effected by gaining the Self-knowledge or the knowledge of the Absolute Reality. See BG 4.35:

yajjñātvā na punarmohamevaṁ yāsyasi pāṇḍava /
yena bhūtānyaśeṣeṇa drakṣyasyātmanyatho mayi //

Arjuna, gaining this [Self] knowledge, you will not be deluded again.
By this knowledge, you will see all beings in your Self and in Me.

Gandhi's Unique Interpretation of the Gītā

Gandhi interprets the war of the Bhagavad Gītā as a symbolic inner duel. The human heart is the battlefield on which are marshaled the divine and demonic impulses—the twin forces of knowledge and ignorance. The Gītā says that one should first fight the real enemy within, and then venture to wage the external war. The enemy is in league with the senses and their objects—within the mind. Hence, mind matters the most.

The key to understanding Gandhi's analysis of the message of the Gītā lies in his interpretation of the epic Mahābhārata as an allegory. Gandhi states again and again that for him the great epic is "*not* a historical work" in the accepted sense of the word[45] and that the "epic described the eternal duel that goes on between the forces of darkness and of light"[46] and that "physical warfare was brought in merely to make the description of the eternal duel more alluring."[47] Gandhi takes his firm stand on interpreting the Gītā as an allegory also, which is abundantly clear from the way he interprets the very opening verse of the Gītā (1.1): "The human body is the battlefield where the eternal duel between Right and Wrong goes on....The Kauravas represent the forces of Evil, the Pāndavas the forces of the Good";[48] and that, "All the names given in the First Chapter of the Gītā, are, in my opinion, not so much proper nouns as names of qualities. In describing the eternal warfare between the heavenly and the devilish natures, the poet has personified them as the characters in the Mahābhārata."[49] It is important to bear in mind that this is a very unique interpretation of the epic war and it determined how Gandhi understood certain key concepts of the Gītā such as *ahiṁsā* (nonviolence), *svadharma* (self-duty), and *aparigraha* (non-possession).

It is beyond the scope of this chapter to enter into a scholarly debate here regarding the correctness of Gandhi's exegetical position. What is important for us is to know that once Gandhi accepts the Mahābhārata as an allegory, he then consistently and boldly takes great pains to prove that the central principle of its philosophy is nonviolence (*ahiṁsā*)—the doctrine that is the be all and end all of Gandhi's philosophy. It is important to remember that, for Gandhi, *ahiṁsā* is a positive force of loving kindness to all beings, not merely "non-injury." He agrees that the Gītā is not written to preach *ahiṁsā* (nonviolence)

[45] M. K. Gandhi in John Strohmeier (Ed.), *The Bhagavad Gītā According to Gandhi* (Berkeley, CA: Berkeley Hills Books), 16.

[46] Ronald Duncan (Ed.), *Selected Writings of Mahatma Gandhi* (New York, NY: Beacon Press, 1951), 46.

[47] M. K. Gandhi in John Strohmeier (Ed.), *The Bhagavad Gītā According to Gandhi*, 16.

[48] Mahadev Desai, trans., *The Gospel of Selfless Action or The Gītā According to Gandhi* (Ahmedabad, India: Navajivan Publishing House, 1956), 135. As stated earlier, Gandhi views the setting of the Gītā in a battlefield as an allegory for the moral struggles of the human life. The Bhagavad Gītā's call for selfless action inspired many leaders of the Indian independence movement including Mahatma Gandhi.

[49] *The Diary of Mahadev Desai*, 172 [Cited in Anand T. Hingorani (Ed.), *Gandhi for 21st Century: The Teachings of the Gītā* (Mumbai, India: Bharitya Vidya Bhavan, 1998), 9.].

even when it accepts the basic tenet of *ahiṁsā*; but then, even if "it is difficult to reconcile certain verses with the teaching of Non-violence, it is far more difficult to set the whole of the Gītā in the framework of violence";[50] and that "the author of the Mahābhārata has not established the necessity of physical warfare; on the contrary, he has proved its futility. He has made the victors shed tears of sorrow and repentance, and has left them nothing but a legacy of miseries."[51] It is hard to disagree with this viewpoint as it seems to be intuitively right, especially in the wake of Gandhi's persistent following of nonviolence as the key message of the Gītā.

These are then the two unique ways in which Gandhi interprets the message of the Gītā: (1) the doctrine of *ahiṁsā* denotes a positive force of loving compassion; and (2) the context of the Gītā is an allegorical war that is constantly fought within the human heart, between the forces of the good and evil. Which of these two forces wins depends upon what we care to cultivate. The original epic of Mahābhārata was called *jaya*, victory. In fine, it represents victory over oneself.

Gandhi and the Central Teachings of the Gītā

Gandhi was a man of action, a *karma yogi*. For him, the key message of the Gītā was, unequivocally, selfless action. That is why he titled the introductory essay that accompanied his Gujarati translation of the Gītā *Anāsaktiyoga*—The Gospel of Selfless Action.[52] This is also the most commonly held meaning of the Gītā. When asked about the message of the Gītā, every Indian, even if he or she has a very cursory acquaintance with the text, would immediately venture to say: *niṣkāma karma*—selfless action. In simple words, do your duty diligently without worrying about the results. At first this may sound counter-intuitive: how can one be motivated to do one's duty without any expectation of reward or result? Should one, then, give up actions? Not at all, the Gītā says. This calls for a little explanation.

The Gītā tells us that every human being has to do some work. So, what is the way to free oneself from the bondage of action? Gandhi goes right to the heart of the matter without mincing words: "That matchless remedy [i.e. the way to self-realization] is *renunciation* of fruits of action: Do your allotted work but renounce its fruit. Be detached and work. Have no desire for reward and work."[53] This interpretation is consistent with the generally accepted meaning

[50] Cited in Hingorani, *Gandhi for 21st Century*, 10.

[51] Ibid., 19.

[52] This introduction was written in 1929 to accompany Gandhi's Gujarati translation of the Bhagavad Gītā. He later translated the essay into English and published it in 1931 in the pages of his periodical, *Young India*, under the title *Anāskatiyoga: The Gospel of Selfless Action* [Strohmeier (Ed.), *The Bhagavad Gītā According to Gandhi*, 14].

[53] Strohmeier (Ed.), *The Bhagavad Gītā According to Gandhi*, 18.

of *karma yoga*: renunciation of the sense of doership and, by extension, the desire for the fruits of actions. This renunciation of the fruits of action, Gandhi avers, is the "central Sun, round which devotion, knowledge, and the rest revolve like planets."[54] Gandhi was quintessentially a man of action, and this interpretation does full justice both to him and to the Gītā.

Selfless Action and Ahiṁsā Are Interdependent

Gandhi then links the renunciation of the fruits of action with his two favorite concepts, truth and nonviolence. When there is no desire for reward, Gandhi tells us, "there is no temptation for untruth or *himsa*....He who is ever brooding over results often loses nerve in the performance of his duty. He becomes impatient and then gives vent to anger and begins to do unworthy things.... He who broods over results is like a man given to objects of senses; he is ever distracted, he says good-bye to all scruples, everything is right in his estimation and he therefore resorts to means fair and foul to attain his end."[55] Further, in Gandhi's estimation, *ahiṁsā* is the key to the renunciation of the fruits of action. He tells us about his discovery: "But after forty years' unremitting endeavor fully to enforce the teaching of the Gītā in my own life, I have, in all humility, felt that perfect renunciation is impossible without perfect observance of *ahiṁsā* in every shape and form."[56] Selfless action is only possible when one renounces the desire for the fruits of action, and all selfish action is in effect violent action. Thus, in the Gandhian scheme of things, selfless action and nonviolence mutually reinforce each other.

Gandhi as the Gītā's Sage Steadfast in Wisdom

Gandhi believed that the last 18 verses of chapter 2 represented the quintessence of the entire art and science of ethics and spirituality. These verses were recited during his daily prayers and magnificently describe the marks of the sage steadfast in wisdom—*sthitaprajña*—"unparalleled in the spiritual literature of the world."[57]

All his life, Gandhi strived very hard to put the essence of these verses into practice. For those who came into close contact with him, Gandhi was a living embodiment of the central archetype of the Gītā—a person of steady wisdom, who has so conquered his carnal desires, subdued his senses, disciplined his mind, purified his heart, and attained the highest levels of virtuous living that there is no trace whatsoever of the ego left behind. Steadfast in the wisdom of the Self, such a person functions in life spontaneously and equanimously, free

[54] Ibid.
[55] Ibid., 21.
[56] Ibid., 23.
[57] Eknath Easwaran, cited in Louis Fischer (Ed.), *The Essential Gandhi* (New York, NY: Vintage Books, 2002), xvi.

from the tug of the warring pairs of opposites such as success and failure, good and bad, happiness and sorrow, gain and loss. This is the summit of the teachings of the Gītā.

Let us first look closer at these 18 magnificent verses (2.55–2.72) that Gandhi used for his daily prayers and meditation, in order to understand their true import for Self-knowledge and Self-realization. In these verses, the marks of a sage established in wisdom (*sthitaprajña*) are described:

> When one completely casts off all selfish desires of the mind, finding contentment by the Self in the Self alone; neither agitated by sorrow nor hankering after the sense pleasures; free from lust, fear, and anger; free from attachment; neither elated by good fortune nor depressed by bad; with senses subdued and mind ever absorbed in the Divine within—such a person is truly wise.[58]

In this part of the description of the traits of a person of steady wisdom, we notice three main things: freedom from self-centered desire (and the resultant anger, greed, and attachment: the triple gates of hell), an attitude of equanimity, and absorption in the wisdom of the Self or the Divine. Then, the Gītā goes on to explain the psychology of anger and the glory of a person who has gone beyond self-interest and egotism:

> Brooding on sense objects leads to attachment; from attachment comes desire; and from (unfulfilled) desire ensues anger. Anger clouds judgment and leads to loss of reason; and loss of reason brings utter ruin….One who has given up all desires and moves about free from longing, without self-interest and egotism, such a person attains peace. Attaining this state even at the time of death, one passes from death to immortality.[59]

According to Gandhi, these verses contain the essence of the Gītā: "If the rest of the scripture were lost, these verses alone will be enough to teach a complete way of life."[60] It is important to note that the description of a person of steady wisdom starts and ends with casting off all the selfish desires of the mind. *Yogavāsiṣṭha Mahāramāyaṇa* also states succinctly: "Wisdom proceeds from the curtailing of desires."[61]

There are at least four places where the characteristics of an ideal sage are presented in the Gītā from different perspectives: 2.55–72; 12.13–20; 14.21–27; and 18.49–56 (in addition, we also find reaffirmation of the same theme in selected verses of two other chapters: 13.7–11 and 16.1–3). For

[58] Ibid., xvi.

[59] Adapted from Eknath Easwaran, trans., *The Bhagavad Gītā* (New York, NY: Vintage Spiritual Classics, 2000), 67–69; Franklin Edgerton, trans., *The Bhagavad Gītā* (New York, NY: Harper & Row Publishers, 1964), 15–17; Dhiman, *Sahaja-Gītā: The Essential Gītā*, 36–39; See also, Strohmeier (Ed.), *The Bhagavad Gītā According to Gandhi*; Hingorani, *Gandhi for 21st Century*. Also see, Betai, *Gītā and Gandhi*.

[60] Easwaran, trans., *The Bhagavad Gītā*, 59.

[61] Vihari-Lala Mitra, trans., *Vālmīki's Yoga-vāsiṣṭha-mahārāmāyaṇa*. Online edition, Retrieved February 10, 2015: http://www.wisdomlib.org/hinduism/book/yoga-vasistha-volume-2-part-ii/d/doc118202.html

example, chapter 12 (verses 13–20) describes the marks of a devotee (*bhakta*); these have a striking similarity to the qualities of a person who has transcended the sway of three modes of material nature—*guṇātīta* (14.21–27), which in turn bear a great similarity to the characteristics of a person steadfast in wisdom (*sthitaprajña*) as described in chapter 2 (verses 55–72) as follows:

> That person is dear to me who is free from ill-will, friendly and compassionate; free from the sense of "I" and "mine"; equanimous in joy and sorrow, forgiving, ever-content, firm in faith with his mind ever united with Me; who has subdued his mind, senses, and body; and has surrendered heart and mind to Me....Not agitating the world, nor agitated by it, above the sway of delight, envy, desire, and fear; who regards equally friend and foe, praise and blame, pain and pleasure, free from selfish attachments; quiet, ever-content, in harmony everywhere, firm in faith—such a person is dear to Me.[62]

What is noteworthy in the above-quoted verses is that almost all of these qualities of an ideal sage more or less focus on emotional maturity—the ability to manage emotional disturbances and reactions calmly. Cultivating these qualities is important for everyone, in both personal and professional arenas. For example, being friendly and compassionate and free from malice (*adveṣṭāsarva bhūtānāṃmaitraḥkaruṇa*: 12.13), being free from attachment, fear, and anger (*vītarāgabhayakrodhaḥ*: 2.56, 4.10), and neither being a source of annoyance to our fellow beings nor feeling vexed with them (*yasmānnodvijatelokolokānno dvijatecayaḥ*: 12.15)—all these are signs of emotional stability which is the key to harmony in personal and professional relationships.

This is a tall order of personal qualities for any leader to cultivate, and requires years and years of dedication, commitment, and perseverance. These qualities represent the highest level of emotional maturity, self-awareness, self-discipline, equanimity, and detachment that may appear to be unattainable by any leader according to modern standards. In the estimation of Eknath Easwaran, who was present at one of the prayer meetings that Gandhi regularly held, Gandhi "fulfilled every condition that the Gītā lays down."[63] An exemplary leader like Gandhi acts as a "witness" of high moral leadership without whom the limits of higher human possibilities would neither be known nor sustained.

It is important to understand that the key to life's fulfillment, according to the Gītā, lies in Self-realization through Self-knowledge. Self-realization is the means as well as the end. The net result of cultivating these qualities is peace, fulfillment, and real happiness. This is the desideratum and the summum bonum of all human aspiration and quest.

[62] Easwaran, cited in Fischer, *The Essential Gandhi*, xvii [author's adaptation].

[63] Ibid., xvii.

Gandhi: On Humility as a Key Leadership Virtue

Service without humility is selfishness and egoism.[64]

Perhaps there is no arena where the dictum "pride hath a fall" is truer than leadership. Without humility, a talented leader can slip into arrogance and situational narcissism. Humility can serve as a powerful antidote to arrogance and guard leaders from such a "fall from grace." The principles of humility advocated by Gandhi may provide a useful framework for contemporary leaders both in their personal and professional life. Gandhi writes, "Who that has prided himself on his spiritual strength has not seen it humbled to the dust?"[65] For Gandhi, a life of service must be one of humility. He was of the view that a leader, who is to serve others, must be humble. Gandhi consistently embodied the perennial values of authenticity/personal integrity, transparency, harmlessness (*ahiṁsā*), truthfulness (*satyāgraha* or truth-force), humility, self-discipline, and selfless service in and through his life and death. His leadership effectiveness proceeded from his categorical adherence to these values and his openness to learn from his own mistakes.

His leadership style was "follower-centric" and "contextual."

Humble leaders do not think that simply being leaders makes them any better than their followers. Nor do they view themselves as being "above" their followers. They do not dismiss an excellent idea put forth by one of their employees simply because they didn't come up with it themselves. They put others first and respect all good ideas regardless of the hierarchical status of the messenger. They subordinate their personal interest to the good of the whole team.

Effective leaders credit their team for success and take full responsibility when things don't go as planned. In leadership literature, this is generally denoted by the metaphor of the mirror versus window mentality. Jim Collins discusses this in his classic book *Good to Great.* Collins found that leaders of great organizations looked out the "window" when things went well (to give credit to others), and looked in the "mirror" when things were not going so great (to take responsibility). The "window" humbles the enlightened leaders to recognize the contribution of others; the "mirror" serves only to magnify the already oversized egos of the arrogant leaders.

Humility is unquestionably the most essential requirement when it comes to learning: without being humble, one cannot learn at all. And learning is one of the most seminal competencies for leadership success.

[64] P. H. Burgess, *Sayings of Mahatma Gandhi* (Singapore: Graham Brash, 1984), 47.

[65] J. B. Kriplani, *Gandhi: His Life and Thought* (New Delhi, India: Publications Division Ministry of Information and Broadcasting Government of India, 1970), 8.

What Is Humility?

Humility does not necessarily mean to think of oneself as insignificant, timid, or worthless. In fact, humility signifies utter sincerity with oneself, requiring one to think of one's abilities as no greater, and no lesser, than they really are. Humble people know what they can and cannot do. They take note of both their gifts and their limitations in a realistic manner. True humility is definitely not about self-deprecation.

We are taught to think pride is a good thing whereas humility is the absence of pride. Pride has meaning only when comparing others to yourself. By comparing ourselves to others, we learn to play the ubiquitous game of "one-upmanship." A humble person does not base his or her self-worth on how he or she stacks up to others. Such a person is content to make their honest contribution without raising a flag. Thus, such a person feels no need to play the game of one-upmanship.

Most people often tend to confuse humility with false modesty. We all have been guilty of this at one time or another. We have a tendency to devalue what we've done under the pretense of humility. In fact, refusing to accept genuine appreciation is often a cover for seeking more praise from others. That is perhaps why true humility is very hard to come by.

No Humility: Only Different Shades of Pride!

Many wiser souls, somewhat jaded with cynicism, have pointed out that there is no humility; only, different shades of pride. We recall an interesting remark by a colleague: "Enough of me talking about myself. Tell me what you think of me!" Real humility is a very hard virtue to cultivate. More often than not, humility may be a cover for subtle pride. In the classic *Autobiography of Benjamin Franklin*, the author tells us how he embarked upon a rather ambitious regimen of cultivating various life virtues such as temperance, silence, order, frugality, sincerity, justice, and humility. He has noted that, although a seemingly simple quality, humility is the most difficult virtue to cultivate because, by the time one gets to master it, one becomes proud of it! A story is told about Frank Lloyd Wright, the famous architect, who was once testifying in court for his friend. While taking the oath, he is reported to have said, "My name is Frank Lloyd Wright, the greatest architect on the planet!" Later when his friend questioned him about his exaggerated sense of self-importance, Frank Lloyd Wright maintained, "I was under oath to tell the truth!"

The human ego is always good at finding new avenues of manifesting itself, especially under the covert cover of humility. Such are the ways of the master magician—"our skin-encapsulated ego"—the socially induced hallucination of a separate self, to use a phrase coined by Aldous Huxley.

The teachings about compassion, frugality, and humility find their closest parallel in the naturalistic philosophy of Taoism. Lao Tzu calls them "three treasures." They first occur in chapter 67 of the Chinese classic *Tao Te Ching*, which Lin

Yutang says contains "Laotse's most beautiful teachings."[66] In Lao Tzu's view, nature arms with humility those it would not see destroyed: An axe first falls on the tallest tree. There is a poem by Chuang Tzu transliterated by Thomas Merton that beautifully underscores the value of the virtue of humility as follows:

> If a man is crossing a river and an empty boat collides with his own skiff,
> even though he be a bad-tempered man he will not become very angry.
> But if he sees a man in the boat, he will shout at him to steer clear.
>
> If the shout is not heard, he will shout again, and yet again, and begin cursing.
> And all because there is somebody in the boat.
>
> Yet if the boat were empty, he would not be shouting, and not angry.
> If you can empty your own boat crossing the river of the world,
> no one will oppose you, no one will seek to harm you....
>
> ...Such is the perfect man:
> His boat is empty.[67]

Gandhi never claimed himself to be special in any way. He credited his success to his hard work and his constant awareness of his own limitations. Johann Sebastian Bach, the great German composer, is reported to have said, "I was obliged to be industrious. Whoever is equally industrious will succeed...equally well."[68] In a similar vein, Gandhi wrote, "I claim to be no more than an average man with less than average abilities. I have not the shadow of a doubt that any man or woman can achieve what I have, if he or she would make the same effort and cultivate the same hope and faith."[69] This humility and openness gave Gandhi the understanding to be on the side of the truth rather than insisting for the truth to be on his side.

Until the last days of his life, Gandhi remained aware of his limitations. He had enough humility to acknowledge his errors and to retrace his steps. He kept working on the ultimate task of shedding his ego. He was fully aware that treading the path of truth means reducing oneself to zero, to a non-entity. Only then can one experience the limitless and be liberated. In his own words, "I know that I have still before me a difficult path to traverse. I must reduce myself to zero. So long as man does not of his own free will put himself last among his fellow-creatures, there is no salvation for him. *Ahiṁsā*, nonviolence, is the farthest limit of humility."[70] For Gandhi, humility was the sine qua non to nonviolence.

[66] Lin Yutang, *The Wisdom of Lao Tzu* (New York, NY: Random House, Modern Library, 1948/1976), 292.

[67] Thomas Merton, *The Way of Chuang Tzu* (New York, NY: Penguin New Directions Books, 1965), 114–115.

[68] "The Greatest Music Leaders." Retrieved July 20, 2018: http://www.greatmusicleaders.org/home/johann-sebastian-bach

[69] R. K. Prabhu & U. R. Rao (Ed.), *The Mind of Mahatma Gandhi* (Ahmedabad, India: Navajivan Publishing House, 1996), 13–14.

[70] M. K. Gandhi, *An Autobiography: The Story of My Experiments with Truth* (New York, NY: Dover Publications, Inc., 1983), 454.

If influence is any measure of a leader's success, the power of humility and gentleness is amply illustrated through the life of this "little brown man in a loincloth"[71] who brought the mightiest empire on earth to its knees—even though he did not hold any official title, office, or position.

Gandhi was no saint. He had his share of failings and favorites. Yet, for his abiding passion constantly to "remake" himself until his last breath, his dogged determination to walk the straight and narrow path of truth and nonviolence, his exceptional ability to reduce his personal self to zero, his disarming humility, and his excruciating self-honesty, he will continue to shine as a beacon for humanity as long as might oppresses right. Whenever a soul peacefully raises her voice against any kind of oppression, Gandhi's legacy will continue.

Aldous Huxley once said that the central technique for humans to learn is "the art of obtaining freedom from the fundamental human disability of egoism."[72] Gandhi achieved that freedom. Only those who dare achieve this freedom can truly serve.

Humility: The Touchstone of Great Leadership

Humility is the cause and consequence of true learning, for nothing can go in a full vessel. Humility is indeed the touchstone of great leadership. A tree with fruits bends. Humility is also a precondition for serving others for, without it, even service could be but an inflation of ego. Lack of humility leads to cluelessness and cluelessness quickly leads to a leader's derailment and demise. Humble leaders are great contributors. True humility is more like self-forgetfulness than false modesty—it means *emptying* ourselves of false pride and pretense.

It has been said that the function of leadership is to produce more leaders, not more followers. What is the alchemy of producing more leaders? Most of the time, it is about leading from behind. In his autobiography entitled *Long Walk to Freedom*, Nelson Mandela, equated a great leader to a shepherd: "A leader…is like a shepherd. He stays behind the flock, letting the most nimble go out ahead, whereupon the others follow, not realizing that all along they are being directed from behind."[73] Elsewhere, Mandela states that "It is better to lead from behind and to put others in front, especially when you celebrate victory when nice things occur. You take the front line when there is danger. Then people will appreciate your leadership."[74] Within the short compass of these two quotes, Mandela encapsulates the leadership lessons he learnt having spent 10,000 days in jail over a period of 50 years of struggle (1944–1994) for ending bondage. Leading from behind is a leadership style whose time has come. It is a style that puts followers at the forefront of the leadership line. However, it requires supreme humility.

[71] J. B. Severance, *Gandhi: Great Soul* (New York, NY: Clarion Books, 1997), 100.

[72] J. H. Bridgeman (Ed.), *Aldous Huxley: Huxley and God, Essays* (New York, NY: HarperSanFrancisco, 1992), 4.

[73] Nelson Mandela, *Long Walk to Freedom: The Autobiography of Nelson Mandela* (New York, NY: Little, Brown and Company, 1995), 22.

[74] Ryan Lizza, Leading from Behind, *New Yorker*, April 26, 2011. Retrieved July 21, 2018: http://www.newyorker.com/news/news-desk/leading-from-behind

The following Sufi story highlights the dangers of self-conceit and the need to stay humble in all pursuits. The Sufi—the one who is *not*—narrates the story as follows:

> *...and my third Master was a small child. I entered into a town once and a small child was bringing a candle, a lit candle, hiding it in his hands. He was going to the mosque to put the candle there. In the lighter vein, I asked the boy, "Have you lit the candle yourself?" He said, "Yes, sir." And I asked, jokingly, "Since you saw the light coming when you lit the candle, can you tell me from where the light came?"*
>
> *The boy became serious first and then laughed and blew out the candle, and said, "Now you have seen the light going, where has it gone? You tell me!"*
>
> *My ego was crushed, and my whole knowledge was shattered. And that moment I felt my own foolhardiness. Since then I dropped all pretense to knowledgeability.*[75]

Does Humility Mean Low Self-Regard?

To be humble does not mean to have a *low* opinion of oneself, it is to have an *accurate* opinion of oneself, says the psychologist Robert Emmons. Emmons describes humility as the "realistic appraisal of one's strengths and weaknesses—neither overestimating them nor underestimating them."[76] True humility is a matter of the right perspective.

Is humility the most important quality to cultivate in life and leadership? Both history and current research testify that the best leaders are humble. In their recent *Harvard Business Review* study, Prime and Slib clarify that humble leaders should not be mistaken for weak ones, for it takes tremendous courage to practice humility. These authors cite Google's SVP of People Operations, Lazlo Bock, who says *humility is one of the traits he is looking for in new hires.* Based on their current research and their ongoing study of leadership development practices at Rockwell Automation, they share the following practices to garner a humble, inclusive leadership style:

Engage in dialog, not debates. Engaging in dialog is good way to practice humility. When people debate to sway others to win them over to their viewpoint, they miss out on the opportunity to learn about *other* points of view. When leaders are humble enough to suspend their own agendas and beliefs, they not only enhance their own learning, but they validate their followers' unique perspectives.

Embrace uncertainty. When leaders humbly admit that they don't have all the answers, they create a space for others to step forward and offer solutions. They

[75] A Traditional Sufi Tale. Author unknown.

[76] R. A. Emmons, *The Psychology of Ultimate Concerns: Motivation and Spirituality in Personality* (New York, NY: The Guilford Press, 2009), 171.

also engender a sense of interdependence. Followers understand that the best bet is to rely on each other to work through complex, ill-defined problems.

Role model being a "follower." Inclusive leaders empower *others* to lead. By reversing roles, leaders not only facilitate employees' development, but they model the act of taking a different perspective, something that is so critical to working effectively in diverse teams. Inclusive leaders are humble enough to admit that they do not have all the answers and that the present-day problems are too complex for any one person to tackle single-handedly. Doing so, they garner the wisdom of the followers and allow them to come up with shared solutions.[77]

Lao Tzu, the great Chinese sage, stated it so well, "A leader is best when people barely know he exists, when his work is done, his aim fulfilled, they will say: we did it ourselves." He recognized the importance of humility as the key ingredient of leadership, for only the humble can truly serve a cause higher than themselves.

Leading Effectively: Seven Exemplary Gandhian Values

The need for leaders who are authentic, principled, and spiritually grounded is greater now than ever. Leadership has always been more challenging during difficult times. In a world beset with rising international terrorism, economic uncertainties, flagrant violation of human values, and rampant character crises among leaders, everybody is searching for the Holy Grail, the silver bullet that will save the world. The unique leadership challenges facing organizations throughout the world today call for an even greater renewed focus on what constitutes "values-based leadership."

The following section will attest that Gandhi embodied the exemplary values-based leadership qualities to the highest degree.

Gandhi and the Value of Values in Leadership

Values represent the heart of leadership and guide behavior and performance. As Samuel Blumenfeld has clearly pointed out, "You have to be dead to be value-neutral." Values are like a lighthouse; they do not change. It is the ship of practices that has to find its way guided by the lighthouse of values. Can an evil leader be an effective leader? The answer to this question depends on whether we consider ethics to be a necessary condition for leadership. It also begs the fundamental question, "What good is leadership if it is not ethical?"

Since leadership is an expression of who we are, in discovering, living, and sharing our deepest values lies the fulfillment of our life and leadership.

In his seminal essay titled "Notes toward a Definition of Values-Based Leadership," James O'Toole calls Gandhi the "*most manifestly values-based of*

[77] Jeanine Prime & Elizabeth Salib, The best leaders are humble leaders. *Harvard Business Review*, May 2014. Retrieved July 22, 2018: https://hbr.org/2014/05/the-best-leaders-are-humble-leaders

all leaders."[78] Besides Gandhi, the author's shortlist of such leaders includes Abraham Lincoln, Martin Luther King, Jr., Nelson Mandela, Vaclav Havel, Mother Teresa, Eleanor Roosevelt, and Jean Monet.

Gandhi consistently embodied the perennial values of authenticity/personal integrity, transparency, harmlessness (*ahiṁsā*), truthfulness (*satyāgraha* or truth-force), humility, self-discipline, and selfless service in and through his life and death. He believed that the universe is not amoral, and that it has a structural bias toward good. His leadership effectiveness proceeded from his categorical adherence to these values and his openness to learn from his own mistakes. Gandhi's innovation lies in extending them from the personal to the public arena. His was essentially a values-based, principle-centered approach to leadership. Despite his faults, or perhaps because of them, we find there is much to learn about Gandhi's development as a leader—who *lived* and *died* for the values he held most dear.

Authenticity and Transparency

Personal authenticity has been explored throughout history, from Greek philosophers ("Know Thyself"—Socrates) to Shakespeare ("To thine own self be true"—Polonius, *Hamlet*). Authenticity as defined in this context seems to be closely linked with self-awareness, sincerity, truth, and transparency. An authentic leader operates from a strong personal and moral stance embodying the unity and purity of thoughts, words, and deeds.

Gandhi underscores this alignment by noting: "I say as I think and I do as I say." He viewed his life and work as an undivided whole and approached his lifework in an utterly selfless manner, renouncing the usual trappings of title, authority, and position. If true living or leadership is an expression of who we are, authenticity becomes the most essential value in life and leadership. According to Warren Bennis, "The 'Dean' of Leadership Gurus," the real task of becoming a leader boils down to becoming an authentic individual first: "At bottom, becoming a leader is synonymous with becoming yourself. It's precisely that simple, and it's also that difficult."[79]

Authenticity does not mean being perfect. It is accepting oneself (and others) as one truly is, warts and all. It is about being aware of one's flaws and learning from them. In fine, it is about leading from within. Gandhi led from within—from the deep moral and spiritual core of his being. His life and leadership were inseparably one. His life was an open book for all to see. His autobiography is an exemplary model of candidness and transparency. Such a level of "transparency" has not been observed in the life of any other public leader before or after.

[78] James O'Toole, Notes toward a definition of values-based leadership. *The Journal of Values-Based Leadership*, 2008, 1 (1), 4, Article 10.

[79] Warren Bennis, *On Becoming a Leader* (New York, NY: Basic Books, 2009, Fourth edition), xxxvii.

Harmlessness or Nonviolence

As is evident from the foregoing, Gandhi believed that the only test of truth is action based on the refusal to do harm—*ahiṁsā*. The commonly used English equivalent "nonviolence" may be misleading as it seems to give the impression that *ahiṁsā* is just a negative virtue. *Ahiṁsā* is not mere abstention from injury in thought, word, and deed; it also implies the positive virtues of compassion and benevolence.

For Gandhi, *ahiṁsā* was a positive force of love. In addition, nonviolence is not a cover for cowardice. Gandhi has said, "Where there is only a choice between cowardice and violence, I would advise violence." Gandhi's distinctive contribution in this area lies in his unique interpretation of "passive" forms of violence such as hatred and anger. The passive violence that we commit consciously and unconsciously every day causes the victims of passive violence to get angry, and their anger eventually leads to physical violence.

We have been told by experts that anger instigates almost 80% of the violence that we experience either in our personal lives or as a society or nation. Anger leads to conflict and conflict to violence. Learning how to use the powerful energy of anger intelligently and effectively is the foundation of Gandhi's philosophy of nonviolence. When used properly, rightly channeled anger can go a long way in reducing the passive violence at the workplace. Nonviolence is both the end and the means. For Gandhi, nonviolence was the means and truth was the end.

Truth

Truth and nonviolence are interrelated, for there is no spirituality without morality. Taken together, truth and nonviolence constitute the alpha and omega of Gandhi the man, as well as Gandhi the leader; every form of discipline or vow that Gandhi observed in his life was just a variation on these themes. Based on all the available evidence, Gandhi remained true to both of these vows in both letter and spirit.

For Gandhi, there was the "relative truth" of truthfulness in human interactions, and the "absolute truth" of the Ultimate Reality. This ultimate truth is God (as God is also Truth) with ethics as expressed in the moral law as its basis. Gandhi was humble enough to acknowledge that the truth we experience at the level of human interactions is "relative, many-sided, plural, and is the whole truth for a given time. Pure and absolute truth should be our ideal." This humility gave Gandhi the understanding to be on the side of the truth rather than insisting for the truth to be on his side. Such humility and courage of conviction are object lessons for contemporary leaders. Even while committing to truth and nonviolence as the absolute ideals, leaders should remain open to the fact of the many-sidedness of the relative truth encountered at the level of human interactions.

Humility

Many spiritual traditions speak about the need to "be poor in spirit and pure in heart." Of all the leadership qualities, humility is perhaps the most difficult to develop. Ben Franklin tells us in his legendary *Autobiography of Benjamin Franklin* that the reason humility as a virtue is hard to cultivate is because by the time one gets to be good at it, one becomes proud of it!

Gandhi strongly believed that the "truth is not to be found by anybody who has not got an abundant sense of humility. If you would swim on the bosom of the ocean you must reduce yourself to a zero." In fact, humility is both the means and the goal. In the field of leadership, the importance of humility can hardly be overemphasized. Only humble leaders can serve a cause higher than themselves. Howard Schultz, the founder and chairman of the Starbucks chain of coffee shops, says that the great leadership expert, Warren Bennis, once told him that to become a great leader you have to develop "your ability to leave your own ego at the door, and to recognize the skills and traits that you need in order to build a world-class organization."[80]

As someone has rightly said, "True humility is not thinking less of yourself; it is thinking of yourself less."[81]

Self-Discipline

Gandhi once said, "Our greatness lies not so much in being able to remake the world as being able to remake ourselves." Every time Gandhi confronted human frailties in the outer world, he turned his moral searchlight within (a phrase Gandhi loved using) to find answers in the deep recesses of his soul. This spiritual and moral anchorage was the key to Gandhi's political potency and innovation and became his most important discovery: A person's capacity for self-discipline enhances his capacity to influence the environment around him. And no power on earth can make a person do a thing against his will. He who disciplines himself gains the strength to shape the environment. Peter Senge concurs and regards self-mastery to be the key aspect of growing as a leader.

Through prayer, contemplation, self-abnegation, and self-purification, he cultivated his being to such an extent that it emanated a gentle soul-force that endeared him even to his severest critics and detractors. Even Gandhi's critics agree that his strength lay in his towering spirit that resided in his frail frame. With his indomitable spirit, Gandhi was able to win his ideological wars in the long run, even when he seemed to be losing his battles in the short run.

[80] Guru: Warren Bennis. *The Economist*, July 25, 2008, Online extra. Retrieved: July 22, 2018: http://www.economist.com/node/11773801

[81] This quote is often misattributed to C.S. Lewis. According to the C.S. Lewis Foundation, this quote belongs to the category of misattributed quotes and is NOT by C.S. Lewis. See: http://www.cslewis.org/aboutus/faq/quotes-misattributed/

Self-Less Service

A leader's true inspiration comes from doing selfless work. Selfless work brings equanimity of mind which in turn contributes to leadership effectiveness. Exemplary leaders are not motivated by personal desires or interests. They recognize that selfless service is the highest principle of life and leadership. They become instruments of the Whole and selflessly work for the wellbeing of all beings. This is where their true fulfillment lies. Gandhi was right: the best way to find oneself is to lose oneself in the service of others.

Gandhi believed that only by not regarding anything as their own can leaders truly devote themselves, body and soul, to the selfless service of others. For, unless the mind is purged of personal desire and attachment, even service is but an inflation of the ego. These are all valuable lessons for contemporary leaders to emulate.

The path to leading others starts with self-awareness through self-discipline and ends with self-transcendence through selfless service. It is paved with authenticity, humility, and compassion.

Concluding Thoughts

> The best way to find yourself is to lose yourself in the service of others. (Gandhi)

This quote sums up Gandhi's position as a servant leader. The greatest road to fulfillment begins and ends with selfless service. This is the essence of ***karma yoga***. This is the key lesson that Gandhi learned from his life-time study of the Gītā.

The Gītā was a spiritual reference book for Gandhi. He studied it all his life; he lived, worked and died according to the spirit of the Gītā. Eknath Easwaran writes about the significance of the Gītā in Gandhi's life:

> He knew it by heart, knew it in his heart, studied it over and over every day, used it in prayer until it became a living presence.…Those years in South Africa were a studio in which Gandhi worked every day like an artist, studying his model and chipping away at the block of stone that hid the vision he was striving to set free, painstakingly removing everything that was not Gītā.[82]

The most distinctive spiritual tenet Gandhi learned from the Gītā was perhaps the truth of One Reality that pervades all and everything in the universe. This nondual Reality is called *Brahman* (the Absolute) and is the very Self (*Ātman*) of everyone and everything. He who perceives the one Divine Principle dwelling in all beings as their very Self cannot harm another, for the Self cannot harm itself. This provided the ontological support for Gandhi's categorical adherence to non-violence and selfless service. This understanding in turn paved the way for him to strive for spiritual and moral perfection, the twin preconditions to Self-realization, signifying the ***summum bonum*** for Gandhi.

[82] Eknath Easwaran, cited in Louis Fischer (Ed.), *The Essential Gandhi* (New York, NY: Vintage Books, 2002), xvi.

Only when we perceive the self as the Self of all, through the discipline of selfless action—actions done with devotion and without desire—we come to the realization of Truth or God, for "to realize God is to see Him in all that lives, and to recognize our oneness with all creation."[83] This, then, is the essence of the path of action (*karma yoga*), the path of devotion (*bhakti yoga*), and the path of knowledge (*jñāna yoga*). In enshrining the teachings of the Gītā in his life, Gandhi personified the essence of these threefold means to Self-realization.

In sum, the Gītā teaches us to become an instrument of the Divine in all that we do, to let all our actions be for the wellbeing of all (*sarvabhūtahiteratāḥ*: 5.25); to be role models for bringing together the communities of the world and maintaining the world order, and above all, to accept the results of our actions with engaging equanimity, as the Grace of the Lord. Then, our actions will never taint us, and we will attain the highest pure knowledge by which the One Imperishable Being is seen in all forms of existence, undivided in the divided: *avibhaktaṃvibhakteṣu*. This knowledge of the essential oneness of all existence (*sarvabhūteṣuyenaikaṃbhāvam*) the Gītā regards as the purest (*sāttvik*) knowledge: *tajjñānaṃviddhisāttvikam* (18.20). Living with this understanding, by the Divine Grace, we will attain the communion of the individual self with the Supreme Self.

Gandhi had his human failings and favorites. Yet for his abiding passion to constantly "remake" himself until his last breath, his dogged determination to walk the straight and narrow path of truth and nonviolence, his exceptional ability to reduce his personal self to zero, his disarming humility, and his excruciating self-honesty, he will continue to shine as a beacon for humanity as long as might oppresses right.

By dedicating his life unconditionally to the service of humanity, Gandhi sought the true value of Self-realization through the teachings of the Bhagavad Gītā. By reflecting deeply on the import of the Gītā's teachings, it became clear to Gandhi that his path was the path of Self-realization through service to humanity, and he made efforts and experiments at every moment of his life to come nearer to this goal. Gandhi's goal was to become *sthitaprajña* (2.55–72) and *triguṇātītaḥ* (14.19, 14.22–27). He succeeded.

If we want to bring about any change in the world, we have to begin with ourselves: we have to *be* the change that we wish to *see* in the world. This was Gandhi's most important discovery and his greatest gift to humankind.

When we delve deep into the core of our being, we come upon the core of all—the Self. Then we come to realize that not only this world, but all life, is one. This is the true wisdom of the Self, the art and science of Self-realization. The Gītā is a clarion call to return to and act from the wisdom of the Self.

This is the timeless message of this manual for life, leadership, and liberation.

[83] M. K. Gandhi, *Selected Works*, vol. VI (Ahmedabad, India: Navajivan Publishing House, 1968), 153; 176.

CHAPTER 11

Epilogue: Timeless Teachings of the Gītā—Maxims for Life and Leadership

Introduction

The Bhagavad-Gītā is a true scripture of the human race, a living creation rather than a book, with a new message for every age and a new meaning for every civilization. (Sri Aurobindo, *The Message of the Bhagavad Gītā*)

The Gītā is a non-sectarian spiritual text with a universal message. Its subject matter is the truth regarding our essential nature which can be verified by everyone right here and now, in this very lifetime. The Gītā teaches us how to be "yoked" to the Divine within through the path or discipline of action (*karma yoga*), devotion (*bhakti yoga*), meditation (*dhyāna yoga*), and knowledge (*jñāna yoga*). It is a gem of a scripture in which we can find the complete essence of the paths of selfless action, knowledge, and devotion. The Gītā says that all our existential problems ultimately stem from self-ignorance—not knowing who we truly are. Just as knowledge of physics cannot destroy the ignorance of biology, even so self-ignorance cannot be dispelled by any other means except Self-knowledge.

The path to leading others starts with self-awareness through self-discipline and ends with self-transcendence through selfless service. The Gītā calls it enlightened leadership. Enlightened leadership is essentially servant leadership. It represents a shift from followers serving leaders to leaders serving followers. Enlightened leaders are not motivated by personal desires or interests. They become instruments of the whole and selflessly serve for the wellbeing of all beings (*sarvabhūta hite*, BG 5.25; 12.4). Only those who have relinquished personal ambition can truly serve. According to the Gītā, the path to enlightened leadership is paved with authenticity, humility, service, and compassion.

The Gītā introduces us to the joy of giving joy to others. It teaches that unless the mind is purged of personal desire and attachment, even service is but

S. Dhiman, *Bhagavad Gītā and Leadership*,
Palgrave Studies in Workplace Spirituality and Fulfillment,
https://doi.org/10.1007/978-3-319-67573-2_11

an inflation of the ego. The Bhagavad Gītā teaches us that true peace can only come by serving the common good and surrendering to the Divine *within* us. The Gītā teaches that "be good, do good" is all that one needs to "be" and "do" to foster happiness in oneself and others. This body is given to do good (परोपकार अर्थम् इदं शरीरम्). We should act with the welfare of the entire universe in view, according to the Gītā 3.20.

The Gītā assures us that on the path of goodness, one never loses (6.40) न हि कल्याणकृत् कश्चित् दुर्गतिं तात गच्छति: One, who follows the path of goodness, there is no misery or misadventure (*durgati*) for such a person.

Two Fascinating Facts About the Gītā

1. The very first letter of the very first word of the Gītā (BG 1.1) is "dh" (*dharmakṣeytre*) and the very last letter of the last word of the Gītā (BG 18.78) is "ma" (*mama*). When we combine them, we get "dh-ma" which signifies "dharma." "Dharma" literally means that which "upholds, supports or maintains the regulatory order of the universe." By extension, it also means righteousness: those behaviors that support and maintain (and are conducive to) the order of the universe. The concept of duty originates from this understanding. Dharma in essence means the innermost law of our being, our natural, innate duty.

   Therefore, the Gītā takes place within the decorum, "*maryāda*," of Dharma. From this, we should learn that the message of the Gītā is about the eternal laws of the universe and our rightful duty toward maintaining those laws. That is why the teachings of self-less service (*niṣkām karma yoga*), as presented from verse 39 of chapter 2 (BG 2.39) through verse 43 of chapter 3 (BG 3.43), are so unique that they are not found in this form (and in such an elaboration) anywhere else in any other scriptures of even India or the world. This is a matter of great significance!
2. The message of the Gītā starts with verse 11 of chapter 2 (BG 2.11) and concludes with verse 66 of chapter 18 (BG 18.66). If we look at the first word of BG 2.11 and the last word of BG 18.66, they tell an interesting tale: The first word of BG 2.11 is *aśocyān*, which means "not worth worrying about..." The last word of BG 18.66 is (*mā*) *śucaḥ*, which means do not worry.

Śrī Kṛṣṇa starts the sublime teachings of the Gītā telling Arjuna that he was worrying about people/things/situations "not worth worrying about" (BG 2.11) and concludes his message by stating, "do not worry" (BG 18.66). Why "not worth worrying about?" It is because they are transient, perishable, subject to change, impermanent, and, hence, non-real, whereas the Self, the indwelling essence, is eternal. When we identify ourselves with what is fleeting—and changing constantly—we live a life of constant worry.

Throughout the Gītā, the Lord helps us (through Arjuna) to understand what is Real: eternal, changeless, imperishable essence underlying the fleeting phenomenon. When we really understand what is Real, we give up our fascination/association with what is unreal (*sarvadharmān parityajya* 18.66) and take refuge in the Real, the Lord dwelling in us all (*mām ekaṃ śaraṇaṃ vraja*). This is the alpha and omega of the Bhagavad Gītā: *Relinquishing the unreal, and abiding in the Real.*

Uniqueness of the Bhagavad Gītā

The Bhagavad Gītā is an endearing dialog (*saṁvād*) between two friends—the warrior prince, Arjuna, and the Lord in human form, Śrī Kṛṣṇa. So, if we want to understand the true import of the Gītā, we have to befriend Śrī Kṛṣṇa. There is no room for contention, *vivāda,* among friends.

It is probably the only scripture in human history that lays exclusive importance on intellect (*buddhi*) and in which the reader is not asked to accept anything on faith. There is a dictum in Indian spirituality that underscores this point splendidly: "Follow the guidance of one who speaks with clarity without asking you to believe in anything." The Gītā strictly adheres to this refrain. Every question is examined insightfully, and diverse perspectives are presented for reflection. It offers food for thought *without* interfering with the intellectual appetite of the reader. At every step, the freedom of choice of the listeners/readers is respected. After the entire teachings of the Gītā have been imparted, Śrī Kṛṣṇa tells Arjuna at the very end, "now that the most profound wisdom has been imparted; deeply ponder over it and do as you wish (18.63)." Do as you wish; not as I say. Teachers open the door; we have to enter by ourselves.

Throughout the entire Gītā, Arjuna asks good questions (*paripraśnena*) and Śrī Kṛṣṇa answers them lovingly and objectively, without growing upset or deprecating. The student has humility and respect for the teacher and the teacher has caring concern for the wellbeing of the student. This makes it a great treatise on the art and science of effective communication.

The Gītā uses a very special teaching methodology. It presents the highest teachings—the "big picture"—first. Arjuna's was confused about his duty and wanted to know "the right thing to do" (*śreyas*). Śrī Kṛṣṇa starts the teaching with the highest good (*param-śreyas*)—the nature of the Self. Arjuna was mostly worried about the outer kingdom; Śrī Kṛṣṇa gently guides him to the inner Kingdom—the inner treasure of the fullness of our being (*puraṇattvam*).

So, if we truly want to understand the Gītā, we have to take our stand in the highest principle of existence—the Supreme Self. We have to stand at the same height from which the Gītā was discoursed. We have to examine our belief system in the light of the truths presented in it rather than scrutinizing its truths in the light of our preexisting notions. We have to be on the side of the truth, rather than insisting that the truth be on our side. This is the most important key to understanding any profound work of philosophy, including the Gītā.

Timeless Teachings of the Bhagavad Gītā

Abraham Maslow once said, "If you plan on being anything less than you are capable of, you will be unhappy all the days of your life." Vedānta and the Gītā make a small, friendly amendment: "If you plan on being anything less than what you are, you will be unhappy all the days of your life." The Bhagavad Gītā is the ultimate self-help book, which teaches eternal Truths about our true nature (Gītā 3.3, 4.1–3). It presents us with the most complete template for liberation from all limitations and conditioned existence!

The sole purpose (and the goal supreme) of the Gītā is Self-realization or God-realization. The Gītā 3.3 recognizes two broad categories/means/courses of spiritual discipline, *sādhanā*, leading up to the Goal Supreme: (1) *yoga-niṣṭhā* (path of Self-less actions) and (2) *sāṅkhyā niṣṭhā* (path of Self-knowledge).

Since the ultimate goal of the Gītā is God-realization, bhakti yoga (path of devotion) becomes a necessary concomitant of both of these disciplines. Dhyāna yoga (path of meditation), likewise, is postulated as an aid in realizing the goal of God-realization. If "Vāsudevaḥ" is "*sarvam iti*" [BG 7.19]—Vāsudeva Śrī Kṛṣṇa is all there is—then all the actions, all the knowledge, all the devotion, and all the meditation should converge at this vital point. All the *yogas* of the Gītā are geared toward helping the seeker see the Divine in all and all in the Divine.

This is the master key to understanding the mysteries of the Gītā.

It is also helpful to bear in mind that in the Gītā, *karma* (action) does not always equate with the path of action (*karma yoga*), and *jñāna* (knowledge) does not always signify the path of knowledge (*jñāna yoga*). Secondly, as pointed out earlier in this book, the word yoga is used in several shades of meanings in the Gītā. However, at two places, Śrī Kṛṣṇa presents the word yoga in its truest sense: BG 2.48 and BG 6.23. In BG 2.48, Śrī Kṛṣṇa states that "equipoise of mind" is called yoga: *samatvaṃ yoga ucyate*. According to Swami Ramsukhdasji, *samatā* (equanimity) is the "fulcrum" around which the entire practice, *sādhanā*, of the Gītā revolves. Wherever the Lord has mentioned the highest peaks of the paths of action, knowledge, and devotion, He has very carefully interspersed "*samatā*" with it. Therefore, this is the litmus-test of perfection (*siddhi*) in all the paths to God-realization. If equanimity is not there, the goal is still far away—regardless of which yoga one may be practicing![1] And this equanimity of mind is the most essential quality for any leader in their task of leading effectively.

The second important sense the word "yoga" is used in the Gītā is in verse BG 6.23: *taṃ vidyād duḥkhasaṃyogaviyogaṃ yogasaṃjñitam*—freedom from contact with sorrow (of this body and material world) should be known as yoga. The complete freedom from sorrow is only possible when one attains to the stage of God-realization or Self-realization.

Yogas of the Bhagavad Gītā have nothing to do with *twisting* the body; it is all about *straightening* the mind. The message of the Gītā fosters the holistic development of human personality on all its dimensions (physical-psychological, emotional, intellectual, and spiritual) by providing guidance about the three

[1] This section about the true import of various *yogas* in the Gītā and the importance of *samatā* draws upon the excellent commentary in Hindi on the Bhagavad Gītā by Pujya Swami Ramsukhdasji Maharaj, titled *Sādhaka Sañjīvanī*. For further details, see: Introduction to *Sahaja Gītā*, translated by this author.

essential spiritual practices: "training the mind," "transforming the passions," and "guarding the heart." This conforms to the threefold disciplines enunciated in various Indian wisdom texts—path of knowledge (*jñāna yoga*), the path of action (*karma yoga*), and the path of devotion (*bhakti yoga*).

The Gītā defines *karmayoga-niṣṭhā* (steadfastness on the path of action) as follows: Considering everything verily God's, steadfastly performing actions selflessly as an "offering" to the Lord (BG 5.10), without attachment to actions or fruits thereof [BG 2.47], and remaining equipoised in success and failure (BG 2.48).

According to the Gītā, *sāṅkhyā niṣṭhā* (steadfastness on the path of knowledge) consists of considering every object transient, perishable (and hence non-real), as belonging to material nature (*prakṛti*), and knowing that the modes of nature (*guṇas*)—being the effect of *prakṛti*—are operating upon the modes ([BG 3.27, 28; 13.29; 14.19]; performing all actions by relinquishing the sense of doership (BG 5.8–9); and transcending the triad of the modes of *prakṛti* (BG 2.45).

The end result of both *karmayoga-niṣṭhā* (path of selfless action) and *sāṅkhya niṣṭhā* (path of knowledge) is exactly the same [BG 5.4–5]. These two paths are prescribed based on the difference in the level of readiness of the spiritual aspirant (*adhikāri-bheda*).

To dispel any misgivings about these two paths, we quote two important verses from chapter 5 below that show the Lord's categorical stance on this vital point:

> It is the ignorant, not the wise, who declare that *sāṅkhyayoga* (path of knowledge and renunciation of actions) and *karmayoga* (path of selfless action) lead to different results. A person well established in anyone of these attains the common goal of Self-realization. (BG 5.4)
>
> The state (of Self-realization) that is reached by the *sāṅkhya yogī* is also attained by the *karma yogī*. One who perceives *sāṅkhya yoga* and *karma yoga* as one (in their end results), sees the Reality. (BG 5.5)

The Bhagavad Gītā teaches that the only spiritual practice you need is *not to react*—to favorable/unfavorable circumstances. This is called *samatā*. What can be favorable or unfavorable for the wise? The wise welcome all situations as opportunities for self-learning and growth.

The Gītā teaches that the seers of Truth behold the One, Unchanging Reality amidst all the changing manifoldness of the universe (*vinaśyatsv avinaśyantaṃ yaḥ paśyati sa paśyati* 13.27). The purpose of all the *yogas* in the Gītā is to "yoke" us to the One Witnessing Divine Consciousness within, the Supreme Absolute Reality.

War and Peace in the Gītā

The Gītā teaches how to attain the Highest Peace—the peace of the Eternal Self—the peace which passeth all understanding.

Some scholars have opined that the Gītā teaches war under the pretext of the immortality of soul. This we take to be the misinterpretation and misunderstanding of the main message of the Gītā (2.18–30). The purpose of the Gītā is neither war nor peace, but to establish *Dharma* (righteousness). As the story of the Mahābhārata reveals, the Pāṇḍavas, under the guidance of Śrī Kṛṣṇa, had tried every possible peaceful means to avoid war. Śrī Kṛṣṇa himself went as a messenger of peace to avoid the war, but Duryodhana was not willing to listen; so much so he even tried to arrest the messenger of peace! Thus, the war became inevitable as a last resort.

When one knows oneself to be the One only reality, that I am the truth of the whole universe (*Tattvamasī*); when a person knows that, how can such person slay anyone when he sees only himself in all and everything?

The Gītā 2.21 clarifies that one who has realized that the One Self residing in one and all to be imperishable, eternal, free from birth and death, how can such a person kill or cause anyone to kill? Because It, the Self, is the only reality, It cannot kill anything, since there is nothing else besides Itself. No two things here, it is all pure non-duality. How can one who has known the Self, the imperishable, the eternal, the unborn, the unchanging, cause anyone to be slain? And how can the Self be slain?

Until one knows this—that I am the unchanging Witnessing-Consciousness—one *must* act.[2] That is why Arjuna is instructed to act initially—to fight (*yudhyasva* 2.18; 3.30). It is also important to note that after chapter 3, Arjuna's questions do not pertain to war. He wants answers to his ultimate existential questions. In 8.7, the refrain is to remember the Lord and fight (*yudhya*); here the word "fight" is used in the general sense of performing one's duties, appropriate to one's *svadharama*—and Arjuna's being one from the warrior class (*khaṣatriya*), is asked to fight the battle of life. And, in B.G.11.34, Arjuna is asked to fight, as an instrument of the Divine (*nimitta mātraṁ* 11.33). At no other place is Arjuna asked to fight. The Bhagavad Gītā is not about war. War is the setting in which the teachings of the Gītā happen to be presented. Later on, when the complete and clear knowledge of the Self has been imparted, Arjuna is finally exhorted to deeply ponder over the teachings and do as he likes (*yathecchasi tathā kuru* 18.63).

Arjuna was no ordinary fighter; he was a consummate warrior. He knew exactly what his dilemma was. A fighter fights with others; a warrior's war is with himself. A warrior knows that all wars are first fought *within* the mind. The mind matters the most. A fighter always thinks in terms of *ends*, namely, winning or losing; a warrior focuses on *perfecting the means*.

[2]For further clarification on this point, please refer to Ira Schepetin's three excellent talks on Bhagavad Gītā on YouTube. See: Ira Schepetin gives a talk about The Bhagavad Gītā: https://www.youtube.com/watch?v=D5Vl6OUezVY&t=2070s

https://www.youtube.com/watch?v=VHbiTNsoYi4&t=1s

https://www.youtube.com/watch?v=uxamejEBPQ4&t=2063s

A fighter is focused on the *results*; a warrior's concern is the propriety of the *process*. A warrior understands that when the process is right, right results follow inevitably. A warrior *knows* that the universe has a structural bias toward goodness. That is, when you do the right thing, right things happen to you.

A fighter fights with the inexorable laws of the universe. A warrior has a deep trust in the divine order—an order modulated by the cosmic laws of cause and effect. A fighter keeps on collecting *needless* karma by fighting with the inevitable; a warrior triggers no unwanted causes and fears no unintended consequences. At every failure, the fighter gets into the blame-game and contemplates quitting; the warrior confronts the enemy *within*, resolutely perseveres, and finally prevails.

When a master-archer fails to hit the target, he does not blame the target. He steps back, *realigns* his purpose, works resolutely on his technique, and comes back—*extra* renewed.

By all thy becoming, *become* a warrior—a peaceful warrior of spirit!

The Gītā teaches us how to engage in the world strategically (1.25) and in a most pragmatic way, but that pragmatism is principled (rooted in *dharma*), and informed by certain mental clarity and intrinsic goodness in which all actions are performed in the full wakefulness of Self-knowledge. The philosophy of the Gītā is but an invitation to the practice. Knowledge must lead to an inner transformation. The inner change must express itself in our conduct.

The Essence of Spirituality, According to the Gītā

The highest spirituality is regarding every being as Divine (*Vāsudevaḥ sarvam iti*: 7.19), and the highest service is treating everyone as one treats oneself (6.32) and being naturally and spontaneously engaged in the wellbeing of all beings (*sarvabhūtahite ratāḥ*: 5.25; 12.4). The Gītā says that such a great-souled person is rare indeed (BG 7.19) and attains to the Highest, the Lord of All (*labhante brahmanirvāṇam*: 5.25; *te prāpnuvanti māmeva*: 12.4).

Śrī Kṛṣṇa extols equanimity as the highest virtue in the Gītā at several places (2.48, 53, 57; 5.6, 18–20; 12.13–19; 14.24, 25; 18.10, 26). Therefore, *samatā* is the crest-jewel of perfection (*siddhi*) in all the paths to spirituality—path of action (*karmayoga*), the path of knowledge (*jñānayoga*), path of meditation (*dhyānayoga*), and path of devotion (*bhaktiyoga*). All virtues obtain in a mind that has cultivated equanimity. Whatever the spiritual practice, if evenness of mind (*samatā*) is not attained, the goal is still far away.

How Wise Leaders Should Act?

The Gītā states that the wise leader acts to set an example to the masses; so that the unwary do not go astray (3.26); for the unification of the world at large (*lokasaṃgraham*: 3.20, 3.25); for the welfare of all beings (*sarvabhūtahite*: 5.25); and for the purification of the mind (*ātmaśuddhaye*: 5.11). These four goals together furnish a touchstone for leadership success in any setting. Wise leaders do their duty for duty's sake (cf. Kant's Duty Ethics), to set an example for others, to bring communities together, and for the wellbeing of all; and above all, for the purification of their mind and their heart. No higher teaching on the sublimity of a leader's work ethic can be conceived.

In the ultimate analysis, leadership is not about changing outer conditions or others. In most cases, there is not much that we can do to change that which is external to us. However, we have full control over our own conduct. "When we are no longer able to change a situation," writes psychotherapist Viktor E. Frankl, "we are challenged to change ourselves."[3] And when we are able to do that, in due course of time, we are also able to change the situation, unexpectedly. This is the alchemy of all social change.

According to the Gītā, wise leaders have several key attributes, such as:

- They act, offering their actions for the good of others (3.9; 5.25; 12.4)
- They lead by example and serve as role-model (3.21)
- They cultivate a high sense of equanimity, *samatā* (2.38; 2.48–50). No great leadership is possible without developing evenness of mind, *samatvam* (2.57; 2.64; 2.68)
- They practice the principle of mutual inter-dependence (3.11)
- They are not afraid of anyone; nor do they generate any sense of fear in others (12.15)
- They bring together world communities by working for the universal welfare (*lokasaṃgraham* 3.20)

The Gītā 3.20 and 3.25 teaches that the highest ethical ideal for the spiritual seekers and leaders is *lokasaṅgraha*—the upliftment of the entire world: You should act with the welfare of the entire universe in view (*loka saṅgraham-evāpi saṃpaśyan kartum arhasi*: 3.20).

The Gītā's ideal is not indifference to the world, but love and compassion born out of realizing the identity of oneself with all beings (*ātmaupamyena sarvatra samaṃ paśyati* 6.32). The following verse of the Gītā presents the quintessential paradigm for both ethics and spirituality, by way of Golden Rule, for life and leadership:

> *ātmaupamyena sarvatra samaṃ paśyati yorjuna /*
> *sukhaṃ vā yadi vā duḥkhaṃ sa yogī paramo mataḥ* //6.32//
>
> He who looks on all as one, on the analogy of his own self, and looks on the joy and sorrow of all equally (that is, treats the joy and sorrow of all, as he treats his own joy and sorrow); such a Yogī is deemed to be the highest of all.[4]

[3] Viktor E. Frankl, *Man's Search for Meaning: An Introduction to Logotherapy* (New York, NY: A Touchstone Book, 1984, Third edition), 116.

[4] See: *Śrimad Bhagavadgītā* (with English Transliteration and Translation) (Gorakhpur, India: Gītā Press, 2011), 114.

The Gītā and the Art of Happiness

Observation and reflection make it evident that half of our unhappiness is caused by not appreciating what we have; the other half by pinning for what we do not have. This is the enigma of unhappiness. This deceptively simple analysis shows that 100% of our unhappiness is caused by self-ignorance. Therefore, whether one is looking for material happiness or for supreme bliss, Self-knowledge seems to be the key. Self-knowledge by definition is an inner quest. The Bhagavad Gītā (2.55) starts the description of a person of steady wisdom (*sthitaprajñā*) as one who, casting off all the desires of the mind, is "content in the joy of the Self by the Self."

When one has found the *inner* font of peace and joy, then one acts *with* fulfillment and not *for* fulfillment! Recipes of happiness do not come any better than this.

The Bhagavad Gītā frees us from the syndrome of "more-ism"—wanting more and more of more and more in more and more ways—from the compulsive habit of, from the torment of, the relentless pursuit of chasing after myriad objects compulsively. It also frees us from the "destination-addiction"—it invites us to focus on the *process* rather than obsessing about the *goals*. Stress comes from misalignment between our actions and results. The Gītā says do your allotted duty conscientiously and leave the results to the workings of the Cosmic Order. It asks us to focus on the process and the outcome will take care of itself. The Gītā teaches us that cultivating equanimity, *samatā*, is the best antidote to the "slings and arrows of outrageous fortune." (2.48)

The Gītā introduces us to the intrinsic fullness of our being, *puraṇattvam*. It teaches us that running after desires is a race without a finish line—it is like trying to put out the fire by adding oil to it! The Gītā says that our happiness will increase in proportion to the decrease in our desire for objects. Only those who are content are happy.

The Gītā teaches us that the path of greed leads to unhappiness, as one can never have enough.

The Gītā teaches us that the fulfillment of any particular desire does not free us from craving or greed because desire increases with enjoyment even as a fire grows stronger with the addition of fuel (3.39). It further states that a mind tormented by desires cannot find peace (2.66). The Gīta likens the mind of sage, steadfast in wisdom (*sthitaprajña*), with an ocean that remains undisturbed despite the raging rivers of desires.

The Gītā teaches that "be good, do good" is all that one needs to "be" and "do" to foster happiness in oneself and others. Greek thinkers of yore have defined happiness as exercising of human faculties along the lines of excellence. In the same manner, the Bhagavad Gītā defines yoga as dexterity or excellence in action (*yogaḥ karmasu kauśalam*: 2.50). It is common to experience a feeling of a soaring spirit when we are doing excellent work. The converse is also true. It has been observed that the best way to kill human motivation is to expect and accept mediocre work from others. Expecting less than excellent work is the greatest disservice we can do to ourselves and to others. We owe excellence to ourselves, as much as we owe it to society.

No mere ideology, this passion for excellence has far-reaching implications for leaders and for workplace performance. Nobody comes to work to put in a shoddy performance. Everyone is looking for creative self-expression. And when we create opportunities for meaningful self-expression, we help build a workplace where people act *with* self-fulfillment and not merely work *for* it. Creating such a liberating work environment is the real job of a leader.

In chapter 18, the culminating chapter of the Bhagavad Gītā, the expression with "God's Grace" occurs at least five times: 18.56, 58, 18.62, 18.66, and finally in 18.73. Wherever it occurs, it is mentioned that, through God's Grace, one attains supreme peace, *parāṁ śāntiṁ* (18.62). This is one of the key pointers to attain abiding peace and fulfillment in life. We need both the self-efforts and God's Grace to experience Supreme Peace of Self-Realization—self efforts verily being an expression of God's Grace!

The main topic of the Gītā is *śarnāgati*, or total surrender. It starts with Arjuna's surrender in verse 7 of chapter 2, when Arjuna implores Śrī Kṛṣṇa to accept him as His disciple and to teach him. It ends in *śarnāgati*, when Arjuna says, at the end, "I will do Thy bidding"—*kariṣye vacanaṃ tava* (18.73). True peace can only come by surrendering to the Divine within.

The spiritual peace—the peace that passeth understanding—is more of a gift than a reward!

Alchemy of Karmayoga According to the Gītā

It is a timeless spiritual truth: release attachment to outcomes, and—deep inside yourself—you'll feel good no matter what. (J. Krishnamurti)

Within the compass of a short sentence, J. Krishnamurti hands over all the keys to the spiritual kingdom. The only way to be peaceful is to release attachment to outcomes. This is the core of the Gītā's message about *karma yoga*. No better philosophy of *freedom in action* can be conceived.

Usain Bolt, the Jamaican athlete, is the fastest man who ever lived. He is the winner of nine Olympics gold medals. His net worth is around 60 million dollars. In three Olympic finals combined, he has run for less than 2 minutes. However, it took him 20 years to get those 2 minutes right! Such is the alchemy of all great work. Nature exacts a price from us before it bestows its bounties. Subtle is the Lord, said Einstein, and added that the Lord does not play dice. The Gītā exhorts us to commit to excellence (*karmasu kauśalam*, 2.50) in all we do, work hard and wait, leaving the results in the hands of the Divine.

What is the alchemy of *karmayoga* according to the Gītā? It is action without attachment to the results and without even a sense of being a doer (*kartāpan*). Then, our actions will become holy and whole. When the actions of people are whole and holy, then we have secured the foundations of a harmonious society and happy people.

Mother Teresa once said, "I alone cannot change the world, but I can cast a stone across the waters to create many ripples." The Gītā says, cast the stone of your good deeds in the waters of life, and let the Divinity work out the ripples for you! The great American transcendentalist, Emerson, once said, "The purpose of life is not to be happy. It is to be useful, to be honorable, to be compassionate, to have it make some difference that you have lived and lived well." Amen, says the Gītā, on all counts!

Life and Leadership Maxims from the Bhagavad Gītā

Know yourself, do good, and be fulfilled.[5]

The Bhagavad Gītā is a treasure trove and a gem of Indian spiritual wisdom and contains eternal truths about life and liberation. The beauty of the Gītā lies in its ability to harmonize the spiritual and the temporal, in the art and science of attaining the highest good (*param śreyas*) while remaining fully engaged in everyday practical matters (*vyavahāra mein paramārtha kī kalā*). This blend of the spiritual and the practical is the key to the Gītā's universal appeal over the centuries. Gītā teaches us that there is no progress on the spiritual path if there is no harmony and unity between our *vicāra* (thought process) and *ācāra* (conduct). The Gītā's ideal is not indifference to the world, but love and compassion born out of the identity of oneself with all beings, *ātmaupamyena sarvatra samaṃ paśyati* (6.32).

It contains practical guidance for every aspect of our life, secular as well as sacred. Consider the following verse alone, which may guide us in most of our practical life:

> *yuktāhāravihārasya yuktaceṣṭasya karmasu /*
> *yuktasvapnāvabodhasya yogo bhavati duḥkhahā* //6.17//
>
> Yoga which destroys sorrow, is accomplished only by one who is regulated in diet and recreation, regulated in performing actions, and regulated in sleep and wakefulness.[6]

Gītā teaches three *yogas* (paths or disciplines) to realize our destiny. The purpose of all the *yogas* in the Gītā is to "yoke" us to the One Witnessing Divine Consciousness within, the Supreme Absolute Reality. The Gītā's spirituality is not an abstract affair, but a lived experience. It has to be imbibed from those who have realized its tenets directly. It teaches us that spiritual freedom (*mokṣa*) can be realized only through knowledge (*jñānam*) gained from a teacher who is established in the vision of Truth [of the Self] (*tattvadarśinaḥ*) (4.34). Otherwise, Śrī Kṛṣṇa would have asked Arjuna to meditate!

The Gītā teaches us how to live in the world and yet remain untouched by its worldliness—like a lotus leaf in the water (5.10). The Gītā teaches us the art of doing our duty diligently without the tag of doership—as an offering to the Supreme.

[5] For further information, see author's webpage: http://foreverfulfilled.com/

[6] See: *Śrimad Bhagavadgītā* (with English Transliteration and Translation) (Gorakhpur, India: Gītā Press, 2011), 108.

One Hundred-and-One Maxims of Life and Leadership

We present below 101 maxims of life and leadership distilled from a concerted study of the Gītā. Each maxim is a little nugget that can illumine our path by showing us the right thing to do in life and leadership.

1. The Gītā teaches the path of *śreyas* (doing our duty for duty sake) that is good in the beginning, good in the middle, and good in the end. This is the foundation of a leader's work.
2. The Bhagavad Gītā teaches us that the greatest project you will ever undertake is You! To study the Gītā is to study yourself—the real "You," with "Y" capital, "O" capital, and "U" capital. This is the beginning and end of all authentic life and leadership.
3. The Gītā teaches that nothing can give you happiness except yourself (2.55). It introduces us to the intrinsic fullness of our being, *puraṇattvam*.
4. The Gītā teaches us that running after desires is a race without a finish line, and a mind tormented by desires cannot find peace (2.66). Only those who are content are happy.
5. The Gītā warns us that the path of greed leads to unhappiness, as we can never have enough of anything. Experience and observation will convince us that pining for more and more is a race without a finish line and a weariness of spirit.
6. The Gītā teaches us that the fulfillment of any particular desire does not free us from craving or greed, because desire increases with enjoyment even as a fire grows stronger with the addition of fuel (3.39). The Gītā declares, "With the attainment of peace, all sorrows come to an end" (*prasāde sarvaduḥkhānāṃ hānir asyopajāyate*: 2.65). This peace is the peace of understanding.
7. The Gītā teaches us that true peace can only come by serving the common good and surrendering to the Divine *within* us. That our happiness multiplies by making others happy has been widely confirmed by various studies on subjective wellbeing in positive psychology.[7] Every traditional system of wisdom has recognized the importance of surrendering to a higher principle/being/intelligence in fostering abiding joy and peace.
8. The Gītā tells us that although the Supreme Lord of the universe has nothing to attain personally in the three worlds, still, the Lord keeps on performing his duties for the benefit of all (3.22). Even so, those in power should model their behavior, since a majority of the people follow whatsoever an important person does (3.21). What an object lesson for leaders to follow!

[7] See Sonja Lyubomirsky, *The How of Happiness: A Scientific Approach to Getting the Life You Want* (New York, NY: Penguin Press, Reprint edition, 2008).

9. The path to leading others starts with self-awareness through self-discipline and ends with self-transcendence through selfless service. Recent studies on emotional intelligence confirm the importance of self-awareness in the leadership equation. The Gītā calls it enlightened leadership.
10. Enlightened leadership is essentially servant leadership. It represents a shift from followers serving leaders to leaders serving followers. According to the Gītā, the path to enlightened leadership is paved with authenticity, humility, service, and compassion. This is one good recipe for effective leadership.
11. The Gītā teaches us that unless the mind is purged of personal desires and attachments, even service is but an inflation of the ego. Only those who have relinquished personal ambition can truly serve. Selflessness is the greatest gift leaders can give to society. Selflessness is also the best thing one can do for oneself! This is the path of *niṣkāma karma*, the discipline of disinterested action.
12. Enlightened leaders are not motivated by personal desires or interests. They become instruments of the whole and selflessly serve for the wellbeing of all beings (*sarvabhūta hitae*, BG 5.25; 12.4).
13. The Gītā teaches us that our innate lifework, *svadharma*, is a supreme means to discover who we are. The goal is Self-knowledge; service is the means to it.
14. The Gītā teaches us how to be "yoked" to Divine within through the discipline of action (*karma yoga*), devotion (*bhakti yoga*), meditation (*dhyāna yoga*), and knowledge (*jñāna yoga*). Yoga brings a certain measure of "integration" in human personality. Only a well-integrated (*yoga-yukta*) person can be an effective leader.
15. The Gītā teaches us that all our existential problems ultimately stem from self-ignorance—*not knowing who we truly are*. According to the great Indian philosopher, Ādi Shaṅkarācārya, "self-ignoracne is the cause of human bondage; Self-knowledge is the remedy."
16. The Gītā teaches us that spiritual freedom (*mokṣa*) can be realized only through knowledge (*jñānam*) gained from a competent teacher who is established in the vision of Truth [of the Self] (*tattvadarśinaḥ*) (4.34). Likewise, the goal of leadership is not to gather more followers, but to inspire more leaders. However, leaders first must practice what they preach. Like Gandhi, they must embody the change they wish to see in the organizations; they must make life their message.
17. The Gītā teaches us that the dictum of "be good, do good" is all one needs to "be" and "do" to foster happiness in oneself and others. It introduces us to the joy of giving joy to others. When we have joy in our heart, we act *with* fulfillment, and not merely *for* fulfillment.
18. According to the Gītā 3.20, leaders should act with the welfare of the entire universe in view. When one becomes a leader, the responsibility for doing the right thing grows tremendously. The stakes are raised

immediately. For a leader, the question is never, what do I like? It is always, what needs to be done. The common good is the guiding star of a leader's conduct in this terrain.

19. The Gītā 6.40 assures us that on the path of goodness, one does not lose ever (न हि कल्याणकृत् कश्चित् दुर्गतिं तात गच्छति): There is no misery or misadventure (*durgati*) for such a person who follows the path of goodness. This understanding accords internal strength and helps leaders remain steadfast on the path of righteousness, when the going gets tough.
20. The Gītā is probably the only scripture in human history where the reader is not asked to accept anything on faith. Every question is examined insightfully, and diverse perspectives are presented for reflection. Likewise, leaders should offer diverse perspectives for the followers to consider, rather than promoting their own pet ideas.
21. After the entire teachings of the Gītā have been imparted, Śrī Kṛṣṇa tells Arjuna at the very end, "…now that the most profound wisdom has been imparted; deeply ponder over it and *do as you wish* (18.63)." Do as you wish, not as I say. Teachers open the door; we have to enter by ourselves.
22. Throughout the entire Gītā, Arjuna asks good questions (*paripraśnena*) and Śrī Kṛṣṇa answers them lovingly and objectively, without becoming upset or deprecating. The student has humility and respect for the teacher and the teacher has caring concern for the wellbeing of the student. As a master teacher, Śrī Kṛṣṇa shows great *passion* for the subject, and great *compassion* for the student. This makes the Gītā a great treatise on the art and science of effective communication.
23. The Gītā uses a very special teaching methodology. It presents the highest teachings—the "big picture"—first. Arjuna was confused about his duty and wanted to know "the right thing to do" (*śreyas*). Śrī Kṛṣṇa starts the teaching with the highest good (*param-śreyas*)—the nature of the Self. Arjuna was mostly worried about the outer kingdom; Śrī Kṛṣṇa gently guides him to the inner kingdom—the inner treasure of the fullness of our being (*puraṇattvam*). Likewise, leaders who are able to garner a vision of the "big picture" are able to create a high level of buy-in.
24. The Bhagavad Gītā is the ultimate self-help book; it teaches eternal Truths about our true nature (Gītā 3.3, 4.1–3). The sole purpose (and the goal supreme) of the Gītā is Self-realization, or God-realization. By following this philosophy, leaders are able to attain their highest good, while discharging their duties diligently in the full wakefulness of Self-knowledge.
25. The beauty of the Gītā lies in its ability to harmonize the spiritual and the temporal, in the art and science of attaining the highest good (*param śreyas*) while remaining fully engaged in the everyday practical matters (*vyavahāra mein paramārtha kī kalā*). This practical orientation is responsible for the Gītā's universal appeal and abiding influence.

26. The Gītā teaches us that there is no progress on the spiritual path if there is no harmony and unity between our *vicāra* (thought process) and *ācāra* (conduct). Its spirituality is not an abstract affair, but a lived experience. How often do we hear these days that the leaders need to "walk the talk" to attain a measure of authenticity. Effective leaders' conduct is authentic: their thoughts, speech, and deeds are well aligned. Ultimately, right thinking and right conduct serve as the two unshakable pillars of leadership.
27. Gītā's ideal is not indifference to the world, but love and compassion born out of the identity of oneself with all beings, *ātmaupamyena sarvatra samaṃ paśyati* (6.32). The writer, speaker, and the listener of the Gītā were all householders, and not renunciates.
28. Gītā 6.17 teaches that the *yoga* that destroys sorrow is accomplished only by those who are regulated in diet and recreation, regulated in performing actions, and regulated in sleep and wakefulness. This object lesson in moderation is also the mainstay of all secular ethics.
29. The Gītā teaches us how to live in the world and yet remain untouched by its worldliness—like a lotus leaf in the water (5.10). This wisdom fosters a certain sense of detachment that is so essential for leaders to carry out their work objectively.
30. The Gītā teaches us the art of doing our duty diligently without the tag of doership, without hankering after results, as an offering to the Supreme. At first, this may seem to be an idealistic, lofty goal. Understood properly, this becomes the most practical strategy in carrying out all functions of life and leadership. When our mind is too focused on the outcome, it is not able to give its full attention to the process at hand. And our work suffers in consequence.
31. The Gītā invites us to focus on the *process* rather than obsessing about the *goals*. This alone can serve as a sure guide in life and leadership.
32. The Gītā teaches us how to act without being attached to the outcomes. The attachment to outcomes—desiring a specific result—sets the stage for anxiety. One gets elated by favorable results and feels dejected when the results are unfavorable. This is to live a life of perpetual emotional roller coaster. When we release ourselves from the attachment to outcomes, we develop certain mental equipoise to deal with "the slings and arrows of outrageous fortune."
33. The greatest practical lesson that the Gītā teaches us is karma yoga—the highest discipline to live by: use the right means for a just cause, and leave the results in the hands of God.
34. Stress comes from misalignment between our actions and results. The Gītā says do your allotted duty conscientiously as an offering to the Supreme and leave the results to the workings of the Cosmic Order.
35. The Gītā considers the attainment of equanimity as the litmus test for perfection in all the three *yogas*: *karma yoga*, *jñāna yoga*, and *bhakti yoga*.

36. The Bhagavad Gītā frees us from the syndrome of "more-ism"—wanting more and more of more and more in more and more ways—from the compulsive habit and the torment of, the relentless pursuit of, chasing after myriad objects compulsively. It frees us from the "destination-addiction."
37. The Gīta likens the mind of a sage steadfast in wisdom (*sthitaprajña*) with an ocean that remains unruffled despite the raging rivers of desires.
38. The Gītā declares in no uncertain terms that, for anyone born, death is certain (*jātasya hi dhruvo mṛtyur*), and for that which is dead, birth is certain (*dhruvaṃ janma mṛtasya ca*, 2.27). Therefore, one should not grieve over the inevitable. This understanding helps us overcome the greatest fear in life, the fear of death.
39. The body is gifted to us to practice righteousness, *dharma*: *Sarīra mādhyam khalu dharma sādhanam* (the purpose of the human body is to practice dharma). This is evident from the very first word of the Gītā, that is, *dharma*.
40. The Gītā teaches us that whatever the spiritual practice, if equanimity of mind (*samatā*) is not attained, the goal is still far away.
41. The Gītā urges us to see things in the correct perspective—*yaḥ paśyati sa paśyati*: One who sees thus, truly sees (5.5; 13.27, 13.29). It helps us to develop foresight and self-insight, two cardinal qualities required of all managers and leaders.
42. The Gītā teaches us that the highest ethical ideal for the spiritual seekers and enlightened leaders is *lokasaṅgraha*—the upliftment of the entire world (3.20, 3.25). One should act with the welfare of the entire universe in view (*loka saṅgraham-evāpi saṃpaśyan kartum arhasi*, 3.20).
43. Knowing that both prosperity and adversity are temporary, the wise welcome them, fully understanding that "this too shall pass." They enjoy prosperity with humility and bear adversity with equanimity.
44. The Gītā teaches us that our choice lifework (*svadharma*) is a supreme means to discover who we are. The goal is Self-knowledge; service is the means.
45. The Gītā teaches the high art of detached engagement—to focus on the actions rather than the results. When we shift our attention from goal-orientation to process-orientation, the results take care of themselves.
46. Effective leaders know that self-awareness is the key to leading from within. They manage their awareness alertly to lead others effectively.
47. Self-awareness ultimately depends upon Self-knowledge. The Gītā presents detailed instructions about attaining steady abidance in Self-knowledge (2.52–72; 13. 7–11).
48. Self-knowledge means the knowledge of one's true self at the "soul-level"—beyond senses, mind, and intellect. While all other knowledge pertains to knowing everything that can be objectified externally, Self-knowledge is about knowing the knower.

49. Selfish desire obscures self-awareness and meddles with achieving life's true ends. Self-aware leaders are not motivated by personal desires or interests. Their goal is contribution through service.
50. The Bhagavad Gītā says, "Cast the pebble of your karma in the pond of life and wait for the Cosmic Laws to work out the ripples for you." This is a perfect recipe for our lifework and work life, a surefire way to free oneself from over-anxiety about the results.
51. Stress comes from misalignment between our actions and results. The Gītā says do your allotted duty conscientiously and leave the results to the workings of the Cosmic Order. The Gītā says focus on the process and the outcome will take care of itself.
52. The Gītā teaches us that cultivating equanimity (*samatā*) is the best antidote to the "slings and arrows of outrageous fortune." (2.48)
53. The Gītā teaches us to be patient with ourselves, for we are the greatest obstacle in our way. We are our own best friend and our own worst enemy. This is a mature understanding based on self-responsibility and not blaming others.
54. The Gītā teaches us that an unruly mind is our greatest enemy and a restrained mind is our best friend (6.5).
55. The Gītā teaches that the wise work, without attachment, for the well-being of all beings (*sarvabhūtahite ratāḥ* 5.25, 12.4) and for the welfare of the world (*lokasaṁgraham* 3.20). This comprises the complete template for *spiritualizing* life and leadership. This is the message the leaders need to hear and practice to lift themselves out of the present-day *selfie* culture.
56. How can I serve the world with my gifts? That's all, says the Gītā, you need to know to live a fulfilled life. The recipes for living a fulfilled life do not come any better than this.
57. The gist of the message of the Gītā is: Always and in everything, keep your mind fastened on the Truth of the Supreme Self and fight the battle of life. सर्वेषु कालेषु माम् अनुस्मर युध्य च *sarveṣu kāleṣu mām anusmara yudhya ca* (8.7).
58. The Gītā teaches us that the world of becoming is fleeting and unreal; the world of being is unchanging and real (2.16).
59. The Gītā introduces us to the joy of giving joy to others.
60. The Gītā teaches that unless the mind is purged of personal desire and attachment, even service is but an inflation of the ego.
61. The path to leading others starts with self-awareness through self-discipline and ends with self-transcendence through selfless service. It is paved with authenticity, humility, and compassion.
62. "The best way to find yourself is to lose yourself in the service of others," said Gandhi. This is an important lesson he learned from the Gītā.
63. Know that your actions are really not "your" actions—just the expressions of the Divine within. And you will become *nimita-mātra* (11.33), a mere instrument, a vessel, in the hands of the Divine.

64. Only actions performed in full wakefulness of Self-knowledge, in the remembrance of the Self (*māmanusmara*), do not bind.
65. The Gītā tells us that all actions are orchestrated by the interplay of the threefold properties of the material nature (*triguṇātamaka prakṛti*). Only those who are confused about the true nature of the Self appropriate all actions to themselves (3.27). No better pointers on spiritualizing life can be conceived!
66. The Gītā says that most of the humanity is running incessantly—either running *after* (*rāga*) or running *from* (*dveṣa*)—in the whirlpool of *saṁsāra*. It provides the diagnosis of the malady and presents an effective solution in the form of *karmayoga*, the art of working selflessly for the common good, offering actions to the Divine and accepting the results gracefully.
67. The Gītā says that the wise ones transcend the sway of likes and dislikes (*rāga-dveṣa*) and live a balanced life, a life of equanimity (*samatā*).
68. The Bhagavad Gītā teaches that the only spiritual practice you need is *not to react*—to favorable/unfavorable circumstances. What can be favorable or unfavorable for the wise? The wise welcome all situations as opportunities for self-learning and growth.
69. Most stress in life comes from misalignment between our actions and results and misdirected expectations. Gītā says do your duty diligently and leave the results to the workings of the Cosmic Order.
70. The Bhagavad Gītā teaches that wisdom (*prajña*) has two aspects: *puraṇattvam* and *samattvam*. It is only when both of these are present that wisdom (*prajña*) becomes steady (*stithaprajña*).
71. The Bhagavad Gītā teaches us that happiness is an inside job. It lies in steady abidance in the contented self (*ātmany evātmanā tuṣṭaḥ* 2.55).
72. The Bhagavad Gītā teaches us that all existential problems are centered on the lack of understanding of "Who am I?"
73. The Gītā teaches us that a spiritual quest starts and ends with asking and answering the question, "Who am I?" In fact, the spiritual journey starts and ends with asking and answering this question.
74. The Bhagavad Gītā 2.40 teaches us that the knowers of the Self and the practitioners of the yoga of selfless action are freed from the greatest fear: the fear of repeated conditioned existence: स्वल्पम् अप्य् अस्य धर्मस्य त्रायते महतो भयात्: *svalpam apy asya dharmasya trāyate mahato bhayāt*: even a little practice of this art of selfless action (born of Self-knowledge) saves one from the great terror of *saṃsāra* (repeated conditioned existence).
75. The Bhagavad Gītā teaches us that a restless mind and an anxious heart know neither peace nor happiness. Tranquility comes to a heart, which is no longer stirred by desires.
76. The three *guṇas*—*sattva*, *rajas*, and *tamas*—belong to the mind only. We should strive to rise above the *guṇas* and know the Self.

77. The Bhagavad Gītā teaches us that you can raise yourself by yourself (*uddhared ātmanātmānaṃ*: 6.5). This is the soul-uplifting message of the Gītā: You can raise your destiny by pulling your own shoestrings. This is very different from what goes for easy self-esteem in most overly simplistic self-help guides.
78. The Gītā says that nothing can give you real happiness except your Self (*ātmany evātmanā tuṣṭaḥ*: BG 2.55).
79. The Bhagavad Gītā teaches us that you are your best friend and your worst enemy. In fact, our mind is our best friend and worst enemy. An unruly mind brings ruin in its wake, whereas a restrained mind saves one from all trouble (*uddhared ātmanātmānaṃ nātmānam avasādayet; ātmaiva hy ātmano bandhur ātmaiva ripur ātmanaḥ* 6.5).
80. The strongest person is not the one who has subjugated the whole world; the strongest person is one who has subdued his/her mind. This is an object lesson in self-mastery through self-discipline.
81. The Bhagavad Gītā 17.15 teaches us that when you speak austerely, sincerely, and politely from the heart, you touch the soul. However, such speech should be truthful, beneficial, and pleasing.
82. The Bhagavad Gītā teaches us that we should face challenges of life and leadership like a peaceful warrior and not like a fighter. Both enter the battle, but there is a fundamental difference in their approach. A fighter fights with others; a warrior's war is with himself. A warrior knows that all wars are first fought *within* the mind. Mind matters the most. A fighter always thinks in terms of *ends*, namely, winning or losing; a warrior focuses on *perfecting the means*. Arjuna was one such consummate warrior.
83. The Bhagavad Gītā teaches us that wise leaders work for the wellbeing of all beings and for bringing people and communities together—*without hankering after the results*. They find fulfillment in their work itself; they are glad to be of some service.
84. The Bhagavad Gītā teaches us that only a self-aware person is free and happy. Only happy individuals create a harmonious society. These teachings hold the key to individual happiness and social harmony.
85. The Bhagavad Gītā teaches us that we should accept nothing on faith. Throughout the verses, Arjuna asks good questions and Śrī Kṛṣṇa answers them sincerely without reproach. The Gītā teaches us to examine everything under the microscope of reason before accepting or acting upon it.
86. The Gītā teaches us the art of attaining the highest good (*param śreyas*) while fully engaged in everyday practical matters. This is where its uniqueness lies. All the yogas of the Gītā are geared toward this aim.
87. The Bhagavad Gītā teaches us that through proper attitude and discipline, we can achieve perfection (*siddhi*) in any field of life. According to the Bhagavad Gītā 18.46, we can attain the highest perfection (*siddhi*)—here and now—by worshiping our common Creator through our allotted work and by being true to ourselves (*svakarmaṇā/svadharma*).

88. In the Gītā's view, only those who know themselves are truly wise (*paṇḍitāḥ*, 2.11). Knowing the Self, the wise do not grieve. This is the message of the Gītā.
89. The Gītā extols equanimity (*samatvaṁ*) above all. In all the three main yogas presented in the Gītā, *samatā* is offered as the benchmark of their perfection (*siddhi*). No matter what the path, if evenness of the mind is not attained, the goal is still far away.
90. Favorable or unfavorable, success or failure, gain or loss—these epithets do not sway the one steady in the wisdom of the Self (*sthita-prajñaḥ*). Such a person remains unshaken amidst even the greatest sorrow (*na duḥkhena guruṇāpi vicālyate*).
91. The Gītā says that all our existential problems ultimately stem from self-ignorance—not knowing who we truly are. Just as knowledge of physics cannot destroy ignorance of biology, even so self-ignorance can only be dispelled by Self-knowledge.
92. Realizing our true Self as immutable, eternal, and imperishable constitutes [Self-] knowledge according to the Gītā. Put differently, realizing our true nature as the Absolute, unchanging, limitless consciousness constitutes Self-knowledge. Liberation through this knowledge is the sole purpose of the teachings of Vedānta and the Bhagavad Gītā.
93. The Bhagavad Gītā teaches us that the ego is one of the biggest barriers to the achievement of peace. The one who moves free from the shackles of ego and attachment attains peace (2.71).
94. Our experience and reflection dictate that wealth and happiness are not related to each other as cause and effect. The very fact that we are constantly in pursuit of happiness shows that we are not content with the current situation. Constantly pining for more is called greed, which the Gītā counts among the three gateways to hell, the other two being lust and anger.
95. Enlightened leaders master their senses instead of letting their senses master them. The leader should manage his anger and should not let anger gain control over him. Śrī Kṛṣṇa explains that from anger, delusion arises, and from delusion bewilderment of memory. When memory is bewildered, reasoning power is lost and, with the loss of reasoning, one falls from one's status as a human being.
96. Therefore, enlightened leaders do not lead by anger or fear. They practice forbearance and use forgiveness as their principal armor. They are well aware that leading by anger and fear is unproductive and leads to disempowerment and disengagement.
97. The Upaniṣads and the Gītā have one central theme or teaching: Supreme bliss as a result of the complete cessation of sorrow (आत्यंतिक शोक निवृत्ति पूर्वक सुख प्राप्ति). The Gītā 6.23 calls it yoga. When we have attained complete separation (*viyogaṃ*) from sorrow, we enjoy supreme bliss. This bliss (*ātma-sukha*) is the result of Self-knowledge alone, and does not depend upon the contrivance of outer circumstances or things.

98. When told about Self-knowledge, one gets upset because one is accustomed to knowing things other than oneself, although it is presumed that a person knows who s/he is.

    Sorrow is caused by the lack of knowledge about our true Self. We suffer because of self-ignorance. The Gītā aims to remove this sorrow by removing the self-ignorance that is causing it. The removal of self-ignorance is the fruit of Self-knowledge (विद्या फलं असत् निवृत्ति). In Indian philosophy, that which liberates is called true knowledge (सा विद्या या विमुच्यते).
99. To know the Truth is to see the oneness of the Self with God. (Śrīmad Bhāgavatam)
100. The lot of an ignorant person is that he goes through life blaming others for all the bad in life while pocketing all the credit for the good.
101. The Bhagavad Gītā teaches us that *all except God perishes* (2.17; 13.27). Accordingly, the wise find joy in serving and surrendering to the Divine, the impressable principle that resides as witnessing consciousness in all, as the innermost Self of all (*pratyagātmā*). In one of the most important verses of the Gītā (10.20),[8] Śrī Kṛṣṇa says, "Arjuna, I am the universal Self seated in all beings": *aham ātmā guḍākeśa sarvabhūtāśayasthitaḥ*. This is why Sureśvarācāya, the foremost disciple of Ādi Saṅkara, says that when the innermost self is known, nothing remains unknown: *Pratyagātmani vijñāte nājñātam avashiśyate* [BUBV 1.4.1007]. The Gītā 7.2 likewise assures that having known the innermost Self, nothing else remains yet to be known in this world, and knowing it, one is released from all that is inauspicious in life (9.1).

Concluding Thoughts

Only two paths are available to man: the path of wisdom and the path of suffering. (Paul Deussen)

Paul Deussen, the great German Indologist and a friend of Friedrich Nietzsche and Swami Vivekananda, sums up the entire philosophy of life in this quote. This quote also represents a running commentary on the glory of the Bhagavad Gītā. Indeed, only two paths are available to us: the path of Self-knowledge and the path of suffering. Arjuna in the very beginning of the Gītā beseeches Śrī Kṛṣṇa to teach him what is decidedly good for him (BG 2.7). He was in a state of deep sorrow. Śrī Kṛṣṇa removes Arjuna's suffering by showing him the path of wisdom (especially in BG 2.11–30), the profound wisdom of the Self. At the very end of the Gītā 18.73, Arjuna confirms that his doubts and delusion have been dispelled (*naṣṭo mohaḥ...gatasaṃdehaḥ*), he has regained the remem-

[8] Sri Ramana Maharshi used to say that this verse (BG 10.20) contains the essence of all the Bhagavad Gītā.

brance of his true Self (*smṛtir labdhā*), that he abides in that wisdom of the Self (*sthitosmi*), and that he is now ready to fulfil the Divine command of duty (*kariṣye vacanaṃ tava*). May this sublime message ring equally true for us as it did for Arjuna!

This book is humbly dedicated to the great change master, Śrī Kṛṣṇa, who, 5000 years ago, proactively impelled political change from the prevailing unjust order to that of righteousness. He became the greatest exemplar of servant leadership by agreeing to humbly serve as Arjuna's charioteer in the epic war of Mahābhārata. Where else can we find the Supreme Lord of the universe leading by example in human form to fulfil his promise of establishing righteousness (*dharmasaṃsthāpanārthāya*), of the protection of the virtuous (*paritrāṇāya sādhūnāṃ*), and of disciplining the wrong-doers (*vināśāya ca duṣkṛtāmto*) [4.8].

Śrī Kṛṣṇa provides the greatest *raison d'être* for managers and leaders to act in the following verses:

> Arjuna! For me there is nothing whatsoever to achieve in the three worlds. Nor is there anything worth attaining, unattained by Me. Yet, I remain engaged in action [to set an example for others so that they do not go astray] (3.22). Arjuna, as the unwise act, attached to the results, even so should the wise act, (but) without attachment, with a view to maintain the world order. (3.25)

Within the compass of one short paragraph, Śrī Kṛṣṇa has handed over all the keys of effective leadership to Arjuna. Servant leaders have nothing left to achieve for themselves. They engage in action to help others, unattached to the results. Yet, they act as role models with same dedication as those who act out of self-interest. Their motivation comes from serving a cause much higher than their narrow personal aims and ambitions. They find their fulfillment in immersing themselves in the wellbeing of all beings and by bringing the world communities together. They become instruments of the Whole and live a life of service, contribution, and purpose. They have passion for their work and compassion for others. Their actions are graced by Self-awareness born of Self-knowledge. Their specialness lies in their ordinariness. They find their joy in giving joy to others.

Leadership guidance does not come any better than this!

The final message of the Bhagavad Gītā:
Know yourself, *serve* all, and *surrender* to the Divine *within*.

To invoke peace of mind and to garner peace in the world, we conclude this book with two Peace Invocations.

Shanti Mantra (Prayer for Peace)

ॐ असतो मा सद्गमय ।
तमसो मा ज्योतिर्गमय ।
मृत्योर्मा अमृतं गमय ।
ॐ शान्तिः शान्तिः शान्तिः ॥

oṁ asato mā sadgamaya /
tamaso mā jyotirgamaya /
mṛtyormā amṛtaṁ gamaya /
oṁ śāntiḥ śāntiḥ śāntiḥ //

Lead me from unreal to the Real.
Lead me from darkness to light.
Lead me from death to immortality.
Oṁ! Peace. Peace. Peace. (*Bṛhadāraṇyaka Upaniṣad* 1.3.28)

Peace Invocation:
ॐ सर्वे भवन्तु सुखिनः सर्वे सन्तु निरामयाः ।
सर्वे भद्राणि पश्यन्तु मा कश्चिद्दुःखभाग्भवेत् ।
ॐ शान्तिः शान्तिः शान्तिः ॥

oṁ sarve bhavantu sukhinaḥ sarve santu nirāmayāḥ /
sarve bhadrāṇi paśyantu mā kaścidduḥkhabhāgbhavet /
oṁ śāntiḥ śāntiḥ śāntiḥ //

May all be happy, May all be free from misery.
May all realize goodness, May none suffer pain.
Oṁ! Peace. Peace. Peace.

श्री कृष्णार्पणमस्तु
Śrī Kṛṣṇārpaṇamastu

Index[1]

A
Absolute Consciousness, 84
Absolute Reality, 37, 43–47, 51, 52, 54, 57, 63, 65, 89, 99
Absolute Truth, 43, 259
Action (*karma yoga*), 266
Actionless-Self, 119, 229
Adamson, Sailor Bob, 94
Adhyaropa-apavāda (Superimposition-Negation), 93
Adhyātma-yoga, 49
Ādi Śaṅkarācārya, 28, 32, 32n40, 33, 40, 41n9, 42, 43, 47n38, 48n40, 52n51, 53, 56, 65n82, 68, 71n3, 72, 81, 118, 129n9, 137, 141n59, 283
Advaita philosophy, 73
Advaita Vedānta, 5n7, 17, 30, 35, 71–102, 106, 107, 123, 183–185
  Bhagavad Gītā and, 31–34
Āgāmī karma, 109
Ahiṁsā, selfless action and, 260
Akṣarabrahmayogaḥ, 63
Al Gini, 243
Alston, A. J., 46
Altruism: The Power of Compassion to Change Yourself and the World, 208
Ānanda Giri, 52, 53n52, 56n65, 184n5
Anāsaktiyoga, 239, 248
Anvaya-vyatireka (Co-presence and Absence), 91–93
Appearance, 94, 95
Aristotle, theory of golden mean, 200–201
Arjuna, xi, 43, 46, 51–57, 61, 62, 66, 115, 160, 161, 163, 165–167, 174, 176, 235, 238, 244–246, 264, 265, 268, 272, 273, 276, 281, 283, 284
Arjunaviṣādayogaḥ, 61–62
Arnold, Sir Edwin, 29
Art of Happiness, 271
Āsana, 182
Asaṅgaśastreṇa, 170
Aspirant (*sādhaka*), 164, 172
Aṣṭāṅga Yoga, 43n16, 181–183
Aṣṭāvakra Gītā, 113, 121
Aśvattham (*Pīpal*), 170
Aśvamedha Parva, 56
Ātma-jñāna, 46
Ātman, 74, 76n31, 81, 85, 89, 98, 261
Ātmasaṁyamayogaḥ, 63, 180
Ātmaśuddhaye, 238, 269
Ātmaupamyena sarvatra samaṃ paśyati, 273, 277
Attribution, 111

[1] Note: Page numbers followed by "n" refer to notes.

S. Dhiman, *Bhagavad Gītā and Leadership*,
Palgrave Studies in Workplace Spirituality and Fulfillment,
https://doi.org/10.1007/978-3-319-67573-2

Austerity (*tapas*), 105, 196
Authenticity, 65, 258
Authentic leadership, 142
Authentic Self, 23, 24, 28, 38
Autobiography of a Yogi (Paramahansa Yogananda), 145–147
Autry, J. A., 234
Avatār, 169
Avidyā, 87, 99

B

Bach, J. S., 254
Bacon, F., 39n1
Basham, A. L., 25
Beginning and conclusion of the text (*upakramo upasaṁhāra*), 51–52
"Be good, do good," 264
Be Here Now (Ram Das), 145
Being-centered leadership, 127–155
  Gandhi, Mahatma, 151–153
  Jobs, Steve, 144–148
  Mandela, Nelson, 148–151
  sage steadfast in wisdom, 141–144
  self-knowledge and, 129–140
Benioff, Marc, 146
Bennis, Warren, 141, 192, 258, 260
Bhagavad Gītā, 1–22, 71–73, 81, 96, 209, 224, 227–229
  and Advaita Vedānta, 31–34
  alpha and omega of, 265
  Art of Happiness, 271
  attributes of, 270
  and being-centered leadership, 127–155
  and Buddhism, 34–37
  colophon of, 43
  dictionary of daily conduct for Gandhi, 239–241
  18 chapters, essence of, 61–67
  ethical and spiritual disciplines (Yogas) of, 226–227
  facts about, 264
  Gandhi and, 233–235
  and Gandhian values, 257–261
  and hermeneutics, 42, 42n12
  and human freedom to action, 112–113
  and leadership, 23–38
  life and leadership of, 273
  message of, 39–70
  one hundred-and-one maxims of life and leadership, 274
  perennial appeal of, 25–28
  personal happiness and fulfillment, 263
  spirituality, 269
  subject matter of, 40
  syndrome of "more-ism," 271, 278
  teachings of, 160–162, 244
  text and context of, 28–30
  timeless teachings of, 265
  transcendent sage of, 216–217
  uniqueness of, 265
  war and peace in, 268
  way of, 236–237
  yogas of, 27, 33, 37, 266
  as Yoga Śāstra, 47–50
Bhagavad Gītā and Management: Timeless Lessons for Today's Managers, 4
The Bhagavad Gītā: Old Text, New Leadership Context, 4
Bhakta, 157
Bhakti-ṣaṭkam, 2
Bhakti yoga (*bhaktiyogaḥ*), 2, 13n28, 18, 43n16, 47–49, 64, 157, 161–163, 180, 188, 192n13, 210, 217–221, 262, 266, 267, 269, 277
  art and science of leadership, 173–175
  essentials of, 163–173
Bhīṣma Parva (The Book of Bhīṣma), 28, 29
Bhōga-saṅgraha, 171
Binding effect, 106–107
"Blind" faith, 157n2
Bliss (*ātma-sukha*), 282
Blumenfeld, S., 257
Bock, L., 256
Bodily postures (*āsanas*), 43n16
Body-conceit (*dehābhimān*), 168
Bohm, 7
Bolt, U., 272
Brahmā, 165
Brahmacārya, 164
Brahman, 74, 76, 84, 85, 89, 93, 99, 107, 158, 159, 261
Brahma-nirvāṇaṃ, 34
Brahma Sūtras, x, 30, 32, 40, 41, 71–73, 89

Brahma-vidyā, 44–47, 82
Bṛhadārańyaka Upaniṣad, 109, 111
Buddha, 24, 99
Buddhi, 265
Buddhism, Bhagavad Gītā and, 34–37
Buddhist Nirvana, 34
Buddhist psychology, 179
Buddhī-yoga, 166

C
Carlin, J., 150, 151
Catuḥślokī Bhāgavatam, 92
Center for Inner Development Resources, 4
Chakra Meditation, 185
Chāndogya Upaniṣad, 29, 224
Chappel, Christopher Key, 29
Chariot (*rathakalpanā*), 193
Charity (*dānaṃ*), 105, 196, 238
Chuang Tzu, 254
Cogito, ergo sum, 131
Collins, J., 141, 147, 252
Colophon of the Gītā, 43
Compassion, 24, 65, 135, 154
Conditioned existence (*saṁsāra*), 60
Conduct (*ācāra*), 236, 273, 277
Conducting affairs without doership, 119–120
Conscious principle, 32n40, 171
Cook, T., 144
Cosmic Order, 271
Cosmic sacrifice (*yajñārthātkarmaṇo*), 237
Covey, S. R., 234
Crest-jewel of perfection (*siddhi*), 269
Cynicism, 253

D
Daivāsurasampadvibhāgayogaḥ, 65
Dalai Lama, 24, 234
Dānaṃ, 224
Darśana, 73n12
Das, R., 145
Das, S., 145
De, S. K., 70
de Klerk, F.W., 150
de Mello, A., 79, 80
De Pree, M., 17, 234
Delusion (*mōha*), 48, 52–55, 59, 61, 66
Desai, N., 240, 241n29
Detachment, 143
Determinism, 110–112
Deussen, P., 73, 283
Deutsch, E., 28
Devanāgarī, xv
Devotee (*bhakta*), 157, 164, 251
Devotees (*yogīs*), characteristics of, 168–169
Devotion (*ananyā bhakti*), 158, 162, 167, 263, 275
Dhāranā, 182
Dhārayate uddhāryateva iti dharma, 221
Dharma, 37, 54, 54n57, 67, 105, 221–222, 264, 269
Dharmakṣetre, 209, 264
Dharma: Sarīra mādhyam khalu dharma sādhanam, 278
Dharmo rakṣati rakṣitāḥa, 10, 221
Dhruvaṃ janma mṛtasya ca, 278
Dhyāna yoga (the path of meditation), 43n16, 63, 180–182, 217–219, 266, 269
Digestive fire of life (*vaiśvānara*), 171
Discipline of action (*karma yoga*), 263, 275
Disciplines of speech, 238
Discrimination (viveka), 184
Distressed (*ārta*), 164
Divine Command (*hukam*), 66
Divine refuge (*śaraṇāgati*), 164
Divine vision (*divya-driṣṭi*), 176
Divinity (*Nirākār-rupa*), 165
Doership, 113, 119, 121, 125
Do not worry ((*mā*) *śucaḥ*), 264
Dreaver, J., 103n1
Durant, W., xvn10, 32n40
Duryodhana, 268

E
Easwaran, E., 242n34, 251, 261
Edgerton, F., 176n25, 180, 181n1, 218n8, 245
Ego, imposter, subduing, 197–198
Egotism, 142, 197
Eightfold Path, The, 181–183
Einstein, A., 7, 154, 155n112, 222
Embodied soul (*jīvātman*), 171

Emmons, R., 256
Emotional intelligence, 21, 175, 231, 275n9
Emotional maturity, 129, 142, 143, 154, 199, 201
Emotions, negative, managing, 194–196
Enlightened leadership, 263, 275
Equanimity (*samatvaṁ*), 62, 63, 143, 167, 201, 240, 266, 278, 282
  attaining through karma yoga, 201–203
  yogas and, 203–204
"Equipoise of mind," 266
Eternal Witness principle, 137
Ethics, 236
Eulogy (*arthavāda*), 60
Evenness of mind (*samatā*), 38, 48, 62, 116, 124, 175, 188, 201, 203, 204, 231, 269, 270
Examples or illustrations (*upapatti*), 61
Exegetical analysis of the Gītā, 50
Exhaling (*apāna*), 171
Existence, 32n40

F
"Faith," 157n2
Fifth Discipline, The (Peter Senge), 26, 192
Fight (*yudhya*), 268
Fortitude, 65
Frankl, V. E., 239, 270
Franklin, B., 260
Freedom from the commanding ego, 121–123
Free will, 110–112
Frydman, M., 113n23, 138n49
Fulfillment, 129, 132, 133, 135, 144, 149, 153, 154
Fundamental teaching of the Gītā, 69

G
Gandhi and Leadership: New Horizons in Exemplary Leadership, 3, 233
Gandhian hallmark, 238
Gandhi, Mahatma, 23–26, 29, 38n57, 104, 123, 124n35, 144, 151–153, 226
  and central teachings of Gītā, 248–249
  and the Gītā, 233–235
  on humility as key leadership, 252–257
  leadership, 238–239
  life an offering to divine, 237–238
  as sage steadfast in wisdom, 249–251
  and servarnt leadership, 243
  unique interpretation of Gītā, 247–248
George, Bill, 142
Gītāmāna Verse, 28
Gītāpadārthakōṣa, 239
God (*Paramātmā*), 160, 162
God-realization, 47, 160
  goal of, 266
God's Grace, 272
Golden Rule, for life and leadership, 270
Goode, G., 75n30
Good to Great (Jim Collins), 141, 252
"Gospel of Selfless Action" (Anāsaktiyoga), 226, 241–242
Grace of the Lord (*Ishvara-prasādabhāvanā*), 66, 68, 116, 173, 221, 262
Greed, 179
Grief (*śōka*), 53, 55
Guardians' of Plato's *Republic* (Al Gini), 243
Guṇas, 163, 164, 170, 171, 215–216, 280
Guṇātīta, 251
Guṇatrayavibhāgayogaḥ, 65
Guru Nanak, 153

H
Happiness (*sukhaṃ*), 129, 133, 135, 141, 153, 154, 166
Harmlessness (*Ahiṁsā*), 258, 259
Harvey, P., 204
Hatred, 179
Havel, V., 258
Herman, A. L., 26
Hermeneutics, 42, 42n12
Hill, W. D. P., 35, 174
Hinduism, 157, 242n34
Hiriyanna, Mysore, 41, 114, 125
Holistic Leadership: A New Paradigm for 21st Century Leaders, 3
Human freedom to action, 112–113
Humility, 24, 142, 143, 260
  defined, 253
Humphreys, Christmas, 108
Huxley, A., 25, 253, 255

I

Ignorance (*avidyā*), 32n40, 107, 123, 179
Iliad, 28, 29
Imperishable, 171
Impermanent (*anityam*), 166
Individual self (*jivātmā*), 45, 48, 67, 69, 75, 76, 84, 98, 107, 160, 173, 214, 215, 221, 262
Infinitude, 32n40
Inhaling (*prāna*), 171
Innermost Self (*pratyak ātmā*), 45, 85, 129, 188, 283
Inposter ego, subduing, 197–198
Intellect (*buddhi*), 51n49, 193
International Alphabet of Sanskrit Transliteration (IAST), xv, 1n1
International Society for Krishna Consciousness (ISKCON), 145
  Ratha Yatra, 149, 149n92
Invictus (film), 150
Isaacson, W., 146
Īśvara, 161, 223
Īśvara arpaṇa bhāvanā, 173
Itihāsas, 29

J

Jagat, 223
James, M., 113n23
Jaspers, K., 72n10, 74
Jātasya hi dhruvo mṛtyur, 278
Jaya, 248
Jijñāsur, 164
Jīva, 165
Jīvanmukta, 122
Jñāna (knowledge), 75n28, 266
Jñāna yoga (path of knowledge), 13n28, 161–163, 210, 262, 267, 269
Jñānakarmasaṁnyāsayogaḥ, 62
Jñāna-mārga (the path of knowledge), 184
Jñāna-ṣaṭkam, 2
Jñānavijñānayogaḥ, 63
Jñāna yoga (path of knowledge), 2, 18, 43n16, 47–49, 62, 65, 154, 157, 162, 163, 180, 192n13, 201, 213–215, 217, 277
Jñānī, 164
Jñāninaḥ (the wise ones), 62

Jobs, S., 26, 144
  karma yoga lessons, 147–148
  spiritual quest of, 144–148
Julka, H., 146

K

Kāmdhenū, 20, 233
Kariṣye vacanaṃ tava, 160, 272, 284
Karma
  defined, 108
  as destiny, 108–109
  and free will, 110–112
  law of, 232
  and passive resignation, 110
  types of, 109–110
Karmaphalatyāga, 168
Karma-ṣaṭkam, 2
Karma yoga (*karmayogaḥ*), 2, 13n28, 17, 18, 33, 43n16, 47–49, 62, 103–125, 147–149, 157, 161–163, 180, 192n13, 210–213, 217, 249, 261, 262, 266, 267, 269, 272, 277
  actionless-Self, 119
  alchemy of, 226
  attaining *samatā* throuogh, 201–203
  binding effect, 106–107
  conducting affairs without doership, 119–120
  freedom from the commanding ego, 121–123
  Gītā's key teachings of, 115–123
  selfless service, 123–124
  servant leadership, 123–124
  understanding, 104–106
Karmayoga-niṣṭhā (path of action), 267
Karma yogi, 113, 161, 162, 211, 212, 248
Kartāpan, 113, 125, 227, 272
Kashani, Afdal al-Din, 139
Kaṭhopaniṣad, 51n49, 193
Kauravas, 52n50, 246, 247
Kauśalam, 43n16
Keṇa Upaniṣad, 133, 137
Kesava Krishna dasa, 149
Keyserling, H., 25
King, Martin Luther, Jr., 24, 154, 234, 258
Knowers of the Self (*panḍitāḥ*), 53, 53n52
Knowing Mandela (John Carlin), 150

Knowledge (*jñāna yoga*), 57, 158, 263, 266, 273, 275
Knowledge of Ultimate Reality (*tattva-jñāna*), 44–47, 50, 61, 62
Krishnamurti, J., 103, 103n1
Krishna Warrier, A. G., 42
Kriya aur padāratha, 161
Kriya Yoga, 146, 186
Kṣatriya, 244
Kṣetrakṣetrajñavibhāgayogaḥ, 64–65
Kundalini Meditation, 185
Kuntī, 163
Kurukṣhetra war, 28, 226

L

Lamotte, 159
Lao Tzu, 131, 154, 253, 254, 257
Law of Garbage Truck, The (David J. Pillay), 195
Law of karma, 104, 107–111, 114–115
Leadership, 2, 4, 257
  authentic, 142
  authentic self-leadership, 192
  being-centered, 154–155
  Bhagavad Gītā and, 23–38
  self-leadership, 179, 193
  servant, 123–124
  three dimensions of, 14–15
Leitmotif, 11
Liberation, 226
Life and leadership of Gītā, 273
Likes and dislikes (*rāga-dveṣa*), 59, 128, 189
Lin Yutang, 253–254
Lincoln, A., 258
Litmus test of perfection (*siddhi*), 266
Lokasaṃgraham, 176, 238, 243, 269
Long Walk to Freedom (Nelson Mandela), 149, 255
Lord Nārāyaṇa, ix
Love, 24

M

Mahābhārata, 28–31, 40, 224, 244, 246–248, 268, 284
Mahadeva Sastry, A., 42
Maitra, S. K., 70, 105, 113, 158, 173, 210, 212
Maitreyī, 132
Mama, 264
Mām ekaṃ śaraṇaṃ vraja, 265
Mandela, Nelson, 24, 25, 144, 148–151, 154, 255, 258
Mantra-draśtās, 73n12
Mantra Meditation, 185
Maru Jivan Ej Mari Vani, 241n29
"Maryāda," of Dharma, 264
Maslow, A., 265
Material nature (*triguṇātamaka prakṛti*), 13, 64, 143, 148, 171, 199, 215–217, 229, 251, 267, 280, 280n65
Maxwell, J. H., 234
Māyā, 9, 63, 164
McKenzie, J., 209
Meditation (*dhyāna* yoga), 63, 179, 181–188, 204, 263, 275
  path of, 180–181
  path of, mastering, 188–191
Mental body' (*mānsīka śarīra*), 164
Merton, T., 254
Message of the Gītā, 39–70
  beginning and conclusion of the text (*upakramo upasaṁhāra*), 51–52
  determination of, 41–43
  eulogy (*arthavāda*), 60
  examples or illustrations (*upapatti*), 61
  originality, novelty or uniqueness of the text (*apūrvatā*), 55–57
  repetition (*abhyāsa*), 52–55
  result (*phalaṁ*), 57–60
Mind (*manas*), 179–205
  controlling, 191
Mindfulness Meditation, 186
Minor, Robert N., 25
Misadventure (*durgati*), 276
"*Mithyā*," 84
Modern leadership, 3
Modes of nature (*guṇas*), 267
Modesty, 65
Modus operandi, 73
Mokṣa, xi, 68, 99, 158
Mokṣasaṁnyāsayogaḥ, 66–67
Monet, J., 258
Moon (*soma*), 171
Mother Teresa, 24, 123, 125, 154, 234, 258, 272
Mulla Nasruddin Hodja, 79

Muṅḍaka Upaniṣad, 73, 133
Murthy, Satchidananda K., 74
My Life Is My Message, 241n29

N
Nānuśocanti paṇḍitāḥ, 173
Negative emotions, managing, 194–196
New Testament, 25
Nicomachean Ethics, 12
Nietzsche, F., 283
Nimitta mātraṁ, 243, 268, 279
Nirguṇa-Nirākār, 164
Nirvāṇa
  Bhagavad Gītā, 34
  Buddhist, 34, 35
Nirvāṇa-paramāṃ, 34
Nisargadatta Maharaj, 77, 80–81, 86
Niṣkāma karma, 103, 103n2, 104, 119, 248, 275
Nitya-anitya-vastu-viveka, 90
Nitya naimita karma, 105, 212
Niyamas, 181–182
Non-duality, 32
Nonpossession (*aparigraha*), 240, 241, 247
Non-real (*mithyā*), 32n40
Non-self (*anātmā*), 137
Nonviolence (*ahiṁsā*), 241, 245–248, 254
North America, 4
No-self (*anattā*), 35
"Not worth worrying about..." (*aśocyān*), 264
Novelty (*apūrvatā*), 55–57

O
Objective knowledge, 130
Odyssey, 28, 29
One Witnessing Divine Consciousness, 273
Orage, A. R., 29
Originality if the text, 55–57
O'Toole, J., 257

P
Panchama Veda, 29
Pāṇḍavānāṃ dhanaṃjayaḥ, xi
Pāṇdavas, 246, 268
Paramaḥ, 175
Param-prem, 165
Parāṁ śāntiṁ, 272
Paramśraddheya Swāmī Rāmsukhdāsjī Mahārāj, x
Param śreyas, 265, 273, 276, 281
Parāyā ghar, 171
Paripraśnena, 265, 276
Paritrāṇāya sādhūnāṃ, 284
Parks, R., 24
Parthasarathy, A., 24, 40, 234
Passion for excellence, 200
Patañjali, 43n16
  Aṣṭāṅga Yoga, 181–183
  Yoga Sūtras of, 183–185
Peace, 226
Perfection (*siddhi*), 62
Perishable, 171
Personal mastery, 198–201
Personal transformation, 132
Philosophia perennis, 90
Plato, 134
Playing the Enemy: Nelson Mandela and the Game that Made a Nation (John Carlin), 150
Pleasure (*arthārthī*), 164
Pollay, David J., 195, 196
Prakriyās, 81, 183
Prakṛti (matter), 183, 190n10, 216, 267
Prāṇaśaktī, 163
Prāṇāyāma, 182
Prārabdha karma, 109
Prasthāna-traya, 39, 41, 71
Pratyagātmani vijñāte nājñātam avashiśyate, 283
Pratyāhāra, 182
Prem, K., 44
Presence (Peter Senge), 192
Preyas, 14, 193
Pujya Śrī Sreenivāsa Mūrthy jī, x
Purāṇas, 29, 171, 224
Puraṇattvam, 59, 265, 271, 274, 276, 280
Pure Consciousness (*shuddha chaitanya-svarūpa*), 128, 138
Purity of mind, 65
Puruṣa (consciousness), 171, 183
Puruṣottma, 169, 183
Puruṣottamayoga, 65, 169

Q
Qigong Meditation, 186

R
Radhakrishnan, S., 108, 114, 177
Rāga-dvēṣa, 207
Rajas, 163, 164
Rājavidyārājaguhyayogaḥ, 63–64
Rāja yoga, 43n16
Ramakrishna Order, 37n56
Rāmānuja, 158, 159
Rāmāyaṇa, 224
Ramsukhdasji, S., 266
Rānāde, R. D., 35
Raychand Bhai, 241
Reality, 73, 74, 76, 76n31, 98
Realization of Truth, 75n30
Reasoning (*viveka*), 62
Remembrance (*ātma-smṛti*), 66
Renunciation of actions (*sāṅkhyayoga*), 267
Repetition (*abhyāsa*), 52–55
Resilience, 24
Result (*phalaṁ*), 60
Retribution, 111
Reward, 123
Righteousness, 54
Roosevelt, E., 258
Ṛtaṃ, 221
Russian court, 243
Russian Orthodox Church, 243
Ruysbroeck, 204

S
Sacrifice (*yajña*), 105, 161, 176, 196, 238
Sādhaka-Sanjīvanī (Swāmī Rāmsukhdāsjī), x, 52n50, 69
Sādhanā, 204, 266
Sage (*jñāni*)
  leader as enlightened, 127–155
  steadfast in wisdom, 141–144
Saguṇa-Sākār, 164, 168, 191
Sahaja avasthā, 211
Sākār, 167
Salinger, J. D., 153
Samādhi, 183
Samapardāya, 90n69
Samatā, 8, 10, 175, 230–231, 266, 267, 269–271, 279, 280, 282
Samatava-sthitiḥ, 211
Samattvam, 270, 280
Samatvaṃ yoga ucyate, 104, 203, 209, 266
Sama Veda, 29
Samkhya School, 183
Samma sati, 10
Saṁnyāsayogaḥ, 62–63
Sampardāya, 2
Saṃsāra, 106
Saṁvād, 265
Sanchita karma, 109
Śaṅkara Bhāṣya, x, 158, 176
Śaṅkarācārya, 158, 234
Sāṅkhyā niṣṭhā (path of knowledge), 267
Sāṅkhya yoga (path of knowledge), 62, 267
Saṅsāra, 165, 170, 171
Sanskrit, xv, 159
Saraswati, Madhusudana, 47
Śaraṇāgati, 158, 173, 272
Sarva bhūta hita, 208, 237, 238, 244, 269, 275
Sarvabhūtahite ratāḥ, 173, 243, 262
Sarvadharmān parityajya, 265
"*Sarvam iti*," 266
Sarvātmabhāva, 158, 173
Śāsti ca trayate ca iti śāstram, 7
Śāstra, 7, 169
Sāstra-driṣṭi, 7
Sattva-guṇa, 163, 164, 232
Satyāgraha in South Africa, 241
Schepetin, Ira (*Ātmachaitanya*), 36–37
Schlender, B., 144
Schultz, H., 141, 260
Schweitzer, A., 123
Scriptural doctrine (*Üāstra*), 172
Scriptures, 171
Security, 226–231
Self (*jīva*), 160, 164
Self (*sthita-prajñaḥ*), 282
Self-awareness, 20, 21, 127, 129–131, 136, 139, 142, 143, 153, 154, 179, 199, 231, 263, 278
Self-development, 25
Self-discipline, 24, 143, 260
Self-discovery, 132
Self-duty (*svadharma*), 247
Self-effort, 193
Self-esteem, 136
Self-freedom, 37n56
Self-fulfillment, 154
Self-gratification, 123
Self-ignorance, 53–55, 107, 131, 134, 137

Self-inquiry (*ātma-vicāra*), 91, 130, 131, 138
Self-interest, 142
Self-knowledge (*ātma-jñāna*), xi, 2, 2n2, 21, 24, 32n40, 37n56, 38, 43–47, 46n32, 50, 51, 53, 55, 57, 59–61, 67, 68, 70, 72, 73, 77, 80–82, 89, 97, 99, 100, 105, 107, 109, 110, 115, 117, 124, 125, 127–129, 142, 143, 148, 153, 154, 179, 197, 200, 207, 208, 229, 232, 246, 263, 269, 271, 278, 282, 283
  alpha and omega of spiritual quest, 137–139
  as already accomplished fact, 139–140
  defined, 129–132
  importance of, 133–134
  modus operandi of, 136–137
  need for, 132–133
  reasons for seeking, 134–135
Self-leadership, 179, 193
  authentic, 192
Selfless action (*niṣkāmakarma*), 32n40, 125, 241
Selflessness, 143
Self-less service (*niṣkām karamyoga*), 24, 123–124, 243, 261, 264
Self-management, 179, 193
Self-mastery, 2, 14, 24, 127, 141, 179, 180, 191–193
Self-pride (*ahaṁkāra*), 197
Self-purification, 189
Self-realization, 20, 26, 38, 38n57, 46n32, 47, 66n84, 68, 81–83, 124n35, 128n6, 139, 145, 146, 200, 251, 266, 267
Self-recognition, 123
Self-remembering, 130
Self-responsibility, 179
Self-sufficiency, 68
Self-transcendence, 263
Self-transformation, 24
Self-victory, 180, 193
Senge, P., 26, 192, 260
Senses (*indriya*), 51n49, 193
Servant leadership, 123–124, 243
Service (*upāsana*), 159
Seven Habits of Highly Fulfilled People: Journey from Success to Significance, 3
Severance (*viyoga*), 190
Shanti Mantra (Prayer for Peace), 284
Short History of Chinese Philosophy, A (Yu-Lan Fang), 12, 128
Shri Pranipāta Chaitanya, x
Siberia, court in, 243
Siddhi, 282
Skillfulness (*kauśalam*), 62
Śloka, 76
Smith, H., 9, 27, 42
Smṛtir labdhā, 284
Smṛtis, 40, 171
Socrates, 127, 134
Sorrow, 46, 49, 53, 55, 59, 67, 69
Sorrow and delusion (*śōka-mōha*), 160
Soul (*ātmā*), 162, 171
Spiritual aspirant (*adhikāri-bheda*), 267
Spiritual freedom (*mokṣa*), 40, 119, 234, 235, 273, 275
Spirituality, 269
Spiritual quest, alpha and omega of, 139
Śraddhātrayavibhāgayogaḥ, 66, 66n83, 157n2, 168, 169
Śreyas, 14, 265, 274, 276
Sri Atmananda, 75n30
Śrī Bhagavān, 163–170
Śrī Dakṣiṇāmūrti Stotram, 92
Śrī Dyālu Swāmījī, x
Sri Krishna Prem, 105
Śrī Kṛṣṇa, xi, 43, 48, 51–57, 60, 62, 63, 65–67, 69, 115, 159, 160, 160n12, 163, 167, 169, 171, 173–175, 180, 189, 193, 195, 197, 235, 238, 244–246, 264–266, 268, 269, 272, 273, 276, 281, 283, 284
Śrīmad Bhāgavatam, xi, 162
Sri Nisargadatta Maharaj, 94, 137
Śrī Rāmakrishna Paramahansa, 11
Sri Ramana Maharshi, 45n24, 77, 81, 97, 113, 131, 136, 138, 138n49, 139, 139n56, 140n57, 183, 184
Śrī Śaṅkarācārya, ix, x
Śrī Sreenivāsa Murthy-jī, 44n17, 46n32
Śruti, 40
Steadfast in wisdom (*sthitaprajña*), 251, 271, 278
Steadfastness in truth (*sthitaprajñatā*), 241
Sthitaprajña (sage of steady wisdom), 68, 228, 230, 249, 250, 262, 280

Subject matter of the Bhagavad Gītā, determination of, 40
Summum bonum, 208
Supreme Abode, 170
Supreme Person (*Puruṣottama*), 65, 171, 172
Supreme Science of Reality (*brahmavidyā*), 60
Supreme Self (*brahma-vidyā*), 128
Supreme Self (*Paramātmā*), 44, 45, 47n37, 48, 49, 67, 69
Sure path to sagehood, 114–115
Sureśvarācāya, 283
Svadharma, 55, 105, 246, 268, 275, 278
Svakarmaṇā tam abhyarcya siddhiṃ vindati mānavaḥ, 161, 232
Svānubhava, x
Svarupa, 165, 189–191
Swāmī Akandānand jī Mahārāj, 66n83
Swāmī Brahmātmānand Saraswati, x
Swāmī Dayānanda Saraswati jī, x, 139
Swāmī Gambhīrānanda, 34, 42
Swāmī Gyānajīvandāsjī, x
Swāmī Krishnananda, 48n41
Swami Nikhilananda, 90
Swami Paramārthānanda, x, 60n75, 100, 138
Swāmī Rāmsukhdās jī, 27n21, 52n50, 69, 162, 165n14, 210
Swami Ram Tirath ji, 64n81
Swami Satchidanandendra Saraswati, x, 36
Swāmī Śharṇānandjī Mahārāj, x
Swāmī Shrī Rāmsukhdāsjī, 157n1, 158, 173, 220
Swami Sivananda, 138
Swāmī Śrī Brahmātmānand Saraswati, 121, 122
Swāmī Tejomayananda, 50n48, 67, 71n3
Swami Vivekananda, ix, 283

T

Tagore, R., 33n45
Taittirīyopaniṣad, 74n22
Taṃ vidyād duḥkhasaṃyogaviyogaṃ yogasaṃjñitam, 209
Tamas, 163
Tamas guṇas, 164
Taoistic Meditation, 186
Tao Te Ching, 253
Tattvadarśinaḥ, 275
Teitsworth, S., 40
Tetzeli, R., 144
Theravada Buddhism (doctrine of the Elders), 35
Thompson, C. M., 234
Thoreau, Henry David, 25
Thought process (*vichāra*), 236, 273, 277
Timeless teachings of Bhagavad Gītā, 265
Transcendental Meditation, 186
Transparency, 258
Trigunatita, 262
Truth, 259
Truthfulness, 65
Tutu, Desmond (Archbishop), 24, 150, 151, 234
2017 Global Bhagavad Gītā Convention, 4

U

Udaghośha, 100
Uddhared ātmanātmānaṃ, 281
Ultimate purpose of life (*mokṣa* or liberation), 27
Ultimate Reality (*tattva-jñāna*), 128
Uniqueness of the text, 55–57
Universe (*Tattvamasī*), 268
Upaniṣads, x, 13, 14, 30, 32, 33, 39–41, 43, 66, 70–73, 71n3, 73n13, 81, 132, 133, 159, 224, 282
Upaniṣad teaching, kernel of, 46

V

Vāk tapas, 238
Values-based leadership, 257–258
van Buitenen, J. A. B., 25, 48, 104, 221n26
Vasishtha, 111
Vāsudevaḥ (*vṛṣṇīnāṃ vāsudevosmi*), xi
Vāsudevaḥ sarvam, 164
Vāsudeva Śrī Kṛṣṇa, 266
Vasudhaiva Kutumbakam, 222–223
Vedānta, 4, 5, 7, 10n15, 11n20, 16, 17, 30–32, 35–37, 41, 44n17, 46, 46n32, 47n35, 56n64, 59, 59n74,

60n75, 68n87, 69n90, 71–74, 73n12, 75n30, 76, 80, 81, 81n48, 84, 85, 87–91, 92n73, 93, 94, 94n79, 96–100, 101n93, 107, 121, 128n6, 131, 134n37, 137–140, 139n56, 183–185, 265, 282
Vedas, 66, 70, 72, 163–165, 167, 170, 171
Veda Vyāsa (*munīnām apy ahaṃ vyāsaḥ*), xi, 28
Vedic epistemology, 86–88
Vedic ontology, 84–85
Vibhūtiyogaḥ, 64
Vidhān, 166
Vināśāya ca duṣkṛtāmto, 284
Vipassana, 186
Viśvarūpadarśanayogaḥ, 64, 167
Vivāda, 265
Viveka, 39
Vivekacūḍāmaṇi, 158
Vivekacūḍāmaṇi: The Crest Jewel of Wisdom, 4
Viyoga (disassociation), 49
Vyavahāra mein paramārtha kī kalā, 231, 273, 276

W
Wadhwa, H., 150
Waḥdat al-wujūd, 90n66
Wallenda, K., 174
Wants, psychology and tyranny of, 194
War and peace in Gītā, 268
Warne, J., 221
Warrior class (*khaṣatriya*), 268
Watts, A., 174
Wellbeing, 128, 149
Wheeler, J., 94, 95
Wilkins, Sir Charles, 29
Wisdom (*prajña*), 280
Wisdom of the Self (*sthitaprajña*), 129, 141, 198
Wise leadership, 147, 148, 151
World (*jagat*), 160, 162
World Confluence of Humanity, Power & Spirituality, 4
Wright, F. L., 253

Y
Yajñās, 165, 224
Yājñavalkya, 132
Yamas, 181
Yathecchasi tathā kuru, 246
Yoga, 10, 13n28, 43n16, 47–49, 61, 176, 180, 273
  adhyātma-yoga, 49
  akṣarabrahmayogaḥ, 63
  arjunaviṣādayogaḥ, 61–62
  Aṣṭānga Yoga, 181–183
  ātmasaṁyamayogaḥ, 63, 180
  bhakti yoga (*bhaktiyogaḥ*), 2, 13n28, 18, 43n16, 47–49, 64, 157, 162, 163, 180, 188, 192n13, 210, 217, 218, 277
  daivāsurasampadvibhāgayogaḥ, 65
  dhyāna yoga (the path of meditation), 43n16, 63, 180–182, 217–219, 266, 269
  guṇatrayavibhāgayogaḥ, 65
  jñānakarmasaṁnyāsayogaḥ, 62
  jñānavijñānayogaḥ, 63
  jñāna yoga (path of knowledge), 2, 18, 43n16, 47–49, 62, 65, 154, 157, 162, 163, 180, 192n13, 201, 213–215, 217, 277
  karma yoga (*karmayogaḥ*), 2, 13n28, 17, 18, 33, 43n16, 47–49, 62, 103–125, 147–149, 157, 162, 163, 180, 192n13, 217, 249, 261, 266, 267, 272, 277
  Kriya Yoga, 146, 186
  kṣetrakṣetrajñavibhāgayogaḥ, 64–65
  mokṣasaṁnyāsayogaḥ, 67
  path and the goal of, 49–50
  puruṣottamayogaḥ, 65
  rājavidyārājaguhyayogaḥ, 63–64
  and *samatā*, 203–204
  saṁnyāsayogaḥ, 62–63
  sāṅkhyayogaḥ, 62
  śraddhātrayavibhāgayogaḥ, 66, 66n83, 157n2, 168, 169
  vibhūtiyogaḥ, 64
  viśvarūpadarśanayogaḥ, 64, 167
Yoga karmasu kauśalam, 209, 212, 271
Yogananda, Paramahansa, 145–147
Yoga-niṣṭhā (path of self-less actions), 266

Yoga of the Bhagavat Gītā, The (Sri Krishna Prem), 27, 33, 37, 105, 209, 266
Yoga Śāstra, Bhagavad Gītā as, 47–50
Yogas for salvation, 162–163
Yoga Sūtras, 181
 of Patañjali, 48, 48n41, 183–185
Yogavāsiṣṭha Mahāramāyaṇa, 143, 199, 250
Yoga-yukta, 275
Yoking the Self, 43
"Yuj," 222n26

Z
Zaehner, R. C., 159
Zazen, 186
Zen Buddhism, 145

CPSIA information can be obtained
at www.ICGtesting.com
Printed in the USA
LVHW030427211218
601307LV00007B/61/P

9 783319 675725